C for java programmers

Tomasz Müldner

Acadia University

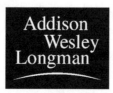

Addison
Wesley
Longman

Reading, Massachusetts • Menlo Park, California • New York
Don Mills, Ontario • Wokingham, England • Amsterdam • Bonn
Sydney • Singapore • Tokyo • Madrid • San Juan • Milan • Paris

Acquisitions Editor:	Maite Suarez-Rivas
Associate Editor:	Katherine Harutunian
Project Manager:	The Publisher's Group
Executive Marketing Manager:	Michael Hirsch
Composition:	Michael and Sigrid Wile
Text Design:	Delgado Design, Inc.
Copyeditor:	Trillium Project Management
Technical Artist:	Delgado Design, Inc.
Proofreader:	Trillium Project Management
Design Supervisor:	Gina Hagen
Cover Design:	Leslie Haimes
Indexer:	Bernice Eisen

Library of Congress Cataloging-in-Publication Data

Müldner, Tomasz.
    C for Java programmers / Tomasz Müldner.
        p. cm.
    ISBN 0-201-70279-7
        1. C (Computer program language) I. Title.
    QA76.73.C15 M853 2000
    005.13'13—dc21

                                99-089910

Many of the designations used by manufacturers and sellers to distinguish their products are claimed as trademarks. Where those designations appear in this book, and Addison-Wesley was aware of a trademark claim, the designations have been printed in initial caps or all caps.

The programs and applications presented in this book have been included for their instructional value. They have been tested with care but are not guaranteed for any particular purpose. The publisher does not offer any warranties or representations, nor does it accept any liabilities with respect to the programs or applications.

Access the latest information about Addison-Wesley titles from our World Wide Web site: http://www.awlonline.com

This book was typeset in QuarkXPress on a Macintosh G4. The font families used were Courier, Officina, Serifa, and Times. It was printed on New Era Matte.

1 2 3 4 5 6 7 8 9 10-MA-03020100

For Kasia and Michał, my daughter and my son,
with love and admiration

PREFACE

C was designed and implemented in 1972, and over the years, it has become one of the most popular programming languages. There is a great deal of software implemented in C, and many universities teach the language, using one of the approximately 500 books that have been written about it. The recent popularity of Java has raised speculation as to whether C will survive, or slowly be replaced. For example, many universities have changed their curricula to teach Java as the first programming language. However, Java is not a language suitable for every application: it requires a great deal of computer memory, is not efficient, and is not appropriate for real-time applications. C continues to be widely used in both industry and research institutions for a broad variety of applications, such as data compression, graphics, compilers, and operating systems. Therefore, at this time, C is very much alive and present.

So why yet another book on C? First of all, we now have the commonly recognized ANSI C standard. Secondly, our understanding of programming techniques has changed considerably, especially with the advent of an object-oriented programming paradigm. Thirdly, we can focus on writing correct, readable, and robust code thanks to current compiler optimization techniques.

This book is called *C for Java Programmers* because it is designed to demonstrate the latest C techniques. Many of the techniques used by C programmers were developed before the ANSI C standard was fully approved, resulting in code that was both difficult to read and to maintain. Today, there are many new techniques available to take advantage of both the efficient low-level constructs that C offers, and to structure them using high-level concepts, such as code modularization. This is the main focus of my book: to apply the techniques that we have learned from working with object-oriented programs to C programs. Since C does not provide built-in high-level constructs, I have taken advantage of its flexibility and designed various coding idioms. An idiom is a template of C code adhering to a rigorous programming style. This book presents a range of idioms, from simple templates such as "Reading until end of line," to more complex templates such as "Function Callback." Idioms both enforce a programming style and allow the programmer to reuse code, instead of finding a new solution each time. Throughout this book, I provide many examples of modules, which are written using these idioms.

C for Java Programmers is designed for readers who know Java, although I would like to stress that this is not a crucial prerequisite to understanding the book. The advantage of knowing Java is that the reader enters the book with a knowledge of many low-level constructs, such as control structures. Such a reader also appreciates the need both to use existing abstractions and to create new ones. Given that knowledge, she or he needs a book that will not only teach C, but also demonstrate how to use it to produce reliable and maintainable programs. In addition, I wanted my book to serve as a reference book for everyday programming tasks. There are several ways in which one could design a book with these criteria in mind. One is to divide the book into two parts: a reference part (construct by construct presentation), and a "topical part," with larger programs useful for understanding the type of programming style required by the language. Another possible structure is to eliminate the reference part completely, and "teach by case studies." The problem with this design is that it would render the book useless as a reference, and so I decided against using it. The first design is appealing because it allows the reader to understand a single section without reading the whole book (or at least the second part does); this is the style I chose, except that I did not divide the book into two parts. I did include some longer programs that demonstrate high-level concepts in several of the chapters.

Java and C are too different to compare construct by construct, and so I only mention some of the differences and concentrate instead on the high level concepts present in Java that may be applied to C. I also focus on the issues that may be particularly challenging to Java programmers, such as memory management, pointer use, exception handling, and code modularization. The book provides a very complete description of these topics, supported by examples that are continually extended as new concepts are introduced.

C for Java Programmers will help you read and understand any large C program (for example, the source code of Linux), as well as to write your own modular programs that can be easily tested and maintained. In order to increase the readability of the presentation, I have decided not to use any of my own libraries. Based on my experience, beginners in C often find it difficult to tell the difference between what functionality is provided in the standard libraries, and what the author has added. For the same reason, I decided against showing complicated and arcane applications of macros to simulate constructs that do not exist in C, such as try blocks.

One of the early design decisions made was to write a book that would cover all of C's constructs but to limit its size to approximately 600 pages, which meant that some topics are covered in more depth than others. At the same time, the book was designed to be self-sufficient, eliminating the need for another book in order to successfully program in C. I spend relatively little time discussing topics that I consider less important or simple, such as preprocessing or bitwise operations. On the other hand, pointers take up almost one third of the book, and modules receive a great deal of attention. At this point, you may be wondering which topics are not covered in this book. First of all, I do not discuss the old C standard, called K&R standard. Secondly, I do not provide a large number of complete case studies and instead demonstrate the techniques that the reader can use to write such programs. Finally, I do not fully describe all of the run-time libraries, but I do provide a table of all functions included in these libraries. Consequently, the book provides a complete description of all the essential ANSI C features, and so is sufficient as a reference and guide.

I decided to focus on several specific modules, used to represent dynamic arrays and lists throughout the book, and use these as a platform for discussing vital concepts, such as:

- extending and modifying modules
- providing alternative implementations
- representing enumerations
- creating concrete and generic modules
- using shallow and deep copying.

Important features of this book include:

- A complete coverage of ANSI C
- Focus on portability; non-portable constructs (that is, constructs that are relevant only in specific implementations, but are useless in others) are avoided
- List of typical errors
- List of 59 idioms
- Over 100 examples of C programs

- Discussion of programming style and recommended lexical conventions, in order to suggest a disciplined way of writing C programs
- Over 190 exercises. Solutions to some of these exercises, as well as complete code for all programs in this book are available from the Addison-Wesley web site. Instructors who adopt the book can use the same site to obtain Power-Point or HTML files, which contain lecture presentations that can be used for teaching in the classroom. Please contact your Addison Wesley Longman sales representative for information on its availability or send an email message to aw.cse@awl.com.

Each of the 14 chapters starts with a preview, which briefly describes the topics to be discussed in that chapter. Most chapters provide lists of common errors, idioms, and guidelines on portability and recommended programming style. To allow the book to be used as a quick reference, these lists are also provided at the end of each chapter, and complete lists appear in the appendices.

Chapter 1 introduces some basic terms and concepts used in the remainder of the book, such as compilation, linking, and preprocessing. It also provides a brief comparison of C and Java. Chapter 2 consists of an example of a C program, which you may wish to read to get a flavor of C. Chapter 3 describes the lexical structure of C, primitive data types, and terminal I/O. Since control structures in C and Java are almost identical, Chapter 4 concentrates on the idiomatic use of these structures using C. Chapter 5 describes text files, which are handled differently in C than in Java. Chapter 6 is on preprocessing, and Chapter 7 talks about functions. This chapter also starts the discussion of module-based programming and describes various kinds of modules, the design of constructors and destructors, alternative implementations, and extensions and modifications of existing modules. Chapter 8 is the longest chapter of this book and covers pointers and their applications. A detailed description of dynamic memory management and pointer arithmetic is provided, and a number of examples are shown to help the reader understand concepts that are fundamental for using other coding techniques. Numerous idioms are introduced to help the reader reuse concepts learned in this chapter. The management of blocks of memory containing either objects of primitive data types or pointers is discussed, followed by the second part of the discussion of module-based programming, which introduces generic modules and enumerations. Chapter 9 discusses strings and applications of string libraries. It also gives an example of a module designed to tokenize strings. Chapter 10 covers arrays and provides a module that implements dynamic arrays. This chapter also discusses testing preconditions. Chapter 11 introduces structures, which together with pointers are the most useful tool for designing abstract modules that have concrete implementations invisible to the client. This chapter re-implements enumerations, and discusses basic list operations. Two modules that represent homogenous collections are presented in this chapter: one that represents generic dynamic arrays with only shallow copying of values, and the other that represents concrete lists with deep copying of values. Chapter 12 covers unions and enumerated data types, and Chapter 13 introduces bitwise operations. Finally, Chapter 14 discusses more advanced topics related to module-based programming, such as exception handling, and provides a summary of the various kinds of previously discussed modules. This chapter also discusses shallow and deep enumeration interfaces, and presents a module supporting generic lists with a shallow and a deep interface.

The appendices contain precedence and associativity tables (Appendix A), alphabetic summary of all standard library functions (Appendix B), glossary of all important terms (Appendix C), the complete list of common errors made by C novices (Appendix D), the complete list of all programming idioms (Appendix E), the complete description of the programming style guidelines (Appendix F), list of portability guidelines (Appendix G), and cross reference index of all useful code fragments, for example, a menu-driven program or a traversal of a binary file (Appendix H).

The reader of the book will be guided by icons placed on the margin of pages, indicating the presence of one of the following discussion topics:

- portability
- programming style
- typical errors
- idioms
- C constructs that are similar to Java, but are handled differently in C **C**

C for Java Programmers does not have to be read sequentially. The reader may wish to first glance over the first four chapters, watching for the "C icons," that appear only in these chapters. Chapters 5 and 6 and the first part of Chapter 7 can also be read quickly. However, the introduction to modules in Chapter 7 should be read more carefully, as should all of Chapter 8, which focuses on pointers and is a real prerequisite for the rest of the book. The next three chapters, 9–11, are also essential. On the other hand, Chapters 12 and 13 are included for the sake of completeness. Chapter 14 is a convenient reference point since it summarizes the different kinds of modules presented in this book.

Notations

In the text, I use the following convention: If `f` is a function, then `f()` is used in the description even if `f` has parameters that are irrelevant for the discussion at hand; otherwise I explicitly list parameters.

Acknowledgments

First and foremost, I would like to thank my daughter Kasia and my son Michał, both of whom graduated several years ago from the Computer Science program at

Acadia University. I have been fortunate indeed to get from them a lot of help and numerous suggestions for improvements. In particular, the style of this book reflects Kasia's input. If there are any remaining mistakes or omissions, then they are unfortunately wholly attributable to the author. Should you find any errors, please send email to tomasz.muldner@acadiau.ca.

I would also like to thank my wife Basia. Without her understanding, constant support, and care, I would not have had enough strength to complete this book. I am grateful for the expertise at Addison-Wesley; specifically, my editor Maite Suarez-Rivas for the valuable input and suggesting the "impossible less-than–6 months-to-completion-deadline," as well as Katherine Harutunian for help during the production process.

I am also appreciative for the useful comments and suggestions that several reviewers provided:

Randy Chow, University of Florida
Nigel Gwee, Louisiana State University
Peter Maurer, University of South Florida
Raj Nagendra, Ryerson Polytechnic University
Paul Sivilotti, Ohio State

Finally, I offer my sincere appreciation to two colleagues from the School of Computer Science at Acadia University: the director, Dr. Andre Trudel, who maximized my productive writing time when assigning departmental duties, and Dr. Leslie Oliver, who a long time ago encouraged me to use programming idioms and had the courage to co-teach a course with me based on theories contained in this book.

CONTENTS

Chapter 9   **Strings   301**

Chapter 1

INTRODUCTION

1.1 ◆ Preview

This chapter will introduce some basic terms and concepts, which may be helpful in understanding later material. I will first describe the history of C. I will then compare two programming paradigms; objected oriented and procedural, and provide a comparison of Java and C. I will next discuss the software development process including issues such as portability, safety, and efficiency, and the need for a programming standard when writing programs in C. To conclude this chapter, I will present the concept of a programming idiom.

1.2 About C

The C programming language was developed by Dennis Ritchie in 1972. The first real test of C came in early in 1973, when it was used to write the Unix operating system. The first standard of the language was given by Kernighan and Ritchie [Ker78], and is known as the K&R standard. In 1989, the American National Standards Institute (ANSI) adopted another standard for C, referred to as ANSI C (formally known as American National Standard X3.159–1989). Although the K&R standard is still used, in this book I will cover the more popular ANSI C standard (for differences between the two standards, see [Har91]).

1.3 Object-Oriented versus Procedural Programming

There are two well-known imperative programming paradigms; object-oriented and procedural. Both paradigms use data and procedures but in a radically different manner. An **object-oriented programming paradigm**, used by Java (see [Arn98]), is based on the following design rule: decide which classes you need, provide a full set of operations for each class, and make commonality explicit by using inheritance. As you probably know, a class allows you to define a new data type according to the needs of the problem to be solved. After defining the data type, you must also define operators to act upon it. For example, to work with two-dimensional arrays, you would define a class `TwoDimensionalArray` and provide various useful operators for this class, such as support for array multiplication, addition, etc. Class operations are defined by methods. Object-oriented programming separates clients and implementors. Public methods are available to the client, and define the user interface; private methods are hidden in the class and define the implementation of that class. Classes may define **concrete** types, with a concrete underlying data type such as a list of integers. They may also define **generic** types that serve as templates from which concrete types can be derived. For example, a generic stack does not specify the type of each element on the stack, and it may be used to instantiate a concrete stack, such as a stack of integers.

A **procedural programming paradigm**, used by C, is based on the following design rule: decide which procedures and data structures you want and use the best algorithms. The language's support is based on functions communicating by passing arguments and returning values. In other words, the only connection between data and its operations is a function invocation. In the procedural programming paradigm there are no classes, no objects, and no inheritance.

1.4 A Brief Comparison of C and Java

In this section, I briefly compare C with Java. C provides the typical *primitive data types*: character, integer, and real. These data types are very similar to the ones found in Java except that they are of different sizes; that is, the language does not define the amount of memory needed to store values of various types. Unlike in Java, there is no Unicode 16-bit character set provided in C, although there is some support for wide characters that need more than one byte. C also provides *structured data types*: arrays, structures (referred to as records in some languages), and unions. Contrary to Java, C's arrays are static, which means that their size has to be defined at compile time. Structures and unions are not present in Java, because they can be represented by classes.

Control structures are similar in both languages. Functions may not be textually nested, but they may be recursive. Java references are called pointers in C. *Pointers* provide quite unexpected power and flexibility; in particular, pointer addition and subtraction is supported.

I mentioned above that C is a procedural language, and so it does not have classes. What other constructs present in Java are missing in C? There are no packages, threads, or exception handling, and no standard Graphical User Interface (GUI) is provided in the standard libraries. There is no garbage collection, no built-in definition of a string, and no standard support for networking, in particular for dynamic loading. Finally, there is no code verifier, and in general no support for program safety.

C provides several *run-time libraries*, which support standard I/O, mathematical operations, and others. (Let's recall that like in Java, a library consists of program fragments that have been compiled and stored for future use.) Many libraries exist that implement some of the functionality present in Java, but they are not a part of standard ANSI C.

1.5 Why Is C Still Useful?

C allows provides ultimate flexibility and power to the programmer. Java forces a more rigorous structure that is meant to impose a particular programming style (one which follows a more object-oriented style). If this style of programming would be the ideal choice for every situation, Java would undoubtedly usurp C and become the language of choice. However, C will continue to survive for a number of reasons. First of all, in many practical situations where a large piece of software has to be developed, Java lacks the efficiency that C can provide. In many instances, it really comes down to practicality, and the resource requirements made by Java simply prove too much. As opposed to Java, C is a language that is designed to take full advantage of a computer, and so C programs can be very efficient (and I am not talking about writing as concise (and often unreadable code) as possible—it is still possible to write elegant, readable, and robust C code that executes very fast). It is ideal for writing applications such as operating systems (the most notable of which is Unix), large applications, databases, and others. Secondly, as I already pointed out, C is renowned for its flexibility, which means it provides many high-level and low-level operations. As a result, it is also used in such areas as data compression, graphics and computational geometry. C assumes that the programmer is intelligent enough to use all of its constructs wisely, and so few things are forbidden. The programmer is allowed to cast types to other types, is responsible for his or her own garbage collection, and memory management. This results in the programmer having a great deal of power, but it also means that inexperienced programmers initially have difficulty in writing correct and clean code. (For example, memory management is always a hurdle for those not used to controlling their own memory; modularity is not enforced, which means it is up to the programmer to choose a "good" programming style.)

Java's popularity can be largely attributed to its platform independence ability. Unfortunately, this concept does not always work as expected because it is very difficult to account for every existing operating system out there. In this book, I will strive to demonstrate how C programs can be written which are also portable.

There are other reasons as to why C is still useful. Many programming languages and shell command languages bear a close resemblance to C. For example, C++ and Java have almost identical concepts for control structures and functions. Java is still young and its standards and environments are changing rapidly. C, on the other hand, is stable and commonly used. Zillions of lines of C legacy code itself will ensure the survival of the language for many years to come.

As a final comment, I would like to add that C can be a very useful and elegant tool. People often dismiss C, claming that it is responsible for a "bad coding style." The bad coding style is not the fault of the language, which is a mere tool for attaining a higher goal, but is instead controlled (and so caused) by the programmer. As you become more proficient in writing code and understanding some of the philosophies essential for creating robust, portable and modular code, you will come to see why C is still powerful after over twenty-five years.

1.6 Development Process

In this section, I review some basic concepts that are not always necessary for writing Java programs, but are required for C programming.

1.6.1 ◆ Compilation, Linking, and Preprocessing

Although the C development process is similar to the Java process, some specific differences warrant a short discussion of the basic steps needed for the development of C programs. To produce an executable C program, three steps are required:

- editing, which produces the source code
- compiling, which translates source code into object code
- linking, which typically produces executable code

The above sequence of steps can be accomplished by using Integrated Development Environments (IDEs). The object code produced in the second step is often not executable, because it contains references to system routines, such as I/O routines. In some specialized environments, the object code does not have such references and may be executed. These are called free-standing environments. It is more common to use a **hosted** environment for creating programs. In such an environment, the object code must be linked with the code of the system in order to produce executable code. An operating system tool called a **linker** or a **loader** performs this task, linking code with the system libraries and reporting appropriate errors if any symbols are left undefined.

C supports a **preprocessing** feature, which from a logical point of view takes place before compilation. This feature allows the user to specify that certain text in the source file is to be replaced by other text. The original text is referred to as a **macro**; the new text is called the **macro replacement** and the process is called a macro substitution. Note that macro substitution is a purely textual, in-place substitution, which does not involve the run-time stack. Macros are useful for defining constants, and can be used for simulating syntactic constructs that are absent in C.

C also provides a preprocessing directive that may be used to include external files in the current file. From the perspective of the compiler, a file containing several **include directives** is a single source file. The use of include directives avoids code duplication and helps code management.

There are many decisions that you will have to make at the onset of any programming project. They will include issues such as portability, efficiency, and even your programming style. The following section briefly discusses these issues.

1.6.2 ◆ Portability, Efficiency, and Correctness

Portable programs will run on any machine. While Java was designed to allow for writing truly portable programs, which may be executed on any machine, C object code runs only on a specific target machine. Portability is difficult to achieve because computer systems differ in a variety of ways; for example, linkers accept different standards for the length of identifiers, and computer memory differs in word size or character size. When you take on the task of writing a C program, you should decide whether this program is to be portable or not. You may decide against portability if your program has to use some very specific features of the target machine, such as the word size. However, it is more likely that you will be striving to write portable programs, and as a result you have to learn how to avoid non-portable constructs. If you find it impossible to write completely portable code, you should isolate machine dependencies into a small portion of the program so that only this part will have to be rewritten in order to move the program to another machine.

Many programmers consider *program efficiency* to be the single most important issue, and seem to forget that correctness and robustness are far more important. I will provide a quote from "A case against the GO-TO" by W.A. Wulf to support my position:

> *More computing sins are committed in the name of efficiency (without necessarily achieving it) than for any other reason—including blind stupidity.*

One should always be more concerned with a program's run-time behavior and its robustness—remember that an efficient program that is also buggy is worthless. Careful testing is crucial in order to avoid program crashes; any cases that can not be fixed should be well documented. In other words, your first goal should always be the development of a correct program. If you reach this goal and find yourself tempted to make it more efficient, consider two things: first, modern compilers can optimize code much better than an average programmer. Secondly, do not optimize a piece of code that appears to be "slow" upon inspection. Instead, use tools such as profilers to identify trouble spots, and only then consider optimization.

Finally, remember that programs should always be *designed for change*—program requirements often undergo modifications while the code is being written and for a long time after. Maintainability is a very important part of the software cycle and should be one of the goals when writing programs.

1.6.3 ◆ Programming Style

It is possible to write bad programs in every programming language, but this is particularly easy in a language that offers the flexibility of doing "everything" at your own risk. Programming in C is like driving a Porsche; you have a lot of power but you have to be more careful than when driving a pick-up truck. That is why care and discipline are so important. In this book, I will recommend a certain programming style. This style includes recommendations for lexical conventions (such as identifiers), a format for control statements, and a convention for writing comments. If you do not like my proposed style, then develop, document, and consistently use your own conventions.

A programming style is important for code maintainability because it makes programs easier to understand and modify. One day you may be asked to read somebody's code (it may even be your own code). You will find that a consistent style will help to develop and maintain your own programs. The proposed programming style will also recommend various idioms.

1.6.4 ◆ Programming with Idioms

In a natural language, an idiom is a phrase that has a specific meaning such as "don't pull my leg", commonly interpreted as "don't try to fool me." In programming, **idioms** are code patterns frequently used and reused, which show the C way of doing things. For example, one of the most famous C idioms tells you how to copy a block of memory using pointers:

```
while (*p++ = *q++)
    ;
```

Idioms are so useful because you can apply and reapply them, as opposed to coming up with a new solution each time. This book provides 59 idioms; a complete list is in Appendix E.

Chapter 2

EXAMPLE OF A C PROGRAM

In this section, I will present a sample C program. The following subsections will describe the various constructs that are used in this program.

```
/*
 * Author:        Tomasz Muldner
 * Date:          August, 1999
 * Version:       2.0
 * File:          Sample.c
 *
 * Program that expects one or two filenames on the command
 *   line and produces a hexadecimal dump of the file whose
 *   name is passed as the first argument. If the second
 *   argument is present, the dump is stored in the file whose
 *   name is passed as this argument. Otherwise, the dump is
 *   displayed on the screen. The format of the dump is as
 *   follows:
 *
 *   Each line contains 16 hexadecimal ASCII codes of the
 *   corresponding 16 bytes read from the file, separated by a
 *   blank. This line is followed by a line containing the 16
 *   corresponding characters, again separated by a blank,
 *   with each non-printable character displayed as a dot and
 *   other characters unchanged.
 */

/* include files */
#include <stdio.h>
#include <ctype.h>
#include <stdlib.h>

/* global definitions */
FILE *outFile;        /* output file */

/* Function declaration */
/*
 * Function: hex(p, max)
 * Purpose: writes to the global output file
 *    outFile the hexadecimal codes of max number of characters
 *    originating at the address given by the pointer p.
 *    This line is followed by the corresponding characters.
 *    Assumes that the file outFile has been opened for output.
 * Inputs:      p, max (parameters)
 *              outFile (global variable)
 * Returns:     nothing
 * Modifies:    outFile
 * Error checking:      none
 */
```

```
void hex(unsigned char *p, int max);

/* main program - here is where the execution starts */
int main(int argc, char *argv[]) {
   FILE *inFile;                   /* input file handle */
   int i, toFile;
   const int SIZE = 16;
   unsigned char line[SIZE];   /* local buffer */

   if(argc > 3 || argc < 2) {
      fprintf(stderr, "usage: %s filename [filename2]\n",
               argv[0]);
      return EXIT_FAILURE;
   }

   outFile = stdout;     /* set default output stream */
   toFile = (argc == 3); /* is there an output file */

   /* open I/O files */
   if((inFile = fopen(argv[1], "r")) == NULL) {
      fprintf(stderr, "Cannot open file %s\n", argv[1]);
      return EXIT_FAILURE;
   }
   if(toFile && (outFile = fopen(argv[2], "w")) == NULL) {
      fprintf(stderr, "Cannot open file %s\n", argv[2]);
      fclose(inFile);
      return EXIT_FAILURE;
   }

   /* main loop; reads SIZE bytes at a time;
    * stores them in line, and calls hex()
    */
   while((i = fread(line, 1, SIZE, inFile)) > 0)
      hex(line, i);

   /* close I/O */
   if(fclose(inFile) == EOF) {
      fprintf(stderr, "Cannot close file %s\n", argv[1]);
      if(toFile)
         fclose(outFile);
      return EXIT_FAILURE;
   }
```

```c
    if(toFile && fclose(outFile) == EOF) {
        fprintf(stderr, "Cannot close file %s\n", argv[2]);
        return EXIT_FAILURE;
    }


    return EXIT_SUCCESS;
}

/* Definition of hex() */
void hex(unsigned char *p, int max) {
    int i;
    unsigned char *paux;

    for(i = 0, paux = p; i < max; i++, paux++)
        fprintf(outFile, "%02x ", *paux);
    fputc('\n', outFile);

    for(i = 0, paux = p; i < max; i++, paux++)
        fprintf(outFile, "%c  ", isprint(*paux) ? *paux : '.');
    fputc('\n', outFile);
}
```

2.1 General Documentation

Comments in C are similar to those in Java, except that there is no standard tool such as `javadoc` to produce documentation in HTML form. Also, an "in-line" comment, starting with `//`, is not supported. The heading comment that starts the sample program follows a particular style convention used throughout this book. It always describes the intended meaning of the program, any known bugs, etc. (other examples of complete programs shown in this book will not include information such as the author, the date, and the version number). Note that I try to avoid "in-line" comments, and use them only when a section of the code is not self-explanatory. Excessive in-line comments are detrimental to program readability—if the meaning a piece of code within the body of a function is clear, do not comment it.

2.2 Run-Time Libraries and Function Declarations

Include directives, starting with `#include`, are practically always needed in C programs to include files, called **header** files, which typically have the ".h" extension. In my example, three files are included, respectively called `stdio.h`, `ctype.h`, and `stdlib.h`.

These header files contain declarations of various standard functions that are defined in the run-time libraries. It is important to remember that there is a difference between the declaration of a function and the definition of a function. A **declaration** merely provides a function prototype, that is, the function header, which includes the return type and the list of parameters. For example:

```
void hex(unsigned char *p, int max);
```

declares `hex` to be a function that returns `void` and has two parameters. The declaration does not say anything about the implementation. The **definition** of a function includes both the function prototype and the function body, where the *body* is the implementation of the function. So why do we include header files for run-time libraries? Header files contain function declarations. A function can not be called before it is defined, or at least declared. Therefore, in order to use a library function in your program, you need to include the header file containing its declaration. For example, since the program uses standard I/O, the `stdio.h` header file has been included (`fread()`, `fprint()`, and other useful I/O functions are declared in `stdio.h`).

2.3 Global Definitions

Global definitions define entities (such as variables), which are available to all the code that follows this definition. In my example there is a single global definition

```
FILE *outFile;
```

that defines a file variable, or handle, used for file-based input/output. This variable is available to all the code that follows it: both the `hex()` and `main()` functions. Java does not allow for global definitions, because their use is against object-oriented encapsulation principles. The C programmer should be careful when using global variables (see Section 7.3.2).

2.4 User-Defined Functions

As you now know, C is a procedural programming language, in which all tasks are performed using functions. If one function, say `f()`, wants to call another function, say `g()`, then as I previously described, `g()` must be either declared or defined before `f()`. In my example, `main()` calls `hex()`, so the following function declaration precedes the code of `main()`:

```
void hex(unsigned char *p, int max);
```

The decision as to whether you first declare a function prototype, then call the function, and finally define it, or you first define the function and then call it, is mainly a matter of personal preference; in my example, the function `hex()` is declared so that it can be used in the `main()` function, and it is defined after `main()`. You could have defined `hex()` before `main()`, in which case you would not have needed its declaration.

Where should a function's documentation be placed? There are three possibilities: before the declaration, before the definition, or in both places. Clearly, there should be documentation in place for any function prototype expected to be seen by the client for the first time indicating what this function is intended to do. In the preceding code, you will find documentation preceding the declaration of `hex()`, but no documentation preceding its definition. While this is justified for a small file, in a larger file you should place another copy of the documentation before the definition of the function. (As you will see later, the prototype and the implementation are usually placed in separate files.) In my opinion, it is better to have two copies of the documentation of a function rather than no documentation at all. The addition of meaningful documentation to your code will not have any negative effect on the resulting executable code, and it will greatly increase maintainability of the program.

2.5 The `main` Function

Every C program must include a function called `main`. This function is the entry point for program execution. Java programmers are used to having more than one main function, each in a separate class. However, in C there must be exactly one occurrence of `main()`. In my example, I used

```
int main(int argc, char *argv[])
```

which shows the main function's command line arguments, very much like in Java. The second argument is an array of strings (`char *` in C represents a string). The first argument specifies the number of string arguments, and is needed because arrays in C can not be queried for their length.

There is also another way of specifying the main function (see Section 3.5), without any arguments, as in

```
int main()
```

Why is `main()` an integer function? Consider a program consisting of several components working in tandem, for example in a pipe. A component may want to know whether or not its predecessor was successful—it is for this reason that typically, the main function returns one of two standard return codes: `EXIT_FAILURE` and `EXIT_SUCCESS`.

The integer variable `toFile` is used as a Boolean variable. (It could not be declared as Boolean because C does not have a Boolean data type.) The definition of the array `line` shows that C arrays have a statically defined size.

The code of the main function consists of four major parts:

1. Error checking, to make sure that the number of command line arguments is correct; here two or three are required. Note that unlike in Java, the very first argument of the C command line is the name of the file containing the executable code itself. In case of an error, a message is displayed using the following call to `fprintf()`, which is a formatted output function:

    ```
    fprintf(stderr, "usage: %s filename [filename2]\n",
            argv[0]);
    ```

    The first argument specifies the name of the output file. Here it is `stderr`, which stands for the standard error stream. This stream is typically the same as the standard output, referred to as `stdout`, but with the exception that it will still send output to the standard output device, likely a terminal, even if the output from the program has been redirected, as in

    ```
    program > file
    ```

    The second argument is the formatted text that is to be sent to the output file. You can use format codes to include variables in the text: each format code is preceded by a '`%`' character, and followed by the type of argument expected. When the text is written to the output file, the format code is replaced by the actual argument provided. There must be a corresponding argument provided for each format code specified in the list of arguments following the formatted text. In my example, I have one format code. The letter '`s`' indicates that the corresponding variable is a string. In the text written, `argv[0]` is the string argument containing the name of the executable code; this is the text which replaces '`%s`'.

2. Opening of input and output files. The second argument in the command line is the name of the input file, which we need to open for reading.

    ```
    fopen(argv[1], "r")
    ```

    is a call to a library function that opens a file. The first argument of this function specifies the name of the file, the second argument specifies the mode in which this file is to be opened. In this case, the mode is `"r"`, which indicates that the file is to be opened for reading. Similarly,

```
fopen(argv[2], "w")
```

opens a file (the third argument from the command line) for writing. Since `fopen()` is a function, its return value can be tested for successful completion; the returned value `NULL` indicates a failure. Note that the second file is opened only if there are two arguments in the command line.

3. The main processing loop reads a chunk of the input file consisting of `SIZE` bytes and calls the function `hex()` to output the required representation:

```
while((i = fread(line, 1, SIZE, inFile)) > 0)
    hex(line, i);
```

`fread()` is a library function that reads from the file specified by its last argument. The third argument specifies the number of chunks, or blocks, that are read, and the second argument specifies the size of each block. The first argument specifies the address of the block of memory where the incoming bytes are to be stored; in this case, a local character array. `fread()` returns the number of bytes that have been successfully read—on encountering end of file, `fread()` will return 0, and the loop will terminate. (`fread()` will also return 0 if an error occurs, but in this example we will not try to differentiate between these two cases.)

4. Closing of input and output files. Here, a library function `fclose()` is tested for its return value; `EOF` indicates a failure.

The above program could have been written in a different way: the function `hex()` could have a third parameter, `FILE *outFile`. This would eliminate the need to have `outFile` as a global variable—it could be declared inside the body of the `main()` function instead. I used it as a global variable to demonstrate that there are two ways of passing arguments to functions. However, in general, using global variables may make programs more difficult to read and debug, and so this practice should be carried out with caution.

2.6 Sample Output

The last section of this chapter shows the script of two sample executions of the provided program. I created an executable file called `a.out`, and used the Unix environment to run the program (although the program source code is fully portable). The Unix command appearing on the first line of the script, `cat ex1.dat`, displays the contents of a small file `ex1.dat`. The third line executes the program with a single argument, `ex1.dat`, using the `a.out` executable. The first line of the output produced shows hexadecimal ASCII codes for the letters "a" and "b", followed by the ASCII code of line feed, used in the Unix environment as a line terminator.

The second execution of the program was done with two arguments; the file with the executable codes itself and a file `ex2.dat`. (Note that the program does not modify the first file provided, and so it is safe to provide the executable itself.) The Unix command

```
more ex2.dat
```

was then used to display the contents of the file `ex2.dat`; here I included only *part* of the output. As you can see, the executable code contains very few printable characters, but from the contents of the output, you can determine that this program used an ELF binary file format.

```
%cat ex1.dat
ab
%a.out ex1.dat
61 62 0a
a  b  .
%a.out a.out ex2.dat
%more ex2.dat
7f 45 4c 46 01 01 01 00 00 00 00 00 00 00 00 00
.  E  L  F  .  .  .  .  .  .  .  .  .  .  .  .
02 00 03 00 01 00 00 00 90 89 04 08 34 00 00 00
.  .  .  .  .  .  .  .  .  .  .  .  4  .  .  .
b4 1b 00 00 00 00 00 00 34 00 20 00 05 00 28 00
```

3

LEXICAL STRUCTURE, PRIMITIVE DATA TYPES, AND TERMINAL I/O

3.1 ◆ Preview

This chapter covers the following topics:

- primitive data types supported by the C language: `int`, `char`, `float`, `double`, and their variants, such as `long double`.

- expressions, including the assignment expressions

- basic terminal I/O

- type conversions and ways of defining synonyms for existing data types.

Since most of C's *control structures* are identical to those in Java, I will use some of these constructs in various examples; for more information on control structures, see Chapter 4.

Remember that those constructs that look similar in Java and in C, but that are handled differently in C, are marked with the C icon in the margin. Typically, it is mainly the most basic terminal I/O that is handled differently in C than in Java.

3.2 Lexical Structure

All programming languages, including C, have a **lexical structure**, defining the set of characters that may appear in a source file. This is the language's **alphabet**. The lexical structure also dictates the way characters are collected into lexical units. (These lexical units are also referred to as **tokens**.) For example, the sequence of characters

```
main()
```

consists of three tokens; respectively `main`, `(`, and `)`.

Tokens are the smallest textual elements of a program that are meaningful to a compiler. When you submit a program to the compiler, it first **scans** the text and extracts tokens. Tokens may be separated by one or more whitespace characters (characters such as spaces, tabs, formfeeds, and newlines are referred to as **whitespace**). C is a free format language, which means that any sequence of whitespace characters can be used in the place of a single whitespace character. For the above example, I could have said

```
main   (
   )
```

Whitespace and comments are used in a program to help a human user read the code but are ignored by the compiler, which replaces any sequence of whitespace characters by a single space. A program is said to be **lexically correct** if it follows the lexical structure of the language: it contains only characters from the language's alphabet, and all its tokens are built according to the language's rules.

Note that during scanning, the *longest* possible translation is chosen. For example,

```
a++b
```

is not scanned into four tokens: `a + + b` (meaning `a+ (+b)`); instead it is scanned into three tokens: `a`, `++`, and `b`, and results in an *incorrect* C construct. Using some whitespace, for example

```
a+ +b
```

would make this expression correct.

3.2.1 ◆ Alphabet

Table 3–1 shows the alphabet of C, which is similar to the Java alphabet (but the latter alphabet includes Unicode character encoding, which C does not use).

TABLE 3-1	Alphabet

```
a b c d e f g h i j k l m n o p q r s t u v w x y z
A B C D E F G H I J K L M N O P Q R S T U V W X Y Z
0 1 2 3 4 5 6 7 8 9
! " # % & ' ( ) * + , - . /
: ; < = > ? [ \ ] ^ _ { | } ~
space, horizontal and vertical tabs, formfeed, newline.
```

3.2.2 ◆ Comments

Comments in C are similar to those in Java, except that there is no standard tool such as `javadoc` provided for the production of HTML documentation. Also, an "in-line" comment, starting with `//`, is not supported.

Comments may contain extra characters not used in the alphabet, including the following characters: $, @, `. Comments can not be nested; for example

```
/* outer /* inner */ */
```

is illegal.

1. My lexical conventions for comments are:

   Short explanations are placed in comments at the right end of a line, for example

   ```
   if(isdigit)  /* error */
   ```

   Multi-line explanations are formatted like this:

   ```
   /*
    * Program to sort integer values
    */
   ```

2. The comments should never echo what is already in the code, for example

   ```
   k++;    /* k is incremented by 1*/
   ```

3. Make every comment count.

4. Don't over-comment.

5. Make sure comments and code agree; there are few things that confuse code readers more than incorrect comments.

3.2.3 ◆ Trigraphs

The standard seven-bit ASCII character set supports all characters in the alphabet from Section 3.2.1. Some computer systems support a smaller set of characters, and for these systems, there is a standard called the ISO 646–1083. In this standard, the following nine characters from the alphabet are not included:

    # [\ ] ^ { | } ~

In order to write ANSI C programs using all characters from the alphabet, *trigraphs* can be used to represent the missing symbols. A **trigraph** starts with two consecutive question marks (see Table 3–2).

It is likely you will never use trigraphs, but you should be aware of their existence. Note that most modern C compilers by default do not use trigraphs, and you may have to turn on a special compiler switch to use them. I cover trigraphs here for the sake of completeness.

TABLE 3–2	Trigraphs
Symbol	**Trigraph**
#	??=
{	??<
|	??!
[	??(
}	??>
~	??-
]	??)
\	??/
^	??'

Any string that includes `"??"`, may be treated by the compiler as a trigraph, and replaced according to the rules in Table 3–2; for example, the string

```
"(How many characters??)"
```

will be replaced by

```
"(How many characters]"
```

3.2.4 ◆ Line Structure

It is possible to break lines anywhere in the program by using the sequence `\newline`.

For example, the two lines shown below

```
my\
id
```

are *joined* during compiler translation into

```
myid
```

3.2.5 ◆ Tokens

There are five classes of tokens:

- identifiers, such as `toFile`
- keywords or reserved words, such as `int`
- constants, such as `1123`
- operators, such as `*`
- separators, `( )  [ ]  { }  ,  ;  :`

In the next section, I will describe identifiers and keywords; other tokens will be described in the following sections.

3.2.6 ◆ Identifiers

As in Java, an **identifier** is a sequence of letters, digits, and underscores that does not start with a digit. Recall that in Java, identifiers are case-sensitive, can use Unicode, and have unlimited length.

In C, identifiers are also case-sensitive, but only the first 31 characters are significant. This means that two identifiers that are identical in the first 31 characters and different in remaining characters are considered to be identical. In addition,

C

identifiers with the storage class `extern` (see Section 7.4.2) may on some systems be case-independent, and have only the first 6 characters significant. This is a very serious limitation, because long identifiers contribute to readability, but may potentially create portability problems. Programs in this book will typically use identifiers that are more than six characters long, but you should remember that before you move such programs from one system to another, you should check how many characters are significant in both systems.

The documentation of programs, which are available to clients, should make it clear whether you are using identifiers whose length exceeds 6 characters. You should never use identifiers that have more than 31 characters.

Leading underscores should be avoided, because most compilers reserve them for their own use.

1. It is important to use a consistent style throughout your code. Variables should have meaningful names when appropriate (a control variable in a `for` statement may be called `"i"`, but a variable representing a filename should not be called `"r"`).

2. You are encouraged to mix cases to make your identifiers more readable, for example:

   ```
   longIdentifier
   ```

3. Always avoid using two identifiers that differ from each other only by one character, or in case only, for example

   ```
   setIns and setInt
   ```

   Unfortunately as you will see in Chapter 6, C does not follow this rule and uses both `ifdef` and `ifndef` as two of its preprocessor commands.

4. Since C does not have classes, you have to take extra precautions to avoid name conflicts. For example, it is best to avoid the general name

   ```
   insert
   ```

   because many functions may want to insert something. Instead, use specific names such as `insertList` (more on this issue in Section 7.4.4.).

TABLE 3-3	Keywords			
auto	default	float	register	struct
break	do	for	return	switch
case	double	goto	short	typedef
char	else	if	signed	unsigned
const	enum	int	sizeof	void
continue	extern	long	static	volatile
while				

3.2.7 ◆ Keywords

The list of C keywords shown in Table 3–3 is shorter than that in Java.

C

3.3 Primitive Data Types and Declarations

3.3.1 ◆ Primitive Data Types

C provides several primitive data types: `char`, `int`, `float` and `double`. There are two important differences between Java and C:

C

- C provides no built-in Boolean type. Instead, Boolean values are represented by integers: The value 0 stands for false, any non-zero value stands for true (this includes both positive and negative integers).
- C does not guarantee that a specific amount of memory will be allocated to a particular data type. Instead, all implementations of C must follow certain rules (described later in this chapter). For example, the `int` type must always occupy at least 16 bits.

In order to help you understand the above description, a brief review of the computer's memory is provided below.

Computer Memory

Computer memory consists of words; each word consists of a number of bytes, and a byte consists of a number of bits (usually 8 bits). In this book, I consider only a byte-oriented memory architecture, in which the smallest addressable unit is one byte. (Other less popular memory architectures are word-oriented.) During program execution, every data object is stored in some memory area consisting of several consecutive bytes. For example, an integer may be stored in 4 bytes of memory starting from the address 100 to the address 103. The size of a data object is the number of bytes it occupies. All data objects of the same type need the same amount of memory (although this amount of memory may not be the same between different platforms), and therefore it makes sense to talk about the size of a data type; for example, the size of integer.

Integer numbers (but not real numbers) come in two flavors: `signed` and `unsigned`. Signed data can use one of the following three encoding techniques:

- two's complement notation
- one's complement notation
- sign magnitude notation

Signed integers use the leftmost bit, called the sign bit, to represent the sign (0 for non-negative values, 1 for negative values). Unsigned integers do not use the leftmost bit as the sign bit, and therefore their positive values can be larger than positive values represented as unsigned integers. For example, the largest unsigned 16 bit integer is $2^{16} - 1$ and the largest signed 16-bit integer is $2^{15} - 1$. For more details of these notations see [Har91].

Range of Values

In various applications, you may need to know the range of possible values for a specific data type. For example, in order to avoid integer underflow or overflow in arithmetic operations, you have to know the maximum possible integer value. C provides a header file `limits.h`, see Appendix B, which defines the various ranges, for example:

`CHAR_BIT` is the width of `char` type in bits, the minimum value is 8.
`INT_MAX` is the maximum value of `int`, at least 32,767.

Integer Types

To specify an integer type, you can either declare it as a plain `int` (i.e. no qualifiers), or precede the `int` (in any order) with one or two *qualifiers* selected from the following list:

`short` or `long`
`unsigned` or `signed`

If you do use qualifications, you can drop the word `int`—it will be assumed by the compiler. Also, a `signed int` is the same as an `int`. Some examples of integer data types are:

```
short unsigned int
signed long
int
```

C guarantees the following:

size(`short`) <= size(`int`) <= size(`long`)

Unsigned integers have wider ranges because their binary representation does not need a sign bit. A word of size n bits is in the range from 0 to 2^n-1. It should be noted that arithmetic operations on unsigned integers follow the rules of arithmetic modulo 2^n and so are different from arithmetic operations on signed integers. In particular, operations on unsigned integers can not produce an overflow. For example the sum of 2^n-1 and 1 does not overflow; instead it is calculated modulo 2^n and results in 0. In addition, for arguments of mixed types, these operations convert all arguments to the unsigned type (see Section 3.9.2).

> To support portability, use only integers in the ranges specified in `limits.h` (see Appendix B). For example, you can always use plain integers in the range from −32,767 to 32,767, since this range is guaranteed by every implementation of C. Any other assumptions, such as that the size of an `int` is 4 bytes, must not be made.

In order to check whether the sum of two integers `i` and `j` *overflows*, do not use

```
i + j > INT_MAX
```

(`INT_MAX` is defined in `limits.h`), because this creates an overflow. Instead, use

```
i > INT_MAX - j
```

Character Types

There are three character data types in C: `char`, `unsigned char`, and `signed char`. A plain `char` may be stored as either a `signed char` or `unsigned` `char`—this is implementation-dependent. C does not have the same *pure* character type as Java; instead its character types are actually represented internally as integers.

Unsigned characters and signed characters are respectively stored as unsigned integers and signed integers. Typically, signed characters are in the range from −128 to 127, and unsigned characters are in the range from 0 to 255.

The most popular character set is ASCII (American Standard Code for Information Interchange). IBM computers use another character set, called EBCDIC. (Sometimes there are only 128 characters, represented by a 7-bit long code.)

Why should you care whether you are using signed or unsigned `char`? The distinction becomes important when the character is converted to an integer—if you are using 8-bit signed characters, then upon conversion, the high order bit will represent the sign and the resulting integer value may be negative (if the sign bit is 1); see the section on type conversions, presented later in this chapter.

In order to write portable code, you should explicitly specify `signed char` or `unsigned char`.

You should never make any assumptions about the code values of characters, such as the value of `'A'` is 65. While this is true for the ASCII code of `'A'`, this assumption is not portable. Thus, use `'A'` rather than 65 in your code.

Floating-Point Types

Floating-point types are similar to those in Java: `float`, `double`, and `long double`; `float` and `double` respectively represent single and double precision, and `long double` may be more precise than `double`.

However, C does not guarantee any specific ranges for these types; instead they are specified in the `float.h` header file (see Appendix B). The only guarantee that C gives you is that

size(`float`) <= size(`double`) <= size(`long double`).

3.3.2 ◆ Declarations of Variables and Constants

Variables

To declare variables, C uses the same syntax as Java. For example:

```
int i;    /* initial value undefined */
double d = 1.23;
```

I recommend that

1. A declaration of a different data type starts on a new line.

2. The lists of identifiers are aligned so that they start in the same column.

3. Each variable identifier (except the last one) is followed by one space.

4. I discourage multiple initializations on the same line, such as:

```
int i = 1, j = 2;
```

or

```
int i = 2, j;
```

and instead recommend that each declaration that contains an initialization appear on a separate line, as in

```
int i = 1;
int j = 2;
```

5. If comments are required, each declaration should be placed on a separate line, for example:

```
int lower;    /* lower bound of the array */
int upper;    /* upper bound of the array */
```

Constants

Constants are like variables except their values cannot be changed. Recall that in order to define constants in Java, you use the `final` keyword. In C, constants are defined as initialized variables, with the additional prefix keyword `const` placed before or after the type identifier. For example:

```
const double PI = 3.1415926;
```

Names of constants will appear in upper case throughout this book, and `const` always appears in front of the declaration.

3.4 Assignment

Assignment is the same in C as in Java, but since understanding it is so important, I will briefly review the most crucial concepts. An **l-value** is an expression that can be interpreted as an address; for example, a variable is an l-value, whereas a constant is not. (Intuitively, an **l**-value is an expression that can appear on the **left**-hand side of an assignment.)

An assignment is an *expression* rather than a statement (its value is the value of the right-hand side), and so it can be used any place an expression is allowed. The assignment operator = associates to the right, so the expression

```
x = y = 2
```

is equivalent to

```
x = (y = 2)
```

I will elaborate more on this topic in the section on type conversion, presented later in this chapter.

I use exactly one blank before and one blank after the "=" operator.

3.5 The main Program

Every C program must include a function called `main`. This function is the starting point for program execution. Java programmers are used to having more than one main function, each in a separate class. In C there must be exactly one occurrence of `main()`.

The main function may have two possible prototypes:

```
int main(int argc, char *argv[])
int main()
```

The first prototype shows the main function with command line arguments, very much like in Java. The first argument specifies the number of string arguments, and is needed because arrays in C can not be queried for their length. The second argument is an array of strings (`char*` represents a string). The second prototype shows the same function, but with no command line arguments.

`main()` is an integer function, which returns one of two standard codes: `EXIT_FAILURE` and `EXIT_SUCCESS`. These are pre-defined constants found in the standard library `stdlib.h` (`main()` can also return other values, but their use would result in non-portable code). The return code allows for the status of the main program to be tested at the level of the operating system (details depend on the system the program is running on—for example, Unix uses the shell variable `$status`).

Note that local variables declared in a function have undetermined values until they are explicitly initialized by the programmer. Unlike the Java compiler, the C compiler typically does not check that the variables have been initialized before their use.

The lexical convention used for the main function is as follows:

```
int main() {          the left brace on the same line as the header
  body               body indented to the right
}                    the matching right brace aligned with int
```

Use return codes `EXIT_FAILURE` and `EXIT_SUCCESS` (other values will not be portable).

MAIN FUNCTION

`main()` is an integer function, which returns one of two standard return codes: `EXIT_FAILURE` and `EXIT_SUCCESS`.

3.6 Constants

A constant is sometimes called a *literal*, because its value is literally what you see in the code—it never changes.

3.6.1 ◆ Integer Constants

Integer constants in C are identical to Java, and may be specified as decimal, octal, or hexadecimal. For example,

```
123
04
0xAF3B
```

The type of a *decimal* integer constant depends on its value V and is defined below:

int	if V does not exceed the largest possible int value
long	if V exceeds the largest possible int value, but does not exceed the largest long value
unsigned long	if V exceeds the largest possible long value but does not exceed the largest unsigned long value
is *undefined*	otherwise (V exceeds the largest unsigned long value)

The actual type of a constant is the first from the following three types

```
int
long
unsigned long
```

that is in the range of this type (does not cause an overflow).

Adding the suffix to the constant can modify these types:

long	with the suffix l or L (e.g. 1234555777L)
unsigned	with the suffix u or U (e.g. 55u)
unsigned long	with the suffix lu or LU (e.g. 2666LU)

Types of *octal* or *hexadecimal* constants are slightly different; the selected type is the first from the following four types

```
int
unsigned int
long
unsigned long
```

that is in the range of this type (does not cause an overflow). For example, a *decimal* integer constant whose value is larger than the maximum value of an int but less than the maximum value of long will have type long; the same constant in a hexadecimal notation may have the type unsigned int.

3.6.2 ◆ Floating-Point Constants

Floating-point constants are similar to those in Java, and can be written using either one of the following two notations:

fixed point notation, for example 3, 3.14, .25

scientific notation, for example 3e+14, 2.75E-20

The type of a floating-point constant is always `double`. Using the suffix can modify it:

f or F	to modify the type to `float` for example `3.23f` is of type `float`
l or L	to modify the type to `long double` for example `37668.668788L` is of type `long double`

I recommend that in order to specify long types, you use the upper case L rather than the lower case l, because the latter can be mistaken for 1, as in

```
1001
```

3.6.3 ◆ Character Constants

Character constants in C are similar to Java's, and are enclosed in single quotes, e.g. `'a'`.

Numeric escape sequences starting with \ are allowed:

octal_number (up to three octal digits), e.g. `'\077'`

hexadecimal_number (any number of hexadecimal digits), e.g. `'\AEC'`

Commonly used escape sequences are the same in C and Java, and are listed in Table 3–4.

TABLE 3-4	Escape Sequences
`\a`	alert (bell)
`\b`	backspace
`\f`	formfeed
`\n`	newline
`\r`	carriage return
`\t`	horizontal tab
`\v`	vertical tab
`\\`	backslash
`\?`	question mark
`\'`	single quote
`\"`	double quote

Character constants have the `int` data type. Unfortunately, these characters may not be used to store characters from other languages, for example Japanese, which require more than one byte. To overcome this restriction, C provides wide characters, specified with a leading `L`, as in

```
L'a'
```

C

Wide characters have type `wchar_t`, defined in the header file `stddef.h`.

3.6.4 ◆ String Constants

A C string constant is enclosed in double quotes (just like in Java), for example

```
"My string"
```

However, the similarity ends here. There are *no* operations provided on string constants, so Java's

```
"one " + "two"
```

is illegal. However, *adjacent* string constants are concatenated; for example, the two strings

```
"one " "two"
```

become

```
"one two"
```

A string constant is converted to a *pointer to a character* (see Section 9.3.1). Wide string constants are provided in C with an `L` prefix.

String constants and character constants are very different. One must take care not to use a string constant

```
"a"
```

if a character constant is required

```
'a'
```

TABLE 3-5	Operators						
=	>	<	!	~	?	:	,
==	<=	>=	!=	&&	||	++	--
+	-	*	/	&	|	^	%
<<	>>	>>	+=	-=	*=	/=	&=
|=	^=	%=	<<=	>>=	>>=		

3.7 Expressions

C expressions are built in the same way as Java expressions (see Table 3–5). However, compared to Java, the evaluation rules are much more relaxed in order to allow the compiler to perform various optimizations. There are only four binary operators that guarantee that the left operand is evaluated *before* the right operand:

logical AND, as in `e1 && e2`

logical OR, as in `e1 || e2`

a conditional expression, as in `e1 ? e2 : e3`

a comma expression, as in `e1, e2`

The comma expression is absent in Java. The first operand of the **comma expression** is always evaluated first, and the result is discarded. The second operand is then evaluated, and the type and value of that operand become respectively the type and value of the comma expression. Comma expressions are often used to perform several updates at once, for example

```
i++, j++
```

This is especially useful in the `for` statement (see Section 4.3).

Appendix A gives the complete **precedence** and **associativity** list of all the operators.

> Do not assume that the evaluation of standard mathematical expressions, such as addition, is performed from left to right.

STOP

Since < is left associative, the expression

```
a < b < c
```

is interpreted as

```
(a < b) < c
```

and has a different meaning than

```
a < b && b < c
```

Note that like in Java, a C variable may be declared `volatile` to signify that it can be modified asynchronously. The compiler does not perform various optimizations of volatile variables; for example, it does not re-arrange variables because it could not assume that the value of `i` would not be changed *asynchronously*.

C provides a library of commonly used *mathematical* functions, such as `sqrt()` and `sin()`. In order to use these functions, you must include the header file `math.h`.

Don't use spaces around the following operators:

```
->      .      []      !      ~      ++      —      – (unary)
 * (unary)   &
```

For example, write

```
a->b            a[i]            *c
```

but not

```
~ a      & c
```

In *general*, use one space around the following operators:

```
=      +=      ?:      +      <      &&      + (binary) etc.
```

For example, code should be written as

```
a = b;
a = a + 2;
```

not

```
a= b+ 1;
```

Although it is not necessary, you may skip spaces to show operator *precedence*. For example, you could write:

```
a = a*b + 1;
```

but you should avoid

```
a = a+b * 2;
```

3.8 Terminal Input/Output

Input/Output operations available in C are so different from those in Java that in this section, I will not even try to refer to Java. You may initially be overwhelmed by the cryptic appearance of C I/O operations, but hopefully as time goes on, you will grow to appreciate their power and flexibility. Recall that all I/O operations are provided through library functions. The principal reason for this approach is that it separates the machine-dependent and machine-independent aspects of the language, and by doing so, makes it simpler to port programs to other computers.

Remember that in order to use I/O operations, you need to include the stdio.h header file, using

```
#include <stdio.h>
```

3.8.1 ◆ Single Character I/O

First, I will define three simple concepts:

- **Standard input** is usually a keyboard, unless it has been redirected, for example from a file
- **Standard output** is usually the screen, unless it has been redirected, for example to a file or a printer
- EOF is a constant defined in stdio.h; it stands for End-Of-File.

Most operating systems use ">" for output redirection and "<" for input redirection. Redirection is particularly useful for **filter** programs—that is programs that are designed to read the standard input stream only and write to the standard output stream only. For example, if F is a filter, then

```
F < test.in > test.out
```

will tell F to read from test.in and write to test.out.

There are two relevant I/O operations:

```
int getchar()        to input a single character
int putchar(int)     to output a single character
```

In more detail:

■ getchar() reads the next character from the standard input, and returns its value (as an integer) or EOF when end-of-file is reached

■ putchar(c) puts character c on the standard output and returns its value, or EOF when a write-error occurs.

I will now provide two examples to give you a better feel for the way these functions work.

Example 3-1

```c
/*
 * File: ex3-1.c
 * Program that reads two characters and prints them in
 *   reverse order, separated by a tab and ending with end of line.
 * Single character, unformatted I/O operations are used.
 * Error checking: none.
 */
#include <stdio.h>
#include <stdlib.h>
int main() {
    int c, d;          /* chars must be read as ints */

    c = getchar();
    d = getchar();

    putchar(d);
    putchar('\t');
    putchar(c);
    putchar('\n');

    return EXIT_SUCCESS;
}
```

I used only one in-line comment, because the rest of the code is self-explanatory. A sample execution follows:

```
ab
b       a
```

If you executed this program by typing 'a' followed by Return, then the output would be an empty line followed by this line

```
a
```

because the second character read is the end-of-line character.

The next example will use a conditional statement to show how to test for values returned by getchar().

Example 3-2

```
/*
 * File: ex3-2.c
 * Program that reads two characters and prints them in
 *   reverse order, separated by a tab and ending with end of line.
 * Single character, unformatted I/O operations are used.
 * Error checking: Program terminates if either of the
 *  input operations fails.
 *  No error checking for the output operations.
 */
#include <stdio.h>
#include <stdlib.h>
int main() {
   int c, d;

   if((c = getchar()) == EOF)
      return EXIT_FAILURE;
   if((d = getchar()) == EOF)
      return EXIT_FAILURE;

   putchar(d);
   putchar('\t');
   putchar(c);
```

```
    putchar('\n');

    return EXIT_SUCCESS;
}
```

Note that the above program quietly terminates when it fails, without printing an error message. If such a program is executed in the context of other components, for example in a pipe, then error messages could create a problem if they are read by another component. Consequently, error messages should be sent to the standard *error* stream which is usually not a part of the redirection (see Section 5.4). In order to save space, some of the sample code provided in this book will not output *any* error messages, but the complete versions of these programs will.

READ SINGLE CHARACTER

```
if((c = getchar()) == EOF) ... /* error, else OK */
```

1. The code fragment presented will show a common error, related to the placement of brackets (notice the lack of any inner brackets):

```
if(c = getchar() == EOF)
```

   Due to the precedence rules, the compiler interprets the code fragment as follows:

```
if(c = (getchar() == EOF))
```

   As a result, c gets assigned a Boolean value, and the character read is not stored in c.

2. Always use an integer variable instead of a char variable c to store the result of getchar().

Blank lines are used to separate logically related sections of code. For example, in the previous program, there are three sections: input, processing, and termination.

3.8.2 ◆ Formatted I/O

In this section, I will introduce two I/O routines:

```
int scanf()     read formatted
int printf()    print formatted
```

Unlike Java, C provides a great deal flexibility when it comes to formatted I/O. Since both `scanf()` and `printf()` are quite involved, I explain only how they can be used to read and write simple data. You will find a complete description in Appendix B.

First, I will describe the `printf()` function in its limited form, used to output a single value:

```
int printf("format", exp)
```

In the above function

"`format`" is a *string constant* called a **format control string**, which specifies the formatting requirements, and exp is the expression to be printed.

A format control string contains **conversion specifications**, preceded by a %. Different data types require different conversion specifications. For example, to output an integer value, you use %d, as in:

```
printf("%d", 123);
```

The format control string may also contain character sequences not preceded by a %; these are simply output exactly as they are given. For example

```
printf("The value of i = %d.\n", i);
```

Assuming that the value of i is 5, this statement outputs:

```
The value of i = 5.
```

The second argument may be omitted if the first argument is just a string, with no conversion specifications; for example

```
printf("Hello world\n");
```

In general, `printf()` can output values of several expressions to the standard output stream; and it returns the number of characters successfully outputted. EOF is returned if an error occurs during the output.

The return value of `printf()` is rarely used, because typically, you assume that the output statement is successful. Consequently, this function is usually called as if it were a procedure, not a function. For the sake of readability, you may use the following *cast* syntax:

```
(void)printf("The value of i = %d.\n", i);
```

On the other hand, if you wish to test the return value of `printf()`, you can use the following:

```
if(printf("The value of i = %d.\n", i) == EOF)   /* error */
```

The *input* function `scanf()` is similar to `printf()`:

```
int scanf("format", &var);
```

but the expression `var` above has to be an lvalue. You have to use `&var` to get the address of the lvalue `var` (for details, see Section 8.15.1). For example

```
scanf("%d", &i);
```

reads an integer value and stores it in the variable `i`.

1. The ampersand `&` preceding the variable `i` is crucial. As I explain in Chapter 8, `&` is the address operator, which returns the address of the memory object specified as its argument. C, like Java, passes function parameters by value, and in order to modify the value of the actual parameter, it has to be "passed by reference," that is, you have to pass its address.

2. `printf()` expects a string, so

```
printf("\n");
```

is correct, but

```
printf('\n');
```

is wrong.

---

scanf(), like printf(), uses various format specifications to read different types.

The first example of formatted I/O routines follows.

Example 3-3

```
/*
 * File: ex3-3.c
 * Program that reads two integers and prints their sum
 *   and difference, each on a separate line
 * Error checking: None.
 */
#include <stdio.h>
#include <stdlib.h>
int main() {
    int i, j;

    printf("Enter two integers:");
    scanf("%d", &i);
    scanf("%d", &j);

    printf("%d\n", i + j);
    printf("%d\n", i - j);

    return EXIT_SUCCESS;
}
```

I now present other conversion specifications, and briefly describe them (a more complete description is provided in Appendix B).

To print integers, the following conversions are used:

d   signed decimal

ld   long decimal

u   unsigned decimal

o   unsigned octal

x, X   unsigned hexadecimal

The conversion character may be preceded by a minimum field width specification (decimal integer constant). It may also include the precision, a period followed by a decimal integer. For example

```
printf("%10.4d\n", i);
```

Here, you have a field width 10, precision 4. For example, if the value of i is 123, then this value will be preceded by a leading zero and printed, right-justified, in a field of length 10 (that is preceded by six blanks, followed by 0123). If the value of i is 17893, then this value will be printed preceded by five blanks.

To print floating-point values, the following conversions are used (the default precision is 6):

f, e, E, g, G   floating-point number in the form:

f   [-] ddd.ddd

e   [-] d.dddde{sign}dd

E   [-] d.ddddE{sign}dd

g   shorter of f and e

G   shorter of f and E

For f, e, and E, the precision is the number of digits to the right of the decimal point; for g and G it is the number of significant digits. For example

```
double d = 123.3456789;
printf("%5.3f\n",d);
printf("%5.3e\n",d);
```

will produce:

```
123.346
1.233e+02
```

1. To print a double, you use %f, but to read the same double value, you use %lf. Similarly, to print a long integer use %d, and to read it, use %ld.

2. Use correct conversions; for example,

```
printf("%d", 3.5);
```

and

```
printf("%g", 4);
```

will both print *garbage*.

To print characters and strings, the following conversions are used:

c   character
s   character string

For example, the code given below will output the character 'a' followed by its character code:

```
printf("%c", 'a');
printf("%d", 'a');
```

The two statements

```
printf("This %s test", "is");
printf("This is test");
```

are equivalent, but in general, for a string mes, the result of the two statements shown below depends on whether or not mes contains any % characters:

```
printf("%s", mes);
```

and

```
printf(mes);
```

The first statement will simply print a string mes, while the second statement will treat any occurrences of % in mes as a control character; for example, if mes is of the form

```
"One %, two %s"
```

the second `printf()` is incorrect.

You can use `%s` to control the format of the output depending on the value of some condition (s). For example,

```
printf("This is %s test\n", flag ? "" : "not");
```

prints

```
This is test
```

when `flag` is not equal to 0, and

```
This is not test
```

otherwise.

Both `printf()` and `scanf()` can be used to output or input *more than one* value. In such a case, the number of conversion specifications in the format control string must be equal to the number of expressions, or the result is undefined.

For example, the two statements

```
printf("%c", 'a');
printf("%d", 'a');
```

can be replaced by a single one:

```
printf("%c%d", 'a', 'a');
```

Similarly, the two statements:

```
scanf("%d", &i);
scanf("%d", &j);
```

can be replaced by a single one:

```
scanf("%d%d", &i, &j);
```

`scanf()` returns the number of items that have been successfully read, and EOF if no items have been read and end-of-file has been encountered. For example,

```
scanf("%d%d", &i, &j)
```

returns the following value:

2   if both input operations were successful, and so two integer values have been successfully read, respectively into `i` and `j`

1   if only the first input operation was successful, and so one integer value has been successfully read into `i` (the value of `j` is undefined)

0   if the input operation failed, for example because the first input value was not an integer

`EOF`   if an end-of-file has been encountered.

Let's rewrite Example 3-3, this time using double values, and check the return value of `scanf()`. Since the program is expecting two double values, if `scanf()` does not return the value 2, the program has failed.

Example 3-4

```c
/*
 * File: ex3-4.c
 * Program that reads two doubles and prints their sum
 *   and difference, each on a separate line
 * Error checking: Terminates if either of the read operations fails.
 */
#include <stdio.h>
#include <stdlib.h>
int main() {
    double i, j;

    printf("Enter two double values:");
    if(scanf("%lf%lf", &i, &j) != 2)
        return EXIT_FAILURE;

    printf("sum = %f\ndifference = %f\n", i + j, i - j);
    return EXIT_SUCCESS;
}
```

READ SINGLE INTEGER

```
if(scanf("%d", &i) != 1 ) ...   /* error, else OK */
```

Above, I have not included a prompt. If you want to use a prompt in your program, use the following idiom:

READ SINGLE INTEGER WITH PROMPT

```
printf("Enter integer: ");
if(scanf("%d", &i) != 1 ) ...   /* error, else OK */
```

The above idiom is used to read a single integer into a variable. It can be easily modified to read other data types, and the number of these data types, by changing the control format string. For example

READ TWO INTEGERS

```
if(scanf("%d%d", &i, &j) != 2 ) ...   /* error, else OK */
```

You may wish to skip leading whitespace when reading some data (for example, when reading integers). Fortunately, scanf() is designed to do exactly that—it skips whitespace and looks for the longest data field that matches the specification given in the corresponding control string (for all conversions except %c). For example, assume that the user enters

```
a    13b
```

when the following code is executed:

```
char c, d;
int i;

scanf("%c%d%c", &c, &i, &d);
printf("%c%d%c\n", c, i, d);
```

The output will be

```
a13b
```

because the two blanks that precede `13` will be skipped. The careful reader will notice that the input character 'b' that did not match the specification is pushed back, and can be read in the future. (Specifically, the first `%c` gets the character `c`, then `%d` skips two spaces, gets `13`, reads the character `b`, and then pushes it back, so that the next `%c` reads it.) Note that if `scanf()` fails to assign a value, then the corresponding variable has an undefined value; for example, for the input

```
12a
```

and the code

```
scanf("%d%d", &i, &j);
```

the value of `i` is `12` and the value of `j` is undefined.

The above discussion should give you some idea as to how to deal with erroneous input.

The number of conversions must be equal to the number of arguments; for example

```
printf("%d%d", i)
```

is incorrect. Remember that with `scanf()` you need to pass the address of the variable, therefore

```
scanf("%d", i);
```

is incorrect.

As a final note, keep in mind that a format control string for `scanf()` may contain any characters, not only conversion specifications. If such characters exist, the control string represents a *pattern*, and `scanf()` will read the input trying to match this pattern.

For example, for the input

```
12 , 4.5
```

and the code

```
scanf("%d,%lf", &i, &f);
```

the ',' character in the format control string will be matched to the one in the input line; the value of i will be 12 and the value of f will be 4.5.

Spurious characters in scanf()'s format control string are a source of errors that are very hard to spot. Use them with caution!

3.9 Type Conversions

C is very flexible when it comes to using data types. Operands of arithmetic expressions do not need to have the same type, arguments of a function may be of a different type from the specified list of formal parameters, and the programmer has the option of modifying the type of a variable that has been previously specified in a declaration, using a cast.

By now, you will likely expect that a discussion of all possible type conversions will be very complicated. Indeed, a full coverage of this topic is fairly involved. However, some of these conversions lead to non-portable code—since portability is one of my goals, such conversions will not be discussed here. I will begin by presenting several basic concepts that you will need to understand this section.

3.9.1 ◆ sizeof

As I explained earlier in this chapter, a computer's memory consists of bytes. All data objects of the same type occupy the same amount of memory. The **size** of a type is the number of bytes occupied by an object of this type. C provides an operator to compute this size:

```
sizeof(type name)
```

or

```
sizeof expression
```

returns the size of the data type or object represented by the expression.

For example

```
sizeof(int)
```

and, assuming `int i;`

```
sizeof i
```

both return the number of bytes used to store integers. The `sizeof` operator returns an unsigned integer type `size_t`, as defined in the header file `stddef.h`. As a result, printing its return value is implementation dependent, but `sizeof` is really indispensable for reasons other than printing. One its main functions is to determine the amount of memory to be allocated to a pointer of a specific type (see Section 8.11.1). If you do need to print this value, use a cast (see Section 3.9.2); for example:

```
printf("Size of double is %ld\n",
            (unsigned long)sizeof(double));
```

3.9.2 ◆ Conversions

Operations on two values of different types cannot be performed until one of the values is converted to the type of the other value.

In Java, there are four kinds of conversion: arithmetic conversion, assignment conversion, function call conversion, and casting conversion. The first three types are performed by the compiler and are known as **implicit** conversions. A casting conversion is performed by the programmer and is known as **explicit** conversion. In C, conversions can be divided in a similar way, and they are explained below. The function call conversions are explained in Section 7.2.3.

First, I provide a general description of conversions, and then provide details of various specific conversions.

The `sizeof()` operator can be used to compare the sizes of two types: a type T is **wider** than type S (and S is **narrower** than T), if

```
sizeof(T) >= sizeof(S).
```

You can say that the narrower type is *promoted* to the wider type, and conversely the wider type is *demoted* to the narrower type. Clearly, when you promote values you avoid losing precision, but when you demote values you invariably lose some information about this value. For example, the value 2.3 demoted to an integer value results in the value 2, and the integer value 3 promoted to the real value results in 3.0. Note that

an `int` value can be safely promoted to `double`

a `double` value can *not* be safely demoted to `int`

You may think that a safe way to demote a `double` to `int` is to simply drop the fractional part. However, the result will still be undefined if the original double value (minus the fractional part) is larger than the largest possible integer (overflow), or smaller than the smallest integer (underflow).

Arithmetic Conversions

If operands of an expression are of different types, then these operands will have their types changed, using *arithmetic conversions*. C does not perform arithmetic operations at a precision shorter than that of an `int`, and `char` values are always converted to `int`.

Even the simple matter of converting characters to integers using their character set representations is a bit involved. Unsigned chars may be converted using sign extension. This does not cause problems with converting 7-bit long characters to integers. However, an 8-bit long *signed* character converted to an integer may result in a negative value. Consider the following example:

```
signed char sc = '\xdb';
```

Since the decimal value of `sc` is 229, its sign bit is 1, and in the expression

```
sc + 1
```

`sc` is converted to `int`; therefore the resulting integer is negative.

When a conversion is applied, a lower precision type is *promoted* to a higher precision type according to the following hierarchy:

```
int
unsigned
long
unsigned long
float
double
long double
```

For example, in an expression

```
int_Operand + unsigned_Operand
```

the `int_Operand` is converted to `unsigned`. Similarly, in an expression

```
float_Operand + double_Operand
```

the `float_Operand` is converted to `double`. Various methods may be used to perform the above promotion.

Note that unsigned arguments are particularly tricky, and should be avoided if possible. For example

```
unsigned1 > unsigned2
```

works as expected, but

```
unsigned1 - unsigned2 > 0
```

does not, because the right-hand side gets converted to an `unsigned` and is always positive, and so the above comparison is always true. Similarly,

```
unsigned u = ...;
... (u != -1) ..
```

may have unexpected results, because -1 is converted to the largest positive unsigned value.

Assignment Conversions

Assignment conversions occur when the expression on the right-hand side of the assignment has to be converted to the type of the left-hand side. These conversions are simpler than arithmetic conversions, but you have to be more careful. In general, type promotions are valid, but type demotions may produce undefined results. For example, the `double_Operand` will be demoted in the following assignment:

```
int_Operand = double_Operand;
```

and the result may be undefined if the demotion results in overflow or underflow.

For the next example, I will assume the ASCII character set is used, and show various `char`-to-`int` conversions.

```
char c = 2;              /* c is ^B */
int i;
```

```
c++;                    /* ^C */
c += '0';               /* 3 */
i = c - '0';            /* 3 */
c = 'a' + i;            /* d */
c += 'z' - 'a';         /* D */
```

Type Cast Conversions

The **type cast** expression

```
(typ) exp
```

converts the expression exp to the type typ. For example

```
(int) 2.5
```

results in

```
2
```

Casting is useful for documentation, and is also needed to overrule standard semantics of various operations. For example, to convert from Fahrenheit to Celsius, you use the formula

```
5/9*(F - 32)
```

Coding this formula as

```
double f, c;
f = 100.2;
c = (5/9)*(f - 32);
```

produces zero, since when the expression (5/9) is evaluated, integer division is used.

In order to obtain the desired result, you need to force one of the operands of the division to be of a double type:

```
c = ( (double)5/9 ) * (f - 32);
```

Avoiding arithmetic overflow may requires a cast, as in

```
long i = 19309399 * 39393883;
```

which should be coded as

```
long i = 19309399 * (long)39393883;
```

Note however that

```
(long)19309399*39393883
```

may be incorrect because * has higher precedence than a cast.

3.10 **Type Synonyms: `typedef`**

C provides a tool to define a *synonym* for an existing type, using the following syntax:

```
typedef existingType NewType;
```

For example, if you want to use a Boolean type, define

```
typedef int Boolean;
```

and now you can use Boolean as if it were a new type (which it is not; it is merely a *synonym* for `int`):

```
Boolean b = 1;
```

(In the presented example, it would be better to use 'true' rather than the integer 1; I will later show how this can be done using macros.)

When specifying a new type using `typedef`, identifier names start with an uppercase letter.

Type definitions are useful for writing programs that can not be fully portable (ones that may require some minor modifications when moved from one machine to another). For example, let's assume that you need to work with large integer values such as 100,000 and add the additional constraint that your program is supposed to be time and space efficient. One safe solution is to always use `long` values, but this would not satisfy the latter goal of efficiency. A better solution would involve using an `int` type on a "large" machine, which you know supports your large values as int types (you need 32-bit integers), and the long type on other machines, which do not provide such support.

To accomplish this, you need to define two data types: on a large machine a data type MyInteger, using

```
typedef int MyInteger;
```

on a small machine, using:

```
typedef long MyInteger;
```

When the code gets moved from the large machine to the small machine, the definition of MyInteger would be modified to the second definition. This technique is also useful for compilers. For example, compilers define

```
typedef char w_char;
```

because they are computer specific. However, this technique is not necessarily convenient for moving *user* programs, because they have to be edited before they can be recompiled on the target machine. If you can foresee all the types of architectures you will be moving your program to, then it is possible to define conditional directives that give a correct definition of your data type depending on the machine; for more details, see Section 6.6.3.

TYPE SYNONYM

```
typedef existingType newType
```

Use typedef to define synonyms for data types that are not portable.

3.11 List of Common Errors

1. In order to check whether the sum of two integers i and j *overflows*, do not use

```
i + j > INT_MAX
```

(INT_MAX is defined in `limits.h`), because this creates an overflow. Instead, use

```
i > INT_MAX - j
```

2. String constants and character constants are very different. One must take care not to use a string constant

```
"a"
```

if a character constant is required

```
'a'
```

3. Since < is left associative, the expression

```
a < b < c
```

is interpreted as

```
(a < b) < c
```

and has a different meaning than

```
a < b && b < c
```

4. The code fragment presented below will show a common error related to the placement of brackets (notice the lack of any inner brackets):

```
if(c = getchar() == EOF)
```

Due to the precedence rules, the compiler interprets the code fragment as follows:

```
if(c = (getchar() == EOF))
```

As a result, `c` gets assigned a Boolean value, and the character read is not stored in `c`.

5. Always use an integer variable instead of a `char` variable `c` to store the result of `getchar()`.

6. The ampersand `&` preceding the variable `i` in `scanf("%d", &i)` is crucial.

7. `printf()` expects a string, so

```
printf("\n");
```

is correct, but

```
printf('\n');
```

is wrong.

8. To print a double, you use `%f`, but to read the same double value, you use `%lf`. Similarly, to print a long integer use `%d`, and to read it, use `%ld`.

9. Use correct conversions; for example,

```
printf("%d", 3.5);
```

and

```
printf("%g", 4);
```

will both print *garbage*.

10. The number of conversions must be equal to the number of arguments; for example,

```
printf("%d%d", i)
```

is incorrect. Remember that with `scanf()` you need to pass the address of the variable, therefore

```
scanf("%d", i);
```

is incorrect.

11. Spurious characters in `scanf()`'s format control string are a source of errors that are very hard to spot. Use them with caution!

3.12 List of Idioms

MAIN FUNCTION

`main()` is an integer function, which returns one of two standard return codes: EXIT_FAILURE and EXIT_SUCCESS.

READ SINGLE CHARACTER

```
if((c = getchar()) == EOF) ... /* error, else OK */
```

READ SINGLE INTEGER

```
if(scanf("%d", &i) != 1 ) ...  /* error, else OK */
```

READ SINGLE INTEGER WITH PROMPT

```
printf("Enter integer: ");
if(scanf("%d", &i) != 1 ) ...  /* error, else OK */
```

READ TWO INTEGERS

```
if(scanf("%d%d", &i, &j) != 2 ) ...  /* error, else OK */
```

TYPE SYNONYM

```
typedef existingType newType
```

3.13 List of Programming Style Guidelines

1. My lexical conventions for comments are:

   Short explanations are placed in comments at the right end of a line, for example

   ```
   if(isdigit)  /* error */
   ```

   Multi-line explanations are formatted like this:

   ```
   /*
    * Program to sort integer values
    */
   ```

2. The comments should never echo what is already in the code, for example

```
k++;      /* k is incremented by 1*/
```

3. Make every comment count.

4. Don't over-comment.

5. Make sure comments and code agree; there are few things that confuse code readers more than incorrect comments.

6. It is important to use a consistent style throughout your code. Variables should have meaningful names when appropriate (a control variable in a `for` statement may be called "`i`", but a variable representing a filename should not be called "`r`").

7. You are encouraged to mix cases to make your identifiers more readable, for example:

```
longIdentifier
```

8. Always avoid using two identifiers that differ from each other only by one character, or in case only, for example

```
setIns and setInt
```

Unfortunately, C does not follow this rule and uses both `ifdef` and `ifndef` as two of its preprocessor commands.

9. Since C does not have classes, you have to take extra precautions to avoid name conflicts. For example, it is best to avoid the general name

```
insert
```

because many functions may want to insert something. Instead, use specific names such as

```
insert_List
```

10. I recommend that

1. A declaration of a different data type starts on a new line.

2. The lists of identifiers are aligned so that they start in the same column.

3. Each variable identifier (except the last one) is followed by one space.

4. I discourage multiple initializations, such as:

```
int i = 1, j = 2;
```

or

```
int i = 2, j;
```

and instead recommend that each declaration that contains an initialization appear on a separate line, as in

```
int i = 1;
int j = 2;
```

5. If comments are required, each declaration should be placed on a separate line, for example:

```
int lower;    /* lower bound of the array */
int upper;    /* upper bound of the array */
```

11. Names of constants will appear in upper case throughout this book, and `const` always appears in front of the declaration.

12. I use exactly one blank before and one blank after the "=" operator.

13. The lexical convention used for the main function is as follows:

`int main() {`   the left brace on the same line as the header

`  body`   body indented to the right

`}`   the matching right brace aligned with `int`

14. I recommend that in order to specify long types, you use the upper case L rather than the lower case `l`, because the latter can be mistaken for `1`, as in

```
100l
```

15. Don't use spaces around the following operators:

```
->     .      []      !     ~      ++      --      - (unary)
* (unary)      &
```

For example, write

```
a->b        a[i]        *c
```

but not

```
~ a    & c
```

In *general*, use one space around the following operators:

```
=      +=      ?:      +      <      &&      + (binary) etc.
```

For example, code should be written as

```
a = b;
a = a + 2;
```

not

```
a= b+ 1;
```

Although it is not necessary, you may skip spaces to show operator *precedence*. For example, you could write:

```
a = a*b + 1;
```

but you should avoid

```
a = a+b * 2;
```

16. Blank lines are used to separate logically related sections of code; for example, three sections: input, processing, and termination.

17. When specifying a new type using `typedef`, identifier names start with an uppercase letter.

3.14 List of Portability Guidelines

1. The documentation of programs, which are available to clients, should make it clear whether you are using identifiers whose length exceeds 6 characters. You should never use identifiers that have more than 31 characters.

2. To support portability, use only integers in the ranges specified in `limits.h` (see Appendix B). For example, you can always use plain (not `short` or `long`) integers in the range from –32,767 to 32,767, since this range is guaranteed by every implementation of C. Any other assumptions, such as the size of an `int` is 4 bytes, must not be made.

3. In order to write portable code, you should explicitly specify `signed char` or `unsigned char`.

4. You should never make any assumptions about the code values of characters, such as the value of `'A'` is 65. While this is true for the ASCII code of `'A'`, this assumption is not portable. Thus, use `'A'` rather than 65 in your code.

5. Use return codes: `EXIT_FAILURE` and `EXIT_SUCCESS` (other values will not be portable).

6. Do not assume that the evaluation of standard mathematical expressions, such as addition, is performed from left to right.

7. Use `typedef` to define synonyms for data types that are not portable.

3.15 Exercises

Note: In all exercises, a prompt should be included whenever your program has to read a value. You should remember to use the "Main function" idiom. Follow all programming guidelines described in this chapter; in particular, comments should properly document your programs.

Exercise 3-1

What's the meaning of
a) `x+++y`
b) `x++>=++y`
Show how the compiler would split these expressions into tokens.

Exercise 3-2

Determine the decimal value of the following constants:
a) `034`
b) `0xA`
c) `0xBA`
d) `12.3E+3`
Write a program to verify your calculations.

Exercise 3-3

Given the declarations

```
int i = 4;
int j = 6;
```

find the values of the expressions and variables `i` and `j` after each of the following expressions is evaluated:
a) `++i - j--`
b) `i += j/2`
c) `i % 2 + (j+=4)`

Exercise 3-4

Find the values of the following expressions:
  a) `1+(3-2)*4 / 5 % 6`
  b) `9 % 2 % 3 % 4 % 5`
  c) `(int)((double)5 + 3.14) % 2`

Exercise 3-5

What's the output produced by the `printf()`:

```
printf("What did you ask ??(do not whisper)??");
```

Exercise 3-6

Write a program that tests whether the following relations hold on your system:

$$size(\text{short}) < size(\text{int}) < size(\text{long})$$

$$size(\text{float}) < size(\text{double}) < size(\text{long double})$$

Exercise 3-7

Write a program that prints the smallest and the largest double value available on the system that the program is running on.

Exercise 3-8

Give the `printf()` call that produces the following output:

```
 T. Muldner  Apt. #07    Moon\Moon    "Agent" Password:''
```

Exercise 3-9

Use the precedence and associativity tables from Appendix A to answer the following questions, and then write a program to verify your answers.
  What are the values of the variables check, d, e, and f after the following code has been executed:

```
int condition1 = 1;
int condition2 = 0;
int check;
double d, e, f;

check = condition1 && condition2 != 0;
d = 1 / 2 * check;
e = (double)1 * 2;
f = double(3/2);
```

Exercise 3-10

Write a program that reads a distance in inches and outputs this distance in centimeters (use the "Read Single Integer with prompt" idiom). If the input is incorrect, the program should output a message, and exit.

Exercise 3-11

Write a program that reads in a user-provided radius of a circle and outputs the area of this circle (use the "Read Single Integer with prompt" idiom, modified to read a double value). If the input is incorrect, the program should output a message and exit. Assume that the value of π is 3.1415926535. The area should be output 5 times, using the following format specifications:

- fixed-point notation, field width 10, left justified in the field, precision 4
- fixed-point notation, field width 10, right justified in the field, precision 4
- fixed-point notation, field width 10, right justified in the field, precision 4, padded with leading zeros
- scientific notation, field width 10, left justified in the field, precision 4
- scientific notation, field width 10, right justified in the field, precision 4.

Exercise 3-12

Write a program that reads a character and outputs the integer value of this character (use the "Read Single character" idiom). If the input is incorrect, the program should output a message and exit.

Exercise 3-13

Write a program to find the area of a rectangle. This program should prompt the user to enter the values of both sides, perform basic error checking, and output the area (use the "Read Two Integers" idiom and add a prompt). If the input is incorrect, the program should output a message and exit.

Exercise 3-14

Write a program that reads two double values (use the modified "Read Two Integers" idiom to read doubles and include a prompt) and outputs their product, or a message if the product creates an overflow. Then, write the same program for float and long values. Finally, write a program containing several test cases that demonstrate what happens when the sum of two unsigned values overflows.

Exercise 3-15

Write a program that reads up to five characters from the standard input stream (include a prompt), and then outputs the second and the fourth character. Describe what happens if you enter the end-of-file symbol as your third character (you have to find which character represents end-of-file on your system). Then, test your program with its input redirected to read from a file, and show its output for the following files: an empty file, a file consisting of only two characters, and a file consisting of 6 characters.

Exercise 3-16

Write a program that checks whether the equation

```
(x+y)² = x² + 2xy + y²
```

is true for all double values. If you find any two values for which the equation is not true, then explain why this is so.

Exercise 3-17

The other day I went to the bank to cash a cheque for $5.89. I asked the cashier to give me as *few* coins as possible. She did not have any dollar coins; instead she gave me quarters (25c), dimes (10c), nickels (5c), and pennies (1c). How many of each kind of coin did I get? Write a program that inputs the value in dollars and outputs the type and number of each coin. Assume that the cashier does not have any coins larger than a quarter, and that she always gives the minimum number of coins possible. For example, given 46 cents, the program outputs 1 quarter, 2 dimes, and 1 penny.

Exercise 3-18

Two cities, A and B, are connected by a straight road of length 200 miles. At noon, a car leaves A heading for B and going with the constant speed of 30 miles/hour. Then, t minutes later, another car leaves city B heading for city A, with the constant speed of 40 miles/hour. Now, consider a function

meet(t) = distance from A to the point where the two cars met

Write a program that shows the various values of the function `meet()` depending on the time t; in particular, for t equal to 0, 3, and 6. Provide an interpretation of these results.

Chapter 4

CONTROL STRUCTURES

4.1 ◆ Preview

Since C's control structures are very similar to those in Java, this chapter will concentrate on the minor differences, such as the absence in C of two constructs that are present in Java: the boolean type and the labeled `break` and `continue` statements. I will also provide various examples and idioms for C's control structures.

4.2 Logical Expressions

Instead of having a Boolean type, C uses integers to represent logical values; a zero value represents false, any nonzero value represents true.

All the relational and logical operators are the same as in Java, see Appendix A.

Remember that `i = 8` is very different from `i == 8` (assignment vs. equality).

4.3 Control Statements and Their Idiomatic Use

Java and C control structures differ in only one respect: C does not support *labeled* `break` and `continue` statements, which are useful for controlling program flow through *nested* loops (such as loop exit). Instead, C provides the infamous `goto` statement that unconditionally transfers control to the statement with the given label. Note that labeled `break` and `continue` statements are simply limited forms of the more general `goto` statement.

A *label* is any user-specified identifier followed by a colon, for example,

```
done:
```

The definition of the identifier occurs when it is used as a label. Its scope is limited to a single function. Labels can overload other identifiers in the same scope; that is, the same identifier can be used for a label and for a variable, a function, etc., because they can be used only in the context of the `goto` statement.

Consider the following Java statement that uses a labeled `break` to terminate the outer loop:

```
done:
    for(i = 0; i < length; i++)
        for(j = 0; j < length1; j++)
            if(f(i, j) == 0)        /* f() represents a condition */
                break done;
```

In C, the above code would be written as follows:

```
for(i = 0; i < length; i++)
   for(j = 0; j < length1; j++)
      if(f(i, j) == 0)        /* f() represents a condition */
         goto done;

done:
```

I believe that 'jumping out of nested loops' is the only situation, which justifies the use of a `goto` statement (i.e. to emulate a labeled `break` or `continue`); otherwise its use leads to unreadable programs, like the one shown in the next example. (You should try rewriting this code using a `while` statement).

Example 4-1

```
/*
 * File: ex4-1.c
 * Program that demonstrates the use of gotos.
 * Finds the sum of all positive numbers and the
 *     sum of negative numbers individually, as well
 *     as the sum of both. Stops when it encounters zero.
 * For example: 5 3 -4 5 -2 1 0 would give the result:
 *        Total: 8
 *        Positive: 14
 *        Negative: -6
 */
#include <stdio.h>
#include <stdlib.h>
int main() {
   int count, n, sum, sumPos, sumNeg;

   sum = sumPos = sumNeg = count = 0;
   printf("Enter integer values, to stop enter 0\n");
loop:
   scanf("%d", &n);
   if(n == 0)
      goto print;
   count++;
   if(n < 0)
      goto negn;
   sumPos += n;
   goto cont;
negn:
```

```
    sumNeg += n;
 cont:
    sum += n;
    goto loop;
 print:
    if(count == 0)
       printf("No values have been entered\n");
    else {
       printf("%d values have been entered\n", count);
       printf("The total sum is %d\n", sum);
       printf("The sum of positives is %d\n", sumPos);
       printf("The sum of negatives is %d\n", sumNeg);
    }

    return EXIT_SUCCESS;
}
```

The remainder of this section provides examples of conditional expressions and statements (and their idiomatic use) through short programs. I will comment on possible testing techniques for these programs, and provide descriptions of the recommended programming style used for control structures.

The first example uses a conditional expression of the form

```
condition ? expression1 : expression2
```

to find the maximum of two integer values.

Example 4-2

```
/*
 * File: ex4-2.c
 * Program that reads two integer values, and outputs the
 *     maximum of these values.
 * No error checking for valid integer numbers.
 */
#include <stdlib.h>
#include <stdio.h>
int main( ) {
    int i, j;

    /* "Read Two Integers with prompt" idiom from Chapter 3. */
```

```
    printf("Enter two integers:");
    scanf("%d%d", &i, &j);

    printf("The maximum value of %d and %d is %d\n",
              i, j, i > j ? i : j);

    return EXIT_SUCCESS;
}
```

As in Java, C conditional statements may suffer from the *dangling else* problem. Assuming that the variable x has a *non-negative value*, the code

```
if(x < 0)
    if(y > 0)
        z = 1;
else z = 2;
```

will never change the value of z if x is > 0. Above, I deliberately used misleading indentation. Indentation should always indicate which `if` an `else` is associated with (this is always the closest previous `if`):

```
if(x < 0)
    if(y > 0)
        z = 1;
    else z = 2;
```

---

1. The body of the `if` statement is indented to the right, and all its instructions are aligned.

2. Some programmers always use curly braces within a conditional statement, even if only one statement is present:

    ```
    if(condition) {
        single statement1;
    } else {
        single statement2;
    }
    ```

In my opinion, this clutters a program with too many braces.

4.3.1 ◆ Testing and Debugging

Testing and debugging are very important topics, but unfortunately can not be reasonably covered in a book such as this one, which mainly concentrates on portable programming techniques in C. Programmers often use **symbolic debuggers** to test their programs. Debuggers are software tools that allow you to use certain operations on your code (such as changing variable values), without actually modifying that code. Debuggers support many useful operations, such as step by step execution of code, the insertion of breakpoints that halt program execution at a particular point, and the examination and even modification of the values of program variables. Unfortunately, debuggers are not portable. At this point, there isn't a single debugger available that would provide the same interface for all or even most computer platforms. For this reason, I do not include any examples of a symbolic debugger, but I do encourage you to find and experiment with one that is suitable for your platform. I do provide a description of an application of conditional compilation to debugging in Section 6.6.1.

The following example solves a quadratic equation $ax^2 + bx + c = 0$ (a warning, this version is not quite correct).

Example 4-3

```
/*
 * File: ex4-3.c
 * Program that outputs the roots of the equation
 *    Ax^2+Bx+C = 0.
 * No check for valid real coefficients.
 */
#include <stdio.h>
#include <stdlib.h>
#include <math.h>
int main() {
    double a, b, c, delta, xr, yr;

    printf("Enter three real values: ");
    scanf("%lf%lf%lf", &a, &b, &c);

    delta = b*b - 4*a*c;
    delta = sqrt(delta);
    xr = (-b - delta)/(2*a);
    yr = (-b + delta)/(2*a);
    printf("\nFirst solution:  %f\n", xr);
    printf("\nSecond solution:  %f\n", yr);
```

```
    return EXIT_SUCCESS;
}
```

Now, I will use the above program to discuss *testing* and *debugging*. In order to test a program, a user typically enters some "reasonable" value. For example, in order to find the roots of the equation $x^2 - 2x + 1 = 0$, the user would execute the following steps:

Enter three real values: `1 -2 1`

First solution: `1`

Second solution: `2`

You should keep the following guidelines in mind when testing:

- always test programs at their boundary values
- add messages that inform the user of the state of the program. Code must not "do nothing" quietly, leaving the user confused as to why things stopped working the way they were expected to
- test input for validity.

What are the limitations of the program presented in the above Example 4.3? Moreover, what are the values that exercise any boundary cases that arise? Does the program successfully solve the quadratic equation $ax^2 + bx + c = 0$ in all cases? Consider the following execution:

Enter three real values: `10 -2 1`

* run time error *

Since you are computing the square root of `delta`, you have to make sure that the value of this variable is never negative. For a quadratic equation, this means that you need to consider two cases: one where there is a solution, and the roots exist and are *real* numbers, and one where there is no solution, and the roots do not exist (here, I do not consider complex numbers).

The next bit of code tries to improve the original example by adding some *error checking*:

```
if(delta >= 0) {
    delta = sqrt(delta);
    xr = (-b - delta)/(2*a);
    yr = (-b + delta)/(2*a);
    printf( . . . );
}
```

A sample execution follows:

```
Enter three real values: 10 -2 1
```

Now the user may be puzzled by the lack of output. If you inspect the code, you will notice that if `delta` is negative, the program exits without printing anything (since all the I/O is inside the `if` clause). A definite improvement would be to print some message if `delta` is negative. (In this case, the roots of the equation are *complex* numbers—for now, it would be satisfactory to inform the user that the program can not deal with such input.)

Before I show code that deals with all types of input more gracefully, I will discuss the boundary values for this example. *Boundary values* generally represent special cases such as empty input, input values equal to zero (when you expect nonzero values), etc. For the quadratic equation, a special case arises when some coefficients are zero. Specifically, for $ax^2 + bx + c = 0$, if $a = b = 0$, then we have the so-called degenerative equation of the form $c = 0$. If $a = 0$ but $b \mathrel{!}= 0$, then there is only one solution, and if $a \mathrel{!}= 0$, $b = 0$, and c is negative, there is one "double" root (that is the same root is counted twice).

Here is the improved code, which deals with all these cases, and also shows solutions that are complex numbers.

```c
/*
 * File: ex4-32.c
 * Program that outputs the roots of the equation
 *    Ax^2+Bx+C = 0
 * Roots may be real values or complex values
 */
#include <stdio.h>
#include <stdlib.h>
#include <math.h>
int main() {
    double a, b, c, delta;
    double xr = 0;
    double xi = 0;
    double yr = 0;
    double yi = 0;

    printf("Enter three real values: ");
    if(scanf("%lf%lf%lf", &a, &b, &c) != 3)
        return EXIT_FAILURE;

    if(a == 0)
        if(b == 0)
            printf("Degenerate equation %f = 0\n", c);
```

```
         else printf("Only one solution: %f\n", -c/b);
     else {  /* a != 0 */
        delta = b*b - 4*a*c;
        xr = yr = -b/(2*a);
        if(delta == 0)
           printf("\nOne double solution:  %f\n", xr);
        else if(delta < 0) {
           printf("Complex solutions\n");
           delta = sqrt(-delta);
           xi = delta/(2*a);
           yi = -xi;
        } else {     /* delta > 0 */
           delta = sqrt(delta);
           xr += delta/(2*a);
           yr -= delta/(2*a);
        }
        printf("\nFirst solution:  %f + i*(%f)\n", xr, xi);
        printf("\nSecond solution: %f + i*(%f)\n", yr, yi);
     }

     return EXIT_SUCCESS;
}
```

4.3.2 ◆ Loops

I will now move on to the topic of loops. The first example is a program which simply reads characters until some condition is met, specifically until a "special" value is encountered, here it is ".", or an end-of-file is encountered. Such a value is called a *sentinel* (guard) value. This program outputs the ASCII values of the largest input character.

Example 4-4

```
/*
 * File: ex4-4.c
 * Read characters until "." or EOF and output the ASCII value
 *   of the largest input character.
 */
#include <stdio.h>
#include <stdlib.h>
int main() {
   const char SENTINEL = '.';
```

```
    int aux;
    int maxi = 0;

    printf("Enter characters, enter . to terminate\n");
    while(1) {
        if((aux = getchar()) == EOF || aux == SENTINEL)
            break;

        if(aux > maxi)
            maxi = aux;
    }

    printf("The largest ASCII value: %d\n", maxi);

    return EXIT_SUCCESS;
}
```

It is common practice in C to write "infinite" loops like the one above. These loops continue until some condition is met. In this example, I used a version of the "Read Single Character Idiom" from Chapter 3. Due to short-circuit evaluation rules, the second operand of the || operator is not evaluated if the first one evaluates to true. As suggested in my programming style section, I used blank lines to separate the code into various sections.

Note that the above style supports *multiple* exit points. Some programmers prefer to use as single exit point, which is maintained using Boolean variables. It is a matter of preference as to which style you use; personally, I found loops with multiple exits points to be much easier to read, understand, and maintain.

The initialization of the above variable maxi is a bit tricky; above, it works because all values are expected to be positive. It would not work in the case where all input values were negative (I will show the solution that deals with this case later).

Is the code correct? An example of a *boundary case* for this program is a situation where the very first input operation either fails or returns the sentinel value. For both these cases, the program prints 0 as the maximum value. This behavior can be modified through the addition of a flag, which would be used to test if anything has been read:

```
    int flag = 0;    /* nothing read yet */

    while(1) {
        if((aux = getchar()) == EOF || aux == SENTINEL)
            break;
```

```
    flag = 1;     /* if here, we have read something */
    if(aux > maxi)
        maxi = aux;
}
if(flag)
    printf("The largest ASCII value: %d\n", maxi);
else printf("No value read\n");
```

Instead of testing a flag in each step of the loop, you can try to read once, and *then* enter the loop:

```
if((maxi = getchar()) == EOF || aux == SENTINEL)
    printf("No value read\n");
else {
    while(1) {
        if((aux = getchar()) == EOF || aux == SENTINEL)
            break;
        if(aux > maxi)
            maxi = aux;
    }
    printf("The largest ASCII value: %d\n", maxi);
}
```

The code does not try to differentiate between an error in the input operation and an exit due to an end-of-file. In the later chapters, I will show a technique to do so.

I will now use this example to discuss programming style and programming idioms.

1. Use indentation to improve readability of your code.

2. There are at least three alternatives to write the `while` statement, shown in the examples below:

```
while(expr) {
    stats
}


while(expr)
{
    stats
}
```

```
while(expr)
  {
      stats
  }
```

I will always use the first format in my code.

3. Some programmers prefer to use the `for` statement to represent a `while(1)` loop:

```
for(;;) {
   body
}
```

The two are identical.

4. Instead of writing

```
while(expr != 0)
   statement;
```

some programmers write

```
while(expr)
   statement;
```

but I find this style to be less readable and will not use it in this book. The same conventions apply to the expression in the `if` statement. For example, I will write

```
if(expr != 0). . .
```

rather than

```
if(expr)
```

READ CHARACTERS UNTIL SENTINEL

```
while(1) {
   /* read in a value and check it */
   if((aux = getchar()) == EOF || aux == SENTINEL)
      break;
```

```
    /* further processing */
}
```

In some cases it may be more convenient to split the test for loop exit into two parts, using the so-called *multi-exit loop*:

```
while(1) {
    /* read in a value and check it */
    if((aux = getchar()) == EOF)
        break;
    if(aux == SENTINEL)
        break;
    /* further processing */
}
```

The next example is similar to Example 4–4, but it finds the maximum *integer* value rather than the character value. As I mentioned earlier, in general it is not safe to initialize the variable maxi to 0. Instead, I will initialize it to the first value read, using the technique described above.

Example 4-5

```
/*
 * File: ex4-5.c
 * Read integers until 0 and output the largest integer
 * It also stops on an incorrect integer and end-of-file
 */
#include <stdio.h>
#include <stdlib.h>
int main() {
    const int SENTINEL = 0;
    int i;
    int maxi;

    printf("Enter integers, 0 to stop\n");
    /* first read */
    if(scanf("%d", &maxi) != 1 || maxi == SENTINEL) {
        printf("No value read\n");
        return EXIT_SUCCESS;
    }
```

```
/* first value read, start looping */
do {
    if(scanf("%d", &i) != 1 || i == SENTINEL)
        break;
    if(i > maxi)
        maxi = i;
} while(1);

printf("The largest value: %d\n", maxi);

return EXIT_SUCCESS;
}
```

READ INTEGERS UNTIL SENTINEL

```
while(1) {
    if(scanf("%d", &i) != 1 || i == SENTINEL)
        break;
    . . .
}
```

I'll now show some examples of the for statement. The first example uses a comma expression and computes the sum of integers from 1 to 10.

Example 4-6

```
/*
 * File: ex4-6.c
 * Use the for loop and a comma operator to compute the
 *    sum of integers from 1 to 10.
 */
#include <stdlib.h>
#include <stdio.h>
int main() {
    int i, sum;

    for(i = 1, sum = 0; i <= 10; i++, sum += i)
```

```
    ;
    printf("sum of integers from 1 to 10 = %d\n", sum);

    return EXIT_SUCCESS;
}
```

There are two comma expressions in the `for` statement; the first one is responsible for the initialization of both the control variable `i` and the variable `sum` used to accumulate the sum. (A control variable in a loop is the one used to stop the loop, like the variable `i` above.) The second comma expression is responsible with the update (here, an incrementation) of both the `i` and `sum`.

REPEAT N TIMES

```
for(i = 1, further initialization; i <= N; i++, processing)
```

with `i` as a control variable.

If the body of the loop is empty, then the corresponding semicolon is always placed on a separate line, indented to the right:

```
for(i = 1, sum = 0; i <= 10; i++, sum += i)
    ;
```

1. The code in the above example assumed that the range of numbers includes the two end values: 1 and 10. If you want to exclude both values, you would have to change the initialization and the stop condition. In general, watch for off-by-one errors.

2. Avoid the following errors:

`e1 & e2`	bitwise "and"; likely what you want is	`e1 && e2`
`e1 | e2`	bitwise "or"; likely what you want is	`e1 || e2`
`if(x = 1)`	should be	`if(x == 1)` ...

3. Be careful with loops that have empty bodies. It is easy to write

```
while(condition)
    statement
```

when what was really intended was

```
while(condition)
    ;
statement
```

For example, compare

```
while((c = getchar()) != 'a')
    putchar(c);
```

with

```
while((c = getchar()) != 'a')
    ;
putchar(c);
```

In the first case, input characters will be output until 'a' is encountered, but in the second case, only the character 'a' will be output.

Before I show the next example, I will introduce a variant of the "Read Until Condition" idiom. This idiom uses a multi-exit loop to exit if one of the input values is incorrect, or these values satisfy a certain condition (here, a >= b):

READ UNTIL CONDITION

```
while(1) {
    printf("enter two integers a and b, a < b:");
    if(scanf("%d%d", &a, &b) == 2)
        break;
    if(a < b)
        break;
    . . .
}
```

Example 4-7

In this example, the program finds the sum and the product of all *odd* integers in the interval (a,b), that is integers that are greater or equal to "a" but less than "b". For example, given a=2 and b=7, there are two odd values in the interval (2,7), namely 3 and 5. The program uses the "Read Until Condition" and starts off by continually prompting the user to enter two integer values "a" and "b", such that a<b, until the user enters values that satisfy this condition. If the user enters values that are not valid integers, the execution of the program is aborted.

```c
/*
 * File: ex4-7.c
 * Read two integers a and b and output the sum and the product
 *  of odd integers from a (inclusive) to b (exclusive).
 * Error checking: Keep reading when a >= b.
 *      Aborts if an incorrect integer has been entered
 */
#include <stdlib.h>
#include <stdio.h>
int main() {
   int i, a, b;
   int sum = 0;
   int product = 1;

   while(1) {
      printf("enter two integers a and b, a < b:");
      if(scanf("%d%d", &a, &b) != 2)
         return EXIT_FAILURE;
      if(a < b)
         break;
      printf("a must be smaller than b\n");
   }
   /* check if there are any values between a and b */
   if(a%2 == 0 && a+1 == b) { /* if a is even */
      printf("There are no odd values between %d and %d\n", a, b);
      return EXIT_SUCCESS;
   }
   if(a%2 == 0)  /* if a is even, then start from a+1 */
      a++;
   for(i = a; i < b; product *= i, sum += i, i += 2)
      ;

   printf("The sum = %d, the product = %d\n", sum, product);

   return EXIT_SUCCESS;
}
```

The above code deals with the boundary case, in which there are no odd values in the interval [a,b):

```
if(a%2 == 0 && a+1 == b) {
    printf("There are no odd values between %d and %d\n", a, b);
    return EXIT_SUCCESS;
}
```

Before entering the loop that calculates the sum and the product, the code checks if `a` is even, and if so, increments it by one so that it becomes odd:

```
if(a%2 == 0)   /* if a is even, then start from a+1 */
    a++;
```

To understand the need for the above statement, consider the case `a == 2`, and `b == 4`. Note that the variables used to accumulate the sum and the product have been initialized in their declarations rather than in the first expression of the `for` statement, as in

```
for(sum = 0, product = 1, i = a;...)
```

It is matter of personal taste as to which of these techniques is better.
The stop condition in the above `for` statement is

```
i < b
```

because according to the specification of this program, the value of `b` is to be excluded—if I had used

```
i <= b
```

the `for` statement would be off by one.

The examples I have presented show that by using a *comma* expression, you can have more than one control variable in the `for` statement.

I will now discuss code inspection. You should read the next example and try to guess the program's meaning based on your inspection.

Example 4-8

```
/*
 * File: ex4-8.c
 * Read two integers a and b
 *       ???
```

```
 * Error checking: Keep reading if either of two
 *    integers is invalid or a >= b.
 */
#include <stdlib.h>
#include <stdio.h>
int main() {
   int i, j, a, b;

   while(1) {
      printf("enter two integers a and b, a < b:");
      if(scanf("%d%d", &a, &b) == 2 && a < b)
         break;
   }
   for(i = a, j = b; i <= j; i += 2, j -= 2)
      printf("%d\n", i + j);

    return EXIT_SUCCESS;
}
```

Consider this loop:

```
for(i = 20, j = 300; i <= j; i += 2, j -= 2)
   printf("%d\n", i + j);
```

What are the values of `i` and `j` after this loop terminates? I have found that a general strategy for answering this question is also useful for testing and debugging programs with `for` statements. First of all, consider *small* and *manageable* boundary values as in

```
for(i = 2, j = 10; i <= j; i += 2, j -= 2)
   printf("%d\n", i + j);
```

and examine values of `i` and `j` in each step of the loop:

i	2	4	6
j	10	8	6
output	12	12	12

Since the two variables `i` and `j` are both updated in the same way in each step of the loop, the output is always the same: the sum of the lower and the upper bounds. How many times will this sum be printed? Judging from the above example, you can hypothesize that the sum will be printed

(number of even numbers between the bounds) / 2
times.

To verify this calculation, I will show how you can modify the `for` statement to additionally count the number of outputs:

```
for(i = 2, j = 10, count = 1; i <= j; i += 2, j -= 2)
    count += printf("%d\n", i + j);
```

The variable `count` is updated in the body of the `for` statement; specifically it is incremented by one if `printf()` succeeded, otherwise its value is left unchanged. Now, try to execute this code using various values for the lower and the upper bounds.

Below, I considered several combinations of odd and even numbers.

lower	upper
3	6
2	5
3	9

Boundary values should also be considered:

lower	upper
2	2
3	3
4	1

The sample testing data does not cover all the important cases; negative input data or mixed positive and negative data are missing. Despite this, you should be able to convince yourself that the program is correct based on the data that I used to test with.

I will conclude this chapter with an example of the `switch` statement.

Example 4–9

This program reads characters from the standard input until 20 characters are read or the end-of-file is encountered. It then outputs the number of blanks, tabs, asterisks, and any lowercase letters.

```
/*
 * File: ex4-9.c
 * Program that reads at most 20 characters and prints the number
```

```
 *      of blanks, tabs, asterisks, and lowercase characters.
 */
#include <stdio.h>
#include <stdlib.h>
int main() {
   const int LIMIT = 20;
   int i, c;
   int cblank = 0;
   int ctabs  = 0;
   int cstars = 0;
   int clower = 0;

   printf("Enter at most 20 characters\n");
   for(i = 1; i <= LIMIT; i++) {
      if((c = getchar()) == EOF)
         break;  /* break the loop on end-of-file */
      switch(c) {
      case ' ' : cblank++;
                 break;
      case '\t': ctabs++;
                 break;
      case '*' : cstars++;
                 break;
      default  : if(c >= 'a' && c <= 'z')
                    clower++;
                 break;
      }
   }

   printf("\nNumber of blanks \t%d\n", cblank);
   printf("Number of  tabs \t%d\n", ctabs);
   printf("Number of asterisks \t%d\n", cstars);
   printf("Number of lower case letters \t%d\n", clower);

   return EXIT_SUCCESS;
}
```

There are two stop conditions for the main loop. These occur when the maximum allowed number of characters is read or when an input operation fails. I used the "Repeat N times" idiom to code the former condition and the "Read a single character" idiom to code the latter condition.
If I had wanted to use

```
switch(c = getchar())
```

I would need to add code to exit from the `for` loop; the `break` statement merely completes the execution of the `switch`. One of the ways of doing this is by using a `goto` statement

```
for(i = 1; i <= LIMIT; i++) {
    switch(c = getchar()) {
    case EOF  : goto end;
    case ' '  : cblank++;
                break;
    case '\t' : ctabs++;
                break;
    case '*'  : cstars++;
                break;
    default   : if(c >= 'a' && c <= 'z')
                    clower++;
                break;
    }
}
end:
```

An alternative solution that avoids the `goto` statement involves adding another case statement to the `switch`—it prints the results and terminates the program if an `EOF` has been encountered.

```
case EOF:    printf(. . .)
             return EXIT_SUCCESS;
```

I recommend using the original version of the code from Example 4–9—it is easier to read and it also uses several of the programming idioms.

It is possible to omit the `break` from one or more `case` statements. As in Java, all the `case` statements are executed until the `break` is encountered, or end of `switch` is encountered. For example, assuming that initially `i` is equal to 1, the following code

```
switch(i) {
case 1: putchar('1');
case 2: putchar('2');
}
```

prints 12, because `putchar('1')` is *not* followed by `break`, and the next case will be executed.

4.4 List of Common Errors

1. Remember that `i = 8` is very different from `i == 8` (assignment vs. equality).

2. Watch for off-by-one errors.

3. Avoid the following errors:

`e1 & e2`	likely should be	`e1 && e2`
`e1	e2`	likely should be	`e1 || e2`
`if(x = 1) ...`	should be	`if(x == 1) ...`

4. Be careful with loops that have empty bodies. It is easy to write

```
while(condition)
    statement
```

when what was really intended was

```
while(condition)
    ;
statement
```

For example, compare

```
while((c = getchar()) != 'a')
    putchar(c);
```

with

```
while((c = getchar()) != 'a')
    ;
putchar(c);
```

In the first case, input characters will be output until `'a'` is encountered, but in the second case, only the character `'a'` will be output.

4.5 List of Idioms

READ CHARACTERS UNTIL SENTINEL

```
while(1) {
   /* read in a value and check it */
   if((aux = getchar()) == EOF || aux == SENTINEL)
     break;
    /* further processing */
}
```

or:

```
while(1) {
   /* read in a value and check it */
   if((aux = getchar()) == EOF)
       break;
    if(aux == SENTINEL)
       break;
    /* further processing */
}
```

READ INTEGERS UNTIL SENTINEL

```
while(1) {
    if(scanf("%d", &i) != 1 || i == SENTINEL)
      break;
    . . .
}
```

REPEAT N TIMES

```
for(i = 1, further initialization; i <= N; i++, processing)
```

with i as a control variable.

READ UNTIL CONDITION

```
while(1) {
    printf("enter two integers a and b, a < b:");
    if(scanf("%d%d", &a, &b) == 2)
        break;
    if(a < b)
        break;
    . . .
}
```

4.6 List of Programming Style Guidelines

1. The body of the `if` statement is indented to the right, and all its instructions are aligned.

2. Some programmers always use curly braces within a conditional statement, even if only one statement is present:

```
if(condition) {
    single statement1
} else {
    single statement2
}
```

In my opinion, this clutters a program with too many braces.

3. Use indentation to improve readability of your code.

4. There are at least three alternatives to write the `while` statement, shown in the examples below:

```
while(expr) {
    stats
}

while(expr)
{
    stats
}

while(expr)
    {
        stats
    }
```

I will always use the first format in my code.

5. Some programmers prefer to use the `for` statement to represent a `while(1)` loop:

```
for(;;) {
    body
}
```

The two are identical.

6. Instead of writing

```
while(expr != 0)
    statement;
```

some programmers write

```
while(expr)
    statement;
```

but I find this style to be less readable and will not use it in this book. The same conventions apply to the expression in the `if` statement. For example, I will write

```
if(expr !=0)...
```

rather than

```
if(expr)
```

7. If the body of the loop is empty, then the corresponding semicolon is always placed on a separate line, indented to the right:

```
for(i = 1, sum = 0; i <= 10; i++, sum += i)
    ;
```

4.7 Exercises

Note: In all exercises, a prompt should be included whenever your program has to read a value. Follow all of the programming guidelines described in this chapter, including comments that properly document your programs. Test your programs carefully.

Exercise 4-1

Show the output produced by the following program (justify your answer):

```
int main() {
 double x = 16.5;
 double y = 2.5;
 int z = 0;
 while(x > y) {
    x -= y;
    z++;
 }
 printf("%d %g\n", z, x);
 return EXIT_SUCCESS;
}
```

Exercise 4-2

Show the output from the following statement and justify your answer assuming that the input was 3 and the read operation was successful.

```
int i;

switch(sscanf("%d", &i)) {

case EOF: printf("see %d\n", i);
          break;

case 1:   printf("\tyou");

case 0:   printf("\tlater");
          break;

default:  printf("printed %d\ntimes\n", i);
}
```

Exercise 4-3

Show the output produced by the following statements (justify your answer):

```
int i = 3;
int j = 7;

if(i > j);
    printf("i = %d\n", i);

if(i + 1 == j)
    if(i > 1)
        printf("One\n");
else printf("Two\n");
```

Exercise 4-4

Show the output produced by the following statements (justify your answer):

```
int i = 3;
int j = 7;

while(j++, i += 3, i < j);
    printf("i = %d, j = %d\n", i, j);

for(; ;)
    break;
for(i = 1, j = 3; ;i++, j--)
    if(i == j) {
        printf("end: i = %d, j = %d\n", i, j);
        break;
    } else printf("within: i = %d, j = %d\n", i, j);

i = (j = 5) + 4;

for(; i > j;) {
    j++;
    printf("%d\n", j);
}
```

Exercise 4-5

Write a complete program that reads three double values (include a prompt) and outputs the largest value (for the output, use a field of width 10, and 4 significant digits). Full error checking should be provided. Then, write the same program using float values.

Exercise 4-6

Write a complete program that reads a single integer value n, and then prints the values of the variables sum and product, where:

sum is the largest int value for which n+sum does not overflow

product is the largest int value for which n*product does not overflow

Exercise 4-7

Write a program that reads integer values from standard input and writes to standard output the smallest of the input values and the average input value. Reading should stop when either a value equal to −1 or greater than 100 is encountered; it should also stop when an incorrect integer value is entered. If there is no integer value in the input, the program should output the following message "no integer values found." Use the "Read Until Condition" idiom. Describe the boundary cases for this program.

Exercise 4-8

Write a program that reads double values from standard input and writes the smallest of the input values and the average input value to standard output. Reading should stop when 10 values have been entered, or an incorrect double value is encountered. If there is no double value in the input, the program should output the following message "no double values found." Use the "Repeat N times" idiom. Describe the boundary cases for this program.

Exercise 4-9

Write a complete program that keeps on reading integer values from the standard input stream (include a prompt). It should read three integer values in a single read operation, and every time the three values have been successfully read, output the sum of these values. If less than three values have been successfully read, the program should output the appropriate message. The program should terminate when no values have been successfully read. Describe the boundary cases for this program.

Exercise 4-10

Write a complete program that reads values from the standard input stream. You can assume that the input is of the following form:

each input line starts with any number of spaces; then it contains a double value, followed by any number of spaces, followed by a single character, and then again followed by any number of spaces and an integer value.

The program stops reading if incorrect input data has been encountered. Once it finishes reading, the program outputs the average of all integer values and the average of all double values. Describe the boundary cases for this program.

Exercise 4-11

Write a complete program that first reads an integer value n less than 10 and then outputs a multiplication table for numbers from 1 to n. Include full error checking. For example, for n equal to 3, the program should output:

	1	2	3
	1	2	3
1	1	2	3
2	2	4	6
3	3	6	9

Exercise 4-12

Write a complete program that can be used to test your knowledge of multiplication; it keeps reading two integer values and then prompts you for the value of the product, and finally verifies your answer. Limit input values to those less than 20. Reading stops if 20 values are read, or if an incorrect value is entered. In the latter case, the program should display a message. For both cases, prior to termination, the program displays the number of correct answers and the number of incorrect answers.

Exercise 4-13

Write a complete program that inputs the integer value representing a year, and prints whether this year is a leap year. Include full error checking.

Exercise 4-14

Write a complete program that inputs three integer values representing a year, a month, and a day, and prints the day of the week for the given date. Include full error checking.

Exercise 4-15

Write a complete program that reads a number in the following form

integer fraction (in the form: integer/integer)

For example

2 1/2

and outputs the corresponding double value. Include full error checking.

Exercise 4-16

Write a complete program that reads a double value, and outputs this value in the format shown in Exercise 4–15. The fraction should be reduced to lowest possible terms.

Exercise 4-17

Write a complete program that reads an integer value n, and then prints all of the prime numbers less than n.

Exercise 4-18

Write a complete program that reads an integer value, and then prints a message indicating whether or not this value is prime.

Exercise 4-19

Write a complete program that reads integer values and finds the smallest value read. The program stops reading when an incorrect int value is encountered, or 10 integer values have been read. Then, the program outputs a message if no values have been read (the very first value was incorrect), or it prints the largest value. Implement your program by initializing a variable used to hold the largest value to the smallest possible int value, i.e. INT_MIN. Describe the boundary cases for this program.

Exercise 4-20

Write a program that prompts the user to enter a double value, which represents the value of an item, an integer value N representing the number of years, and the rate of depreciation (an integer value R). The program should then output this value depreciated after N years, assuming that the rate of depreciation is R% a year. Describe the boundary cases for this program.

Exercise 4-21

Write a program that reads five double values; the first two values represent the coordinates of a point, say P, the next two values represent another point, say Q, and the last value represents the radius of a circle that has its origin on point Q. Your program should check whether or not point P is inside the circle. Include full error checking and describe the boundary cases for testing this program.

Exercise 4-22

Write a program that reads six double values; the first two values represent the coordinates of a point, say P, the third value represents the radius of a circle that has its origin on point P, the next two values represent another point, say K, and the last value represents the radius of a circle that has its origin on point K. Your program should check whether or not the two circles intersect. Include full error checking and describe the boundary cases for this program.

Exercise 4-23

Write a program that reads six double values; the first two values represent the coordinates of a point, say P, the third value represents the radius of a circle that has its origin on point Q, the next three values represent the coordinates of a line. Your program should check whether or not the line intersects the circle, and if so, it should display the coordinates of the intersection point. Include full error checking and describe the boundary cases for this program.

Chapter 5

TEXT FILES

5.1 ◆ Preview

The Java I/O package provides an extensive set of classes that handle input and output to and from many different devices, see Appendix B. The Java model is based on the concept of a stream, which can be thought of as a physical stream of water flowing to and from the program. In reality, data in the stream consist of bytes, or Unicode characters. The power of Java I/O operations stems from the fact that streams can be wrapped around other streams to create more powerful combinations.

In C, you can also think about I/O operations as streams, but they consist only of bytes, and their operations are much more primitive. In particular, there is no clear division of all operations into input streams and output streams. This chapter describes text files; Chapter 8 describes binary files.

5.2 Introduction

The standard I/O is typically used to perform input/output from the keyboard and to a monitor, but it can be combined with filter programs to read from and write to a file. In Section 3.8.1, I stated that *filter* programs are designed to read the standard input stream only and write to the standard output stream only, and they can be made to read or write to a file by using I/O redirection. However, doing so may be inconvenient, or you may need to operate on more than one I/O file, in which case you need to use file I/O.

Files are simply sequences of bytes. Programmers often talk about two types of files: text and binary. In reality, there is only one type of a file, but its *processing* may be line-oriented (for text files), or not line oriented (for binary files). What's special about **line-oriented** file processing? It assumes that the file contains end-of-line terminators and uses this assumption to process the file. On the other hand, **binary** file processing disregards end-of-line terminators and treats all the bytes on an equal basis. For example, the text of this book is clearly line oriented. The first complete C program, presented in Chapter 2, is an example of binary file processing. It allows for the processing and output of any file type, such as an executable file, which may not have any line-based structure. In Unix, both types of files are stored in the same way; other operating systems may handle binary files and text files differently. As a result, it is a good idea to indicate whether a file is a text file or a binary file.

If you are working with any existing file-based programming tools, you must always remember to check if they are line-oriented. I once remember trying to use a Unix diff program (which is a line-oriented filter) to compare two *binary* files, and for some time, not being able to understand why the result was meaningless.

Different operating systems use various strategies to deal with the end-of-line terminator. These are some of the strategies used:

- a single carriage return symbol
- a single linefeed symbol
- a carriage return followed by a linefeed symbol

For example, if you create a file using an editor in a Windows environment, and then move this file to a Unix environment, upon editing this file you will see a number of occurrences of ^M, which is the end-of-line symbol in Windows, but not in Unix.

In Java, you can write portable programs by using a system property, which specifies the end-of-line terminator. Unfortunately, C does not provide this facility. In many cases, the only solution is to write filter programs that convert from one convention into another. (For the Windows/Unix example, the filter would have to remove all occurrences of ^M's.)

Now, a few words about end-of-file. Modern operating systems, such as Unix or Windows, do not store any special character to signify end-of-file; instead the file system maintains information about the length of the file. Various operating systems have different conventions for representing end-of-file, useful for interactive input (input coming in from the keyboard). For example, Unix uses ^D; Windows typically uses ^Z.

For the sake of efficiency, file operations are **buffered** by the operating system. This means that writing a character using some C-provided I/O function does not immediately write it to disk; instead, it places it in an appropriate buffer. When the buffer becomes full, its entire contents are written to disk. When a file is closed, or when the main C function terminates, all buffers are **flushed** (that is, written to disk). Sometimes, you may want to flush buffers while executing the program (for example, when writing a program that has to quickly update the users screen); this operation, `fflush()` is supported in C.

5.3 File Handles

The `FILE` type, declared in the header file `stdio.h`, allows you to define variables that represent files:

```
FILE *fileHandle;
```

Here, the variable `fileHandle` (which happens to be a pointer to a `FILE`) is called a **file handle**. In order to access files, the user first declares the required number of file handles, and then uses these handles in file operations, described below.

To declare more than one `FILE` variable, the asterisk must be repeated, for example,

```
FILE *f, *g;
```

If you find this annoying, you can define a synonym for `FILE *`, for example,

```
typedef FILE* FILE_P;
```

and then use it like this:

```
FILE_P f, g;
```

5.4 Opening and Closing Files

Files that reside in the external memory must be associated with a file handle before they may be accessed. This is accomplished by *opening* a file, using the provided `fopen()` function:

```
fileHandle = fopen(fileName, fileMode);
```

Above, `fileName` is a string representing the name of the file, and `fileMode` is a string that specifies the mode(s) in which the file will function. Valid modes are:

`"r"` open file for input; the file must exist

`"w"` open file for output; if the file exists it will be overwritten, otherwise a new file will be created

`"a"` open file for output; no matter whether or not the file exists, writing will append to this file

`"r+"` like `"r"` for I/O: open file for both input and output; the file must exist

`"w+"` like `"w"` for I/O: open file for both input and output; if the file exists, it will be overwritten, otherwise a new file will be created

`"a+"` like `"a"` for I/O: open file for both input and output; no matter whether or not the file exists, writing will append to this file

In addition, the above modes may be used to specify a *binary* mode, by using the character `b`, for example

```
"r+b"
```

Consequently, to read from a text file `test.dat`, use

```
f = fopen("test.dat", "r");
```

and to write to a binary file `test.out`, use

```
g = fopen("test.out", "wb");
```

When a file is opened for *both* input and output, I/O operations must be "separated" by the call to one of the following functions: `fseek()`, `fsetpos()`, `rewind()`, or `fflush()`. These functions are useful for binary files and will be further described in Section 8.14.

If `fopen()` fails, it returns a `NULL` value. This value is defined in several header files, including `stdio.h`. It is a special "zero" value (see Section 8.8). It is one of your responsibilities to test if a call to `fopen()` was successful; in the case where it failed, all successive I/O operations will be meaningless (and will typically result in run-time errors).

OPENING A FILE

```
if((fileHandle = fopen(fname, fmode)) == NULL)
   /* failed */
```

A file name may include a *path*. For example, in a Unix environment, you may write

```
fopen("/usr/home/solid/test.c", "r");
```

You should remember that in a DOS environment, the call to

```
fopen("\usr\home\solid\test.c", "r");
```

is incorrect because \ is a special character and has to be preceded by an escape character:

```
fopen("\\usr\\home\\solid\\test.c", "r");
```

The maximum length of a file name is limited by FILENAME_MAX defined in stdio.h.

Once you have opened and processed a file, you must remember to close it. The operating system maintains only a limited number of files (FOPEN_MAX, defined in stdio.h) that may be open at one time—if this number is exceeded, then fopen() will fail. To close an opened file, use its handle and the provided fclose() function:

```
fclose(fileHandle);
```

fclose() returns EOF if it fails, which may happen, for example, when you do not have appropriate permission or run out of disk space to save the file.

CLOSING A FILE

```
if(fclose(fileHandle) == EOF)
   /* failed */
```

Be very careful of the spelling of file operations; do not use `open()` or `close()`. These are low-level file operations that are often accessible from C, but do not have the same functionality.

You can use three predefined file handles in your programs:

`stdin`	to refer to the standard input stream
`stdout`	to refer to the standard output stream
`stderr`	to refer to the standard error stream

These streams do not need to be explicitly opened and closed; they may be used at any time in your programs. The above file handles are not l-values and so may not appear on the left-hand side of an assignment. This means that while the following is legal

```
fileHandle = stdout;
```

this is not:

```
stdout = fileHandle;
```

5.5 Basic File I/O Operations

The basic file operations provided in C are similar to those described in Section 3.8, which deal with terminal-oriented character and formatted I/O. The summary below presents terminal I/O on the left-hand side, and file I/O on the right-hand side:

```
int getchar()              int fgetc(fileHandle)
int putchar(int)           int fputc(int, fileHandle)

int scanf(...)             int fscanf(fileHandle, ...)
int printf(...)            int fprintf(fileHandle, ...)
```

In order to use file I/O, you just add the letter "f" to the front of the operation name, and then add a defined file handle as the very first argument.

Note that C also supports `getc()` and `putc()` respectively, identical to `fgetc()` and `fputc()`.

Below, I show idioms introduced in Chapter 3, modified to read to and write from a file, rather than from the standard I/O streams.

READ SINGLE CHARACTER FROM A FILE

```
if((c = fgetc(fileHandle)) == EOF) /* error */
```

READ SINGLE INTEGER FROM A FILE

```
if(fscanf(fileHandle, "%d", &i) != 1) /* error */
```

The first example in this Section shows basic file I/O in action. Note that error messages are printed to the standard error stream, `stderr`, instead of the standard output stream, `stdout`. This is the preferred method, because the standard output stream may have been redirected, which would result in any output written to it having been redirected also. Note that most operating systems provide a separate command to redirect the error stream, for example Unix uses `>&`.

Example 5–1

This program reads double values from the file `TEST1.TXT`. It aborts program execution if the file does not exist, can not be opened, or three double values can not be read from this file. If the read operation was successful, the program outputs the sum of the three values. This program uses three idioms, respectively "Opening a file", "Reading integers", and "Closing a file".

```
/*
 * File: ex5-1.c
 * Program that reads three real values from the file TEST1.TXT
 *  and displays the sum of these values on the screen
 */
#include <stdio.h>
#include <stdlib.h>
int main() {
    FILE *f;
    double x, y, z;
```

```
    if((f = fopen("TEST1.TXT", "r")) == NULL) {
        fprintf(stderr, " can't read %s\n", "TEST1.TXT");
        return EXIT_FAILURE;
    }

    if(fscanf(f, "%lf%lf%lf", &x, &y, &z) != 3) {
        fprintf(stderr, "File read failed\n");
        return EXIT_FAILURE;
    }

    printf("%f\n", x + y + z);

    if(fclose(f) == EOF) {
        fprintf(stderr, "File close failed\n");
        return EXIT_FAILURE;
    }

    return EXIT_SUCCESS;
}
```

5.6 Testing for End-of-Line and End-of-File

The next example deals with the end-of-line terminator, which in C is represented by the '\n' character. The program reads a single line from the standard input, and outputs this line to the standard output.

Example 5-2

```
/*
 * File: ex5-2.c
 * Program which copies a single line from the keyboard and
 *    redisplays it
 */
#include <stdio.h>
#include <stdlib.h>
int main() {
    int c;
```

```
    printf("Enter a line of characters\n");

    while((c = getchar()) != '\n')
        putchar(c);
    putchar(c);        /* to print end-of-line */

    return EXIT_SUCCESS;
}
```

READ A LINE

```
while((c = getchar()) != '\n')
```

READ A LINE FROM A FILE

```
while((c = fgetc(fileHandle)) != '\n')
```

The code presented above suffers from one problem: the loop does not terminate on end-of-file. This problem is corrected in the next example, by changing the `while` statement as follows:

```
while ((c = getchar()) != '\n')
  if(c == EOF)
     break;
   else putchar(c);

if(c != EOF)
   putchar(c);
```

Typically, you would expect that the last line of a text file is terminated by the end-of-line character \n. However, this may not be the case; for example, a file may look like this:

abc\nde

It has two characters "de" at the end of the file, and no terminating \n. You should avoid writing programs that create such files.

Now, I will introduce idioms that deal with end-of-file.

READ UNTIL END -OF-FILE

```
while((c = getchar()) != EOF)
```

READ FROM A FILE UNTIL END-OF-FILE

```
while((c = fgetc(fileHandle)) != EOF)
```

Note that the above idioms can be easily modified, for example, to read integers until end-of-file you will use:

```
while((flag = fscanf(fileHandle, "%d", &i)) != EOF) {
    if(flag == 0) /* error */
```

My next example uses several familiar idioms to find the length of the longest line in a given file; the "Open a file" idiom is used twice, then "Read until end-of-file" is used, and finally the "Close a file" is used twice. This length is written to another file.

Example 5–3

```
/*
 * File: ex5-3.c
 * Program that reads text from the file TEST until end-
 *   of-file and outputs to the file TEST2 the length of
 *   the longest line and the number of this line
 */
#include <stdio.h>
#include <stdlib.h>
int main() {
    typedef FILE* FILE_P;
    int     c;
    int     len     = 0;
    int     maxlen  = 0;
    long    longest = 0;
    long    line    = 0;
    FILE_P  f, g;
```

```
    if((f = fopen("TEST", "r")) == NULL) {
        fprintf(stderr, "The file TEST cannot be opened\n");
        return EXIT_FAILURE;
    }
    if((g = fopen("TEST2", "w")) == NULL) {
        fprintf(stderr, "The file TEST2 cannot be opened\n");
        fclose(f);
        return EXIT_FAILURE;
    }

    while((c = fgetc(f)) != EOF) {
        if(c == '\n') {
            line++;
            if(len > maxlen) {
                maxlen = len;
                longest = line;
            }
            len = 0;  /* reset running length */
        } else len++;
    }

    if(line == 0) {  /* no line read */
        fprintf(stderr, "TEST has no line\n");
        return EXIT_SUCCESS;
    }

    if(fclose(f) == EOF) {
        fprintf(stderr, "File TEST cannot be closed\n");
        fclose(g);
        return EXIT_FAILURE;
    }

    fprintf(g, "\nThe longest line is ## %ld, ", longest);
    fprintf(g, "it has %d characters\n", maxlen);

    if(fclose(g) == EOF) {
        fprintf(stderr, "File TEST2 cannot be closed\n");
        return EXIT_FAILURE;
    }

    return EXIT_SUCCESS;
}
```

When discussing the correctness of this program, we should consider its boundary cases: empty input file, or an input file in which there is an "incomplete" last line, that is a file where the last line is missing the end-of-line character. Upon inspection, you should be able to see that the program in Example 5-3 behaves correctly in both cases.

C also provides a function that can be used to test if end-of-file has been encountered. The function feof(fileHandle) returns EOF if an attempt has been made to read and end-of-file has been detected, and 0 otherwise. Note that you must perform *at least one* input operation before you use feof():

```
while(1){
    c = getc(f);
    if(feof(f))
        break;
    else putc(c, f);
}
```

When performing buffered input, the programmer must be aware that although a particular operation may request only a single character (for example, getchar() expects one character), an entire line may actually be entered by the user. When the user hits the Enter key, all of these characters, including end-of-line, are stored in an input buffer. Whenever an input operation, such as getchar(), is performed, it first checks if there are any characters in this buffer; and if so, it will read from this buffer rather than from the keyboard until the buffer becomes empty. Thus if the user wants to force input to come from the keyboard, the buffer must first be cleared. To aid in writing code to skip to the end-of-line, I designed a new idiom.

CLEAR UNTIL END-OF-LINE

```
while(getchar() != '\n')
    ;
```

Note that this code assumes that end-of-line will eventually be encountered.

Example 5-4

This program gives the user the option of reading the input from the standard input stream or from the file TEST1, and sending the output to the standard output stream or to the file TEST2. In addition, if the user chooses to direct the output to a file, the program checks if this file already exists and, if so, asks the user for confirmation before rewriting it. The program then copies the contents of the selected input stream to the selected output stream. In order to implement the part of the program in which the user is asked to enter an option, I use the following technique:

- prompt
- read a single character c; then clear until end-of-line
- test the value of c.

```c
/*
 * File: ex5-4.c
 * Reads from stdin or the file TEST1, write to stdout
 * or the file TEST2.
 */
#include <stdio.h>
#include <stdlib.h>
int main() {
    FILE *f, *g;
    int c;
    int fromFile = 0;  /* reading from a file ? */
    int toFile = 0;    /* writing to a file ? */

    /* prompt */
    printf("Enter Y or y to read from the standard input stream, ");
    printf("any other character to read from TEST1: ");

    /* read a single character c */
    c = getchar();

    /* skip until end-of-line */
    while(getchar() != '\n')
        ;

    /* test the value of c */
    if(c == 'y' || c == 'Y')                /* reading from stdin */
        f = stdin;
```

```
else {
   if((f = fopen("TEST1", "r")) == NULL) {
      fprintf(stderr, "can't open TEST1\n");
      return EXIT_FAILURE;
   }
   fromFile = 1;        /* reading from TEST1 */
}

/* prompt */
printf("Enter Y or y to write to the standard output stream, ");
printf("any other character to write to TEST2: ");

/* read a single character c */
c = getchar();

/* skip until end-of-line */
while(getchar() != '\n')
   ;

/* test the value of c */
if(c == 'y' || c == 'Y')
   g = stdout;
else {
   /* to see if TEST2 exists, open it for reading, then close it */
   if((g = fopen("TEST2", "r")) != NULL) { /* TEST2 exists */

      fprintf(stderr, "File exists, overwrite? (Y/N) ");
      c = getchar();
      while (getchar() != '\n')
         ;

      if(fclose(g) == EOF) {
         fprintf(stderr, "error in closing\n");
         if(fromFile)
            fclose(f);
         return EXIT_FAILURE;
      }

      if(!(c == 'y' || c == 'Y')) {
         fprintf(stderr, "Leaving TEST2 intact; terminating\n");
         return EXIT_SUCCESS;
      }
   }
```

```
    /* overwrite TEST2 */
    if((g = fopen("TEST2", "w")) == NULL) {
        fprintf(stderr, "can't open TEST2\n");
        if(fromFile)
            fclose(f);
        return EXIT_FAILURE;
    }

    toFile = 1; /* set the flag */
}

/* Now, both I/O files are ready */
while((c = fgetc(f)) != EOF)
    putc(c, g);

if(fromFile && fclose(f) == EOF) {
    fprintf(stderr, "error in closing TEST1\n");
    if(toFile)
        fclose(g);
    return EXIT_FAILURE;
}
if(toFile && fclose(g) == EOF) {
    fprintf(stderr, "error in closing TEST2\n");
    return EXIT_FAILURE;
}
return EXIT_SUCCESS;
}
```

As can be seen from the previous example, the "Clear until end of line" idiom can be used to implement menu-driven programs. For example, suppose that you are implementing a line editor that supports various commands, such as append a line, delete a line, etc. The user is presented with a menu of available editor commands, and is supposed to enter a single character representing a command; for example

a - to append a line
d - to delete a line

You can implement this menu using the following code (functions such as e_append() are programmer-defined operations)

```
c = getchar();                    /* get option */
while(getchar() != '\n')          /* clear */
    ;
switch(c) {                       /* test option */
case 'a' :
            e_append();
            break;
case 'd' :
            e_delete();
            break;
}
```

I will conclude this chapter with a description of the function related to buffered input and called automatically by fscanf() when reading numerical values:

```
ungetc(c, f)
```

ungetc() pushes the character c back on the input stream f (practically, this means that the character is returned to the file input buffer described earlier). If successful, this function returns the character c, and EOF if the character c cannot be pushed back.

In many applications, you want to read and possibly process input characters that satisfy a certain condition, and stop when you encounter the first character that does not satisfy this condition, leaving it in the input stream. For example, to compose an unsigned integer, you need to read characters that are digits, as in:

```
value = 0;
while(isdigit(c = getchar()))
  value = value * 10 + (c - '0');
ungetc(c, stdin);
```

(isdigit() is a standard function explained in Section 9.2). This code is so useful that I will formulate it into an idiom.

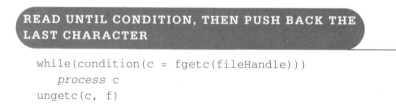

READ UNTIL CONDITION, THEN PUSH BACK THE LAST CHARACTER

```
while(condition(c = fgetc(fileHandle)))
    process c
ungetc(c, f)
```

Now, consider an example in which you would like to modify an existing file, say to remove all occurrences of ^M (control-M, or carriage return) from the file. There are several ways to accomplish this task. First, you can write a filter program that copies all characters with the exception of ^M:

```
while((c = getchar()) != EOF)
    if(c != '\r')
putchar(c);
```

Now, if you store a complete program in a file (say dos2unix), then to remove ^M from this file, you can not do the following:

```
dos2unix < test1 > test1
```

Instead, you have to use a temporary file, say junk:

```
dos2unix < test1 > junk
```

It is also possible to write a program that will internally perform the above operations. This program uses a standard function tmpfile() that creates a temporary file; it opens this file with the "w+" mode. This file is automatically deleted when it is closed, or when the program terminates. The basic idea of this program is to copy all characters with the exception of ^M's to the temporary file, then rewind the file and copy all characters back to the original file. The code snippet is shown below:

```
int c;
FILE *inOutFile;
FILE *temp;

if((inOutFile = fopen("test1", "r")) == NULL)
    return EXIT_FAILURE;
if((temp = tmpfile()) == NULL)
    return EXIT_FAILURE;

/* filter out all ^M */
while((c = fgetc(inOutFile)) != EOF)
    if(c != '\r')
        fputc(c, temp);

if(fclose(inOutFile) == EOF)
    return EXIT_FAILURE;
```

```
/* now, rewrite test1 and copy back */
if((inOutFile = fopen("test1", "w")) == NULL)
    return EXIT_FAILURE;

rewind(temp);
while((c = fgetc(temp)) != EOF)
    fputc(c, inOutFile);

if(fclose(inOutFile) == EOF)
    return EXIT_FAILURE;
```

Note that the above example shows how you can read and write respectively from and to the same file. The file that was originally opened for reading had to be closed before it was reopened for writing. Also notice that there is no simple way to write this program to modify the file "in place," that is, without using a temporary file.

5.7 Handling Errors

There are two file operations designed specifically to deal with errors. First, errors can be reported by the function

```
int ferror(FILE *f);
```

which returns a non-zero value if an error has occurred; otherwise it returns 0. Since the error could have occurred during the last operation or several operations before, there is a function

```
void clearerr(FILE *f);
```

that clears any error indications. These two functions are used as follows:

```
clearerr(f);
I/O operation
if(ferror(f))
    there has been an error
```

The above functions are not used very often because the error state can be tested using the return value of the library I/O function used.

5.8 List of Common Errors

1. To declare more than one FILE variable, the asterisk must be repeated, for example,

   ```
   FILE *f, *g;
   ```

2. Be very careful of the spelling of file operations; do not use open() or close(). These are low-level file operations that are often accessible from C, but do not have the same functionality.

5.9 List of Idioms

OPENING A FILE

```
if((fileHandle = fopen(fname, fmode)) == NULL)
    /* failed */
```

CLOSING A FILE

```
if(fclose(fileHandle) == EOF)  ...
    /* failed */
```

READ SINGLE CHARACTER FROM A FILE

```
if((c = fgetc(fileHandle)) == EOF) /* error */
```

READ SINGLE INTEGER FROM A FILE

```
if(fscanf(fileHandle, "%d", &i) != 1) /* error */
```

READ A LINE

```
while((c = getchar()) != '\n')
```

READ A LINE FROM A FILE

```
while((c = fgetc(fileHandle)) != '\n')
```

READ UNTIL END-OF-FILE

```
while((c = getchar()) != EOF)
```

READ FROM A FILE UNTIL END-OF-FILE

```
while((c = fgetc(fileHandle)) != EOF)
```

CLEAR UNTIL END-OF-LINE

```
while(getchar() != '\n')
    ;
```

Note that this code assumes that end-of-line will eventually be encountered.

READ UNTIL CONDITION, THEN PUSH BACK THE LAST CHARACTER

```
while(condition(c = fgetc(fileHandle)))
    process c
 ungetc(c, f)
```

5.10 Exercises

Note: In all exercises, follow all of the programming guidelines described in this chapter; use comments to properly document your programs. Test your programs carefully and all consider boundary cases.

Exercise 5-1

Write a program, which compares two text files, f1 and f2, one character at a time. Use the "Opening a file," "Closing a file," and "Read Single Character from a file" idioms.

Exercise 5-2

Write a program, which reads int values from a file IN1.dat and writes to the file OUT1.dat, the sum of all of the positive input values. Reading should stop when an end-of-file is encountered. The program should issue an error message if the input file cannot be opened. Use the "Read Single Integer from a File" idiom.

Exercise 5-3

Consider a text file money.txt, which represents your expenses. Every line (except for the last line) is of the following form:

```
number[newline]
```

Here, a number is a double value. The last line is empty. Write a program that writes the sum of all the expenses to the standard output stream. Then, the program asks the user whether that value should also be *appended* to a file called expenses.dat, and if so, writes this value to the file. Make sure that you handle boundary cases.

Exercise 5-4

Write a filter program that replaces all occurrences of \n with \r\n. This program should not create any temporary files that will be left after it terminates.

Exercise 5-5

Write a filter program that replaces all sequences of consecutive whitespace characters by a single space.

Exercise 5-6

Write a filter program that replaces all occurrences of the tab character by two blanks.

Exercise 5-7

Write a program that merges two data files; i.e. it outputs the contents of the first input file, followed by the contents of the second input file, to an output file.

Exercise 5-8

Write a program that merges two files containing sorted lists of double values; the output file should contain a sorted list; for example, given the following two input files:

```
1.2   3.4   6
2.4   5     9
```

the output file would contain:

```
1.2   2.4   3.4   5   6   9
```

Exercise 5-9

Write a filter program that removes all empty lines (i.e. lines containing only the end-of-line character).

Exercise 5-10

Write a filter program that outputs the contents of the input with each line numbered.

Exercise 5-11

Write a filter program that outputs the contents of the input with all C comments removed.

Exercise 5-12

Write a menu-driven program, which provides all of the operations described in Exercises 5–9 to 5–11.

Exercise 5-13

Write a menu-driven program that can be used to test your knowledge of addition, subtraction, and multiplication. For addition and subtraction, limit input values to those less than 100, for multiplication, limit input values to those less than 10. The program should display a message if an incorrect value has been entered, and then it should terminate, displaying the number of correct answers and the number of incorrect answers (also, add an exit option to the menu that allows the user to exit from the program).

Exercise 5-14

This exercise has two parts:

a) Write a program that reads the file "Rawin", encodes it and stores the encoded version in the output file junk1.out. The encryption algorithm is a simple one: a positive integer N ($0 < N < 128$) is added to the ordinal value of each character. The user supplies the encryption code N at run time.

b) Write a program that reads the encrypted file junk1.out, decodes it and stores the decoded version in the output file junk2.out. The decryption algorithm is a simple one: a positive integer N ($0 < N < 128$) is subtracted from the ordinal value of each character in the input. The decryption code N is supplied by the user at run time and must be the same as the one used for encryption, or the file will not be decoded properly.

Exercise 5-15

Write a program that provides a simple menu to perform Roman numeral to Arabic numeral conversion, and/or Arabic numeral to Roman numeral conversion (assume that the values are less than 1000).

Exercise 5-16

Write a program that reads the standard input stream and terminates on encountering end-of-file. This program writes a message stating whether the number of left brackets '(' is equal to the number of right brackets ')'. It also displays a message stating whether or not the brackets are balanced. For example, for the input:

( ))) ((

the number of left and right brackets is the same, but they are not balanced.

Exercise 5-17

Write a program that reads a file and splits it into two files; the first file contains the first half of the lines of the input file, and the second file contains the remaining lines.

Exercise 5-18

Write a program that reads a text file and counts the length of every line in the file. After reading the file, your program should output a message that states how many lines had more than 20 characters.

Chapter 6

THE C PREPROCESSOR

6.1 ◆ Preview

This chapter introduces the commands supported by the C pre-processor (which is absent in Java). I cover the topic of macros (with and without parameters), and then discuss conditional compilation and file inclusion. You will find that most examples that appear in this chapter are rather short, but they should be studied closely. Preprocessing is used in the remainder of this book, and it is important for both supporting program portability and software maintenance.

6.2 Introduction

Any line of C code that begins with the # (pound symbol) contains a preprocessing command. These lines are referred to as preprocessor command lines, and they have their own syntax, which does not adhere to C's syntax rules. From a logical point of view, preprocessing is performed before compilation, and as a result, these lines are removed and the source file is accordingly processed. The preprocessor has three uses. First, the user can specify that certain text in the source file is to be replaced by other text. The original text is referred to as a **macro**; the new text is called the **macro replacement** and the process is called a macro substitution. Note that macro substitution is a purely textual, in-place substitution, which does not involve the run-time stack.

Secondly, C provides a preprocessing directive which may be used to *include* other external files in the current file. Finally, C supports **conditional compilation**, which tells the compiler that a *part* of the source file is included conditionally (that is, the compiler will ignore it if some condition is met). This technique is useful for debugging (see Section 6.6.1).

6.3 Macros

This chapter introduces parameterless macros, macros with parameters, predefined macros, and the process of undefining and redefining macros.

6.3.1 ◆ Parameterless Macros

To define named constants, you can use macros, following this syntax:

```
#define  macroName  macroValue
```

During preprocessing, each occurrence of macroName in the source file will be replaced with the text specified in macroValue. Here, macroName is a single string (that is, one word), and macroValue is any sequence of tokens. The definition of macroValue ends when the newline character is encountered. If you want a macro to occupy more than one line, you should use the \ character. If you do use the \ (continuation) character, remember that it has to be the *very last* character on the preprocessor command line.

Examples
```
#define PI          3.14
#define SCREEN_W      80
```

```
#define SCREEN_H          25
#define GUI           Graphical User \
                         Interface
```

Using these definitions, the following line:

```
if(i < SCREEN_W || j > SCREEN_H)
```

would be replaced by the preprocessor with

```
if(i < 80 || j > 25)
```

---

1. To define a macro such as PI, do not use:

```
#define PI = 3.14
```

This replacement for PI consists of two tokens, = and 3.14. For example, the code

```
i = PI;
```

would be replaced by

```
i = = 3.14;
```

Also, remember to omit the ';' from a macro definition. For example,

```
#define PI 3.14;
```

is incorrect.

At this point, you may wonder what the difference is between a declaration of a constant, as in

```
const double PI = 3.14;
```

and a macro definition, such as

```
#define PI 3.14
```

The main difference is the *scope*; the macro can be used, starting with its definition, until the end of the file (unless it is later undefined, see the next section). On the other hand, a declared constant is subject to the same scope rules as any other declared variable. This brings up the question of where to place the macro definition. There are two possibilities: at the beginning of the file, or immediately before the macro is to be used. In my opinion, neither option is necessarily better—it is a matter of personal preference as to which one you use. Finally, the use of typed constants enables type checking to be performed.

Macros names will always appear in upper case.

Any constant value, which might change during software development, should be defined as a macro or as a constant.

Macros can also be used to replace one or more lines of code. For example, I may want to create an *Abort* command, which terminates the program by returning an error status flag. To do this, I would first write the macro:

```
#define ABORT      return EXIT_FAILURE
```

With this in place, the following code segment:

```
if(parityFail)
    ABORT;
else ...
```

would be replaced by

```
if (parityFail)
    return EXIT_FAILURE;
else ...
```

The preprocessor syntax is not the same as C syntax.

The best advice for debugging macros is to remember that it is a straight textual substitution that takes place—if you can't figure out why the compiler is complaining, try temporarily replacing the macro with the actual text (most compilers have a switch that performs this task). I find that in many cases, this makes the problem instantly clear.

Here are a few more examples of macros:

```
#define PROMPT        printf("Enter real value: ")
#define SKIP          while(getchar() != '\n') \
                         ;
```

The second macro defines a "Skip until end of line" idiom.

The example given below shows that one macro can be used in the definition of another macro:

```
#define EMPTY         (maxUsed == 0)

#define ASSERT        if(!(EMPTY ? current == 0 : \
                        0 < current && current <= maxUsed)){\
           fprintf(stderr, "invariant failed; current = %d\t; \
                    maxUsed=%d\n", current, maxUsed); \
                 exit(1); }
```

The condition of the above if statement uses a conditional expression:

```
EMPTY ? current == 0 : 0 < current && current <= maxUsed
```

Therefore, if EMPTY evaluates to true, then the value of the condition is the same as the value of

```
current == 0
```

otherwise it is the value of

```
0 < current && current <= maxUsed
```

The next example, presented below, recommends that you enclose the macro value with parentheses, at least when you use arithmetic expressions. For example, in the macro definition

```
#define A      2 + 4
#define B      A * 3
```

B is expanded to

```
2 + 4 * 3
```

and, perhaps what you wanted is:

```
(2 + 4) * 3
```

This can be achieved with

```
#define A      (2 + 4)
#define B      (A * 3)
```

6.3.2 ◆ Predefined Macros

There are four predefined macros:

__LINE__	current line number of the source file
__FILE__	name of the current source file
__TIME__	time of translation
__STDC__	1 if the compiler conforms to ANSI C

The above macros are not defined in any header file; instead they are built into the implementation of C. As you can see, each macro name contains two leading and two trailing underscores. These macros are useful for printing information, especially if an error occurs.

Example

```
if(y == 0) {
    fprintf(stderr,
        "divide by zero error on line %d in the file %s\n",
            __LINE__, __FILE__);
    return EXIT_FAILURE;
} else x /= y;
```

6.3.3 ◆ Macros with Parameters

The addition of *parameters* to a macro definition provides even more flexibility. Here is the syntax:

```
#define macroName(parameters) macroValue
```

Any number of parameters, separated by commas, can be used.

Examples

```
#define RANGE(i)              (1 <= (i) && (i) <= maxUsed)
#define R(x)                  scanf("%d",&x);
#define READ(c, fileHandle)   (c = fgetc(fileHandle))
```

Typically, it is a good idea to include parentheses around both macro argu-ments and macro bodies—use the "parenthesize aggressively" approach. Consider the last macro *without* the outer parentheses, used in the code:

```
if(READ(c, fileHandle) == 'x')
```

The expanded text would result in:

```
if(c = fgetc(fileHandle) == 'x')
```

Due to precedence rules, the expression `fgetc(fileHandle) == 'x'` would get evaluated first, and either 0 or 1 would get assigned to c—probably not what you intended.

Now, let's look at another example in which the macro is used to identify whitespace:

```
#define WHITESPACE(ch)       \
   ((ch)==' ' || (ch)=='\t' || (ch)=='\n' || (ch)=='\f')
```

You have to be careful about the manner in which you invoke this macro. For example, the following piece of code will result in an action that is performed "behind the scenes" as a *side effect*:

```
while(WHITESPACE(c = getchar()))
   ;
```

Here is what happens: the first character gets read by `getchar()`, and the macro WHITESPACE is invoked. The first condition in the macro, ch == ' ' is false. Because the parameter to the macro is the expression c = getchar(), a *sec-ond* character is read, and ch == '\t' is evaluated. (If you have trouble seeing this, try substituting the string c = getchar() for every occurrence of ch in the macro body). To avoid the side effect in this example, you can call the macro WHITESPACE as follows:

```
while((c = getchar(),WHITESPACE(c))
   ;
```

By using macros, you are adding new constructs and new functionality to the language—if you do this inappropriately, the readability of your code may suffer.

There should be no whitespace between the macro name and the opening parenthesis '(' for the parameters; otherwise, the preprocessor will interpret the parameters as part of the text to be included.

Enclose the entire macro, as well as each occurrence of a macro argument, in parentheses.

Avoid side effects in macro arguments.

As I mentioned earlier, a function macro is not a true function. It is still a macro substitution with an additional substitution of the parameters. A macro function has the advantage of avoiding the *overhead* of a function call (stack management). A disadvantage is that code within the macro itself is less readable, and so macros should be kept relatively short.

Macros are *not* expanded within comments and string constants. For example, you can try to define a macro that uses various control formats for double values:

```
#define PRINT(width, kind, value) printf("%width.2kind", value)
```

The call

```
PRINT(4, g, 2.33)
```

would not produce

```
printf("%4.2g", 2.33)
```

as expected; instead it will be undefined. In this situation, you need to use the # character to instruct the preprocessor to *convert a token into a string*. If # appears in the macro definition, then it must be followed by the parameter, as in

```
#kind
```

During the macro expansion, the above string is replaced by the corresponding argument of the macro enclosed in string quotes; for example, if the argument for the parameter `kind` is

```
g2
```

then the replacement string will look like this

```
"g2"
```

The previous example should have used the following definition:

```
#define PRINT(width, kind, value) printf("%" #width ".2" #kind, value)
```

Now, when I try invoking the macro,

```
PRINT(4, g, 2.33)
```

the sequence

```
"%" #width ".2" #kind
```

will be replaced by

```
"%" "4" ".2" "g"
```

and since as I mentioned in Section 3.6.4, adjacent string constants are *concatenated*, the above string becomes

```
"%4.2g"
```

Therefore, the macro expansion will be

```
printf("%4.2g", 2.33);
```

There is one more rather rarely used construct that I will mention—namely token *merging*, using `##`. This construct merges the two tokens surrounding the `##` characters into a single token, as in

```
#define TEMP(i)    temp ## i
```

Then,

```
TEMP(1) = TEMP(2)
```

would be expanded into

```
temp1 = temp2
```

6.4 Undefining and Redefining Macros

If you define a macro, for example PI, then what happens if you try to redefine it (i.e., define the macro to be something else later on in the source file)? While this may work, it is best avoided because the legality of the redefinition depends on various details, such as the number of whitespace characters appearing in the original definition and the redefinition. A macro redefinition typically makes the code more difficult to debug—the programmer sees the first definition and assumes that it remains constant throughout the file. If you must redefine a macro, you should first undefine it, using the undef command:

```
#undef PI
```

6.5 File Inclusion

The #include command specifies that the text of some file is to be included in the current source file. From the perspective of the compiler, a file containing several **include directives** is a single source file. There are two formats for the include command:

```
#include "filename"
```

and

```
#include <filename>
```

These two formats differ in how the specified file is located by the compiler. If the first format is used, the system will typically scan the *current* directory (the directory in which the source file I am compiling is located), and if it does not find the file, it continues to look for it in other directories—the exact search rules are implementation dependent and vary from system to system. If the second format is used, the compiler will typically look for the file in special *system* directories—

again which directories depends on both the system and the programmer's specifications. The main difference between these two methods is that the first one is used for *user defined* include files, while the second method is used for *system include* files.

INCLUDE FILES

Use

```
#include <filename>
```

for system files, and

```
#include "filename"
```

for user-defined files

File inclusion is a useful mechanism for increasing the readability of programs. For example, all relevant definitions may be grouped in a single file, typically referred to as the **header** file, which should be included in the main file. I will now provide an example.

Consider a file screen.h:

```
#define SCREEN_W      80
#define SCREEN_H      25
```

and a second file, containing the main program:

```
#include "screen.h"
int main() {
. . .
}
```

The main program includes the file with all the definitions (screen.h). This allows the programmer to organize and standardize his or her code by placing all of the global definitions, which will be used by (potentially) several files, in one place.

You have already seen various standard header files supplied with a typical C compiler, such as stdio.h, which contain the basic declarations needed to perform I/O. Another useful standard header file is ctype.h, which contains the declarations of several macros (or functions) useful for testing the state of characters, such as the islower() macro. Mathematical functions, such as abs and sin, are declared in another header file called math.h.

File inclusion should *not* be confused with separate compilation. Even if code is divided into several files, the compiler treats it as one complete program and compiles all of the included files. An included file may itself contain include commands, which may lead to including the same file more than once. Section 6.6.2 will explain how to avoid this problem.

6.6 Conditional Compilation

In many cases it is useful to have the compiler ignore portions of the code depending on some specified condition—this is referred to as **conditional compilation**. These portions of code are not compiled and are not part of the executable code. Examples of such situations include debugging and writing portable code—I will expand on these topics later on in this section.

There are two basic kinds of conditional compilation. The first one resembles the syntax of an `if` statement:

```
#if constantExpression1
    part1
#elif constantExpression2
    part2
#else
    part3
#endif
```

There may be any number of `#elif` parts, and this part, as well as the `else` part, may be entirely omitted. If the value of the `constantExpression1` is true (nonzero), the text making up `part1` of the file is included; otherwise, if the value of the `constantExpression2` is true (nonzero), the text making `part2` is included, else `part3` is included.

The second kind of conditional compilation is used to test whether a macro has been defined:

```
#ifdef macroName
    part1
#else
    part2
#endif
```

Here, `part1` is included if `macroName` has been defined; otherwise, `part2` is included. There is a similar command that is the logical negation of `#ifdef`:

```
#ifndef macroName
    part1
```

```
#else
    part2
#endif
```

Finally, there is the `defined` operator that can be used only in `#if` and `#elif` expressions:

> `defined(name)` evaluates to 1 if its parameter is defined; otherwise it evaluates to 0.

For example:

```
#if defined(__STDC__)
...
#endif
```

The predefined `#error` command can be used as shown below:

```
#error textMessage
```

This command produces a compile time error message that includes `textMessage`. For example:

```
#if defined(IBM)
#error "can't use it"
#endif
```

Now, I describe three important applications of conditional compilation: debugging, header files, and portability.

6.6.1 ◆ Debugging

During program development, it is often convenient to *exclude* portions of the code. The best way of doing this is by using an `#if` ... `#endif` syntax:

```
#if 0
    part to be excluded
#endif
```

This is a better solution than commenting out the code. In C, comments must not be nested, so if the piece of code you wish to exclude already contains comments, and you try to enclose it in another pair of comments, a compilation error will result.

For the purpose of debugging a program, you may wish to add some informative output statements that tell you about the state of the program. Once debugging is complete, these statements should probably be removed, because even if they do not produce any visible output, they still increase the size of the executable code. Deleting the debugging output statements may not be a good idea, since at some point you may find some other bug in the code, and so need them again.

A program typically has two versions: the *testing* version and the *production* version. In the testing version, the debugging information is produced; no such output should be produced in the production version. It is possible to have both versions in the same source file, and use a macro to make the compiler toggle between them. Below, I give an outline of this technique.

Create a macro name, say DEB, which, when defined, turns debugging on and, when undefined, turns it off. This is summarized in the following idiom:

DEBUGGING USING CONDITIONAL COMPILATION

```
#define DEB    /* empty, but defined */
#ifdef DEB
   /* some debugging statement, for example */
   printf("value of i = %d", i);
#endif
/* code which will be executed when NOT debugging */
```

One way to turn debugging off and on is to edit the source file. A better way is to use the compiler command line. Many compilers allow the user to define or undefine a macro on the command line used to compile the program; for example, under Unix, the command

```
cc -UDEB filename
```

will undefine the macro DEB when filename is compiled, whereas

```
cc -DDEB filename
```

will define this macro.

I will now provide an example of a program that contains some debugging code. This example is a modification of Example 4-1; the program finds the largest input character and uses conditional compilation to output debugging messages.

Example 6-1

```
/* File: ex6-1.c
 * Read characters until "." and output the ASCII value
 *  of the largest input character.
 * Use conditional compilation for debugging
 */
#include <stdio.h>
#include <stdlib.h>
int main() {
   const  char SENTINEL = '.';
   int    aux;
   int    maxi = 0;

#ifdef DEBUG
   printf("debugging on: copy each input character\n");
#endif
   while(1) {
       if((aux = getchar()) == EOF || aux == SENTINEL)
          break;
#ifdef DEBUG
      putchar(aux);
      putchar('\n');
#endif
      if(aux > maxi)
#ifdef DEBUG
         printf("Now setting largest character to: %c\n", aux);
#endif
      maxi = aux;
   }
#ifdef DEBUG
   putchar('\n');
#endif
   printf("The largest ASCII value: %d\n", maxi);

   return EXIT_SUCCESS;
}
```

6.6.2 ◆ Header Files: Part 1

Header files represent interfaces, very much like Java interfaces. They typically contain declarations of functions and macros. In this section, I will describe the application of conditional compilation to header files; I will present a detailed description of header files in Section 7.4.4.

When a program consists of several included files, it is easy to inadvertently include the same file more than once, which will typically generate a compilation error. To avoid this, the following approach should be used: each included file begins a conditional compilation directive based on the definition of a macro, which specifies whether this file has already been included.

By convention, the name of this macro is made up of the header file name; the period " . " in the file name is replaced with the underscore character. For example, an include file `screen.h` will have the macro name SCREEN_H, and the file might look like:

```
#ifndef SCREEN_H
#define SCREEN_H

/* contents of the header */
#endif
```

Now consider a file called `main.c` that includes `screen.h`:

```
#include "screen.h"
#include "screen.h" /* a second #include by accident */
```

This code will not include the header file twice, because only the first include statement actually includes the `screen.h` file. Once SCREEN_H is defined, the

```
#ifndef SCREEN_H
```

statement is false, and the file is not included for the second time.

HEADER FILE USING MACRO

```
#ifndef SCREEN_H
#define SCREEN_H

/* contents of the header */
#endif
```

Make sure that in a header file you use

```
#ifndef
```

rather than

```
#ifdef
```

6.6.3 ◆ Portability

The final application of conditional compilation is for developing programs that run under different environments. For example, we could use these definitions for a program that runs either under an IBM environment or any other environment:

```
#if IBMPC
#include <ibm.h>
#else
#include <generic.h> /* use machine independent routines */
#endif
```

If the `IBMPC` macro is defined, this code includes the file `ibm.h` rather than `generic.h` when the program is compiled.

In Section 3.10, I described the use of `typedef` to write portable programs. Assuming that `IBMPC` uses small integers and other computers use large integers, you can use conditional compilation to support portability:

```
#ifdef IBMPC
typedef int MyInteger
#else
typedef long MyInteger
#endif
```

6.7 Line Numbering

There is one more preprocessor command available, which is rarely used, and I mention it here only for the sake of completeness. The preprocessor command

```
#line constantExpression "filename"
```

makes the compiler *think* that it is compiling the file called `filename` and that the current line number is `constantExpression`. The identifier may be omitted, in which case only the current line number changes. For example,

```
#line 100 "FILE1"
```

makes the compiler assume that the next line number is 100, and the name of the file that should be associated with it (for example, in error messages) is `FILE1`. The numbers of subsequent lines read from the current input file will increment starting at this point. These settings will remain in effect until a new `#line` directive is given. This command does not actually change the file being compiled, only the view of the file presented to the compiler.

This preprocessor command is useful if the source file being compiled was created by merging two or more files. As a rather simplistic example, assume you have the following two files defined:

```
s1.c:

int main()
{

s2.c:

integer   i;
}
```

Suppose these two files have been combined, as a result of the execution of another program, say P, into a file called s.c:

```
int main()
{
 integer   i;
}
```

If s.c is compiled, the compiler will issue a message that an error has occurred on line 3. However, the user may wish to know where in the files s1.c and s2.c the error has occurred. This can be done by having the program P, which originally concatenated these two files, insert appropriate #line commands in s.c. Specifically, s.c should look like

```
s.c:

    #line 1 "s1.c"
    int main()
{
#line 1 "s2.c"
   integer   i;
}
```

If this file is compiled, the compiler will produce an error message indicating that an error occurred on line 1 of s1.c, although it is actually on line 3 of s.c. This application of the #line command is used by the Yacc program, a parser generator available on Unix systems [Joh78].

6.8 List of Common Errors

1. To define a macro such as `PI`, do not use:

```
#define PI = 3.14
```

This replacement for `PI` consists of two tokens, `=` and `3.14`. For example, the code

```
    i = PI;
```

would be replaced by

```
    i = = 3.14;
```

Also, remember to omit the ';' from a macro definition. For example,

```
#define PI 3.14;
```

is incorrect.

2. The preprocessor syntax is not the same as C syntax.

3. There should be no whitespace between the macro name and the opening parenthesis '(' for the parameters; otherwise, the preprocessor will interpret the parameters as part of the text to be included.

4. Enclose the entire macro, as well as each occurrence of a macro argument, in parentheses.

5. Avoid side effects in macro arguments.

6. Make sure that in a header file you use

```
#ifndef
```

rather than

```
#ifdef
```

6.9 List of Idioms

INCLUDE FILES

Use

```
#include <filename>
```

for system files, and

```
#include "filename"
```

for user-defined files

DEBUGGING USING CONDITIONAL COMPILATION

```
#define DEB    /* empty, but defined */
#ifdef DEB
   /* some debugging statement, for example */
   printf("value of i = %d", i);
#endif
/* code which will be executed when NOT debugging */
```

HEADER FILE USING MACRO

```
#ifndef SCREEN_H
#define SCREEN_H

/* contents of the header */
#endif
```

6.10 List of Programming Style Guidelines

1. Macro names will always appear in uppercase.
2. Any constant value, which might change during software development, should be defined as a macro or as a constant.

3. By using macros, you are adding new constructs and new functionality to the language—if you do this inappropriately, the readability of your code may suffer.

6.11 Exercises

Exercise 6-1

Find the output produced by the following program:

```
#define LOW -2
#define HIGH (LOW + 5)
#define PR(arg)  printf("%d\n", (arg))
#define FOR(arg) for(; (arg); (arg)--)
#define SHOW(x) x
int main() {
int i = LOW;
int j = HIGH;

    FOR(j)
    switch(j) {
        case 1:   PR(i++);
        case 2:   PR(j);
                  break;
        default : PR(i);
    }
    printf("\n%s\n", SHOW(3));
    return EXIT_SUCCESS;
}
```

Exercise 6-2

(a) Write a macro ERROR(s) that writes the error message s to stderr and then aborts the program.
(b) Write a header file Bool.h that defines true and false.

Exercise 6-3

Write the definitions of the following macros (here, don't use any predefined macros):

```
EOL            /* represents end of line */

ISLOWER(c)     /* evaluates to 1 if c is a lowercase
               * character, to 0 otherwise */
```

```
SHOUT(s)         /* prints the string s and then terminates
                  * program execution */

MED(a, b, c)    /* prints 1 if the value of b is between a
                  * and c; otherwise prints 0 - assume a, b, c
                  * are integers */


OPEN(f)         /* opens file f for reading using "junk" as the
                  * filename. Evaluates to 1 if successful;
                  * 0 otherwise */
```

Exercise 6-4

Suppose that MAX is a macro defined like this

```
# define MAX(x,y)   x < y ? y : x
```

Show the fully expanded form of the following expressions and calculate the values of these expressions:

```
1 + MAX(2,3)
1 + MAX(3,2)
MAX(3,2) + 1
MAX(2,3) + 1
```

Rewrite the definition of MAX so that it works correctly (all the above expressions evaluate to 4).

Exercise 6-5

Is it possible to rewrite the macro MAX from Exercise 6–4 so that it will work correctly even if the evaluation of arguments results in side-effects? Justify your answer.

Exercise 6-6

Write a header file bool.h, which contains the definition of a data type Boolean (use typedef), and two macros TRUE and FALSE. Then, write another header file boolean.h, which contains the same definition for the Boolean data type, and two macros True and False. Finally, write a program that creates a macro BOOL and uses conditional compilation to include bool.h (if BOOL is defined), and boolean.h (if BOOL is not defined). In this program, use the data type and macros to read two double values and output a message informing the user as to whether the second value is larger than the first one.

Exercise 6-7

Use conditional compilation and rewrite Exercise 5–5 so that in a debugging mode, the program displays the first character that precedes the whitespace, the number of consecutive whitespace characters, and the first character that follows the whitespace.

Exercise 6-8

Use conditional compilation and rewrite Exercise 5–8 so that in a debugging mode, the program displays a message informing the user as to which input file is being read, what line of this file is currently read, and the time the program was executed (use predefined macros).

Chapter 7

FUNCTIONS, SCOPE, AND INTRODUCTION TO MODULE-BASED PROGRAMMING

7.1 ◆ Preview

In this chapter, I will cover the following topics:

- a review of functions
- modularization of programs through multiple files and separate compilation
- scope rules
- introduction to module based programming:
  - header files for representing interfaces
  - encapsulation of data in a file
  - kinds of modules
- module maintenance, including modifying and extending existing modules (this discussion will be continued in the following chapters).

7.2 Functions and Their Documentation

A C program consists of one or more function definitions, including exactly one that must be called `main`.

The syntax for C functions is the same as the syntax for Java methods. All functions are *stand-alone*, which means that they are not nested in any other construct, such as a class. As in Java, parameters are passed *by value* (Section 8.15.1 describes how to implement call by reference).

I will start by presenting a relatively simple example of a function, and use this opportunity to introduce various lexical conventions and make comments on the programming style.

Example 7–1

Consider the task of drawing a frame with *'s used for boarders, like this:

```
****
*  *
*  *
****
```

Breaking it down into sub-problems best solves this problem:

> draw the top
>
> draw a line
>
> draw a line
>
> draw the bottom

Thus far, I have not considered the implementation of any of the components, such as how to draw a line. I have only concerned myself with how to solve the original problem. This approach is referred to as the *top-down* design: you start by sub-dividing the original problem into components and only then worry about how to implement the individual pieces. The alternative is *bottom-up* design: you implement the individual sub-components that you think will be required, and only then use them to solve the original problem.

The first and the last components in my example are identical, and could be represented by the following function:

```
/*
 * Function: draw
 * Purpose: print numOfC occurrences of character c,
 *    and then end-of-line
```

```
 * Inputs: c and numOfC (parameters)
 * Returns: void
 * Error checking: Does nothing if numOfC is not positive
 * Sample call:
 *    draw('*', 10); -- draw a line of 10 asterisks
 */
void draw(char c, int numOfC);
```

Note how carefully I documented the semantics of the `draw()` function. In general, the function documentation consists of the following sections:

a short description

input to the function (through parameters and global variables)

the return value, if any

output from the function (through parameters and global variables)

error checking performed by this function

finally, a sample application (call)

While this may appear like overkill, you should remember that the user of the function should be able to read just this documentation in order to use it. If he or she has to inspect the implementation to understand the semantics, then there is something wrong with the documentation. Sometimes, it is also useful to put in a 'Warning' section to alert the user about any additional side effects your function may have.

I have chosen to implement a general `draw()` function that displays the character passed to it, rather then just '*'. Typically, it is more useful to write *general* functions that can be used to solve other problems in the future.

To draw intermediate lines, you could either design a separate function or modify the design of `draw()` so that it handles both cases. To do the latter, you can use the following function:

```
/*
 * Function: draw
 * Purpose:print numOfC occurrences of character c,
 *    followed by numOfD occurrences of character d,
 *    followed by numOfC occurrences of character c,
 *    and then end-of-line
 * Inputs: c, numOfC, d, numOfD (parameters)
 * Returns:void
 * Error checking: if numOfC is not positive then c is not printed
 *    If numOfD is not positive then d is not printed.
 * Sample call: draw('?',2,'$',4);
 *    Prints a line like this:
 *  ??$$$$??
 */
```

```
void draw(char c, int numOfC, char d, int numOfD);
```

Now, to print the box of asterisks specified earlier, you would use the following code:

```
draw('*', 2, ' ', 0);
draw('*', 1, ' ', 2);
draw('*', 1, ' ', 2);
draw('*', 2, ' ', 0);
```

The readability of this solution is questionable; for example, it may take a while to figure out why the second argument in the call to draw() is equal to 2, not 4. As a result, I have chosen to use another function to draw intermediate lines. The complete code follows, in which the first line is created by calling drawFullLine(), and an intermediate line is created by calling drawIntermediate-Line():

```
/*
 * File: ex7-1.c
 * Print a box of N asterisks
 */
#include <stdio.h>
#include <stdlib.h>
/*
 * Function: drawFullLine
 * Purpose:  prints numOfC occurrences of character c,
 *    and then end-of-line
 * Inputs:    c and numOfC (parameters)
 * Returns: void
 * Error checking: Does nothing if numOfC is not positive
 * Sample call: draw('?', 3);
 *     Prints
 *     ???
 */
void drawFullLine(char c, int numOfC);

/*
 * Function: drawIntermediateLine
 * Purpose: prints character c, then numOfD-2 occurrences of d,
 *    then c, followed by end-of-line
 * Inputs: c, d, numOfD (parameters)
 * Returns: void
 * Error checking: Does nothing if numOfD is not positive
 * Sample call: draw('?', '$', 3);
```

```
 *      Prints
 *      ?$$$?
 */
void drawIntermediateLine(char c, char d, int numOfD);


/*
 * main program that calls the above functions
 */
int main() {
   const int N = 4;
   const char STAR = '*';
   const char BLANK = ' ';
   int     i;

   if(N < 3)  /* here, can not happen */
      return EXIT_FAILURE;

   drawFullLine(STAR, N);    /* draw the top line */
   for(i = 0; i < N - 2; i++)
      drawIntermediateLine(STAR, BLANK, N);
   drawFullLine(STAR, N);   /* draw the bottom line */

   return EXIT_SUCCESS;
}

void drawFullLine(char c, int numOfC) {
   int i;

   for(i = 0; i < numOfC; i++)
      putchar(c);
   putchar('\n');
}

void drawIntermediateLine(char c, char d, int numOfD) {
   int i;

   putchar(c);
   for(i = 0; i < numOfD - 2; i++)
      putchar(d);
   putchar(c);
   putchar('\n');
}
```

I included the documentation of both functions only before their declaration because the complete program is relatively short. In general, it may be useful, or even necessary, to provide documentation for both the declaration and the definition. For example, a function definition may appear in a file separate from its declaration (see Section 7.4.3), in which case it requires its *own* documentation.

A careful inspection reveals that the implementation of the function `drawIntermediateLine()` does *not* meet its specification. This function specified that it does nothing if `numOfD` is negative, yet it lacks a check for this condition and in fact does produce output even if `numOfD` is negative. To fix this problem, one more statement should be added to the code of `drawIntermediateLine()` function, right after the declaration of the variable `i`:

```
if(numOfD <= 0)
    return;
```

1. Make sure comments and code agree; in particular, always carefully check that the function implementation meets its specification.

2. In general, a function definition should not exceed one page. Code should be broken up; in particular, lines which are too long should be avoided.

3. Either the function declaration or definition (or both) should be preceded by documentation, which describes the function. The required format of the documentation is as follows:

> Function: name
> Purpose: a general description of the function
> (typically, this is a description of what it is supposed to do)
> Inputs: a list of parameters and global variables read in the function
> Returns: value to be returned
> Modifies: a list of parameters and global variables that are modified; describes any side-effects
> Error checking: describes your assumptions about actual parameters; what happens if actual parameters are incorrect
> Sample call:

In addition, there may also be a Bugs section, which documents cases that the implementation does not handle.

7.2.1 ◆ Declarations and Definitions

In Chapter 2, I briefly introduced the difference between a function declaration and definition. To review, a **declaration** merely provides a function prototype; that is the function header, which includes the return type and the list of parameters. For example:

```
void hex(unsigned char *p, int max);
```

declares `hex` to be a function that returns `void` and has two parameters. The declaration does not say anything about the implementation. The **definition** of a function includes both the function prototype and the function body, that is, its implementation.

A function must be declared or defined *before* it is called. Strictly speaking, this is not true, but only because of the need for backward compatibility with the old K&R standard. I urge you to always avoid calling a function that has not been declared; consequently, in this book, I will not provide a description of what happens when a function has not been declared, but it has been called. In some cases you need to use a declaration as a *forward declaration*; for example, consider two functions `f()` and `g()` that call each other. Since in this case there is no way to define each function before it is called, you have to declare at least one of them before you can define it.

There are two types of function parameters: **formal parameters**, which are parameters appearing in a declaration or a definition of a function, and **actual parameters**, which appear in a call to the function. For example:

```
int f(int x);    here x is a formal parameter
i = f(2*3);      here 2*3 is the actual parameter corresponding to the
                 formal parameter.
```

Some people refer to formal parameters simply as *parameters* and actual parameters as *arguments*.

1. A function must be declared or defined *before* it can be called (strictly speaking this is not true, and a function may be called even if its prototype has not been seen, but the rules that describe this case are complicated, and the technique often leads to programming errors).

2. Remember that a function declaration is terminated with `;` but that in the definition, the function prototype is not terminated with `;`. Instead, the function body is enclosed in braces (this is a very common error when copying

code from a header file to an implementation and then forgetting to make the necessary changes).

C does not require that you provide names of formal parameters in the *declaration*. If you do, you will probably use these names for documentation purposes.

Example

```
int max(int, int);
/* returns the maximum of two integer arguments */
```

Since you can specify the purpose of `max()` without referring to the parameters by name, the names of the formal parameters are omitted. However, the declaration of

```
void drawIntermediateLine(char c, char d, int i);
```

needs the names of its formal parameters in order to properly document the function. My next example is of a function that counts the number of digits in its integer parameter; for example, 123 has three digits.

Example 7-2

```
/*
 * File: ex7-2.c
 * Function: digits
 * Purpose: compute the number of digits in the integer n
 * Inputs: n (parameter)
 * Returns: number of digits in n
 * Error checking: returns 0 if n is not positive
 * Sample call: i = digits(123);
 *        i gets the value 3
 */
int digits(int n) {
   int count = 0;
```

```
    if(n <= 0)
       return 0;

    do {
       count++;
       n /= 10;
    } while(n != 0);

    return count;
}
```

As part of standard testing and debugging, I must consider boundary cases for the code. One such case is when n is equal to 0; upon inspection the code is correct. Note that some C programmers would write:

```
while(n)
```

instead of

```
while(n != 0)
```

The two are equivalent, but the latter seems to be more readable. The problem has a recursive structure:

> if there is only one digit return 1, otherwise
>
> return 1 + function applied to n/10

and therefore I could re-code the function digits() as a recursive function

```
int digits(int n) {

   if(n <= 0)
      return 0;

   if(n/10 == 0)
      return 1;

   return 1 + digits(n/10);

}
```

1. In the `digits()` function of the sample program, I did not choose to write the code as follows:

```
if(n/10 == 0)
    return 1;
else return 1 + digits(n/10);
```

The only difference is that the original code did not use the `else`; the logic is exactly the same. In this case, it is a matter of personal preference—some people, myself included, find the original code more readable, while others argue that by including the `else`, the code has a more logically understandable structure. In the case of a more nested `if` structure, extra `else`'s may make the code more difficult to understand.

2. Brackets in the `return` statement are unnecessary, and in my opinion clutter the code:

```
if(n/10 == 0)
    return (1);
return (1 + digits(n/10));
```

3. As always, the code is as clear as possible. For example, I could have written:

```
if(n /= 10)
    return 1;
return 1 + digits(n);
```

Although the outcome is the same, this is hard to understand, because of the side effect in the `if` condition.

Side effects in loop conditions should be typically avoided. As a second example of a loop-side-effect, I will write a code to print the digits of an integer n reversed. I could write it as follows:

```
do {
    printf("%d", n%10);
} while(n/=10);
```

A more readable solution avoids the side effect in the loop condition:

```
do {
    printf("%d",n%10);
```

```
        n /= 10;
    } while(n != 0);
```

7.2.2 ◆ Functions and Void

Functions that have *no* parameters may specify a `void` list of formal parameters, using the syntax:

type f(void)

The keyword `void` may be omitted.

Example 7-3

This function demonstrates how user-input characters may be filtered and converted. Specifically, the function expects only digits and sign characters to be entered (i.e. any character from the set [0..9,+,-]). It ignores any characters that are spaces, and terminates if the user inputs a character not in the above set. The filtering is performed using the two functions, `isdigit()` and `isspace()`, defined in the standard file `ctype.h` (details may be found in Section 9.2). The function returns the integer representation of the read characters. For example, if the user enters the sequence of characters

−123

the function converts the sequence to the integer value −123, and returns this value.

```
/*
 * File: ex7-3.c
 * Function: getInt
 * Purpose: read characters from the keyboard and
 *    return the corresponding integer value
 * Inputs: nothing
 * Returns: integer value of characters read
 * Modifies: reads in input stream. Any character that has
 *    not been used is pushed back.
 * Error checking: returns 0 if no digits encountered
 * Sample call:  i = getInt();
 * Assuming the input was
 *    -12a
```

```
 *    the value of i will be -12, and 'a' will be the current
 *     input character.
 */
int getInt(void) {
    int c;
    int sign = 1;
    int val  = 0;

    /* skip whitespace  */
    while((c = getchar()) != EOF)
        if(!isspace(c))
            break;

    switch(c) { /* check current character */

    case '-' :  sign = -1;

    case '+' :  c = getchar();

    default  :  if(!isdigit(c)) {    /* error */
                    ungetc(c, stdin);
                    return 0;
                }
    }

    while (isdigit(c)) {
        val = val * 10 + (c - '0');
        c = getchar();
    }

    if(c != EOF)
        ungetc(c, stdin); /* return last character */

    return sign * val;
}
```

For the above program, I used a variant of the "Read until condition" idiom. Note that the above switch statement does not use the break statement. The implementation has one major weakness: when the function getInt() returns 0, the caller does not know whether the value read was 0, or the function failed. I could redesign this function to return an error code, but this would mean that I would have to pass the integer value that was read as a parameter. To do this requires the use of pointers, which won't be discussed until Chapter 8.

It is possible to call a function as if it was a procedure, that is, neglecting its return value. For the sake of readability, you can cast it with `void`:

```
(void)getInt();   /* ignore return value */
```

7.2.3 ◆ Type Conversion

In Chapter 3, I introduced type conversion. I will now describe two more types of conversion: argument type conversion and return type conversion.

The rule for argument conversion is relatively simple: the value of each actual parameter is implicitly converted to the type of the corresponding formal parameter, as if the assignment

```
formal parameter = actual parameter
```

was performed. Thus, type conversions on parameters are the same as those done during assignment.

The same rules apply to return type conversion. Given a function `f()` that has the following `return` statement:

```
return exp;
```

a call to `f()`

```
i = f()
```

can be interpreted as an assignment

```
i = exp;
```

and assignment conversion rules are used.

Examples

```
double sqrt(double);
double w = sqrt(2);
int i = sqrt(2.0);
```

In the first call, the actual parameter `2` is converted to the double value `2.0`. In the second call, the double value calculated by `sqrt()` is demoted (truncated) to the integer value `1`.

A return statement that returns nothing, such as:

```
return;
```

is meaningful only in a procedure; for a function you need to return an expression:

```
return exp;
```

7.2.4 ◆ The exit Function

A `return` statement terminates the execution of the function in which it appears. Thus, a `return` in the main function terminates the execution of the entire program, but a `return` executed in another function simply terminates the execution of that function and returns to its caller. If you wish to terminate the execution of an entire program at some arbitrary point, you can use the `exit()` function with a single parameter:

```
exit(int code);
```

The code parameter of `exit()` should be one of two values:

`EXIT_SUCCESS` or `EXIT_FAILURE`.

7.3 Scope

The scope of an identifier is the region of the program in which it is visible—in other words, in which occurrences of this identifier can be *matched* with the defining declaration. In general, C's scope rules are very similar to Java's, but there are some differences. In this section, I will discuss only programs stored in a single file; I will describe multiple-file programs in the next section.

In order to understand scope rules, it is helpful to understand several concepts first. The **lifetime** of a variable is the period of time during which memory is allocated to the variable. When a function is called, storage for this function (specifically for its parameters and local and auxiliary variables) must be allocated. When this function terminates, this storage is released. Since storage is freed in the reverse order of allocation, a *stack* is a convenient data structure to represent it with. Traditionally, one refers to this stack as the **run time stack**, and any data allocated on it is called stack-based data. Stack-based data is allocated and deallocated implicitly whenever a function starts or terminates.

7.3.1 ◆ Blocks

A **block** is like a compound statement, enclosed in braces, and it may contain both definitions and statements. Blocks can appear anywhere a statement can appear. For example

```
if(flag) {
    int i = 2; /* i is declared here */
    printf("%d\n", i);
} /* i is now out of scope */
```

One possible use of a block is in the definition of a macro that needs a local variable, for example

```
#define SWAP_DOUBLE(x, y)   {double temp = (x); \
                             (x) = (y); (y) = temp; }
```

7.3.2 ◆ Global Variables

Global variables are defined outside the body of every function in the file. For example, in the following piece of code, `flag` and `switch` are both global variables:

```
int flag = 0; /* global */

int f() {
. . .
}
int out = 1; /* global */

int main() {
 . . .
}
```

The *scope* of a global variable starts at the point of its definition, and continues to the end of the file. In my example, the variable `flag` can be used by both functions: `f()` and `main()`, but the variable `out` can only be used by the main function. The *lifetime* of global variables is the same as the lifetime of the main program; memory for global variables is allocated when the program starts executing and is available until the program terminates (the lifetime can be modified by specifying the storage class, see Section 7.3.3).

It is nearly impossible to find a similar construct in Java; the closest Java counterpart is a static variable declared in a class which includes all other classes.

Unlike local variables, which are not implicitly initialized, global variables are initialized to "zero"; that is, integer variables will have initial values of 0, float and double variables will be initialized to 0.0, and so on (more on initialization in Section 7.3.4).

---

1. Global variables should be used with caution and always be carefully documented. In particular, changing the value of a global variable as a result of calling a function should be avoided; these side-effects make testing, debugging, and, in general, maintaining the code very difficult. If the function must change a global variable, it should document this clearly.

   For example, suppose a function `printIt()` changes the value of a global `counter` variable. The following documentation is not adequate:

   ```
   /* Prints the next character */
   void printIt();
   ```

   The documentation must describe all effects of the function:

   ```
   /* Prints the next character
    * Modifies: Global variable counter
    */
   ```

2. The placement of the definition of a global variable defines its scope, but also contributes to the readability of your program. I do not have strict recommendations, but *suggest* that for short files, all global variables are defined at the top; for long files they are defined in the logically related place (before definitions of functions that may need these variables). (Note that this recommendation does not suggest that you use global variables; it says that if you do, you should think about their placement.)

C's scope rules are similar to Java's:

1. It is *illegal* to have the same identifier denoting different objects in the same scope, with the following two exceptions:

   statement labels

   structure and union tags (see Chapter11)

   For example:

   ```
   int f;
   double f();
   ```

   is illegal, but the following code is legal:

   ```
   double f() {
      . . .
      if(condition)
        goto f;
      . . .
     f: return expression;
   }
   ```

   (Note that I do not recommend this use of `goto`, I merely state that it is legal.)

2. Identifier definitions within functions (parameters and local variables) supersede the definitions of global identifiers with the same name. This rule is the same as in Java, and I will not elaborate on it.

7.3.3 ◆ Storage Classes and Lifetime

The lifetime and accessibility of a variable is determined by its storage class. For example, in Java, *instance* variables are declared and allocated within an object and are discarded when this object is garbage-collected, and *static* variables are local to a class; they are allocated when the class is loaded and discarded when the class is unloaded.

In C there are three storage classes:

```
auto
static
register
```

The storage class is specified in the variable definition, for example

```
auto int i;
```

I will begin by providing a definition for the `auto` storage class. By default, local variables defined in functions and blocks have the `auto` storage class, which means that their lifetime is the defining function or block, respectively. Thus `auto` is rarely explicitly stated.

Let's now discuss the `static` storage class. My discussion will be limited to local variables that are declared *inside* a block or function. As I already mentioned, the lifetime of a global variable is the same as the lifetime of the entire program, and its scope is the entire program (from the point of its definition). On the other hand, local variables are allocated and deallocated using the stack storage; their scope is a single block. It is sometimes useful to limit the scope of a variable but not the lifetime. For example, a `login()` function may have a counter to count how many times it was called. The scope of this counter should be limited to the `login()` function, but memory for the counter should not be deallocated each time `login()` terminates. Instead, the lifetime of counter should be the same as the lifetime of the program. Static local variables serve this purpose; they are defined with the `static` storage class:

```
void login() {
    static int counter = 0;
    counter++;
    ..
}
```

When `login()` is called for the first time, the value of `counter` is set to 0 and then incremented. When `login()` terminates, the storage for `counter` is not deallocated; it is retained so that when `login()` is called for the second time, the initialization of `counter` is not performed, and its value is changed from 1 to 2. Static variables are always implicitly initialized to zero (for example, 0 for integers, 0.0 for float and double values, NULL for pointers, etc.).

The keyword `static` can also be applied to functions and global variables, in which case it has a different meaning related to the linkage, described in Section 7.4.3.

The last storage class I will describe is the `register` class. For the sake of efficiency, the C programmer may *request* that the compiler allocate storage for a variable in a machine register rather than in regular memory. For example

```
register int i;
```

Usually there are few, if any, registers available and so the compiler may choose to disregard this storage class request and allocate regular memory for the variable.

In general, you should always consider the "gain versus cost" question when optimizing code, and the level at which optimization takes place. Low-level optimization, such as using registers, is hard to justify for most situations. Unless you are a very experienced C programmer, such optimization should be left to the compiler. Higher-level optimization, such as the effective use of memory, may be more warranted. If you do decide to optimize your code, you should consider using a profiler tool, which tells you how long different components of your code take to complete, and how many resources are used. The golden rule to remember is that readability must never be compromised for the sake of optimization.

7.3.4 ◆ Initialization of Variables

Initialization may occur at compile time or at run-time:

■ compile time. If the value of an initialization expression is known at compile time, a variable can be initialized to that value by using an assignment in the definition; for example:

```
const int a = 3 * 44;
```

■ run time. If the value of an initialization expression is not known at compile time, a variable can be initialized to that value at run-rime; for example:

```
double x = sqrt(2.66);
```

The value of a *local* variable that is declared, but not initialized, is undefined. Global variables are initialized to a "zero" value.

7.4 Module-Based Programming: Part 1

A C program is rarely stored in a single file—typically, it is divided into a number of files. Similarly, a Java program consists of many files; each file typically contains a single class. In C, it is useful to think about dividing a program into **modules,** although C does not have such a syntactic construct. For example, a program that maintains addresses of your friends may consist of three modules: the main module, the hash module (implementing the hash table), and the list module (used by the hash module).

A module is seen differently by the client than by the implementor. The client does not need to see the internal details of the implementation; instead she or he is interested in the interface, which is the list of functions that are *exported* by the module. For example, the client of the hash module is interested in functions such as `insert_Hash()` or `member_Hash()`. In C, this interface is stored in a header file (discussed in detail later). Traditionally, the header file for the module has the extension `.h`, and the implementation file has the extension `.c`, for example `hash.h` and `hash.c` (see Fig. 7–1).

Figure 7–1

Interface and
Implementation

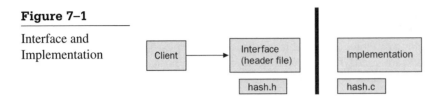

A module can be thought of as a *substitute* for a class. Admittedly, this vision is limited, but it is a step towards class-*like* programming in C.

Java programmers are used to working with a number of different *instances* of a class (these instances are called objects). In the following chapters, I will discuss modules that can only be used to work with a *single* instance, for example, a module that can process a single file. This is not sufficient for some applications. For example, you may need to use two instances of the module LIST to work with two lists, not just one. Chapter 11 describes techniques used for such applications.

7.4.1 ◆ Design for Change

The object-oriented programming paradigm forces the user to think about designing interfaces. It also provides constructs to reuse existing implementations, in particular to extend and restrict them. As a result, object-oriented programming supports *design for change*. This is not the case in a procedural paradigm. In this chapter, I will present several examples that explain how you can emulate this design style in C.

The power of object-oriented programming mainly comes from two constructs: encapsulation and inheritance. Encapsulation supports data hiding—the client of the module gets access to the data only on a need-to-know basis. Inheritance allows the implementor to extend, restrict, or modify the design, and thus have a great deal of control over the interface that the client sees. In an object-oriented paradigm, it is even possible to change the implementation without affecting the user of the module (in some situations, the user may have to re-link her code, but it may also be possible to do it at run-time). Although C does not provide this kind of power, one should still attempt to write programs that are amenable to change.

When you design a C module, you have to decide which variables and functions should be encapsulated and which should be made accessible. In addition, when you are trying to determine who needs access to the data and functions, you have to think about the two types of clients that the module will have: the user of the module and the implementor. At this point, you need to think about how you can encapsulate the data, while still making your design support future modifications. In Java, data encapsulation is supported through the protected keyword. By specifying data as protected, the Java programmer is simplifying future extensions to a particular class, by allowing all inherited classes to use this data, but still hiding it from the user of the module. C does not support inheritance, and so it is much more difficult to both encapsulate the data and provide support for future modifications that will not affect the client.

7.4.2 ◆ Sharing Functions and Variables: `extern`

Java programmers rarely see files that are *explicitly* compiled separately. In C, this technique is fairly standard. **Separate compilation** means that one or more source files may be compiled creating object codes (each source file produces an object file at compilation). This object code may have to be *linked* with other object code to form executable code. This feature is useful for a variety of reasons. First, it contributes to modularization of the program and the reusability of modules. Second, a single modification in a large program requires the recompilation of only the file where the modification was made, not the entire program.

If a program consists of a single file, any functions called by it are either defined in this file, or come from a library. Library functions are defined in separate files, which are *linked* with the main program (note that `#include <math.h>` only includes the header file, and you have to link your code with the implementation of this library, for example using `"-lm"` in Unix). Therefore, several files can share these functions. This concept of function sharing (and even variable sharing) is also useful for user-defined functions. Section 7.4.4 explains how this can be achieved.

A function may be defined in one file and called in another file, as long as the call is preceded by the function declaration. Consider a program that *uses* hash table functions such as `insert_Hash()`, etc. In order to call this function in a separate file, you have to declare it:

```
void insert_Hash();
```

You can also specify that this function is external to your source file:

```
extern void insert_Hash();
```

Above, the `extern` specification may be omitted, because by default, a function *declaration* introduces an external specification. In some situations, you may want to share not only functions, but also variables between several files. These are rare; one example would be of a variable used to determine the number of errors, modified whenever an error occurs (C actually uses such a variable, the `extern` specification is required in order to use a variable that is declared *elsewhere*). For example,

File `errors.c`
```
int myErrorNo;
```

File `main.c`:

```
extern int myErrorNo;
```

The scope of `myErrorNo` consists of two files: `errors.c` and `main.c`.

A program typically consists of one or more files, and when it is printed:

a) each new file should not exceed 500 lines and should begin on a new page.

b) in each source file, the first page should contain the name of the author, date, version number, etc.

c) avoid splitting a function header, a comment, or a type/structure definition across a page break.

7.4.3 ◆ Linkage and the `static` Keyword

Various *entities* that occur in a program may have the same identifier. When creating the executable code, the linker must know whether various occurrences of an identifier refer to the same entity, or several different entities. In order to make this decision, the linker uses the information generated by the compiler. Specifically, the compiler associates various attributes with each entity, one of which is the type of linkage associated with the entity. There are three types of linkage: internal, external, and "no linkage." First, I will describe how these types of linkage are assigned to entities, and then I will explain how the linker uses them.

There are various default rules to specify the type of linkage, and two keywords that can be used to change the default rules: `extern` and `static`.

The three default rules are:

■ entities declared at the outermost level have external linkage

■ entities declared inside a function have no linkage

■ `const` identifiers and `struct`, `union`, and `enum` types (see Chapters 11 and 12) have internal linkage.

The `static` keyword changes the linkage of entities to *internal*. The `extern` keyword changes the linkage of entities to external. Unfortunately, `static` is an overloaded keyword; as I explained earlier, specifying a local variable as `static` will modify its storage class, but it does not change its linkage.

For example (see Figure 7–2)

```
int i;
static int si;
```

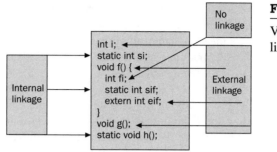

Figure 7–2

Various types of linkage.

```
void f() {
    int fi;
    static int sif;
    extern int eif;
}
void g();
static void h() {
}
```

Above:

- i, f, and g have external linkage because they are declared at the outermost level; also eif has external linkage because it is specified as extern

- si, sif, and h have internal linkage

- fi has no linkage.

As I mentioned above, const has internal linkage, but this can be changed using extern:

file f.c:

```
const int j = 7;
```

file g.c:

```
extern const j;
```

The linker uses the above keywords as follows:

- an identifier with external linkage may be shared by various files, and all occurrences of this identifier refer to the same entity

- all occurrences of an identifier with no linkage are assumed to be referring to distinct entities

- given an identifier with internal linkage, all occurrences in a single file refer to the same entity. If a second file has an internally-defined identifier with the same name, all of those occurrences will be tied to a second entity defined for that identifier; there is no sharing of internally defined entities between modules.

The process of dividing a program into multiple files and then separately compiling and linking them together introduces a different source of errors. In the context of a *single* file, the compiler can carefully check that every used identifier has been defined, and its use is consistent with the definition. For an external declaration of an identifier occurring in a separately compiled file, the compiler is not able to check if this identifier has been defined. It is the linker's responsibility to find matching definitions of all external identifiers. Error messages produced by the linker are usually quite easy to understand; for example, the message

```
undefined symbol   xxx
```

means that one of your files declared an identifier xxx but that none of the files being linked contains the definition of this identifier.

Unfortunately, linkers do not carry out full-proof error checking. For example, I can have a declaration and a matching definition with conflicting data types:

File a.c:

```
int i;
```

File b.c:

```
extern long i;
```

The linker will likely not generate an error or even warning about the fact that the variable i has two types, but the program's behavior is undefined. Similarly, the linker may not recognize that a function is *defined* more than once, such as

File a.c:

```
int f() { ... }
```

File b.c:

```
double f() { ... }
```

Instead of generating a warning about this, the linker may simply arbitrarily choose one of the functions. This can lead to a great deal of confusion, since you expected one function to be executed, and a different one is actually being used. As a result, such syntax should be treated as an error and be avoided at all cost.

I will now describe how to group related function declarations into header files.

7.4.4 ◆ Header Files: Part 2

Essentially, the header file corresponds to a Java interface. Thus, the header file provides the interface between the client and the implementor. Header files play an important role in program modularization and encapsulation.

The client gets the header file and the object code of the implementation file. The header file is included in the application code, and this code is linked with the implementation file. Thus the header file must contain any documentation that is necessary for the client to understand the semantics of all the functions that are declared in it. This documentation should be designed based on a "need to know" principle, and should not include any implementation details. I have already introduced some documentation standards for functions; I will now describe a standard convention for the design and documentation of header files.

I will use the example of a simple line editor to illustrate my conventions. This program will consist of the editor module and the main program. This program accepts input lines that specify various commands, such as "append a line," "delete a line," etc., and then executes these commands. Thus, to begin, you need a function that reads commands and executes them:

```
/* Function: getCommand_Editor
 * Purpose: get a command from the keyboard and skip to EOL
 * Return -1 if incorrect command and 1 otherwise
 */
int getCommand_Editor();
```

Note how the above design follows the need-to-know principle: the client does not have to be aware of the specific techniques needed to read a command and then execute it. Consider another example,

```
/*
 * Function: read_Editor
 * Purpose: read a file fname into the array text
 * Return E_OK, or error code
 */
int read_Editor(char* fname);
```

that tells the client about the array `text`, which is bad documentation style, since the client does not need to know this in order to use the function.

Given the above documentation, the client can now use the function in his or her code; for example:

```
printf("Type h to get help\n");
while(putchar('>'),  i = getCommand_Editor())
    if(i == -1)
        printf("Wrong command\n");
```

I used a comma expression to first print the prompt >, and then to read and execute the command.

The line editor needs to have the ability to get the name of the file to be edited, as well as the ability to read this file, so I will use a read_Editor() function:

```
/* read a file fname and return ... */
int read_Editor(char* fname);
```

What should this function return? Since reading can fail for a variety of reasons, I will show a technique that uses error codes implemented as macros (Section 12.2 shows an alternative implementation using enumerated types):

```
#define E_OPEN      3
#define E_CLOSE     2
#define E_LONG      1
#define E_OK        0
```

In the program, E_OPEN is returned if the input file can not be opened; E_CLOSE is returned when it can not be closed. Another problem that may be encountered is that the file being read is too large, since typically a file is read into some buffer of fixed size. The E_LONG code is returned if the input file is too large.

Here is the entire header file:

```
/*
 * File: editor.h
 * Header file with all editor operations
 */
#ifndef EDITOR_H
#define EDITOR_H

#define MAXI 200          /* number of lines */

/* error codes */
#define E_OPEN      3
#define E_CLOSE     2
```

```
#define E_LONG        1
#define E_OK          0

/*
 * Function: read_Editor
 * Purpose: read a file fname into the array text,
 *     return E_OK, or error code
 * Sample call: if(read_Editor("test.in") == E_OK)
 */
int read_Editor(char* fname);

/* Function: getCommand_Editor
 * Purpose: get a command from the keyboard and skip to EOL
 *     return -1 if incorrect command and 1 otherwise
 */
int getCommand_Editor();

#endif
```

I will now discuss the various details of my header file. First, to avoid problems with multiple inclusion of this file, I used the "Header file" idiom (conditional compilation). Second, the header file provides only function declarations and macros; it does not contain any function or variable *definitions*. This should always be the case. Header files that contain definitions of functions or variables are against the very philosophy of these files: they should provide the interface to the implementation rather than the implementation itself. Third, the header file contains complete documentation for the client. Finally, names of functions are created using the name of the module in which they appear as the suffix; for example, getCommand_Editor() not getCommand(). While this technique does not eliminate the possibility of name clashes, it reduces it and it increases readability.

1. Header files should only include function declarations, macros, and definitions of constants.

2. Avoid compiler dependent features; if you have to use any such features, use conditional compilation.

3. A header file should provide all the documentation necessary to understand the semantics of this file.

4. The documentation for the client is placed in the header file.

5. The documentation for the implementor is placed in the implementation file.

6. The documentation for the client and for the implementor may be different.

FUNCTION NAMES

Use function names that are relevant to the module in which they appear. I recommend using this convention

```
FunctionName_moduleName
```

For example,

```
insert_Hash
```

As I described in Section 3.2.6, in some implementations, only the first six characters are significant for external identifiers. Therefore

```
stack_push
```

and

```
stack_pop
```

may be considered to be identical by such an implementation.

Of course my convention suffers from the same problem; if you have two modules, say M1 and M2, that export the same function insert(), then the two names:

```
insert_M1()
insert_M2()
```

have the *same* first six characters. Nevertheless, to make the programs in this book more readable, I will consistently use the above idiom. The reader should be warned that these modules are not completely portable and may cause problems when moved to systems that consider only the first six characters.

7.4.5 Encapsulation

In order to support encapsulation, some of the variables and functions in a source file should not be accessible to the outside world.

Using Java jargon, you want to make some definitions *private*. To accomplish this in C, you precede *global* variable and function definitions with the keyword `static` (see Section 7.4.3):

```
static int flag_ = 0;
static void read_();
```

As my convention for declaring global static variables, I use identifiers with a trailing underscore. These declarations are not passed to the linker because they have internal linkage. In my previous editor example, the file `editor.c` contains both the implementation of the functions specified in the header file `editor.h`, and the implementation of various local editing functions which are not exported from the module (for example, the function to add a line). These functions are declared and defined with the `static` keyword as follows:

```
static void e_append_()
```

There is a very important difference between encapsulation in Java and in C. In Java, you can encapsulate data in objects, but in C, the smallest encapsulation unit is a *file*. C promotes file-based programming rather than object-based programming.

STATIC IDENTIFIERS

Any functions and variable definitions that are private to a file (and are not accessible outside of this file) should be qualified as `static`.

Global static variables have identifiers with a trailing underscore.

7.4.6 ◆ Using Modules

Consider a program P using two modules P1 and P2. There are two possible scenarios:

- you maintain and have access to all of the source code for every module

Figure 7–3

Program P that uses two modules.

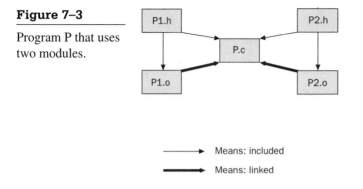

──────▶ Means: included

━━━━━▶ Means: linked

- you have access to the *source* code of the main file P.c and to the *object* code of the remaining modules (for example, these modules are library modules); in other words you do not have access to the source code of P1 and P2.

For the first situation, you will likely use a tool to automate the task of recompiling files that have been changed, such as the make utility in Unix (for a description of make, see any Unix documentation). I will concentrate on the second situation.

For my example, you have four module-related files, P1.h, P1.o, P2.h, and P2.o, as well as the file P.c containing the main program. The P.c file includes both header files, and its code can call functions defined in these modules. To create executable code, you compile P.c, creating P.o, and link the three object files, P.o, P1.o, and P2.o together (see Fig. 7–3).

This approach is not error-proof. If any two modules happen to define functions with identical names, they should not be linked together (multiple definitions are incorrect even if you will not see any error message). For this reason, I will use a specific convention for function names, such as f_P1() for a function f() defined in the module P1.

A module must not be confused with a Java object. I will illustrate my point using an example: let's suppose that I have two modules, P1 and P2. P1 represents an Abstract Data Type (ADT) such as a list. The list is internally represented in the module; the user has the ability to query and modify the list through the provided functions. The second module, P2, wants to create two instances of this list, and does so by declaring two variables of the list type. This is something like what you would do in Java: create a number of objects of the same class. Unfortunately, in C this will not work, since a module is not like a class. For my example, both of the variables in module P2 reference the same list object inside module P1; any operation performed on one affects the other. Unfortunately, if we are using modules, there is really no general solution to this problem.

7.4.7 ◆ Types of Modules

There are various kinds of modules. **Layer modules** add a customized interface to an existing module; for example, a layer module may be used to modify the interface to an existing standard I/O library. **Package modules** define new functions. **Type abstraction modules** provide a new data type, operations on this type, and a set of values; for example, `Fractions` could be one type abstraction module designed to represent fractions. Modules may be **stateless**, that is they are like classes that have functions but no data. If I do not qualify a module as stateless, then this module will have an internal state. For example, an interface module that provides functions to perform simple I/O is likely to be stateless. On the other hand, a module that represents a list has a state, namely the state of the list. Finally, a module is referred to as **singleton** if the client can use only one instance of this module.

These differences are not as apparent to Java programmers, since the class replaces the module. Some classes may be easily represented as modules in C, while for others, it is impossible to do so. In this chapter, I will show the C implementation of some simple modules. In the following chapters, once I introduce pointers and structures, I will present more complicated modules and show how you can construct multiple instances.

In order to demonstrate how to design class-like programs in C, I will show several examples. Whenever appropriate, I will compare the C modules with the corresponding Java class and discuss their reusability and modifiability.

Stateless Package Modules

In this section, I will provide an example of a simple *stateless* singleton package module.

Example 7–4

I will use a module called `Lines` for my first example, which operates on lines of the form $y=ax+b$ (I only consider lines of this form). The module provides the following two operations on lines:

> `parallel_Lines()` to test if two lines are parallel
>
> `perpendicular_Lines()` to test if two lines are perpendicular.

The module `Lines` consists of two files: `lines.h`, which contains the interface and `lines.c`, which contains the implementation. I will first show the code for the header file `lines.h`:

```
#ifndef LINES_H
#define LINES_H
/*
 * File: ex7-4-lines.h
 * A header file for the module with two simple operations on lines
 * Here, a line is of the form y = a*x + b, a!=0, and is represented
```

```
 *    by a pair of double values.
 * Operations:
 *    check if two lines are parallel
 *    check if two lines are perpendicular
 */

/*
 * Function: parallel_Lines
 * Purpose: check if two lines are parallel
 * Inputs: a1, b1, a2, b2 (parameters)
 * Returns: 1 if y=a1*x+b1 is parallel to y=a2*x+b2, 0 otherwise
 * Modifies: Nothing
 * Error checking: None
 * Sample call:
 *    i = parallel_Lines(4,2,4,7);
 * Since the lines y = 4x + 2 and y = 4x + 7 are parallel
 *    the value of i will be 1.
 */
int parallel_Lines(double a1, double b1, double a2, double b2);

/*
 * Function: perpendicular _Lines
 * Purpose: check if two lines are perpendicular
 * Inputs: a1, b1, a2, b2 (parameters)
 * Returns: 1 if y=a1*x+b1 is perpendicular to y=a2*x+b2, 0 otherwise
 * Modifies: Nothing
 * Error checking: None
 * Bugs: Returns 0 if a2=0
 * Sample call:
 *    i = perpendicular_Lines (4,2,4,7);
 * Since the lines y = 4x + 2 and y = 4x + 7 are not perpendicular
 *    the value of i will be 0.
 */
int perpendicular_Lines(double a1, double b1, double a2, double b2);

#endif
```

The documentation of the function perpendicular_Lines() warns the user that this function does not handle lines of the form y=C. In general, your implementation should always avoid run-time errors, and your documentation should always mention the cases that are not handled correctly by the function.

For a Java programmer, this design is quite different from the one supported by objects (you see the function prototypes, but not the actual data). In an object-oriented programming paradigm, you see both the data and the functions that act on the data together in a class. The data is typically protected from the client; you can think of this as the functions surrounding the data, and providing access to it. It is almost never the case that an object's data may be accessed directly without using a function, see Figure 7–4.

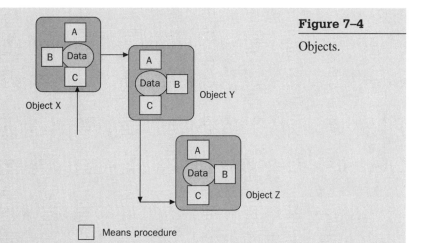

Figure 7–4

Objects.

☐ Means procedure

I'll digress for a moment from the example, and describe a parallel design for the `Lines` module in Java. A Java class, say `JavaLines`, designed to have the same functionality as the lines module, would have the following attributes:

> private, or protected data attributes: line coefficients
>
> public methods: operations on lines.

This design encapsulates the data and gives access to it through a well-defined interface. You can create many objects of the class `JavaLines`, and each of these objects may have a different state (that is, values of local attributes). Unfortunately, this is not possible in C for this particular design because you can not create several instances of a module file. (In Chapter 11, I will explain how you can attempt to model objects using structures).

Before I discuss the implementation of the `Lines` module, I will show the code for the main program (see Fig. 7–5). This figure shows that modules effectively extend the functionality of the language; specifically in this example, the user of the `Lines` module can use two functions that are not standard in C. The application that uses the module includes this module's header file; hence below I included the header file. Note that the user of the main program has to *link* two files together:

- `ex7-4.o` (object code resulting from the compilation of the main program)
- `ex7-4-lines.o` (object code resulting from the compilation of the implementation file)

```
parallel_Lines
perpendicular Lines
Lines
                ↑
    Application
```

Figure 7–5

Application of `Lines`.

```
/*
 * File: ex7-4-lines-main.c
 * An application of the module with two simple operations on lines.
 * The user enters coefficients of two lines, and the program
 *   checks if these two lines are parallel and perpendicular
 */
#include "ex7-4-lines.h"
#include <stdlib.h>
#include <stdio.h>
int main( ) {
   double a1, b1, a2, b2;

   printf("Enter 4 values representing two lines\n");
   if(scanf("%lf%lf%lf%lf", &a1, &b1, &a2, &b2) != 4)
      return EXIT_FAILURE;

   printf("Line1: y = %fx +%f\n", a1, b1);
   printf("Line2: y = %fx +%f\n", a2, b2);
   printf("Lines are %s parallel\n",
         parallel_Lines(a1,b1,a2,b2)? "" : "not");
   printf("Lines are %s perpendicular\n",
         perpendicular_Lines(a1,b1,a2,b2)? "" : "not");

   return EXIT_SUCCESS;
}
```

The above program uses the "Read Values with the prompt" idiom, and allows the user to enter four values. There are several other remaining alternatives for controlling data input:

> provide input values on the command line
>
> loop until the user wants to quit
>
> use a menu-driven program.

The first solution will be described in Section 9.9. The second solution is easy and left as an exercise and the last solution is shown in Example 7–7. The implementation of both functions exported by the module Lines is straightforward:

```
#include "ex7-4-lines.h"
int parallel_Lines(double a1, double b1, double a2, double b2) {
   return a1 == b1;
}
```

```
int perpendicular_Lines(double a1, double b1, double a2, double b2) {
    return (a2 == 0) ? 0 : (a1 == -1/a2);
}
```

Note that the implementation file *always* includes its corresponding header file (here, ex7-4-lines.c includes ex7-4-lines.h).

HEADER AND IMPLEMENTATION

The implementation file always includes its corresponding header file.

Extending Stateless Modules

Often, you may wish to *extend* a module to add some functionality. Stateless modules are easy to extend. For example, you can create a second module Lines1, which provides an additional function to find the area of a triangle, by following these two steps:

1. The header file ex7-4-lines1.h will include ex7-4-lines.h and declare the function

```
double area_Lines1(double x1, double x2,
        double y1, double y2, double z1, double z2);
```

2. The implementation file ex7-4-lines1.c will (as always) include the header ex7-4-lines1.h and it will provide the implementation of the function area_Lines1().

Now the client of Lines1 includes a single header file, the one defined for the extended interface,

```
ex7-4-lines1.h
```

and links her or his code with *two* object code files:

```
ex7-4-lines.o and ex7-4-lines1.o.
```

Note that I used a naming convention consistent with the previous discussion and called the new function area_Lines1(). The client of the module Lines1 will use two functions that have the suffix _Lines: parallel_**Lines**() and perpendicular_**Lines**(), and one function that has a suffix Lines1. I should mention that there are two other alternatives available for extending the interface. First, you can use the original module name, such as `area_Lines()`. With this solution, the client sees names that always end with the same suffix. A second alternative is to change the suffix for all the names to `Lines1`, which would require the following two steps:

1. The header file `ex7-4-lines1.h` will declare three functions,

    `perpendicular_Lines1()`, `parallel_Lines1()`, and `area_Lines1()`

2. The implementation file `ex7-4-lines1.c` will provide the implementation of all the functions; in the case of the first two functions, the call will merely delegate the task to the original implementation. For example, for `parallel_Lines1()`, the code would merely call the original function:

    `parallel_Lines(x1, x2, y1, y2);`

In either case, the client of `Lines1` includes a single header file, `ex7-4-lines1.h` and links her or his code with *two* object code files: `ex7-4-lines.o` and `ex7-4-lines1.o`.

MODULE EXTENSION

To extend a module M to a module M1, define the header file `M1.h` and the interface `M1.c`; `M1.h` includes `M.h` and `M1.c` includes `M1.h`. The client of M1 includes `M1.h` and links the application code with `M.o` and `M1.o`

Layer Modules and Error Handling

In this section, I consider a fairly simple *layer* singleton module built on top of the existing I/O library. In addition, I tackle the issue of maintaining the state of the module used for handling errors.

Example 7–5

This example reuses the existing implementation. A module called `IO` is built on top of the existing standard I/O library, and it is designed to perform just two file I/O operations:

reading an integer value, using `int getInt(FILE *handle)`
printing an integer value, using `void putInt(FILE *handle)`

In either case, the file handle, that is a variable of type FILE*, must point to a file that has been previously opened by the client of the module. In addition, this module deals with *error handling* by maintaining an error flag. This flag will be set when an operation fails; as a result, the module has a state, namely the state of the error flag. The error flag is not directly accessible to the client; instead it is accessible through three accessor functions:

isError_IO()   to test whether or not an error has occurred

clearError_IO()   to clear any error indication

printError_IO()   to print a description of the error on the standard error stream

The client can use these functions after each I/O operation. For example, to test whether printing an integer value was successful, the client uses the isError_IO() function:

```
clearError_IO();
putInt_IO(f, i);
if(isError_IO())
    printError_IO();
```

Note that the error flag was cleared *before* the call to putInt_IO(), in case one of the earlier operations resulted in an error and set this flag. After the call to putInt_IO(), the error flag is tested, and if it is set, then the error is printed. It is up to the client to test for errors after each operation, and even if she or he does, then printing an error message is optional.

Figure 7–6 shows the interface; the documentation provided in the header file describes all the available operations.

```
#include <stdio.h>
#ifndef IO_H
#define IO_H
/*
 * File: ex7-5-io.h
 * A header of the module with two simple I/O operations
 *    to read and print an integer from a file, and possibly
```

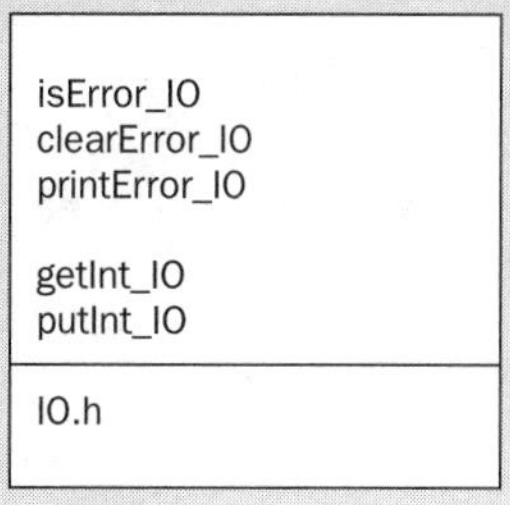

| isError_IO
clearError_IO
printError_IO |
| getInt_IO
putInt_IO |
| IO.h |

Figure 7–6

Interface of IO module.

```
 *    set the error code. The file must be opened for reading.
 * The error code is not explicitly available to the client.
 * There are three functions to deal with errors:
 *   isError_IO() to inquire about error
 *   clearError_IO() to clear any error indication
 *   printError_IO() to print a description of the error
 *          on the standard error stream
 */


/*
 * Function: getInt_IO
 * Purpose:   read from a given file a single integer and return it.
 * Inputs:   file descriptor f, must be opened for reading (parameter)
 * Returns:   the integer read, 0 if fails
 * Modifies: nothing (except the current position in the file)
 * Error checking: If an integer can not be read, the error flag is
 *   raised (see error routines below).
 * Sample call:
 *   clearError_IO();
 *   i = getInt_IO(f);
 *   if(isError_IO())
 *     printError_IO();
 *
 */
int getInt_IO(FILE *f);

/*
 * Function: putInt_IO
 * Purpose: print a single integer to a file (must be opened for output)
 * Inputs: file descriptor f and integer i (parameters)
 * Returns: nothing
 * Error checking: If an integer can not be printed, the error flag is
 *   raised (see error routines below).
 * Sample call:
 *   clearError_IO();
 *   putInt_IO(f, i);
 *   if(isError_IO())
 *     printError_IO();
 */
void putInt_IO(FILE *f, int i);
```

```
/**********  Error routines *******/

/*
 * Function: clearError_IO
 * Purpose:  clear an error flag
 * Inputs:   nothing
 * Returns:  nothing
 * Error checking: none
 * Sample call:   clearError_IO();
 */
void clearError_IO(void);

/*
 * Function: isError_IO
 * Purpose:  test for an error flag
 * Inputs:   nothing
 * Returns:  1 if the error flag is raised, 0 otherwise
 * Error checking: none
 * Sample call:
 *     i = isError_IO();
 */
int isError_IO(void);

/*
 * Function: printError_IO
 * Purpose:  print on the standard error stream an error description
 *    (nothing if the error flag is not set)
 * Inputs:   nothing
 * Returns:  nothing
 * Error checking: none
 * Sample call:   printError_IO();
 */
void printError_IO(void);

#endif
```

The design of an interface is usually difficult, and invariably involves making some architectural decisions. I chose to make the error flag inaccessible to the client. Had I chosen to make it public, I would have needed the following declaration in the header file:

```
extern int errorFlag;
```

This technique is undesirable, because now the client has the power to arbitrarily modify the error flag. In Java, you would restrict the operations that can be performed on this flag through the functions that access it; the same technique should be used in C. The interface shown provides *three* error handling routines that allow testing for an error, clearing an error, and printing it. You may wonder if this many routines are needed; perhaps just one or two more powerful routines would be sufficient. However, I want to demonstrate that in some cases, like this one, a "fat interface" is better than a "lean" interface because it gives the client more flexibility. (Below, I will show how you can use the existing fat interface to create a more limited interface.)

For example, I could rewrite the interface to provide only one function:

```
void errors(void);
```

If the error flag is set, this function prints the error message and then clears this flag. This solution is very limiting: it makes it impossible to just test for error in a Boolean expression. On the other hand, the first interface gives the client more power, but also more responsibility. The error flag has to be cleared explicitly, otherwise `printError_IO()` may print an "old" error message even if the most recent I/O operation was successful. An alternative solution is to give each operation, `getInt()` and `putInt()`, the additional responsibility of clearing the old error flag, and setting the flag only if an operation fails.

I will now show a simple application of the I/O module. The module will read and print a single integer using standard I/O streams. In this application, the error checking is performed only for the input; the output operation merely clears the error flag. This code follows the philosophy used for the design of this program: it is the *client* who decides whether it is worthwhile to test for possible errors (a similar technique is used in Unix).

```
/*
 * File: ex7-5-io-main.c
 * An application of the file I/O module
 * Reads an integer and if this integer is correct, outputs it
 */
#include "ex7-5-io.h"

int main() {
   int d;

   d = getInt_IO(stdin);

   if(isError_IO()) {
      printError_IO();
      clearError_IO();
   } else {
      putInt_IO(stdout, d);
      clearError_IO();
   }
```

```
      return EXIT_SUCCESS;
}
```

I will now discuss some details of the implementation module (the complete code is stored in the file ex7-5-io.c, which includes the header file described above). There are three macros representing error codes. These macros are internal to the implementation file and not made visible to the client, who will only see the error messages, and not the error codes:

```
#define INPUT    1
#define OUTPUT   2
#define OK       0
```

The variable errorFlag_ is private (defined as static) because its scope should be limited to the implementation file:

```
    static int errorFlag_ = OK;
```

The implementation of putInt() and getInt() follows this philosophy: perform the required operation and set the flag if not successful:

```
int getInt_IO(FILE *f) {
   int i;

   if(fscanf(f, "%d", &i) != 1) {
      errorFlag_ = INPUT;
      return 0;
   }

   return i;
}

void putInt_IO(FILE *f, int i) {
   if(fprintf(f, "%d", i) == EOF)
      errorFlag_ = OUTPUT;
}
```

The code for the error routines is similarly straightforward:

```
void clearError_IO(void) {
   errorFlag_ = OK;
}
```

```
int isError_IO(void) {
   return errorFlag_ != OK;
}

void printError_IO(void) {

   switch(errorFlag_) {

   case INPUT:  fprintf(stderr, "input failed\n");
                return;

   case OUTPUT: fprintf(stderr, "output failed\n");
                return;

   case OK:     return;

   default:     fprintf(stderr, "unknown error\n");
                return;

   }
}
```

Note that the `printError_IO()` routine considers all known errors as well as unknown ones. In general, you should always use a *defensive* style of programming: be prepared for the unexpected.

Modifying the Interface

Section 7.4.7 discussed extending existing modules. I will now show how the fat interface in the previous example can be *modified*. The modified interface may use one of the two following designs:

- the error module interface consists of a single function used for the printing of errors, if any
- `getInt()` and `putInt()` always clear the error flag and then set it if needed

For a "do-it-once" job, you may simply write auxiliary macros, and that's what I will do for the first case. For applications which may be used more frequently, you may want to design a new module, and I will do so to implement the second case.

A macro that prints messages and then clears the error flag looks like this:

```
#define ERRORS   { if(isError_IO()) { \
                      printError_IO(); clearError_IO(); \
                  } \
              }
```

I will now discuss the module IO1, which uses the existing implementation of the module IO. Its interface is a restricted version of the IO interface, consisting of most functions in the original interface with the exception of the function to clear the error flag:

```
int getInt_IO1(FILE *f);
void putInt_IO1(FILE *f, int i);
int isError_IO1(void);
void printError_IO1(void);
```

Of course, the documentation of these functions is different. For example, the documentation of the function putInt_IO1() looks like this:

```
/*
 * Function: putInt_IO1
 * Purpose:   clear the error flag and print a single
 *   integer to a given file
 * Inputs:    file descriptor f and integer i (parameters)
 * Returns:   nothing
 * Modifies: the error flag
 * Error checking: If an integer can not be printed, the
 *   error flag is set (see error routines below).
 * Sample call:
 *     putInt_IO1(f, i);
 *     if(isError_IO1())
 *        printError_IO1();
 *
 */
void putInt_IO1(FILE *f, int i);
```

The header file ex7-5-io.h, representing the interface of the module IO, is *not* included in the IO1 interface because the client will not use functions from the module IO (this header file is included in the implementation file). Rather than extending the IO interface with additional functionality, this interface will be *modified*. The client of the module IO1 needs to include a single header file:

```
#include "ex7-5-io1.h"
```

Figure 7–7

Application of IO1.

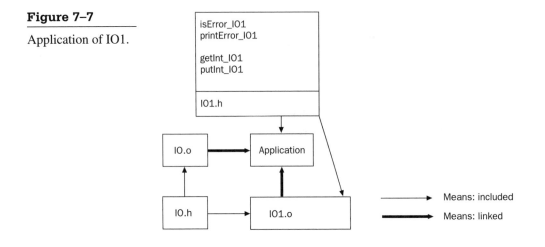

and link two object files `ex7-5-io.o` and `ex7-5-io1.o` with her or his main program (see Figure 7–7).

The application code is stored in the file `ex7-5-io1-main.c`. The complete implementation of the module `IO1` is stored in the file `ex7-5-io1.c`. It includes both header files and delegates some of its work to the existing `IO` module. For example, the function `getInt_IO1()` will clear error messages and then ask the existing function `getInt_IO()` to supply an integer value:

```
int getInt_IO1(FILE *f) {
   clearError_IO();
   return getInt_IO(f);
}
```

On the other hand, error routines merely delegate their work to the corresponding functions from the `IO` module; for example,

```
int isError_IO1(void) {
   return isError_IO();
}
```

MODULE MODIFICATION

To define module M1, which extends an existing module M, follow these steps:

1. Declare the new interface in `M1.h` (`M1.h` does not include `M.h`)

2. `M1.c` includes both `M1.h` and `M.h`

3. The client of M1 includes `M1.h` and links the application code with `M.o` and `M1.o`

It may appear inefficient to have two new error functions, which merely call *existing* error functions from the module `IO`. The advantage of this solution is that it *restricts* the existing interface by making only certain functions available. By providing both interfaces, the client could have called functions from the old one as well, and use functionality that was supposed to be unavailable. This technique is not equivalent to function overriding in Java, the ability to modify the implementation but leave the prototype (header) unchanged. In order to implement function *overriding* in C, you can use pointers to functions (described in Section 8.15.4).

Modules and Constructors

I will now show another layer module, built on top of the module `IO` described in Section 7.4.7, and designed to encapsulate file handles in the implementation file. (For the module `IO` , the client is responsible for opening and closing I/O streams.) To do so, I have two options:

- I/O file names are fixed; the implementation file is responsible for using these names to open I/O streams

- file names are provided by the client and passed to the implementation module before any other I/O operation is performed. For example, the module encapsulates global variables which represent file names; a function `initRead()` is responsible for receiving and initializing the variable representing the name of the input file and a function `initWrite()` is responsible for receiving and initializing the variable representing the name of the output file.

I will use the second option to implement a layer module `IO2` and reuse the existing `IO` module. The module `IO2` is a *singleton module*, which means that the user will be able to work with at most one input stream and at most one output stream.

In order to initialize the streams, the need for a Java constructor that performs all necessary *initialization* is evident. Unfortunately, C does not support constructors and so it is the client's responsibility to perform initialization. The good news is that through careful programming, you can mimic Java's constructor functionality.

For this example, I will implement three constructor functions, which will initialize the internal state of a module. The module's data starts off un-initialized; an error flag is set should the client try to perform an operation before initialization.

The three constructors are listed below (recall that the suffix IO2 is the name of the module):

```
constructRead_IO2(inFilename)
```
to associate the input stream with the inFilename

```
constructWrite_IO2(outFilename)
```
to associate the output stream with the outFilename

```
constructReadWrite_IO2(inFilename, outFilename)
```
to associate the input stream with the inFilename *and* the output stream with outFilename

For example, to open just the input file "in.dat", the client calls:

```
constructRead_IO2("in.dat")
```

By providing these three functions, I have mimicked Java's constructor functionality and provided the user with the maximum possible flexibility. The return values of these functions require special attention. Specifically, the third function may be "partially" successful; for example, when it successfully opens the input stream but fails to open the output stream. Consequently, this function should return more specific return values, which can be used by the client to determine the cause of failure. For the sake of readability, the interface of IO2 defines several macros so that the *client* can use them; for example, FAIL_READ_IO2 indicates that the attempt to open the input stream failed.

In my design, I always follow the rule that in case of an error, a function should return an error code that can be used by its caller, instead of printing to the standard error stream. The interface consists of the following macros and functions:

```
#define OK_IO2              1
#define FAIL_IO2            0
#define FAIL_WRITE_IO2      2
#define FAIL_READ_IO2       3

int constructRead_IO2(char *name);
int constructWrite_IO2(char *name);
int constructReadWrite_IO2(char *inFilename,
                           char *outFilename);
```

Above, I had to use one construct which I have not yet explained, namely a C string. For example, the function

```
int constructRead_IO2(char *name);
```

takes a string representing a file name as a parameter. In C, strings are really pointers to characters (details in Section 9.3.1). By convention, a NULL parameter indicates that standard I/O should be used. For example

```
constructReadWrite(NULL, "test.out");
```

means reading should be done from the standard input and writing should be done
to the file test.out. The full code and the documentation are provided in the file
ex7-5-io2.h. The remaining functions declared in the interface include:

```
int getInt_IO2(void);
void putInt_IO2(int i);

void clearError_IO2(void);
int isError_IO2(void);
void printError_IO2(void);
```

The code for the main program, which uses the module IO2, follows. This program
demonstrates the need for all three constructors. First, the program attempts to establish
an input stream from the file in.dat and the output stream to the file out.dat. If any
of these attempts fails, the standard streams are used instead. Note that macros exported
by the module IO2 significantly increase the readability of the main program.

```
/*
 * File: ex7-5-io2-main.c
 * An application of the file I/O module
 * Initialize I/O streams: read from in.dat and write to a
 *    file out.dat.
 * If any of these files can not be open, use standard
 *    streams instead.
 */
#include "ex7-5-io2.h"
int main() {
   int d;

   switch(constructReadWrite_IO2("in.dat", "out.dat")) {

   case OK_IO2:          break;   /* success */

   case FAIL_READ_IO2:   (void)constructRead_IO2(NULL);
                         break;

   case FAIL_WRITE_IO2:  (void)constructWrite_IO2(NULL);
                         break;
```

```
        case FAIL_IO2:      (void)constructReadWrite_IO2(NULL, NULL);
                            break;
        }

        clearError_IO2();
        d = getInt_IO2();

        if(isError_IO2())
            printError_IO2();
        else (void)putInt_IO2(d);

        (void)putInt_IO2(getInt_IO2());

        return EXIT_SUCCESS;
}
```

The main program disregards the return value of putInt()—no error check-ing is done. It is the client's decision to test function calls for errors.

Now, I will discuss the implementation for the module IO2. Since the imple-mentation deals with two streams (input and output), it maintains two private file handles and two private flags, which are used to test whether the constructor has been called. Macros, which are private to the implementation, are used to increase readability.

```
static FILE *fInput_;       /* file handles */
static FILE *fOutput_;

/* macros for testing initialization */
#define NOT_INITIALIZED    0
#define INITIALIZED        1

static int initializedInput_  = NOT_INITIALIZED;
static int initializedOutput_ = NOT_INITIALIZED;

#define READ    1            /* macros for testing errors */
#define WRITE   2
#define OK      0
```

The implementation of the constructor functions is based on the following algorithm:

  - check if the module has already been initialized; if so, return the failure code

  - try to open the stream; if operation failed, return the failure code.

I will now show the implementation of `constructRead_IO2()`:

```
int constructRead_IO2(char *fname) {
   if(initializedInput_ == INITIALIZED)
      return FAIL_IO2;

   if(fname == NULL) { /* stdin is always opened */
      initializedInput_ = INITIALIZED;
      fInput_ = stdin;
      return OK_IO2;
   }

   if((fInput_ = fopen(fname, "r")) == NULL)
      return FAIL_IO2;
   initializedInput_ = INITIALIZED;

   return OK_IO2;
}
```

The module IO2 maintains its own error flag:

```
static int ioErrorFlag_ = OK;
```

It must do so because it has no access to the error flag from the existing module IO. The flag `ioErrorFlag_` is set in case of an error handled by IO2; handling other types of errors is delegated to the existing functions from the module IO. For example, the code for `getInt_IO2()` looks like this:

```
int getInt_IO2(void) {
   if(initializedInput_ == NOT_INITIALIZED) {
      ioErrorFlag_ = READ;
      return 0;
   }
   return getInt_IO(fInput_);
}
```

All error routines explicitly handle `ioErrorFlag_`, and implicitly handle other error flags maintained by the module IO; for example, the code for testing for the existence of errors looks like this:

```
int isError_IO2(void) {
   return ioErrorFlag_ != OK || isError_IO();
}
```

The complete code for the implementation module is in the file `ex7-5-io2.c`.

This implementation suffers from a rather serious limitation. Once a constructor is used to associate a filename with a stream, there is no way to disassociate it or change the association. The inability to disassociate means that the implementation can never close files, which is against the principle that an allocated resource should be released as soon it is not needed. Both of these limitations may be overcome by adding "destructor" functions, which will perform the required cleanup:

```
int destructRead_IO2();
int destructReadWrite_IO2();
int destructWrite_IO2();
```

All the functions return `OK_IO2` if successful and `FAIL_IO2` otherwise (for example, `FAIL_IO2` is returned when `destructRead_IO2()` is called but the input stream has not been initialized).

The implementation of destructor functions is not difficult; each of them performs some error checking and then clears the error flag. For example

```
int destructRead_IO2() {
   if(initializedInput_ == NOT_INITIALIZED)
      return FAIL_IO2;

   if(fInput_ == stdin)
      return OK_IO2;

   if(fclose(fInput_) == EOF)
      return FAIL_IO2;

   ioErrorFlag_ = OK;
   initializedInput_ = NOT_INITIALIZED;

   return OK_IO2;
}
```

Note that the standard I/O streams should not be closed using `fclose()`; therefore, before `fclose()` is called, I check whether the current file handle points to the standard input stream.

Modules and Caching Data

The following program is another example of a singleton module that maintains its internal state. In this example, I will also show how *caching* data in the implementation file may increase the efficiency of the functions defined in the interface.

Example 7–6

The module `fileOps` defines three file-processing functions:

```
long words_fileOps();    finds the number of words in a file
long chars_fileOps();    finds the number of characters in a file
long lines_fileOps();    finds the number of lines in a file
```

For reasons of efficiency, values computed by these functions are cached (that is, stored by the implementation file) and not recomputed unless the user explicitly clears the cache. The user is also provided with a constructor function to initialize the module, called `construct_fileOps(filename)`, and a destructor function to clean up the module, called `destruct_fileOps()`. Below, I present the documentation of just one function from the interface (the complete code may be found in the file `ex7-6-fileOps.h`):

```
/*
 * Function: lines_fileOps
 * Purpose: read from a file and count the number of lines
 * Inputs:  nothing
 * Returns: number of lines, or EOF if failed
 * Modifies: nothing (the file is rewound before termination)
 * Error checking: fails if the module is not initialized
 *    or input will fail
 * Sample call:    long i = lines_fileOps();
 */
long lines_fileOps();
```

The *implementation* file defines macros (for the sake of readability) and two private variables used by the constructor:

```
#define NOT_INITIALIZED 0
#define INITIALIZED     1
static int initialized_ = NOT_INITIALIZED;
static FILE *f;
```

The code of the constructor is quite simple; if the module has not been initialized, then the constructor attempts to open the specified file:

```
int construct_fileOps(char *filename) {
  if(initialized_ == INITIALIZED)
    return 0;

  if((f = fopen(filename, "r")) == NULL)
    return 0;
```

```
    initialized_ = INITIALIZED;

    return 1;
}
```

In order to improve efficiency, various functions may given additional responsibilities, as long as this extra work does not cause any major overhead. For example, the function that counts lines will be almost as efficient if it also counts all the characters and *caches* this information. This type of a solution (caching) may also be handy for solving other problems. To help support reading and caching, the implementation file defines a single macro and several private variables used to specify if any values have been read and cached:

```
    #define CLEAR -1
    static long words_ = CLEAR;
    static long chars_ = CLEAR;
    static long lines_ = CLEAR;
```

For example, if the value of words_ is not equal to CLEAR, then the cache contains the number of words read, and this value does not need to be recomputed. The destructor function performs some error checking, closes the stream, and clears the flags (including the cache):

```
int destruct_fileOps() {
  if(initialized_ == NOT_INITIALIZED)
     return 0;

  if(fclose(f) == EOF)
     return 0;

  words_ = chars_ = lines_ = CLEAR;
  initialized_ = NOT_INITIALIZED;

  return 1;
}
```

The function words_fileOps() returns the number of words, but it is also in charge of *caching* the number of characters and the number of lines read. It uses techniques introduced in Section 6.6.1 to provide two versions, a *debugging* version and a *production* version:

```
long words_fileOps() {
   int flag = 1;
   int c;

   if(initialized_ == NOT_INITIALIZED)
      return EOF;
```

```
      if(words_ != CLEAR)   /* use cache */
         return words_;

      /* reset cache */
      words_ = 0;
      if(chars_ != CLEAR)
         chars_ = 0;
      if(lines_ != CLEAR)
         lines_ = 0;

      /* read and process the input file */
      rewind(f);
      while ((c = getc(f)) != EOF) {

         if(chars_ != CLEAR) /* cache characters? */
            chars_++;

         if(lines_ != CLEAR && c == '\n') /* cache lines? */
            lines_++;

         if(isspace(c))   /* take care of words */
            flag = 1;
         else if(flag) {
            flag = 0;
            words_++;
#ifdef DEB
            printf("\nword #: %ld\n", words_);
            fputc(c, stderr);
#endif
         }
#ifdef DEB
         else fputc(c, stderr);
#endif
      }
      rewind(f);

      return words_;   /* update cache */
}
```

The documentation for the implementation differs from the documentation provided for the client in the header file. This is appropriate since the client is informed on a need-to-know basis. The implementation details, specifically the caching of local data, are of no interest to the client. The complete code of the implementation module may be found in the file ex7-6-fileOps.c.

Finally, I will present a *menu-driven* application of the module `fileOps`. The main program contains the function `help()`, which displays a list of available file processing functions, and the function `menu()`, which reads user commands. For the sake of completeness, I have included the code that reads a string representing a filename and stores it in the array; a complete explanation of strings will be given in Section 9.3.

```c
#include <stdlib.h>
#include <stdio.h>
/*
 * File: ex7-6-fileOps-main.c
 * An application of the file I/O module
 * The user can enter the following commands:
 *    I - to set the filename
 *    W to count words in the given file
 *    L - to count words
 *    C to count characters
 *    Q to quit.
 */
#include "ex7-6-fileOps.h"

/* Displays available commands */
void help() {
   printf("enter\n");
   printf("\tH for help\n");
   printf("\tI to provide filename\n");
   printf("\tW to count words\n");
   printf("\tL to count lines\n");
   printf("\tC to count characters\n");
   printf("\tQ to quit\n");
}

/* reads in user's command and executes the corresponding command */
void menu() {
   int c;
   int initialized = 0;
   char filename[FILENAME_MAX];
   long result;

   while(1) {
      printf("> (h for help): ");
      c = getchar();

      while (getchar() != '\n')
         ;
```

```
switch (c) {
case 'h':
case 'H':
        help();
        break;
case 'i':
case 'I':
        if(initialized)
          if(destruct_fileOps() == 0) {
             fprintf(stderr, "failed to close previous file\n");
             break;
          } else initialized = 0;

        printf("filename please: ");
        if(scanf("%s", filename) != 1) {
          fprintf(stderr, "can't read file %s\n", filename);
          break;
        }
        while(getchar() != '\n')   /* skip till end of line */
          ;
        if(construct_fileOps(filename) == 0)
            fprintf(stderr, "can't initialize %s\n", filename);
        else initialized = 1;
        break;
case 'w':
case 'W':
        if((result = words_fileOps()) == EOF)
           fprintf(stderr, "failed to execute\n");
        else fprintf(stderr, "number of words is %ld\n", result);
        break;
case 'l':
case 'L':
        if((result = lines_fileOps()) == EOF)
           fprintf(stderr, "failed to execute\n");
        else printf("number of lines is %ld\n", result);
        break;
case 'c':
case 'C':
        if((result = chars_fileOps()) == EOF)
           fprintf(stderr, "failed to execute\n");
        else printf("number of characters is %ld\n", result);
        break;
```

```
        case 'q':
        case 'Q':
                if(destruct_fileOps() == 0)
                    fprintf(stderr, "failed to clean up\n");
                return;
        default :
                fprintf(stderr, "\nunknown command\n");
                break;
        }
    }
}

int main() {
    menu();
    return EXIT_SUCCESS;
}
```

7.5 Overloading Functions: Variable Number of Arguments

Java programmers often *overload* functions, that is, use the same function identifier for two or more different functions. For example:

```
void product(double x, double y);
void product(Vector x, Vector y);
```

C does not support function overloading but it can be simulated, to a limited extent, by using a *variable number* of actual parameters. For example, you may want to write a function `product()` that finds the product of its `double` arguments (the first integer argument specifies the number of remaining double arguments), as in

```
double d;
d = product(2, 2.0, 3.0);
d += product(1, 5.0);
```

or a function `debug()`, which displays values of several variables according to a certain format, such as

```
debug("%d\t%f\n", x, f);
debug("%c", d);
```

A function with a variable number of parameters is declared like this:

```
void debug(char *format, ...);
```

The **ellipsis** ...indicates that there is a variable number of arguments. There must be at least one known (fixed) parameter before the ellipsis. Also, you have to include the standard header file stdarg.h for any file using this syntax.

The header file stdarg.h provides a type va_list, which represents the list of arguments, and several macros for dealing with variable arguments. Assuming that you have a declaration of

```
va_list list;
```

and that the last known formal parameter before the "..." is called par, you use these macros as follows:

va_start(list, par); needs to be called before you can do anything

va_arg(list, typ) must be called to get the value of each variable parameter in order (starting from the first), assuming that this parameter is of type typ (note that different parameters may be of different types)

va_end(list) must be called when you are done processing.

Often the number of variable arguments is passed as one of the known parameters. This is what I will do in the following example, which provides the implementation of the function product().

Example 7–7

```
/*
 * File: ex7-7.c
 * Illustrates a function with a variable number
 *   of arguments.
 */
#include <stdio.h>
#include <stdlib.h>
#include <stdarg.h>
int main() {
    double product(int number, ...);

    printf("%f\n", product(2, 2.0, 3.0) * product(1, 4.0, 5.0));
```

```
      return EXIT_SUCCESS;
}


/* return a product of double arguments */
double product(int number,  ...) {
   va_list list;
   double p;
   int i;

   va_start(list, number);
   for(i = 0, p = 1.0; i < number; i++)
      p *= va_arg(list, double);
   va_end(list);

   return p;
}
```

Note that the above code would not work correctly if you provided a function arguments of an incorrect type; for example:

```
product(2, 3, 4)
```

There is no predefined type conversion between formal parameters and actual parameters for functions containing a variable number of arguments! On the other hand, the call

```
product(2, 3.0, 4.0, 5.0)
```

is correct. The last argument is ignored, and only the two values 3.0 and 4.0 are used. Therefore, the above technique does not support function overloading that involves different *types* of parameters.

There are some limitations of the variable number of arguments:

1. You can not access arguments in the middle.
2. Both the client and the implementor are responsible for the correct usage; in particular, the macros defined in stdarg.h do not know the type of each argument.

OVERLOAD FUNCTION

To overload a function, use a variable number of arguments.

There are various other constructs related to functions that are not covered in this chapter because they require the use of pointers. For example, a function may have function parameters, which are functions themselves; a function may take parameters of a generic data type, which allows it to be called with any data type, and so on (for details see Section 8.15).

7.6 List of Common Errors

1. A function must be declared or defined *before* it can be called (strictly speaking this is not true, and a function may be called even if its prototype has not been seen, but the rules that describe this case are complicated, and the technique often leads to programming errors).

2. Remember that a function declaration is terminated with ; but that in the definition, the function prototype is not terminated with ;, instead the function body is enclosed in braces (this is a very common error when copying code from a header file to an implementation and then forgetting to make the necessary changes).

3. A return statement that returns nothing, such as:

```
return;
```

is meaningful only in a procedure; for a function you need to return an expression:

```
return exp;
```

7.7 List of Idioms

FUNCTION NAMES

Use function names that are relevant to the module in which they appear. I recommend using this convention

```
FunctionName_moduleName
```

STATIC IDENTIFIERS

Any functions and variable definitions that are private to a file (and are not accessible outside of this file) should be qualified as `static`.

HEADER AND IMPLEMENTATION

The implementation file always includes its corresponding header file.

MODULE EXTENSION

To extend a module `M` to a module `M1`, define the header file `M1.h` and the interface `M1.c`. `M1.h` includes `M.h` and `M1.c` includes `M1.h`. The client of `M1` includes `M1.h` and links the application code with `M.o` and `M1.o`

MODULE MODIFICATION

To define module `M1`, which extends an existing module `M`, follow these steps:

1. Declare the new interface in `M1.h` (`M1.h` does not include `M.h`)
2. `M1.c` includes both `M1.h` and `M.h`
3. The client of `M1` includes `M1.h` and links the application code with `M.o` and `M1.o`

OVERLOAD FUNCTION

To overload a function, use a variable number of arguments.

7.8 List of Programming Style Guidelines

1. Make sure comments and code agree; in particular, always carefully check that the function implementation meets its specification.
2. In general, a function definition should not exceed one page. Code should be broken up; in particular, lines that are too long should be avoided.

3. Either the function declaration or definition (or both) should be preceded by documentation, which describes the function. The required format of the documentation is as follows:

Function: name

Purpose: a general description of the function
　　　　　(typically, this is a description of what it is supposed to do)

Inputs: a list of parameters and global variables read in the function

Returns: value to be returned

Modifies: a list of parameters and global variables that are modified;
　　　　　describes any side-effects

Error checking: describes your assumptions about actual parameters;
　　　　　　　　what happens if actual parameters are incorrect

Sample call:

In addition, there may also be a Bugs section, which documents cases that the implementation does not handle.

4. I do not write the code as follows:

```
if(n/10 == 0)
    return 1;
else return 1 + digits(n/10);
```

Instead, I write the code as follows:

```
if(n/10 == 0)
    return 1;
return 1 + digits(n/10);
```

In the above case, it is a matter of personal preference—some people, myself included, find the second code more readable, while others argue that by including the `else`, the code has a more logically understandable structure. In the case of a more nested `if` structure, extra `else`'s may make the code more difficult to understand.

5. Brackets in the `return` statement are unnecessary, and in my opinion clutter the code:

```
if(n/10 == 0)
    return (1);
return (1 + digits(n/10));
```

6. As always, the code is as clear as possible. For example, I could have written:

```
if(n /= 10)
    return 1;
return 1 + digits(n);
```

Although the outcome is the same, this is hard to understand because of the side effect in the `if` condition.

7. Side effects in loop conditions should be typically avoided. As an example of a loop-side-effect, the code to print the digits of an integer n reversed could be written as follows:

```
do {
    printf("%d", n%10);
} while(n/=10);
```

A more readable solution avoids the side effect in the loop condition:

```
do {
    printf("%d",n%10);
    n /= 10;
} while(n != 0);
```

8. The code parameter of `exit()` should be one of two values:

`EXIT_SUCCESS` or `EXIT_FAILURE`.

9. Global variables should be used with caution, and always be carefully documented. In particular, changing the value of a global variable as a result of calling a function should be avoided; these side-effects make testing, debugging, and, in general, maintaining the code very difficult. If the function must change a global variable, it should document this clearly.

10. The placement of the definition of a global variable defines its scope, but also contributes to the readability of your program. I do not have strict recommendations, but *suggest* that for short files, all global variables are defined at the top; for long files they are defined in the logically related place (before definitions of functions that may need these variables).

11. A program typically consists of one or more files, and when it is printed:

    a) each new file should not exceed 500 lines and should begin on a new page.

    b) in each source file, the first page should contain the name of the author, date, version number, etc.

    c) avoid splitting a function header, a comment, or a type/structure definition across a page break.

12. Header files should only include function declarations, macros, and definitions of constants.

13. Avoid compiler dependent features; if you have to use any such features, use conditional compilation.

14. A header file should provide all the documentation necessary to understand the semantics of this file.

15. The documentation for the client is placed in the header file.

16. The documentation for the implementor is placed in the implementation file.

17. The documentation for the client and for the implementor may be different.

18. Global static variables have identifiers with a trailing underscore.

7.9 Exercises

All functions should be well documented. A main program should be included for any exercise that asks you to implement a function and that carefully tests this function.

All functions must be documented following standards introduced in this chapter. You should also use the "Function Names" idiom whenever appropriate.

Exercise 7–1

Write a boolean function:

```
int between(int x, int y, int w)
```

which returns 1 if w is between x and y (including both x and y), that is, $x <= w <= y$; and returns 0 otherwise.

Exercise 7–2

Write a recursive function

```
double power(double x, int n)
```

that implements the following algorithm to compute x^n:

for even values of n, compute

$$x^{n/2} * x^{n/2}$$

for odd values of n, compute

$$x * x^{n/2} * x^{n/2}$$

Exercise 7-3

Write a Boolean function testPrime(), which takes a single integer parameter n, and returns 1 if n is prime, and 0 otherwise. Assume that n > 1.

Exercise 7-4

Consider the following function:

```
int Enigma(int n) {
    int m;

    while(n >= 10) {
        m = 0;
        while(n > 0) {
            m += n % 10;
            n /= 10;
        }
        n = m;
    }
    return n;
}
```

Write a specification for the above function. What's the value of Enigma(1993)?

Exercise 7-5

Write a procedure formatter() which takes an integer parameter n and a string parameter c, and outputs a single line consisting of 2n occurrences of c. Every two consecutive occurrences of c are separated by a single blank and the output line is terminated by the letter E. For example,

for n = 1, and c = "**", we have

****E

for n = 2, and c = "?" we have:

?? ??E

for n = 3, and c = "+*" we have:

+*+* +*+* +*+*E

and so on. If n < 1, then formatter() prints nothing.

Exercise 7-6

Write a procedure `printTriangle()` which takes a single integer parameter n. If n is less than 1, then `printTriangle()` does nothing. Otherwise, `printTriangle()` prints a triangle of n lines; the i-th line contains the integer numbers 1 ... i, separated by at least one blank. For example, for n = 3, `printTriangle()` prints:

```
1
1 2
1 2 3
```

Exercise 7-7

Write the definition of a function `multiplier()`, which has two real parameters n and m, and which returns the value of n multiplied by m.

Exercise 7-8

Consider a sequence of numbers defined by the following formula:

```
a(1)  =   2
a(2)  =   5
a(n)  =   a(n-1) * 2a(n-2) + 2          for    n > 2
```

Write two functions, both of which have an integer parameter n, that compute the value of `a(n)`; the first function should use a loop and the second function should be recursive.

Exercise 7-9

Write the definition of a function `findSum()`, which has two integer parameters, n and m, and returns the sum of all the integers from n up to m (inclusive). You can assume that n <= m.

Exercise 7-10

Write the declaration of a function `Combination(n,r)`, which has two integer parameters n and r, and which returns the number of combinations of r values selected from n values, `C(n,r)`:

$$\frac{n!}{r!\ (n-r)!}$$

Exercise 7-11

Write a function that takes a file handle f as a parameter and returns the number of occurrences of all digits in the file found in the file f. Write a program to show how this function can be used to find the number of digits in the file `"abc.dat"`.

Exercise 7-12

Write a recursive function ssquares() that returns the sum of squares of all integers from 1 to n (your function should have one parameter, used to pass the value of n).

Exercise 7-13

Show the output produced by the statement

```
printf("%d\n", f(14));
```

where f() is defined as follows:

```
int f(int n) {
    return n < 2 ? 1 : f(n-1) + f(n-2);
}
```

Exercise 7-14

Write a procedure compute() that takes two parameters, n and flag, and returns the sum of all odd integers from 1 to n if flag is 1; otherwise it returns the product of all even integers from 1 to n.

Exercise 7-15

A complete polygon with n nodes (n>=3) is a polygon in which there is an arc connecting any two nodes.

Find a recursive formula to compute the number of arcs in a complete polygon with n nodes (n >= 3). Write a function that computes this value, and test this function for n = 5, 6, and 7.

Exercise 7-16

Write an integer function limit() that returns the largest positive integer value n such that:

```
abs(1/(n - 1)) < 0.00001
```

Use iteration.

Exercise 7-17

Write the declaration of a function which has one integer parameter n, and which prints the Pascal triangle for any n > 0; for example, for n = 4, the function prints:

```
1    1
1    2    1
1    3    3    1
1    4    6    4    1
```

Exercise 7-18

Write an integer parameterless function `lines()`, which returns

- the number of lines in the input stream
- negative one if the input stream is not empty but there are no lines in the stream
- 0 if the input stream is empty.

Exercise 7-19

Implement a function

```
int base(int n)
```

which reads one character at a time, using `getchar()` from the standard input, until a non-digit is encountered. n may be either 2 or 8; if n has a different value, then `base()` returns –1.

For n = 2, `base()` accepts only the characters '0' and '1'; other characters are skipped (but reading continues). The function considers the input to be a binary value, and returns this input converted to a decimal value. For example, the call to `base(2)` for the input

```
12016a
```

returns 5 (binary 101 in base 10). Here, don't use `scanf()`.

For n = 8, the semantics is similar, except we assume the input to be octal numbers, and the function again returns the decimal equivalent. Thus, characters '0'–'7' are accepted and others are skipped. For example, the call to `base(8)` for the input

```
194x
```

returns 12 (octal 14 in base 10).

Your program should read an integer value n, and if n is equal 2 or 8, then it should output the value returned by the function `base()`, otherwise it should issue an error message. Test your program using the following input:

```
2   150018a
3   211f
8   129934z
2   001z
8   07a
```

Exercise 7-20

Show the output produced by the program given below (the program is stored in two separate files):

File F1:

```
#include <stdio.h>
#define lim 10
extern char s[lim];
    static int first = 1;

int find(char c) {
    static int posi = 0;

    while(s[posi] != c) {
        if(posi == lim - 1)
            return 0;
        posi++;
    }
    if(first) {
        posi = 0;
        first = 0;
    }
    return 1;
}
```

File F2:

```
#define lim 10
char s[lim];

void get() {
int i = 0;

    while((s[i++] = getchar()) != '\n')
        ;
}

int main() {

    get();
    if(find('a'))
        put('f');
    else putchar('b');
```

```
    if(find('b'))
        putchar('f');
    else putchar('b');

    if(find('a'))
        putchar('f');
    else putchar('b');

    return EXIT_SUCCESS;
}
```

Assume the input passed to the program is:

```
be aware
```

Exercise 7-21

If you calculate the sum

```
1 + 1/2 + 1/3 + 1/4  + 1/5 + 1/6 +  ...  1/n
```

then this sum can be arbitrarily large; that is, for any positive integer M, you can find an integer n for which this sum is greater than M.

Implement a function to test the above claim:

```
int sum(int M);
```

sum() returns the smallest positive integer value of n for which the sum shown above is greater than M (assuming that M > 0). If M <= 0, then sum() returns −1. Use a loop. Next, implement a function sumRec() whose semantics are identical to the ones in the function sum(), except sumRec() is recursive.

Test these functions with the following input values:

a) First for sum(), use the following test values:
   M = 3
   M = 7
   M = 15
b) Then for sumRec(), use the following test values:
   M = 3
   M = 7
   M = 15

Caution! sumRec() may not work for some values of M, although sum() does work for these values (due to the nature of recursion).

Exercise 7-22

Write a stateless module to implement this interface:

```
char encode(char c);
    /* For any ASCII character c, encode(c) is a printable
     * character different from c; for any non-printable
     * character c, encode(c) = c
     */

char decode(char c);
    /* For any character c, decode( encode(c) ) = c       */
```

Use the "Header and Implementation" idiom.

Exercise 7-23

Write a stateless module to implement this interface:

```
int randomInt();
/* Returns a pseudo-random integer value in the range 0 .. 100 */
```

To generate random numbers use the mathematical expression

```
r(i+1) = (a*r(i) + b) mod c
```

where c is 101, a is prime, and $r(i)$ $(i > 0)$ is the value the function returns the i-th time it is called. Choose your own values for the constants a and b (note that a must be prime), and for $r(1)$ (must be between 0 and 100). Use the "Header and Implementation" idiom.

Exercise 7-24

Implement a stateless module with functions to convert pounds to kilograms and back.

Exercise 7-25

Implement a layer module that maintains an error code and uses standard I/O to provide the following functions:

```
error functions as in Example 7.5
```

```
double getDouble(FILE*);
```
reads a double value from a file, and returns it

```
void putDouble(double, FILE*, int width);
```
writes a double to a file, using the field width.

Use the "Header and Implementation" idiom.

writes a double to a file, using the field width, return 1 if successful, 0 if it fails. Use the "Header and Implementation" idiom.

Exercise 7-26

Implement a module that modifies the interface provided by the module from Exercise 7–25 and performs I/O using the standard input/output streams. Use the "Module Modification" idiom.

Exercise 7-27

Modify the module `Lines`, from Section 7.4.7, to handle all kinds of lines, including lines of the form `y=b`. Use the "Module Modification" idiom.

Exercise 7-28

Extend the module `Lines`, from Section 7.4.7, to additionally support functions to support the following two operations:

- find the intersection of two lines (assume that this function is not called if the two lines are parallel)
- find the shortest distance between a line and a point.

Use the "Module Extension" idiom.

Exercise 7-29

Implement a singleton module `Fractions` that represents fractions. This module should provide a constructor and functions respectively to add, subtract, multiply, and divide fractions. Fractions should always be reduced to lowest terms. Use error handling similar to that provided in module `IO`, from Section 7.4.7.

Exercise 7-30

Implement a module `Prime` that provides a function which can be used to test whether its parameter is a prime number. The module uses caching to remember the last three values input and their respective answers, and so does not have to re-test the value if this value was one of the three most recently used.

Exercise 7-31

Implement a module `SetOper` that provides several simple set operations. The module only deals with sets that are closed intervals specified by two real numbers; for example, the pair 2.5, 4.5 represents the interval [2.5, 4.5]. The following operations should be supported:

- check if the value x belongs to the given interval
- check if the value x belongs to the intersection of two intervals
- check if the value x belongs to the union of two intervals.

Exercise 7-32

Implement an overloaded Boolean function `compare()` which takes one or two double parameters. If there are two parameters provided, `compare()` returns 1 if the first parameter is larger than the second parameter; otherwise it returns 0. If there is only one parameter provided, `compare()` compares this parameter with 0, and returns 1 if it is greater than zero, and 0 otherwise.

Chapter 8

POINTERS AND THEIR APPLICATIONS

8.1 ◆ Preview

The time has come to discuss pointers, which are at the heart and soul of C. Consequently, this chapter is quite long and consists of many sections, all of which describe techniques used in subsequent chapters. In order to be consistent with the overall structure of the book, where each chapter is devoted to related C constructs, I have not broken it down into several subchapters.

I will first describe the relationship between Java references and C pointers, and include the main areas of application for pointers. C offers great flexibility with respect to pointers, and so in this chapter you will find a careful description of all relevant operations. These include address and dereferencing operations, dynamic memory allocation and deallocation using pointers, and pointer arithmetic. This chapter will then show how to pass function parameters by reference and how to pass functions as parameters of other functions. This description is followed by an explanation of how you can override a function (i.e. change its implementation without changing the prototype). My next topic will be a continuation of the discussion of module-based programming in C. I will introduce modules that provide enumerations (and resemble Java interfaces), and discuss various applications, for example, an application to override a part of the interface, or make it "final". Next, I will show examples of how you can design modules that handle homogenous collections. Finally, I will discuss alternative implementations of the same interface. The discussion of module design will be continued in Chapter 10. As in other chapters, my discussion concentrates on the *portable* techniques.

8.2 Stack and Heap Based Memory

Although dynamic memory management is covered in detail later in this chapter, at this point I want to introduce various basic concepts. A program can get its memory from one of two *separate* memory areas: the run-time stack and the heap (see Figure 8–1).

Dynamic memory management means that the running program is using memory which is not stored on the run-time stack, which is governed by the First-In-First-Out rule. Instead, memory blocks required by the program come from a memory pool used for this purpose, traditionally called a **heap** (any data allocated on the heap is called heap-based data).

Figure 8–1

Run-time stack and heap

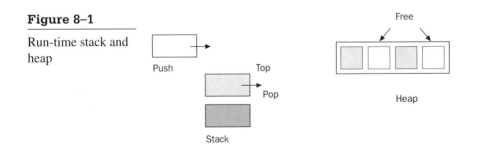

Dynamic memory **allocation** means that block of memory, requested by some program, is removed from the heap, and can be used by it; dynamic memory **deallocation** means that a program returns a block of memory to the heap. The deallocated memory can now be used the next time a memory request occurs.

Java programmers are used to seeing statements like: "A variable of a reference type can hold a reference to any object...". What's a *reference* to an object? Technically speaking, it is a memory address, specifically an *address* of the block of memory allocated for this object on the heap. The programmer decides when objects are created by calling constructors, and the garbage collector decides when these objects are deallocated. Java objects are never allocated on the run-time stack.

I will now compare the strengths and weaknesses of stack-based and heap-based memory management:

1. Stack-based memory: *implicitly* managed by function calls and function returns. The programmer can not explicitly invoke operations that would result in the allocation and deallocation of the blocks of memory on the stack. As a result, an advantage of stack-based data is that you do not have to be concerned with its deallocation. However, this in itself may lead to programming errors, such as the so-called dangling reference problem. This problem is a result of a variable referencing a memory block whose lifetime has expired; in other words, one that has been allocated on the stack and then deallocated.

2. Heap-based memory: *explicitly* managed by the programmer. While in Java, memory for an object is implicitly deallocated by the garbage collector. Other programming languages, such as C, force the user to explicitly deallocate memory. The advantage of heap-based data is that you have control over the management of the data; the disadvantage is that it is easy to introduce errors, caused by forgetting to initialize or free memory, etc. Even if the heap memory is properly managed, a problem exists which is beyond the programmer's control. This problem occurs when a heap gets divided into a large number of small memory blocks, referred to as heap **fragmentation**. These unused blocks are interspersed with used ones, and while the total size of all of them may be quite large, there is not a single free block large enough to satisfy a memory allocation request. *Compacting* the heap does solve this problem; it involves moving all the free blocks to one end of the heap so that they form a uniform whole piece. Unfortunately, few implementations support compaction because it is costly and requires intermediate handles to maintain values of pointers. Since C does not support compaction, in some situations you will need to manage your own heap; that is, allocate a large block of memory and manage it yourself.

C programmers are *responsible* for memory management. One very serious problem with improper memory management is so-called **memory leakage**, which appears when the programmer forgets to deallocate memory. If a small program forgets to free some memory, this will probably not be a problem. On the other hand, a program that runs for a long time and requires large amounts of memory will almost certainly run into trouble if it does not return its *unused* memory. In

Java, dynamic memory management is mainly used for objects, but in general it is useful in various other applications. Here are two examples:

1. Assume that we want to read a text file and store its lines in a character array (which in C have sizes fixed at compile-time). We don't know the size of the file (number of lines and number of characters in each line). In order to use statically allocated memory, we have to:

   - decide on the maximum number of lines (may be too much or not enough)

   - decide on the maximum number of characters on each line (as above).

   Both of these conditions restrict the ability of the program to perform its function. Dynamic memory management does not suffer from these limitations.

2. A great number of applications need to use *lists* (lists of numbers, lists of students, etc.). Lists can be stored in arrays, but since these are static, you have to decide beforehand on the maximum size of the list. An alternative is to dynamically allocate memory for each element of the list when necessary. The second option offers more flexibility and so gives the program more power.

Armed with the knowledge presented thus far, we are ready to formulate a definition of pointers. A **pointer** is a variable whose value is a memory address representing the location of the chunk of memory on either the run-time stack or on the heap. In C, pointers are "first-class" objects (that is, there are pointer types, pointer assignments, etc.) and memory management is done through pointers. The main difference between C pointers and Java references is that pointers are much more versatile and they can point to any memory location, while references can only point to objects (as a result, pointers are also more dangerous).

8.3 Basic Terminology

Like any other variable, pointer variables (or just pointers) have names, types, and values. The *value* of a pointer is the address of a memory **object**; the *type* of a pointer determines the size of that object (the size is essential to access data stored at that address). Note that in this book, an *object* means a block of memory. Figure 8–2 shows a simple graphical representation of pointers; in this figure, the value of the pointer p is 100.

Figure 8–2

Representation of a pointer

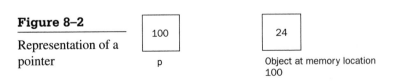

100

p

24

Object at memory location 100

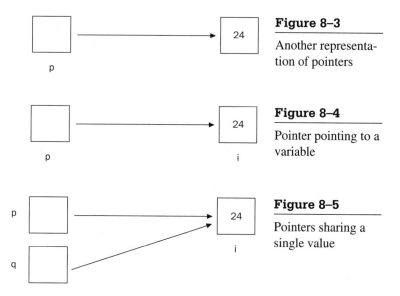

Figure 8–3

Another representation of pointers

Figure 8–4

Pointer pointing to a variable

Figure 8–5

Pointers sharing a single value

The memory location 100 stores another value, say 24. I can say that p **points** to the value 24. Most of the time, the specific value of the pointer is not important, and I use the abbreviated graphical representation shown in Figure 8–3.

In many cases, I talk about pointers pointing to objects, represented by variables, arrays, etc. For example, the representation shown in Figure 8–4 will be used when the pointer p points to the variable i, whose value is 24.

You may recall that in Java, when two references point to the same object, changing the value in this object influences both references. Similarly, in C, given two pointers p and q pointing to the same variable i, like in Figure 8–5, the value of i can be changed through the pointer p, but now the pointer q also points to the new value.

In Java, when you declare variables of a *class* type, these variables are automatically references. In C, when you want to declare a pointer, you have to use special syntax, described in the next section.

8.4 Declaring and Casting Pointers

For any C data type, for example int, you can define a variable of type "pointer to int". For example

```
int *p;      /* pointer to int */
double *q;   /* pointer to double */
char *s;     /* pointer to char */
```

I will sometimes use an alternative terminology, and rather than saying

a pointer to `int`

I will say

an `int` pointer

For the above examples, you have the `int` pointer `p`, `double` pointer `q`, and `char` pointer `s`.

The *type* of a pointer is extremely important because it determines the size of the memory object that it points to (this assumes that the pointer has been initialized, see below). For my previous declarations

> `p` points to an object of size `sizeof(int)`
>
> `q` points to an object of size `sizeof(double)`

The *type* of a pointer is specified in the declaration, but it can be modified by using a cast:

> `(int*)q` is of type `int`, and it points to the block of size `sizeof(int)`
>
> `(double*)s` is of type `double`, and it points to the block of size `sizeof(double)`

Casting pointers is rarely portable, and in general should be *avoided*.

The value of a pointer is rarely printed. If you do need to do so, use the `"%p"` format, for example:

```
printf("%p", p);
```

The placement of the whitespace around the asterisk is just a lexical convention. All of the following are valid declarations of a pointer variable:

`int* p;` — implies that `p` is of type 'pointer to `int`'
`int * p;` — no implication
`int *p;` — implies that `*p` (the value `p` points to) is of type `int`.

Actual placement is not as important as consistency, and I will always use the last alternative.

To declare two pointers of the same type, use

```
int *p1, *p2;
```

The declaration

```
int *p1, p2;
```

declares an integer pointer `p1` and an integer `p2`.

In order to avoid this problem, you may want to use `typedef`, for example

```
typedef int* Pint;
```

and then, use this type when declaring pointers. For example

```
Pint p1, p2;
```

defines two integer pointers.

The following declaration:

```
int **p;
```

defines a pointer to pointer to integer. Such pointers are useful, for example, to pass parameters by reference (see Section 8.15.1). There is no restriction on the number of '*' characters you use, but typically more than two is not practical.

8.5 Dereferencing Pointers and the Address Operator

This section describes two operations that are not available in Java: dereferencing and the address operator. I will start by talking about dereferencing. Once you have a pointer, you may want to access the contents of the memory location pointed to by it; this operation is called **dereferencing**. Dereferencing the pointer p in Figure 8–4 will result in the value 24 (the value of the memory location pointed to by p). In C, in order to deference a pointer, you use its name prefixed with the asterisk *. For example, given

```
int *p;
```

p is an `int` pointer and `*p` is the contents of the memory object p points to; in this example, `*p` is exactly like an `int` variable.

Dereferencing takes a pointer and produces a "regular variable". On the other hand, if you take a regular variable and apply an **address operator** `&` to this variable, you will get a pointer. For example:

```
int i;
```

i is an `int` variable

&i is like an `int` pointer, pointing to the variable i

The address operator can be applied only to l-values, and it can not be used with register variables.

8.6 Pointer Assignments

Pointer assignments are the same as any other assignments. They have to be correct both at compile and run-time. *Compile time correctness* means that the right-hand side and the left-hand side of the assignment have to be pointers to compatible types (for portability, compatible usually means identical). *Run-time correctness* means that you are using the pointer "correctly"; for example that you are not using a pointer that has not been initialized (the value of such a pointer may be any memory location, for example the one that belongs to the operating system rather than to your data). Consider the following declarations:

```
int i;
int *iPtr;
int j = 3;
int *jPtr;
```

Note that j has been initialized, but i, iPtr, and jPtr have not. I can now make the following assignment:

```
jPtr = iPtr;
```

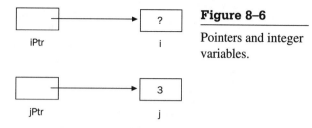

Figure 8–6

Pointers and integer variables.

For this assignment, both sides are of type pointer to int. As a result, jPtr points to the same value as iPptr, but both are still undefined.

```
iPtr = &i;
jPtr = &j;
```

Both sides are of type pointer to int. As a result, iPtr now points to i and jPtr now points to j (see Figure 8–6).

A pointer is said to be **initialized** if it points to a memory block that has been allocated for your program. Although i is not initialized, the pointer iPtr is initialized; specifically it is initialized to point to i. This is an important distinction: the usage of an uninitialized pointer typically results in program crashes (when the pointer accesses memory it is not allowed to). On the other hand, the usage of an initialized pointer, but to a variable that is not initialized will probably mean that while the program will not behave logically, it will probably not crash. I am not implying that either situation is better—variables should always be initialized. On the other hand, the pointer jPtr points to an initialized variable j.

The following assignments are not correct at compile time:

```
i = &j;
jPtr = &i;
```

The problem is that the types of the left-hand side and the right-hand side are not compatible. While the following assignment is correct at compile time, it is not correct at run-time

```
*iPtr = *jPtr;
```

because it would store the "garbage" value pointed to by iPtr into the variable j. I still have not explained why you would want to make a pointer point to some variable, such as:

```
iPtr = &i;
```

The answer is that now you can access and change the value of the variable i without actually using i, but using iPtr instead (later I show the application of this technique to implement "call by reference"). For example,

```
*iPtr = 5;
```

assigns 5 to i.

Thus far, I have only explained how to initialize pointers by making them point to existing variables. I will later show how you can obtain a block of memory using dynamic memory allocation, and initialize a pointer in this way.

This gives you a "technical" description of what you can and can not do with pointer assignments. The understanding of the fundamental concepts behind pointers is crucial to understanding more complicated aspects of C.

1. Never use uninitialized pointers.

2. To increment a dereferenced pointer, use

```
(*p)++
```

   rather than

```
*p++
```

which means: first dereference a pointer, and then increment this pointer (and not its value)—for the discussion of pointer incrementation, see Section 8.12.1.

I will now provide two slightly larger, but somewhat artificial, examples that are designed to help you understand correct and incorrect usage of pointers. The first example uses an int pointer to find the larger of the two integers.

Example 8-1

```
int i, j, *pi;

scanf("%d%d", &i, &j);
pi = i > j ? &i : &j;
printf("%d\n", *pi);
```

The pointer `pi` is set to the *address* of the larger of the two values: `i` and `j`. Then, this pointer is dereferenced to print the larger value.

The second example shows another way to find the larger of the two integers using two pointers.

Example 8-2

```
int i, j;
int *pi = &i;
int *pj = &j;

scanf("%d%d", pi, pj);
printf("%d\n", *pi > *pj ? *pi : *pj);
```

In this example, `scanf()` does not use the `&` operator because its arguments are already pointers. It is very important to notice that both pointers have been initialized to point to integer variables, prior to being used. In fact, this was the only purpose of the variables `i` and `j`. Consider another (incorrect) variant of this program:

```
int *pi;
int *pj;

scanf("%d%d", pi, pj);
```

The result of the call to `scanf()` is undefined, because `pi` and `pj` have not be initialized and have "garbage" values (memory has not been allocated for these pointers). Any input data that is stored in them may or may not belong to your program—if it does *not*, then the program will try to overwrite some other program's memory, and the execution will be aborted, possibly with the "segmentation fault" message.

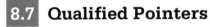 Qualified Pointers

A `const` qualifier applied to a pointer can mean one of three things:

```
const int *p;
```
pointer to a constant integer, the value of `p` may change, but the value of `*p` can not

```
int *const p;
```
constant pointer to integer; the value of `*p` can change, but the value of `p` can not

```
const int *const p;
```
constant pointer to constant integer

There is an alternative syntax for a pointer to constant data; the data type and the qualifier `const` may appear in different order such as:

```
int const *p;
```

but I will use the first alternative.

Pointers can also be qualified as `volatile`, mainly to deal with problems encountered with real-time systems (for a description of `volatile`, see Section 3.7).

8.8 Generic Pointers and NULL

Consider an application in which you want to have a reference to "any" kind of object. In Java, programmers use a variable of type `Object`, and use the cast or `instanceOf` operator to work with the actual type of object this reference points to. The `instanceOf` operator provides a *run-time type identification*, which unfortunately is missing in C. The `Object` type provides a generic reference, and a similar facility does exist in C: a special pointer type called `void*` can be safely converted to any other pointer type. For example:

```
void *p;
```

defines a *generic* pointer p. Recall that a *typed* pointer (for example, given the declaration `int *p`, p is a typed pointer) carries the information about the size of the memory object it points to, and this information is used to dereference it. Generic pointers are really *typeless* and therefore can not be dereferenced, unless a cast indicating the type is used. As I will later show, generic pointers are useful for dynamic memory management.

Example

Consider the following declarations:

```
void *p;
char c = 'c';
char *cp = &c;
```

It is legal to assign a generic pointer to a typed pointer

```
p = cp;
```

but you *still* can not dereference it (use *p); for example

```
putchar(*p);
```

is illegal. In order to dereference a generic pointer, you have to use a cast to indicate the type of value that it is pointing to. For example:

```
putchar(*(char*)p);
```

I will now describe the NULL macro. This is a special "zero" value that can be assigned to any pointer, no matter what its type. NULL is defined as

```
(void*)0
```

in stddef.h (and other header files, such as stdlib.h). The NULL value is usually used to initialize pointers to a *well-defined* "zero" value, and then to compare the pointer's value as in

```
if(p == NULL) ...
```

GENERIC POINTERS

Data stored in a memory object can be recovered as a value of a specific data type. For example, if I have a generic pointer

```
void *p
```

that points to an object containing a double value, I can retrieve this value using the following syntax:

```
*(double*)p
```

Figure 8–7

Little Endian

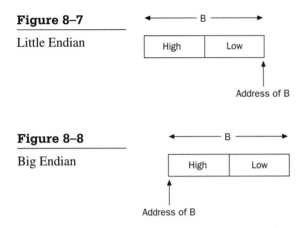

Figure 8–8

Big Endian

Blocks of memory can be copied, etc. using functions described in Section 8.13. Up to this point in our discussion, I have not described *byte ordering* within a memory object. There are two architectures that use different byte ordering, the difference between which I will explain through an example. Suppose I have a block B of memory of type `int`, which consists of two bytes.

The block may use of two architecture types:

> Programs that assume a particular architecture (for example, a big endian) are not portable.

- "little-endian" or *right-to-left byte* ordering architecture (for example, DEC VAX and Intel), in which the address of B is the address to the low-level byte in B (see Figure 8–7).

- "big-endian" or *left-to-right* byte ordering architecture (for example, Motorola 680x0 and SUN SPARC) in which the address of B is the address to the high-level byte in B (see Figure 8–8).

8.9 Pointer Conversions

For the sake of completeness, I have included a description of the type conversions that occur when pointer types are not identical. In practice, I urge you to avoid these situations whenever possible. If you are interested in knowing all of the details of pointer conversion, read the following description; otherwise you can omit this section.

Storage alignment means that storage units must begin on certain addressing boundaries. For example, on a byte-oriented machine, a 16-bit word may have to start on a multiple of bytes, such as 4 (for example, addresses 100, 104, 108, etc.). In order to satisfy this requirement, compilers insert *pad bytes*. Storage alignment is one of the reasons for the lack of portability. Any data type has an **alignment modulus**. Any address of a specific type must be a multiple of its alignment modulus. Now, consider the following definitions:

```
char *pc;
int *pi;
```

and assume that `pc` is initialized in some manner to 1001. Given this information, what is be the value of `(int*)pc`?

The conversion of `pc` to an integer pointer type may require an adjustment to an address that is divisible by 4, accomplished either by scaling down to 1000 or scaling up to 1004. The C language does not specify whether the adjustment is backward or forward, so both possibilities could occur. Whatever the case, the value of `(int*)pc` differs from the value of `pc` because of this scaling.

A third possibility is that no address adjustment is performed when pointers are converted from one type to another. If this is the case, an expression involving the dereferencing of that converted pointer, for example, `*((int*)pc)`, may result in the operating system aborting the program because of illegal addressing (an integer at an address not divisible by 4).

A type A is said to be more **restrictive** than a type B if the alignment modulus for type A is greater than or equal to the alignment modulus for type B. For example, if the alignment modulus of type `char` is 1, and the alignment modulus of type `int` is 4, then `int` is defined to be more restrictive than `char`.

In general, pointers to a type S may be safely converted to pointers to a type T and back if S is more *restrictive* than T. For example, pointers to `int` can be converted to pointers to `char` and back without the value of the pointer involved being changed, as the following illustrates:

```
pc = (char*)pi;
pi = (int*)pc;
```

In this example, after the second assignment is performed, the value of `pi` should be unchanged because no scaling takes place. However, the reverse of this is not necessarily true:

```
pi = (int*)pc;
pc = (char*)pi;
```

In this case, the initial assignment of `pc` to `pi` may cause scaling to occur, and as a result, the reassignment of `pi` to `pc` may change the original value of `pc`. If a particular implementation does not perform the scaling of pointers, these assignments do not change the values of pointers; however, subsequent dereferencing may cause a run-time error to occur. The `NULL` pointer can always be safely used in pointer expressions since its value can be converted to any pointer type regardless of memory alignment restrictions.

You can cast information to and from `void*` without any loss of information, this is helpful in making functions more generic (see Section 8.15.5).

8.10 Standard Type Definitions

Different implementations of C may use different data types to represent values of operations such as `sizeof()`. For the sake of portability, C provides the standard header file `stddef.h` that defines (using `typedef`) several "universal" data types. The programmer should use these universal types and avoid any code that makes assumptions about specific representations of these types. There are two data types used with pointers.

The first type, `size_t` is an unsigned integral type, likely to be defined as `unsigned long`. The second type, `ptrdiff_t`, is a signed integral type (used for pointer difference, see Section 8.12.2), which is `int` or `long`.

Both data types are used in other C libraries. For example, I will shortly describe a function `malloc()` which takes a parameter of type `size_t`. Since `sizeof()` returns a value of type `size_t`, it is perfectly safe to use:

```
malloc(sizeof( ...)).
```

On the other hand, code that uses `malloc(v)`, where `v` is of type `long`, is not portable.

8.11 Heap Memory Management

This section describes those C functions that are used to allocate and deallocate heap storage. All these functions return a generic pointer type, `void*`, and are low-level "typeless" functions; that is, their basic task is to allocate or deallocate a *block* of memory.

8.11.1 ◆ Memory Allocation

C provides two primary methods of allocating memory, accomplished by using the functions `malloc()` and `calloc()`. Both functions return a `void*`:

```
void *malloc(size_t requestedSize);
void *calloc(size_t requestedCount, size_t requestedSize);
```

Both these functions get a contiguous block of memory of the requested size from the heap. Both return the address of this block, or NULL if there is not enough memory available to satisfy the request:

- malloc() gets a block of size requestedSize
- calloc() gets a block of size requestedSize*requestedCount and *additionally* initializes this block to zero values.

Most of the time, you need to use a block of memory to store a value of the specific data type. To obtain a block of memory for type T, you need to allocate a block of size sizeof(T). Therefore for a pointer of type T*

```
T *p;
```

you would use:

```
p = malloc(sizeof(T));
p = calloc(1, sizeof(T));
```

You should always remember to check if a call to a memory allocation function was successful.

Example

Let's suppose I have been given the task of allocating a block of memory for the purpose of storing a single integer, and then storing the value 12 in this block:

```
int *p;

if((p = malloc(sizeof(int))) == NULL)
    exit(EXIT_FAILURE);
*p = 12;
```

In my example, I exit upon memory allocation *failure* (typically, when malloc() fails, there is no point in continuing program execution). In real applications, you may wish to first print a meaningful message regarding the lack of memory, but I will not do so here. After the successful allocation, p points to the memory block allocated from the heap, and you safely store the value 12 in this block.

Note that in the assignment

```
p = malloc(sizeof(int))
```

the right-hand side is of type `void*` and the left-hand side is of type `int*`. For the sake of readability, some programmers use an explicit cast:

```
p =(int*)malloc(sizeof(int))
```

I personally do not believe that it contributes to readability and will usually omit it.

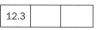

Always pass `sizeof(type)` as a parameter to a `malloc()` call, rather than the absolute value. (For example, use `malloc(sizeof(int))`, instead of `malloc(2)`.)

So far, I have shown you how to allocate memory for a single value of `T`, here called an *object* of type `T`. In order to allocate a block large enough to store n objects of type `T`, you can use one of the following calls:

```
p = malloc(n*sizeof(T));
p = calloc(n, sizeof(T));
```

For my second example, I will write a piece of code to create a block of memory to store three integer objects:

```
#define SIZE 3
double *p;

if((p = malloc(SIZE * sizeof(double))) == NULL)
    exit(EXIT_FAILURE);
```

Since p points to the beginning of the block

```
*p = 12.3;
```

stores the value `12.3` as the first value in this block (see Figure 8–9). In order to access the remaining values, I will have to use pointer arithmetic, specifically an expression such as `p+1`, which points to the second value in the block. The next section explains how this is done.

Figure 8–9

Block of memory that can store three double values

| 12.3 | | |

p

```
int* p;
if((p = malloc(n*sizeof(int))) == NULL)
    error
```

The "Memory Allocation" idiom is used so often that some programmers define a macro:

```
#define MALLOC(p, type, n)    \
    ((p) = malloc((n)*sizeof(type))) == NULL)
```

I will use this macro in various examples throughout the remainder of this chapter.

8.11.2 ◆ Memory Deallocation

Memory should be deallocated once the task it was allocated for has been completed; otherwise this memory cannot be reused, and sooner or later your program will run out of available heap memory. To deallocate memory, you use a procedure `free(void *p)`.

Example

```
int *p;

if(MALLOC(p, int, 1))
    exit(EXIT_FAILURE);
*p = 12;
free(p);
```

`free(p)` does not change the value of p, although after the call has been made, p points to memory that should never be used (it was deallocated). To be on the safe side, it is a good idea to follow the call to `free(p)` with the assignment p = NULL. Then, if you tried to dereference p, that is use *p, the execution will be aborted (this is better than accessing memory that does not belong to your program).

Always follow the call to `free(p)` with p = NULL.

1. You must always avoid *mixing* statically and dynamically allocated memory. For example, the following code:

```
int i;
int *p;

&i = malloc(sizeof(int));
```

is illegal, because you can not allocate memory for non-pointer variables on the heap.

2. Memory deallocation using `free()` should only be used if memory has been previously allocated with `malloc()`. Using the same declarations from the previous example, the code

```
p = &i;
free(p);
```

is also wrong, because memory belonging to non-pointer variables (such as `i` in this example) can not be deallocated (deallocation is implicitly done by the system).

   Both of these examples illustrate that you must always remember where the memory came from: the heap or the stack. It is illegal to get memory from the stack and return it to the heap.

3. The value of a pointer should never be dereferenced after the call to `free(p)`.

4. Do not create "garbage" objects, such as

```
MALLOC(p, int, 1)
MALLOC(p, int, 1)
```

The first object created above is now inaccessible (garbage).

5. Given two pointers `p` and `q`, the assignment `p = q` does not copy the block of memory pointed to by `q` into a block of memory pointed to by `p`; instead it assigns memory addresses (so that both `p` and `q` point to the same memory location; changing the value of that memory location affects both pointers).

6. Remember that after `p = q`, `p` and `q` share the value; therefore if you call `free(p)` this would also deallocate `q`, and now you must not call `free(q)`.

8.12 Pointer Arithmetic

In this section, I will describe pointer arithmetic, which allows for the addition and subtraction of pointer values, as well as general pointer comparisons. Valid operations on pointers include:

- the *sum* of a pointer and an integer
- the *difference* of a pointer and an integer
- pointer *comparison*
- the *difference* of two pointers

Other pointer operations are not valid.

8.12.1 ◆ The Sum of a Pointer and an Integer

Once you have initialized a pointer p to some memory block, you have to remember that it points to the *beginning address* of that block (the first object in this block). It is useful and necessary to access other objects in the block of memory belonging to p. In order to do so, you can use this expression

```
p + n
```

where n is an integer. This expression yields a pointer to the nth *object* beyond the one that p currently points to. Note that the exact meaning of the "object" is determined by the *type* of p (for example, given an integer pointer p, an object is a memory location storing an integer). This operation is well-defined only if the nth object is located within a *single* memory block pointed to by p (allocated by `malloc()`, or obtained as a result of using an array).

The sum of a pointer and an integer is useful for the **traversal** of a block of memory—by traversal, I mean the ability to *access* each object in this block.

Consider the following code:

```
#define SIZE 3
double *p;

if(MALLOC(p, double, SIZE))
    exit(EXIT_FAILURE);
```

Here p points to the beginning of a block consisting of three double objects, as shown in Figure 8–10, and therefore

p points to the first double value

p+1 points to the second double value

p+2 points to the third double value

Figure 8-10

Sum of pointer and
integer

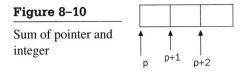

It is important that you understand that p+2 points to the last value in the allocated block, but p+3 is *not* well-defined (by not *well-defined* I mean that accessing that memory location (by dereferencing p+3) is not valid, and may result in a run-time error).

My next example assumes that p points to the beginning of the block of size SIZE; it reads in three real values and stores them in this block:

```
for(i = 0; i < SIZE; i++)
    if(scanf("%lf", p+i) == 0)
        exit(EXIT_FAILURE);
```

Do not access memory locations that have not been allocated by your program; in particular, if you allocated a block of n objects, do not try to access objects beyond this block (this includes any objects in locations p+n and beyond).

You can access the i-th value in a memory block, using the syntax *(p+i). In C, this expression is equivalent to p[i]. Note that p[i] is not a pointer; instead it represents the i-th object of a block pointed to by p. If a block of memory contains integers, then p[i] represents the i-th integer in that block. Since p points to the beginning of the block of memory, and *p represents the first object in that block, p[0] and *p are equivalent.

*(p+i) is not readable and whenever possible should be replaced by p[i].

THE iTH OBJECT

p[i] is like a regular variable representing the *i-th object* in a block whose beginning is pointed to by p. In particular, *p is the same as p[0].

I can use the `[]` operator to rewrite my previous example:

```
for(i = 0; i < SIZE; i++)
    if(scanf("%lf", &p[i]) == 0)
        exit(EXIT_FAILURE);
```

`scanf()` requires a pointer as its argument. `p[i]` is of type `int`; in order to make it a pointer, I have applied the `&` operator to it. Incidentally,

```
&p[i]
```

is the same as

```
&*(p+i)
```

which is the same as

```
p+i.
```

The following code snippet can be used to find the product of the values stored in the block of memory:

```
for(i = 0, product = 1; i < SIZE; i++)
    product *= p[i];
```

Pointers are often used for *traversals* in loops, for example

```
double *pi;
for(i = 0, pi = p; i < SIZE; i++, pi++)
    product *= *pi;
```

The loop control variable `i` in my `for` statement is not really necessary; I will later show how to rewrite this statement using only pointers.

8.12.2 ◆ Difference of a Pointer and an Integer

In some cases, you may want to access objects *preceding* the object pointed to by your pointer. To do so, you can use the expression

```
p - n
```

which yields a pointer to the nth object *before* the one that `p` currently points to. Recall that the exact meaning of "object" is determined by the type of `p`. This operation is well-defined only if the nth object is located within a *single* memory block

Figure 8–11

Difference of
pointer and integer

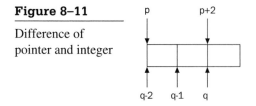

pointed to by p (for example, the block that was allocated by malloc(), or represents an array).

I will use the block of memory pointed to by p from the previous example, and
set another pointer q to point to the *last* element in this block (see Figure 8–11):

```
double *q;
q = p+SIZE-1;
```

In order to output the values stored in this block in reverse order, I can use q to
traverse the block backwards:

```
for(i = 0, q = p+SIZE-1; i < SIZE; i++, q--)
    printf("%f\n", *q);
```

I also could have written the code like this:

```
for(i = 0, q = p+SIZE-1; i < SIZE; i++)
    printf("%f\n", q[-i]);
```

because q[-i] is the same as *(q-i). If q is set to point to the last object in the
block

```
q = p+SIZE-1;
```

then q-1, q-2, ..., q-SIZE-1 are well defined, but q-SIZE is not.

Given a block of memory of SIZE objects pointed to by p, you can set q to point to
the last object in the block using:

q+SIZE-1

rather than

q+SIZE ('off by one' error).

8.12.3 ◆ Pointer Comparison: <, <=, >, >=, ==, !=

Two pointers of the same type, p and q, may be compared as long as *both of them* point to objects within a single memory block; for example a block that has been previously allocated (or belongs to an array or structure). Pointers may be compared using the <, >, <=, >=, == , != operators. When you are comparing two pointers, you are comparing the values of those pointers. These are the memory addresses of the objects the pointers are pointing to. It is important to remember that you are *not* comparing the contents of those memory locations, just the addresses.

Example

Using pointer comparison, I can now rewrite the `for` statement from Section 8.12.1 using only pointers:

```
double *pi;
for(pi = p, product = 1; pi < p+SIZE; pi++)
    product *= *pi;
```

BLOCK TRAVERSAL

```
for(pi = p; pi < p+SIZE; pi++)
    use pi here
```

The comparison of two pointers p and q using p == q does not compare the contents of the memory blocks pointed to by p and q; it merely compares addresses of these blocks.

I will provide a few more examples of loops using pointer arithmetic. For these examples, I will assume that I have already initialized a pointer p to point to a block of memory containing SIZE objects. The loop to output elements of a block backwards may be re-written using a variant of the above idiom:

```
for(pi = p+SIZE-1; pi >= p; pi--)
    printf("%f\n", *pi);
```

I can also use pointer arithmetic to find the largest element in a block:

```
double *max;

for(max = p, pi = p+1; pi < p+SIZE; pi++)
    if(*max < *pi)
        max = pi;
printf("The largest value is %f\n", *max);
```

The first expression in the `for` loop of this example initializes two variables, `max` and `pi`, in a single comma expression. The pointer `max` is initialized to point to the first double object in the block of memory pointed to by `p`; the `for` control variable `pi` is initialized to point to the *second* double object. It is important to understand that this code works, even if there is no second element; that is `SIZE` is equal to 1. In this case, `pi` will be initialized to `p+1` (which points beyond the block), but it will never be dereferenced because the body of the loop will never be executed.

I can also use pointers to write code to copy the contents of a block pointed to by `p` to the contents of another block pointed to by `q`:

```
double *pi;
double *qi;

if(MALLOC(q, double, SIZE))
    exit(EXIT_FAILURE);
for(qi = q, pi = p; qi < q+SIZE; qi++, pi++)
    *qi = *pi;
```

In this example, `qi` is traversing the block `q` and `pi` is traversing the block `p`. The `for` statement may be written in another, not necessarily more readable form:

```
qi = q;
pi = p;
while(qi < p+SIZE)
    *qi++ = *pi++;
```

This form is often used with a memory block that has a *sentinel* value used to terminate the traversal. For example, assuming that 0 is a sentinel value:

```
while(*qi != 0)
    *qi++ = *pi++;
```

Some programmers further condense this loop to:

```
while(*qi)
    *qi++ = *pi++;
```

Since 0 is the sentinel, the loop will terminate when `*q == 0`. I will formulate this code into an idiom, which I refer to as the "Block traversal with a sentinel"; however, in some situations it may be better to use one of the memory functions described in Section 8.13. Note that this idiom can only be used if the sentinel value actually occurs in the traversed block. To be on the safe side, you should also check in the loop if your pointer reached the end of the block.

BLOCK TRAVERSAL WITH A SENTINEL

```
for(pi = p; until sentinel reached; pi++)
    use pi;
```

8.12.4 ◆ Pointer Subtraction

Given two pointers, p and q, which are of the same type, assuming that p is greater than q and that both point to objects in a single memory block, the expression

```
p - q
```

yields the number of *objects* between p and q, *including* the object pointed to by q. The type of the result of pointer difference is `ptrdiff_t`, defined in `stddef.h`. This type is defined in the library because the result of pointer subtraction may have to be represented as a "small" value, if the so-called small memory model is used (for example, the model limited to 64K). It may also have to be represented as "large" value for large memory models. Therefore, for the sake of portability, you can only assume that this type is signed, and avoid making any conversions.

I can use pointer subtraction to help me find the *first* occurrence of the value 0 in a block of doubles. I want to initialize a variable `position` to the position in the block that the 0 occurs, or to –1 if 0 does not occur in the block. The following code will accomplish this:

```
int position;
for(q = p; q < p+SIZE; q++)
    if(*q == 0.0)
        break;
position = (q == p+SIZE) ? -1 : q-(p+1);
```

This code compares q with the pointer pointing to p+SIZE, which points *beyond* the block allocated for p. As I mentioned above, C allows you to do this, as long as you do not try to *deference* such a pointer. To understand this code, consider Figure 8–9 and assume that the second value is 0. Then, p-q is 2 and q-(p+1) is 1 (the difference p-q includes the objects pointed to by p and q).

8.13 Working with Memory Blocks

In this section, I will describe operations on memory blocks pointed to by *generic* pointers. Since these pointers cannot be dereferenced, you can not copy the contents of one block to the other, or compare these blocks, by traversing them. For example, given two generic pointers p and q, you can not dereference p and q, as in *p or *q. Fortunately, C provides library functions that allow you to operate on *untyped blocks*. These functions are declared in the standard header file string.h.

To copy a memory block of size len from a source src to a destination dest, you can use the memcpy() function:

```
void *memcpy(void *dest, const void *src, size_t len);
```

memcpy() should only be used if the two blocks do not *overlap*; otherwise memmove() should be used:

```
void *memmove(void *dest, const void *src, size_t len);
```

Both these functions return the value of src, that is a pointer to the first object in src. I will use the memcpy() function in Section 8.13 to implement a generic *bubble* sort routine.

There are two more functions operating on memory blocks; both of them require that the contents of a block be unsigned characters. This may give unexpected results when applied to other types such as floats.

The first function, memcmp(), compares two blocks of size len using a lexicographical comparison (the same that is used in a dictionary; for example "abc" is less than "abd") :

```
int memcmp(const void *p, const void *q, size_ len);
```

This function returns 0 if the two blocks are lexicographically equal, and respectively a positive or a negative value if the block p is greater than q, or less than q. The second function, memchr(), looks for the value val in a block p, which is of size len:

```
void *memchr(const void *p, int val, size len);
```

The value `val` is converted to an `unsigned char`, and the function returns a pointer to the first unsigned character in the block equal to `val`, or `NULL` if there is no such character.

8.14   File I/O for Memory Blocks: Binary Files

Binary files do not have a line-oriented structure, and as a result they can not be displayed using standard tools, such as the `cat` command in Unix. Instead, they consist of blocks of objects, (for example, double objects) which allows them to store information in a concise way. Many applications can process binary data efficiently, but to display this data in a human-readable form, a specialized program is needed. Unfortunately, binary files are often not portable. For example, assume that you have a binary file "image" on a Vax computer (that uses little endian architecture) and you would like to move this file to a Sun SPARC computer (that uses big endian, see Section 8.8). In this case, you would have to preprocess this file by applying a conversion from the first type of architecture to the second.

Remember that it does not make sense to store values of pointers in a file. Since these values are memory addresses, they do not represent persistent information (the next time this program is run on the same computer, the values will likely be different). Restoring pointers from a file is meaningless; instead, you can store in a file values *pointed* to by pointers.

> When you open binary files, you should always use `'b'` as the second argument for `fopen()` (see Section 5.4); for example, use `"wb"` rather than `"w"`. While this will not make any difference under Unix, it will make your programs more portable.

In this section I will describe operations on binary files. In C, these operations use **random access**, meaning that they can directly operate on data stored at *any* position within the file.

8.14.1 ◆ Current File Position

Once a file has been opened, its file handle provides the current position within the file. Below, I will provide a list of functions that can be used to operate on binary files; these may be found in the standard library `stdio.h`. All the functions assume that the file has been opened:

1. `long ftell(FILE *f)` - returns the *current position* in a file; upon error, `ftell()` returns `-1L` and sets `errno` (see Section 9.7)

2. `int fseek(FILE *f, long offset, int mode)` - sets the current position in a file by the specified `offset`; it returns 0 if successful and a non-zero

value otherwise. The value of `mode` determines the initial position in the file to begin offsetting. There are three *predefined* macros:

- `SEEK_SET`, to specify that the offset is from the beginning of the file
- `SEEK_CUR`, to specify that the offset is from the current position in the file
- `SEEK_END`, to specify that the offset is from the end of the file.

Here are some examples of `fseek()`, given a file of double values

`fseek(f, sizeof(double), SEEK_SET)` - move to the second double value

`fseek(f, sizeof(double), SEEK_CUR)` - move to the *next* double value

`fseek(f, -sizeof(double), SEEK_CUR)` - move to the *previous* double value

`fseek(f, -sizeof(double), SEEK_END)` - move to the last double value

The value returned by `ftell()` is often used by `fseek()`:

```
long currentPosition;
...
currentPosition = ftell(f);
...
fseek(f, currentPosition, SEEK_SET) - move to the saved position.
```

`fseek()` can also be used for text files, but only when the offset is 0, or it has been computed by `ftell()`.

3. `rewind(FILE *f)` moves the current file position to the beginning of the file; equivalent to `fseek(f, 0L, SEEK_SET)`

Example 8–3

The following function computes the size of a file whose name is provided as an argument:

```
fileSize(const char *filename);
```

(for an explanation of string parameters, see Section 9.3.2).

```
long fileSize(const char *filename) {
   FILE *f;
   long size;

   if((f = fopen(filename, "r")) == NULL)
      return -1L;

   if(fseek(f, 0L, SEEK_END) == 0) {
      size = ftell(f);
      if(fclose(f) == EOF)
         return -1L;
      return size;
   }
   /* if here, fseek failed */
   fclose(f);
   return -1L;
}
```

8.14.2 ◆ Binary Reading and Writing

As described in the previous section, binary files consist of blocks of objects. There are two standard library functions declared in `stdio.h` that are used to read and write blocks of objects: `fread()` and `fwrite()`. Both functions assume that the file has been opened for input or output respectively.

The first parameter, `buf`, points to the block of objects; the second parameter, `elSize`, specifies the size of each object; the third parameter, `count`, specifies the number of objects in the block; and the last parameter specifies the file:

1. `size_t fread(void *buf, size_t elSize, size_t count, FILE *in);`

   `fread()` reads from the file `in` up to `count` objects, each of size `elSize` and stores them in the block pointed to by `buf`. It returns the number of objects that have been actually read; 0 on error. You can use the `ferror()` function, described in Section 9.7 to tell the difference between the end-of-file and an error.

2. `size_t fwrite(void *buf, size_t elSize, size_t count, FILE *out);`

   `fwrite()` has the same specification as `fread()`, except it writes to the file `out`.

Example 8–4

In this example, I will show two functions. The first translates a text file containing double values into a binary file; the second translates a binary file of double data into a text file. The main program gives the user various options, for example, the choice of the translations to perform.

The basic loop that translates the text file `in` into a binary file `out` reads one double value at a time and writes the block of memory representing this value to the output file:

```
while(fscanf(in, "%lf", &d) == 1)
    if(fwrite(&d, sizeof(double), 1, out) != 1)
```

The translation from a binary file `in` into a text file `out` is based on another loop, which reads one double object at a time and stores it into the `double` variable d. It outputs up to `Max` values on each line of the output file:

```
while(fread(&d, sizeof(double), 1, in) == 1) {
    i++;
    if(i == Max) {
        putchar('\n');
        i = 0;
    }
    fprintf(out, "%f\t", d);
    ...
}
```

The user of the main program can choose to convert a text file containing double values to a binary file called `"junk.bin"`, or to convert a binary file containing double values to a text file called `"junk.txt"`. Either or both conversions can be skipped.

The main program first allocates memory to store filenames (`FILENAME_MAX` is the maximum length of the filename; it is defined in `stdio.h`). The flag `noSkip` is used to determine whether the user decided to skip the translation:

```
char *tname;
char *bname;
int noSkip = 1;    /* flag */

printf("Converts text files to binary files and back\n");

if((tname = malloc(FILENAME_MAX*sizeof(char))) == NULL)
    return EXIT_FAILURE;

if((bname = malloc(FILENAME_MAX*sizeof(char))) == NULL) {
    free(tname);
```

```
        return EXIT_FAILURE;
}
```

Note that if the second memory allocation request failed, then memory allocated as a result of the first request is freed. While this is not necessary in a small program that terminates in case of a failure, it is essential for a larger program that continue to execute.

Next, the user is asked whether a text-to-binary conversion should be performed:

```
printf("To convert a text file into a binary file\n");
printf("press y or Y, to skip this conversion press");
printf(" any other character\n");
switch(getchar()) {

case 'y':
case 'Y': break;

case '\n': noSkip = 0;
           break;

default: noSkip = 0;
         SKIP
         break;
}
```

If the user chose to perform the conversion, then she or he is asked to provide the file name, and then the conversion takes place:

```
if(noSkip == 1) {
   printf("Enter the name of the text file:\n");
   printf(" (one word, no more than %d characters)\n", FILENAME_MAX);
   if(scanf("%s", tname) != 1)
      return EXIT_FAILURE;
   SKIP

   printf("Text file %s is converted to a binary file %s\n",
           tname, "junk.bin");
   printf("Conversion %s successful\n",
           (textToBinary(tname, "junk.bin") == 0) ? "not" : "");
}
```

A binary-to-text file conversion is similar and it is not shown here. (The complete code is provided in the file ex8-4.c.)

Section 11.4.9 provides one more example of binary file processing using a file of structures.

8.15 Pointers and Functions

In this section, I will cover the use of pointers in functions, pointers as parameters passed by value and by reference, and the use of const parameters, functions returning pointers and functions passed as parameters to other functions, and conclude with a discussion of the dangling reference problem.

8.15.1 ◆ Pointer Parameters

Pointers can be used as function parameters wherever other expressions can be used (as long as they satisfy the general correctness conditions).

Accessing Actual Parameters

I will start with an example of a function that has a pointer as a formal parameter. This parameter is assigned the address of a block of memory through the actual parameter.

Example 8–5

Suppose I have a memory block that contains a sequence of characters terminated by the ASCII null character. To print these characters on a single line, separated by blanks, and enclosed in square brackets, for example

```
[ a b c d ]
```

I can use the following function:

```
void show(char *p) {
    char *q;

    printf("[ ");
    for (q = p; *q != '\0'; q++)
        printf("%c ", *q);
    printf("]\n");
}
```

Above, I used the "Block Traversal with a Sentinel Value" idiom. Since strings constants in C are terminated by the ASCII null character, you can call this function as follows:

```
show("abcd");
```

Now, let's try to use a recursive solution.

```
void show1(char *p) {

    printf("[ ");
    if (*p != '\0') {
        printf("%c ", *p);
        show1(++p);
    }
    printf("]\n");
}
```

This solution is incorrect—it will output an open bracket before every character and follow the whole list with an equivalent number of closing brackets. You only want to output an open bracket in the very first call to show1()—to determine which call you are in, you can use a global flag. An even better solution is to limit the scope of this flag to the function, using a local static variable:

```
void show2(char *p) {
    static int first = 1;

    if (first) {
        printf("[ ");
        first = 0;
    }
    if (*p != '\0') {
        printf("%c ", *p);
        show2(++p);
    } else {
        printf("]\n");
        first = 1;  /* reset first for next call */
    }
}
```

Note that the recursive call must use ++p; indeed show2(p++) would result in infinite recursion.

Modifying Actual Parameters (Call by Reference)

Recall from Section 7.2 that passing parameters *by value* means that on entry to the function, an assignment is performed:

```
formal parameter = actual parameter
```

Since the formal parameter gets the *value* of the actual parameter, any modifications of the formal parameter in the body of the function do *not* modify the actual parameter. In order to modify the value of the actual parameter, you have to use pointers. The assignment of actual parameters to formal parameters then becomes:

```
formal parameter = &(actual parameter)
```

Any modifications of the *dereferenced* formal parameter now change the value of the actual parameter.

I will illustrate how this works through an example of a procedure, used to swap the values of two integer variables. The function prototype:

```
void swap(int x, int y);
```

is wrong, because its two parameters are passed by value, and so the call

```
swap(i, j);
```

does not change the values of i and j. In order to modify the actual parameters, you need to use pointers:

```
void swap(int *x, int *y) {
    int temp;

    temp = *x;
    *x = *y;
    *y = temp;
}
```

Now, you can use swap() to exchange the values of integer variables i and j by passing their addresses as actual parameters:

```
swap(&i, &j);
```

I will trace this call using the graphical representation introduced earlier. Assuming the initial values of the variables i and j are 3 and 4, respectively, the state of memory before the call has been made is shown in Figure 8–12. Immediately after the call has been initiated, the state of memory is shown in Figure 8–13. After the execution of temp = *x, the state of memory is shown in Figure 8–14.

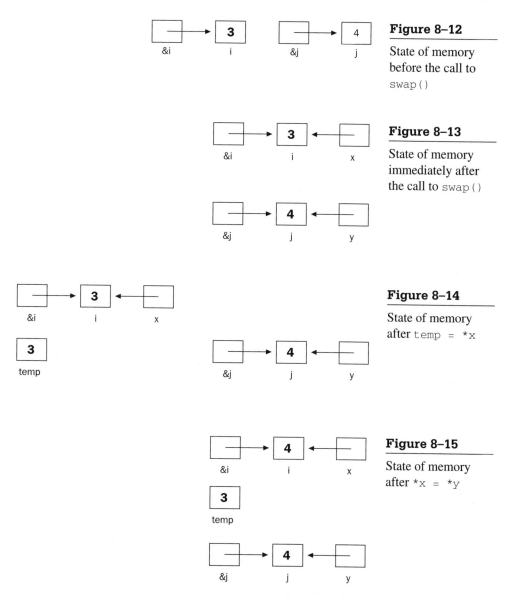

Figure 8–12

State of memory before the call to `swap()`

Figure 8–13

State of memory immediately after the call to `swap()`

Figure 8–14

State of memory after `temp = *x`

Figure 8–15

State of memory after `*x = *y`

After the execution of `*x = *y`, the state of memory is shown in Figure 8–15. And finally, after the execution of `*y = temp`, the state of memory is shown in Figure 8–16.

When the function `swap()` terminates, its local variables x, y, and `temp` "disappear", but the values of i and j are correctly modified.

Figure 8–16

State of memory
after `*y = temp`

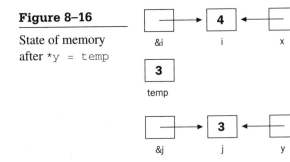

PASS BY REFERENCE

1. Declare the formal parameter `FP` as a pointer, for example `int *FP`

2. In the body of the procedure, dereference `FP`, that is use `*FP`

3. In the call

   if the actual parameter `AP` is a *variable*, use the address of `AP`; for example

   ```
   f(&AP)
   ```

   if the actual parameter `AP` is a *pointer*, use `AP` without the address operator; for example

   ```
   f(AP)
   ```

I would like to now consider some code, which will further illustrate the third point of the "Pass by reference" idiom.

```
int *p;
int *q;

if(MALLOC(p, int, 1))
    exit (EXIT_FAILURE);
if(MALLOC(q, int, 1)) {
    free(p);
    exit (EXIT_FAILURE);
}

*p = 3;
*q = 4;
swap(p, q);
```

To help you understand this code, I recommend that you draw pictures similar to ones in previous figures, and make certain that you understand why the values of *p and *q are exchanged as a result of the call to swap().

Example 8–6

The next example shows one more application of parameters passed by reference. A function get() reads a *single* line and calculates the number of whitespace characters and letters occurring in this line. Since get() has to return two values to its caller (the number of characters and letters), it needs two parameters passed *by reference*:

```
get(int *ws, int *lc);
```

Given two variables

```
int white, letters;
```

this function is called like this:

```
get(&white, &letters);

int get(int *ws, int *lc) {
    int c;

    *ws = *lc = 0;

    while ((c = getchar()) != EOF)
        switch (c) {
        case ' ':
        case '\t': (*ws)++;
                    break;

        case '\n': return 1;

        default:    if(islower(c))
                        (*lc)++;
                    break;
        }
```

```
    return 0;
}
```

Above, I used a function `islower()`, described in Section 9.2.

For my next example, I will write a function that creates a block of memory to store a number of `int` values:

```
int* getBlock(size_t size) {
    return malloc(size*sizeof(int));
}
```

This function returns a pointer to the newly allocated block of memory, or NULL if it fails, and can be used like this:

```
int *p;
if((p = getBlock(10)) == NULL)
    error
```

It is the *client's responsibility* to deallocate memory that has been allocated by this function, using the "Memory Deallocation" idiom:

```
free(p);
p = NULL;
```

> Any memory allocated in a function must be clearly documented so that the function's client is clear as to who is responsible for freeing this memory.

In some situations, you need to modify a pointer parameter, specifically the value of that pointer (rather than the value the pointer points to). To do so, you have to pass this pointer by *reference*, using the same "Call by reference" idiom, but this time applied to a pointer. Therefore, you need to use a *pointer to a pointer*.

You can rewrite the above function `getBlock()` for allocating memory to return the newly-allocated block through the first parameter:

```
int getBlockRef(int **p, unsigned n) {
    if((*p = (int*)malloc(n*sizeof(int))) == NULL)
        return 0;

    return 1;
}
```

This function can be called as follows:

```
int *q;
if(getBlockRef(&q, 10) == 1)
    success
```

Here is the list of steps I used above to apply the "Call by Reference" idiom:

- the formal parameter, FP, in this example is a "pointer to `int`", specifically `int *p`; step 1 one of the idiom specified that I declare FP as a pointer `*FP`, which in this case amounts to `int **p`
- within the code, I used `*FP`, which is the same as `*p`
- in the call to the function, I supplied the address of the actual parameter, that is `&q`

As one last example of passing a parameter by reference, consider a function that is supposed to deallocate a memory block pointed to by its parameter p, and additionally set this pointer to NULL. While the first of the required actions does not modify p, the second one does. Therefore, I have to pass p by reference:

```
void myFree(int **p) {
    free(*p);
    *p = NULL;
}
```

Now, I can use this code:

```
int *q;
if(getBlockRef(&q, 10) == 1) {
...
    myFree(&q);
}
```

8.15.2 ◆ Protecting Return Values and Parameter Values: const

I will now compare and contrast passing parameters by value and by reference. Passing by value has one clear advantage; it does not modify actual parameters, and therefore provides a safe way of passing values *to* a function. This is efficient if the parameters are not very large; when a parameter represents a large object (such as structures, introduced in Chapter 11), a more efficient solution is to pass only the address of the object. The disadvantage of doing so is that the client who calls the function may not realize that the function will potentially modify the actual parameter. Fortunately, there is a solution to this problem—the const qualifier, which provides a safe call by reference. For example, assume that you have created a memory block allocated to store 10 double values, using the following code

```
#define SIZE 10
   double *p;
   if(MALLOC(p, double, 10))
      error
```

Assuming that this block was somehow initialized, you now want to find the product of all its values. You also want to guarantee that the values stored in the block will not change. The following implementation of the function product()

```
double product(double *block, int size) {
   int i;

   for (i = 1; i < size; i++)
      block[0] *= block[i];

   return block[0];
}
```

shows that the programmer attempted an unnecessary (and confusing) optimization that used the first value in the block to accumulate the product. This is bad coding style, but I am using it for the sake of the example. A call to this function will confuse the caller, who most likely does not expect the product() function to modify his or her block of memory. If I had declared the product() function using the const keyword, this could have been prevented:

```
double product(const double *block, int size);
```

const specifies that `block` is a pointer to constant data, and any attempt to modify this data, such as `block[0] = expression` would produce a compiler's warning.

EFFICIENT PASS BY REFERENCE

```
void f(const T* p);
```

This idiom is used by various library functions, for example string functions. When you have a function that returns a pointer to a memory block that should not be modified, you need to prevent the client of this function from using its return value to modify the values in the block. This can be accomplished by specifying the pointer as a `const` pointer. For example, consider a function that initializes a pointer to an `int` object, and returns this pointer through a parameter of this function:

```
const int* f(int p) {
    int *i;

    if((i = malloc(sizeof(int)) == NULL)
        return NULL;

    *i = p;
    return i;
}
```

`f()` returns a pointer to constant data, and any attempt to modify it will fail. Specifically,

```
    int *j = f(2);
```

will produce a compiler *warning*, while

```
    const int *i = f(2);
    *i = 3;
```

will produce an error.

8.15.3 ◆ The Dangling Reference Problem

One of the main dangers of using stack-based data is that it is deallocated as soon as the function which defines the data terminates. Therefore, you should avoid setting values of pointers to such data. The next example demonstrates this problem:

Example 8-7

```
int *pi;
void f() {
    int i = 2;

    pi = &i;
/*
 * global pointer now points to the value
 * allocated on the stack
 */
    printf("Inside f the value pointed to by pi is %d\n", *pi);
/*
 * when f terminates, the location used by i can be reused
 */
}
```

Another, rather trivial example, is:

```
int* f(void) {
    int i = 2;
    return &i;
}
```

8.15.4 ◆ Overriding Functions: Pointers to Functions and Functions as Parameters

Java programmers are used to *overriding* a function—changing the implementation but leaving the prototype unchanged. This technique is useful in many applications. For example, consider an application that switches at run-time between using one of two sorting functions, depending on conditions such as the number of elements. In C you can use **pointers to functions** to emulate function overriding. The syntax of the declaration of a pointer to a function is:

```
returnType (*ptrName)(...);
```

For example

```
int (*fp)(void);
```

Here `fp` is a pointer to an integer function that has no parameters.

The brackets around `*fp` are necessary. By C's precedence rules,

```
int *fp( )
```

is a function returning a pointer to `int`.

Another example:

```
double* (*gp)(int);
```

`gp` is a pointer to a function that returns a pointer to a double and has one integer parameter.

A pointer to a function determines the prototype of this function, but it does not specify its implementation. You can assign an existing function to the pointer *as long as* both have identical parameter lists and return types, using this assignment

```
ptrName = funcName;
```

For example

```
int (*fp)(void);
double* (*gp)(int);
int f(void);
double* g(int);

fp = f;
gp = g;
```

You can call the function `f()` through the pointer `fp`:

```
int i = fp();
```

One application of this technique is to write generic sort functions that make the user provide the required function, such as the comparison function.

OVERRIDE FUNCTION

To override a function, use a pointer to the function.

Pointers to functions may be used to pass **functions as parameters** to other functions. In this case, a formal parameter is explicitly specified as a pointer to a function. For example, suppose I want to write a function `tabulate()` which has a function, say `f()`, as one of its parameters. This function will "tabulate" the values of `f()` within the specified range and the provided step. I can declare `tabulate()` as follows:

```
void tabulate(double low, double high, double step,
        double (*f)(double));
```

The syntax for the function parameter is important—the following definition is *not* correct:

```
void tabulate(double low, double high, double step,
    double f(double) );
```

Example 8–8

This example implements the `tabulate()` function. The function takes as one of its parameters a caller-provided function, and executes a loop (high-low+1) times. At each step of the loop, the caller-provided function is called. The following example shows tabulations of two functions: x^2-2, and x^3-2x+5:

```
void tabulate(double low, double high, double step,
    double (*f)(double)) {
  double x;

  for(x = low; x <= high; x += step)
    printf("%13.5f %20.10f\n", x, f(x));
}

tabulate(-1.0, 1.0, 0.01, pol1);
tabulate(-2.0, 2.0, 0.02, pol2);
```

Using this implementation, you could not provide `tabulate()` with a function whose prototype does not match; for example, providing a function `double f(char*)` would result in a compiler error because its prototype is different.

8.15.5 ◆ Reusability of Functions: Generic Pointers

Functions provide reusability, because they can be called over and over to perform the same task, which prevents the programmer from having to re-write code. Functions are required to specify both return *types* and a list of *typed* formal parameters to help catch various errors at compilation time. This makes sense most of the time, but some situations do arise where you as the programmer would like to have more flexibility when it came to parameter types. For example, it may be very useful to have functions with *typeless* parameters.

In this section, I will describe a technique that uses generic pointers to support typeless parameters, using a fairly simple example. In the following chapters, the same technique will be used for more complex applications.

Assume that you have a block of memory and a given value, and you want to search this block for this value. If you assume that the block contains objects of a particular type, for example a `double`, then writing the code using the "Block traversal" idiom is not hard:

```
for(p = block; p < block+size; p++)
```

Since `p` is a `double` pointer, `p++` will point to the next `double` object.

Example 8–9

In this example, I will show a function `search()` that searches for a particular value in a block of memory of a given size .

```
/*
 * File: ex8-9.c
 * Function: search
 * Purpose: search a block of memory of a given size for a given value
 * Inputs: block, size and value (parameters)
 * Returns: 1 if found, 0 otherwise
 * Modifies: nothing
 * Error checking: Returns 0 if block is NULL
 * Sample call:
 *     if(search(block, 10, 12.3))   ...
 */
int search(const double *block, size_t size, double value) {
    double *p;

    if(block == NULL)
        return 0;

    for(p = block; p < block+size; p++)
        if(*p == value)
            return 1;

    return 0;
}
```

This task becomes more difficult if you want to generalize the previous code so that a single search function can be used with any parameter type: double, int, etc. In Java, you would use polymorphism. (Recall that **polymorphism** is the ability to send the same message to objects of different types and have these objects respond correctly.) C does not support polymorphic programming directly, but it can be simulated using generic pointers (i.e. void*).

A function prototype may specify that a block of memory and the value it is looking for is *not* typed; it looks like this:

```
int searchGen(const void *block, size_t size, void *value);
```

Writing the prototype is easy—the implementation is a little trickier. The problem is that you need to compare two values:

```
if(*p == *value)
```

This is not allowed because generic pointers can not be dereferenced. Since the search1() function does not know how to compare two elements, we have to come up with a different solution. In Java, you could use a virtual function to compare two elements. You can mimic this in C by passing the compare function as a parameter:

```
int searchGen(const void *block, size_t size, void *value,
       int (*compare)(const void *, const void *));
```

The new parameter to searchGen(), the function compare(), can be called a *virtual* function; its implementation is not known to searchGen() but will be provided when searchGen() is called. Sometimes this function is called a **callback** function, because it calls back the function supplied by the client. A callback function is extremely useful in the design of some modules. Recall that a module consists of two parts: an *interface*, represented by the header file, and an *implementation*, represented by the implementation file (see Section 7.4.4). The implementation file may need some information from the client; for example, in order to implement a search() function, the implementation needs to know how to compare two elements. This type of information may be provided by the callback function, which can be called by the implementation file, and defined by the client.

The header file contains the following declaration:

```
int searchGen(const void *block, size_t size, void *value,
    int (*compare)(const void *, const void *));
```

The implementation file does not need to know how to compare two elements, since it is the client who provides the implementation of compare().

CALLBACK

The implementation file may get information from the client using a callback function, passed as a parameter of another function in the interface.

The first attempt at implementing the function `searchGen()` follows:

```
int searchGen(const void *block, size_t size, void *value,
        int (*compare)(const void *, const void *)) {
    void *p;

    if(block == NULL)
        return 0;

    for(p = block; p < block+size; p++)
        if(compare(p, value))
            return 1;

    return 0;
}
```

The above code is **wrong** (I encourage you to compile and test it, and see where it fails). Before I explain why it is wrong, I would like to discuss the client's responsibilities. In order to search a block of `double` values, the client has to first write a function that will be used to compare two double values. The first attempt to do so may look like this:

```
int comp(const double *x, const double *y) { /* wrong */
    return *x == *y;
}
```

The problem is that you can not provide this function as an actual parameter to `searchGen()` because it has a *different* prototype than the corresponding formal parameter, `compare()`.

The following code will work:

```
int comp(const void *x, const void *y) {
    return *(double*)x == *(double*)y;
}
```

Note that function parameters have to be cast to the desired type (in the above code, I cast the formal parameters to `double`). Since the caller provides the function, she or he knows the type of values that will be compared, and thus is able to provide the appropriate cast.

Here is a simple application:

```
#define SIZE 10
double *b;
double v = 123.6;
int i;

if(MALLOC(b, double, SIZE))
    exit(EXIT_FAILURE);

for(i = 0; i < SIZE; i++)
    if(scanf("%lf", &b[i]) == 0) {
        free (b);
        exit(EXIT_FAILURE);
    }

printf("%f was %s one of the values\n",
    v, searchGen(b, SIZE, &v, comp) == 1 ? "" : "not");
```

I had to pass the address of v in the call to searchGen(). Also, you should notice that I remembered to free the block b before program termination. While this was not strictly necessary in this case, because the exit() function takes care of memory deallocation, in general, it is a good habit to deallocate memory that is no longer needed.

I will now go back to the searchGen() function and explain what's wrong with its implementation. The problem lies in the structure of the for statement:

```
for(p = block; p < block+size; p++)
```

The intention was to traverse the block of memory of a given size, consisting of a number of *objects*, and checking the object pointed to by p in each step of the loop. The problem is that because p is a pointer to void, p++ does not give me the next object; in fact, this code does not have enough information to get the next object. For the same reason, block+size is not a pointer to the end of the block. The solution involves adding another parameter, elSize, which represents the size of each object in the block, and interpreting the value of size as the number of objects. Incorporating these changes, the for statement will look like this:

```
for(p = block; p < block + size*elSize; p += elSize)
```

TRAVERSING A BLOCK OF OBJECTS

In order to traverse a block of memory consisting of n objects, where each object is of size elSize, use:

```
for(p = block; p < block + n*elSize; p += elSize)
```

ACCESSING THE iTH OBJECT IN A BLOCK OF OBJECTS

Assuming that each object in the block is of size elSize, to access the ith object, use:

```
p = block + i*elSize
```

The complete code, including the modified searchGen() function, follows.

```
/*
 * File: ex8-92.c
 * Function: searchGen
 * Purpose: search a block of memory of a given size for a
 * given value
 * Generic solution that uses a function compare()
 * Inputs: block, size, value and compare() (parameters)
 * Returns: 1 if found, 0 otherwise
 * Modifies: nothing
 * Error checking: Returns 0 if block is NULL
 */
int searchGen(const void *block, size_t size, void *value,
    size_t elsize, int (*compare)(const void *, const void *));

/* sample compare functions to compare doubles and ints */
int doubleComp(const void *x, const void *y) {
    return *(double*)x == *(double*)y;
}

int intComp(const void *x, const void *y) {
    return *(int*)x == *(int*)y;
}
```

```c
#include <stdlib.h>
#include <stdio.h>
#define SIZE 3
/*
 * Sample application
 * Create a block of SIZE doubles, read in values from the
 *    standard input and then check if 1.0 was one of the
 *    values entered.
 * Then repeat this process for integers.
 */
int main() {
    double *b;
    double v = 1.0;
    int i;
    int *bi;
    int vi = 1;

    if((b = malloc(SIZE*sizeof(double))) == NULL)
        return EXIT_FAILURE;

    printf("Enter three double values:");
    for(i = 0; i < SIZE; i++)
        if(scanf("%lf", &b[i]) == 0) {
            free(b);
            return EXIT_FAILURE;
        }

    printf("%f was %s one of the values\n", v,
        search1(b, SIZE, &v, sizeof(double), doubleComp)
            ? "" : "not");

    free(b);
    b = NULL;

    if((bi = malloc(SIZE*sizeof(int))) == NULL)
        return 0;

    printf("Enter three integer values:");
    for(i = 0; i < SIZE; i++)
        if(scanf("%d", &bi[i]) == 0) {
            free (b);
            return EXIT_FAILURE;
        }
```

```
    printf("%d was %s one of the values\n", vi,
        searchGen(bi, SIZE, &vi, sizeof(int), intComp)
            ? "" : "not");

    return EXIT_SUCCESS;
}

int searchGen(const void *block, size_t size, void *value,
    size_t elsize, int (*compare)(const void *, const void *)) {
    void *p;

    if(block == NULL)
        return 0;

    for(p = block; p < block + size*elsize; p += elsize)
        if(compare(p, value))
            return 1;

    return 0;
}
```

A generic pointer can not be dereferenced. For example

```
    int i;
    void *p = &i;

    *p = 2;
```

is wrong, but

```
    *(int*)i = 2;
```

is correct. Similarly, the code

```
void* f() {
    int *ip;

    if((ip = (int*)malloc(sizeof(int))) == NULL)
        error;
    return ip;
}
```

```
*f() = 2;
```

is wrong, but

```
*(int*)f() = 2;
```

is OK.

8.16 Declarators: Part 1

Function declarators can be combined with other declarators. Since these combinations may be very complex, in this section, I provide only a brief description of a declarator. This description is limited to function and pointer types; in the following chapters, I expand this description to include array and structure types. For a complete description, see [Har91].

There are two basic rules that govern declarators:

- () has higher precedence than *
- for brackets, declarators are parsed from the inside out.

Examples given below explain how to apply these rules.

■ function `z()` that takes an `int` parameter and returns pointer to `double`

```
double *z(int);
```

■ pointer to function `v()` that takes a `char*` parameters and returns pointer to `int`

```
int *(*v)(char*);
```

■ function that returns a function - *illegal*:

```
double f(void)(void);
```

Programmers often use `typedef` to simplify definitions; for example:

```
typedef double (*Func)(void);
```

`Func` is a synonym for a pointer to a function with no parameters, which returns a `double` value. It can be used as follows:

```
Func f = sqrt;
```

8.17 Pointers to Blocks Containing Pointers

At this point, you know how to create blocks of memory containing objects, such as a block of memory containing `double` objects. In some applications it is useful to have a more flexible structure in which the block of memory contains pointers to blocks of memory containing objects. Figure 8–17 shows a block containing three pointers to `double` objects.

Now, in order to access a single object, the code has to apply dereferencing twice. This *double-indirection* is useful for a variety of applications—for example, sorting data of large sizes, since instead of moving data, it is enough to move only the pointers to that data. To create the structure shown in Figure 8–17, I first declare the variable `block`:

```
double **block;
```

Note that `block` is not a pointer to `double`, because its values are *not* doubles; instead its values are pointers to `double`. To initialize the value of `block` to point to the memory block that will contain three pointers, I will use the "Memory allocation" idiom:

```
#define SIZE 3
   if((block = calloc(SIZE, sizeof(double*))) == NULL)
     . . .
```

Above, I used `sizeof(double*)` because the block will store pointers to `double`. The next step allocates memory for *each element* of the block:

```
for(i = 0; i < SIZE; i++)
   if((block[i] = calloc(1, sizeof(double))) == NULL)
      . . .
```

Note the difference between blocks of data and blocks of pointers. Memory is allocated once for the blocks of data. Memory is typically allocated several times for blocks of pointers: first for the block itself, and then for each pointer in the

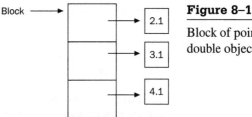

Block ⟶

2.1

3.1

4.1

Figure 8–17

Block of pointers to double objects.

block. Now that the memory has been allocated, I have to think about accessing `double` values, starting with the first value. To do so, you have to use "double" dereferencing:

```
*(*block) = 2.1;
```

Since

```
*block
```

is the same as

```
block[0]
```

you can also say

```
*(block[0])
```

which is the same as

```
(block[0])[0]
```

or simply

```
block[0][0]
```

Note that `block[0][1]` is not well-defined because it translates to `*(block[0] + 1)`, which tries to access the second object in that memory space, but `block[0]` points to a *single* object. To access the second double element, use

```
block[1][0]
```

because the above expression is the same as

```
*(block[1])
```

or

```
*(*(block + 1))
```

I will now present the complete code to initialize the block as shown in Figure 8–17:

```
for(i = 0; i < SIZE; i++)
    block[i][0] = 2.1 + i;
```

Above, memory must be freed in *reverse* order to it being created (because I must not free a block of pointers until I free the memory that these pointers point to), and so I will first free all the double elements, and *then* the block itself:

```
for(i = 0; i < SIZE; i++)
    free(block[i]);
free(block);
block = NULL;
```

BLOCK OF POINTERS

For a block `b` of pointers, use `b[i][j]` to refer to the jth object in a block pointed to by `b[i]`.

The same technique can be used to allocate memory of a "triangular shape" shown in Figure 8–18.

I will show code that creates this block, then initializes it by reading values from the standard input stream, and finally computes the sum of all values stored in the block:

```
#define SIZE 3
if((block = calloc(SIZE, sizeof(double*))) == NULL)
  error
for(i = 0; i < SIZE; i++)
    if((block[i] = calloc(i, sizeof(double))) == NULL)
        error
for(i = 0; i < SIZE; i++)  /* for each row */
    for(j = 0; j <= i; j++)
        if(scanf("%lf", &block[i][j]) != 1)
        error
for(i = 0, sum = 0; i < SIZE; i++)  /* for each row */
    for(j = 0; j <= i; j++)
        sum += block[i][j];
```

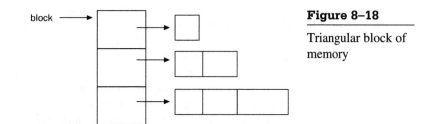

block ⟶

Figure 8–18

Triangular block of memory

8.18 Module-Based Programming: Part 2

In this section, I will present various techniques based on constructs covered earlier in this chapter and show a larger example. First, however, I will introduce some useful terminology.

8.18.1 ◆ Basic Terminology

A data structure (such as the collection of objects, or a hash table) that consists of objects of the *same* type is called **homogenous**. On the other hand, a data structure that stores objects of different types is called **heterogeneous**. For example, a collection of double objects is homogenous, but a collection of both `double` and `int` objects is heterogeneous. Java supports heterogeneous data structures by using the class `Object`. There are two types associated with any data structure:

- the type of each *object*

- the type of the *data structure* itself

A data structure is **concrete** if the type of each element is known; otherwise, it is generic. For example, you may have a generic stack, whose element types are unknown, or a concrete *stack*, which contains character elements.

The internal representation of the type of data structure should be hidden from the client; these types are called *opaque*.

In Section 11.5.1, I will show how opaque types can be implemented in C.

8.18.2 ◆ Homogenous Collection of Objects

In this section, I will present an example of a homogenous generic module, called Ops, designed to operate on an *ordered* collection of objects. In general, a generic module has two important characteristics:

1. It consists of objects of the same type.

2. This type is *not* known at the time the module is implemented.

In other words, the module is designed to operate on a collection of untyped objects of the same size.

The module provides a single implementation, which does not have to be modified to work with various data types. It is the *client* of the module who decides what *types of objects* she or he wants to use, for example doubles, integers, etc.

Ops is a singleton module, which means that at any given time, the client can only use one "instance": two collections can not be operated on at the same time. Section 11.5 shows how to design modules for which multiple instances can be created.

I will now specify the available operations for my example. These include reading data from a file, searching for a given value, and sorting the collection. Since the collection is ordered, the module needs to know how to *compare* two elements, and relies on a callback function to do so.

The client is responsible for both initializing and destroying the collection she or he wants to use. To support this, I use a technique introduced in Section 7.4.7, where the module's interface provides a *constructor* and a *destructor*. The module also supports an "intelligent" search function—this function keeps track of the state of the data (sorted or unsorted), and chooses either a binary or linear search implementation accordingly. The next section describes details of the interface.

Interface

All functions declared in the interface return 1 if successful and 0 if they fail.

In order to initialize the collection, the client has the following duties:

- implement a callback function to *compare* two elements of a selected type

- call a *constructor* to initialize the module and pass the number of elements, the size of each element, and a function to compare two elements:

```
int construct_Ops(size_t nElements, size_t elSize,
    int (*compare)(const void *, const void *));
```

The function `compare()` must return a negative value if the first argument is less than the second argument, a positive value if the first argument is greater than the second argument, and 0 otherwise (arguments are equal). The constructor enforces the fact that the module is a *singleton* module, and does not allow the client to create a second instance; if the constructor has already been called, then a second call will fail.

The client is also responsible for calling the *destructor* when the module is no longer needed:

```
int destruct_Ops(void);
```

In addition, the interface provides the following functions:

```
int read_Ops(const char *fname, size_t *size);
```
- read objects from a binary file `fname`, store them in the collection and return the number of objects that have been read through the parameter `size`

```
int search_Ops(void *value, int *result);
```
- search for the `value`, return the result of the search (success or failure) through the parameter `result`

```
        int sort_Ops();
```
- sort the collection using the current sorting routine (by default quick sort)

```
        int setSort_Ops (
        void (*sort)(void *base, size_t nElements,
            size_t elSize,
            int (*compare)(const void *, const void *))
        );
```

- set a different sorting routine supplied by the user.

The complete code for the interface is in the file ex8-10-ops.h.

Application

Given the interface, I will now provide an example of a program using the module. The program uses the module Ops to operate on a collection of double values. It reads a number of double values from a binary file and stores these values in the collection, then searches the collection for a specific value.

```
/*
 * File: ex8-10-ops-main.c
 * Application of the module Ops to search and sort a
 * collection. The program assumes that there is a
 * binary file "8-10.dat" containing double values
 * It constructs a collection to hold double values,
 * and reads in from the file values to be stored in this
 * collection. Then it asks the
 * user for the value and searchess the collection looking
 * for this value.
 */
#include <stdlib.h>
#include <stdio.h>
#include "ex8-10-ops.h"

/* User-defined callback function */
int doubleComp(const void *x, const void *y) {
    double dx = *(double*)x;
    double dy = *(double*)y;

    if(dx < dy)
        return -1;
```

```
    if(dx > dy)
        return 1;
    return 0;
}


#define SIZE 10  /* 10 elements in the collection */
int main() {
    size_t elements;
    double value;
    int result;

    if(construct_Ops(SIZE, sizeof(double), doubleComp) == 0) {
        fprintf(stderr, "failed to construct\n");
        return EXIT_FAILURE;
    }
    if(read_Ops("8-10.dat", &elements) == 0)  {
        fprintf(stderr, "failed to read data\n");
        return EXIT_FAILURE;
    }
    printf("%d values read from the file\n", elements);

    printf("Enter a value to search for: ");
    if(scanf("%lf", &value) != 1) {
        fprintf(stderr, "invalid double\n");
        return EXIT_FAILURE;
    }

    if(search_Ops(&value, &result) == 0)
        fprintf(stderr, "search failed\n");
    else printf("%f was %s found\n", value,
        result == 1 ? "" : "not");

    if(destruct_Ops() == 0)  {
        fprintf(stderr, "failed to destruct\n");
        return EXIT_FAILURE;
    }
    return EXIT_SUCCESS;
}
```

Looking at the application, you may find that the client of the module has several duties to fulfill, including the implementation of the callback function, calling the constructor, and then calling the destructor. Unfortunately, this is the price to be paid for generality in C, in contrast to the Java environment, in which constructors and destructors are called implicitly by the system.

Implementation

I will now discuss the implementation of the module `Ops`. The module uses the following private variables:

```
static int initialized_ = 0;
```
- checks whether the collection has been initialized

```
static int isSorted_ = 0;
```
- checks whether the collection has been sorted

```
static void *base_ = NULL;
```
- stores the collection

```
static size_t nElements_;
```
- stores the size of the collection

```
static size_t elSize_;
```
stores the size of each element

```
static size_t actualSize_;
```
- stores the current size of the collection

```
static void (*sort_)(void *base, size_t nElements,
    size_t elSize,
    int (*compare)(const void *, const void *));
```
- stores the current sorting routine

```
static int (*compare_)(const void *, const void *);
```
- stores the `compare()` callback function

The constructor function performs some error checking, allocates a block of memory to store the collection, and then saves values passed as parameters in private variables. The default sorting routine `qsort()`, is defined in the standard header file `stdlib.h` (it sorts *blocks of* objects).

```
int construct_Ops(size_t nElements, size_t elSize,
    int (*compare)(const void *, const void *) ) {

if(initialized_)
    return 0;
```

```
    if(nElements == 0 || elSize == 0 || compare == NULL)
        return 0;

    /* now, allocate a block */
    if((base_ = calloc(nElements, elSize)) == NULL)
        return 0;

    /* initialize private variables */
    nElements_ = nElements;
    elSize_ = elSize;
    compare_ = compare;
    sort_ = qsort;    /* set default sort */
    initialized_ = 1;

    return 1;
}
```

The destructor function is simple: in addition to some error checking, its main task is to deallocate memory that is stored in the collection. Since the flag initialized_ is set to 0, any future calls to all functions defined in the module, with the exception of the constructor, will fail:

```
int destruct_Ops(void) {
    if(!initialized_)
        return 0;

    free(base_);
    base_ = NULL;
    initialized_ = 0;

    return 1;

}
```

Private variables in the module make the implementation of the remaining functions straightforward. For example, the implementation of the function sort_Ops() uses the current sorting routine (either the default, qsort(), or a routine that has been set by client of the module). Note that the module caches the information as to whether the collection is sorted or not:

```
int sort_Ops() {
    if(!initialized_)
        return 0;
```

```
      sort_(base_, actualSize_, elSize_, compare_);
      isSorted_ = 1;  /* caching */

      return 1;
}
```

The last function that I will discuss here is the search routine. If the collection is sorted, then the implementation uses a `bsearch()` function, defined in a standard library, which performs a binary search on the block of objects using the provided `compare()` function. If the collection is not sorted, then the implementation resorts to using a less efficient linear search, and finds the value by traversing the block, using the "Traversing a block of objects" idiom:

```
int search_Ops(void *value, int *result) {
   if(!initialized_)
      return 0;

   if(isSorted_) /* binary search */
      *result =
        bsearch(value, base_, actualSize_, elSize_, compare_)
            != NULL;
   else {   /* linear search */
      void *p;

      *result = 0;
      for(p = base_; p < base_+actualSize_*elSize_;
            p += elSize_)
         if(compare_(value, p) == 0)
            *result = 1;
   }

   return 1;
}
```

The complete code for the implementation module may be found in the file `ex8-10-ops.c`.

8.18.3 ◆ Pure Modules: Enumeration

Java programmers use the word "interface" to refer to a class that has no implementation. In order to avoid confusion with terminology, I will use the term "pure module" to describe a module that consists of only a header file and has no accompanying implementation.

To explain this concept, I will emulate, in C, the `Enumeration` interface from Java:

```
int hasMoreElements_Enum();    is there another element
void* nextElement_Enum();      get the next element
void reset_Enum();             reset the enumeration
```

This module is not as useful as the Java `Enumeration` interface, because it supports only a *single* enumeration. Since I have only one enumeration, I added an additional function to the interface, used to reset an enumeration (Chapter 11 will discuss an alternative). The complete `Enumeration` interface may be found in the file `ex8-enum.h`.

So why would you provide *only* the interface? A pure module is useful for the same reason it is useful in Java—it provides the design for a module. For the enumeration example, a programmer uses the interface to implement his or her own enumeration module, say a list. The interface (header file) of a `List` will include the `enum.h` file and the implementation of the `List` module will implement it.

Using Enumerations

The module `Ops`, presented in Section 8.18.2, has some weaknesses (for example, printing functionality is missing). The problem is that the client does not have access to the memory block, so she or he cannot print; the module does not know the type of each element in the block, and so it can't do it either. The module can't use a function such as `printf()` since it does not know the format specification to use. Even if the required format were provided by the client as a string parameter, the module would still not know how to cast the pointer pointing to the block's element. (Recall that in order to dereference a generic pointer, you have to first cast to it to some type.) In other words, the module does not know the type of each element, and C, unlike Java, does not support type *reflection*. One option is to have the module output all of the data stored in the block to a binary file have the client read this file, and finally print the data. This would be a rather convoluted solution. Another possibility is to add an *accessor* function that gives the client access to the beginning of the block:

```
const void *getBlock_Ops();
```

This function returns a pointer to a constant, preventing the client from modifying the block of data. The client can now write code to print all of the values in the block as follows:

```
const double *block;
double *p;
if((block = getBlock_Ops()) == NULL)
   error
```

```
for(p = block; p < block + elements; p++)
    printf("%f\n", *p);
```

Notice that when p is incremented by 1, it points to the next double element because p is a double pointer—C takes care of the memory adjustment for you.

A better and more general solution is to use enumeration, introduced in the previous section. If the header file for the Ops module included the file enum.h and the implementation file implemented the enumeration, then the client could use this enumeration to read or write values in the block.

Enumerations allow the client to read data into a block. In the previous implementation, the *actual* number of objects was set by the function read_Ops() and then could not be changed by the client. Therefore, using an enumeration requires one more function to be added to the interface, which will set the actual number of objects stored in the collection. For example, in order to construct a collection that may hold 10 double objects, and initialize it by reading values from the standard input stream, I can use the following code:

```
#include "ex8-11-ops.h"
#define SIZE 10

if(construct_Ops(SIZE, sizeof(double), doubleComp) == 0)
    return EXIT_FAILURE;

/* set the size of collection */
(void)setSize_Ops(SIZE);
reset_Enum();
while(hasMoreElements_Enum())
    scanf("%lf", (double*)nextElement_Enum());
```

The following code may be used to show all values stored in the collection using an enumeration:

```
reset_Enum();
while(hasMoreElements_Enum())
    printf("%f\n", *(double*)nextElement_Enum());
```

Finally, the module must be destructed:

```
if(destruct_Ops() == 0)
    return EXIT_FAILURE;
```

The complete code of this application is in the file ex8-11-ops-main.c. Other files needed for this example are:

ex8-enum.h, which defines the pure interface for the enumeration ex8-11-ops.h, which defines the interface for the module Ops

ex8-11-ops.o, which is the object code for the interface ex8-11-ops.c
that implements ex8-11-ops.h, and additionally
enum.h

I will now discuss the implementation of the enumeration module. The private variable current_ is the index of the current object:

```
static int current_;
```

In order to check if there are any elements left for enumeration, this variable is compared with the actual size of the collection:

```
int hasMoreElements_Enum() {
   return current_ < actualSize_;
}
```

The function nextElement_Enum() gives access to the next element of the collection. In Java, a related function throws an exception if there is no such element available; in my code, I chose to return the NULL pointer. To access the ith object in the collection, I use the "Accessing the ith object in a block of objects" idiom:

```
void* nextElement_Enum() {
   int i = current_;

   if(current_ >= actualSize_)
      return NULL;

   current_++;

   return base_ + i*elSize_;
}
```

The complete code may be found in the file ex8-11-ops.c.

Alternative Implementation

When you design a module, the interface should not be bound to the implementation, which means that you should be able to change the implementation without modifying the interface. (It is important to remember that any modifications made should have no impact on the client.) I will illustrate this concept by modifying the implementation of the interface from Section 8.18.3.

The implementation will use its own search and sort routines rather than those provided in the standard library `stdlib.h`. Specifically, it will use bubble sort for sorting and linear search for searching.

The code for this implementation follows. In order to implement *bubble* sort, I need to swap two memory blocks. I can do so by using the standard library function `memcpy()`

```
void *memcpy(void *dest, const void *src, size_t len);
```

which copies a memory block of size `len`, originating at address `src` to the address `dest` (see Section 8.13). (Recall that I can't do a direct swap, since I am dealing with generic pointers which can not be dereferenced.) Here, I will use a private buffer to swap values:

```
static void defaultSort_(void *base, size_t nElements,
    size_t elSize,
    int (*compare)(const void *, const void *)) {
    void *p;
    void *q;

    for(p = base_; p < base_+(nElements-1)*elSize;
                        p += elSize_)
        for(q = base_ + (nElements_ - 1)*elSize_; q > p;
                        q -= elSize_)
            if(compare(q, q-elSize_) < 0) { /* swap */
                (void)memcpy(buffer_, q, elSize_);
                /* q to buffer */
                (void)memcpy(q, q-elSize_, elSize_);
                /* q-elSize_ to q  */
                (void)memcpy(q-elSize_, buffer_, elSize_);
                /* buffer to q-elSize_ */
            }
}
```

The complete code may be found in the file `ex8-12-ops.c`.

8.18.4 ◆ Homogenous Concrete Modules

In this section, I will redesign the previous example of a homogenous module, but this time I will assume that the element type is *defined* in the header file provided for the module. This approach should be restricted to a working environment in which the client has access to the header file, is allowed to modify it, and is able to re-compile the source code. The client decides on the type of element he or she wants to store in the collection—say double, and modifies one line in the header file—the line which defines the element types stored in the collection. For example, to use double values, the header file has the following line:

```
typedef double Element_Ops;
```

Suppose the client has decided to store integers instead—the only modification that would have to be made would involve changing the word `double` to `int`:

```
typedef int Element_Ops;
```

The advantage of this solution is that it will simplify the implementation code. The module now knows the type of each object (using my example, each object is referred to as `Element_Ops1`), so that the pointers to the objects no longer need to be cast. There are several serious disadvantages. Any application code may only use *one* version of the module; you can not have a module defining `Elements` as `int`s, and second one defining `Elements` as `double`s. You could create a second copy of the module, give it a different name, and then define a second type for Element, but this solution is not acceptable as far as code maintenance is concerned. (Imagine trying to maintain several copies of virtually identical software!) A second disadvantage is that the client has to *edit* the source of the header file. Although the implementation source does not need to be changed, it has to be *recompiled* to update the modification made to the interface.

I will discuss the code for the header file first. Note that the constructor no longer needs to know the size of each object—it can obtain this information using a call to `sizeof(Element_Ops1)`. On the other hand, the `compare()` callback function is still required. The implementation cannot assume that two elements can be compared using the "<" operator and we do not want to change anything in the implementation code when changing `Element_Ops`. In C, the comparison operators are only defined for primitive data types and for pointers.

The entire interface (see file `ex8-13-ops1.h`) is similar to the one presented in Section 8.18.2 (file `ex8-11-ops.h`), except that all functions operate on values of type `Element_Ops1` rather than `void*`:

```
typedef double Element_Ops1;
int construct_Ops1(size_t nElements,
   int (*compare)(const Element_Ops1 *, const Element_Ops1 *));
int destruct_Ops1(void);
int read_Ops1(const char *fname, size_t *size);
int search_Ops1(const Element_Ops1 *value, int *result);
int sort_Ops1();
int setSort_Ops1(void (*sort)(Element_Ops1 *base,
    size_t nElements));
int setSize_Ops1(size_t size);
```

I will now show an example of the application that uses this module (for the complete code, see file `ex8-13-ops1-main.c`). The macro `nextElement_Ops1` has been defined for the user's convenience; otherwise every call of the function `nextElement_Enum()` would have to be cast to `Element_Ops1`. The application code constructs a collection of double objects, and initializes it by reading double values from the standard input. Next, all the values in the collection are displayed, again using an enumeration. Finally, the collection is sorted and displayed once more using an enumeration:

```
/* User-defined comparison of double values */
int doubleComp(const Element_Ops1 *x, const Element_Ops1 *y) {
   return *x == *y;
}


#define SIZE 3 /* elements in the block */
#define nextElement_Ops1  (Element_Ops1*)nextElement_Enum()

int main() {
   double d;
   double *dp;

   if(construct_Ops1(SIZE, doubleComp) == 0)
      return EXIT_FAILURE;

   (void)setSize_Ops1(SIZE);
   /* read all values */
   reset_Enum();
   while(hasMoreElements_Enum())  {
      printf("enter a double value: ");
      if(scanf("%lf", &d) != 1)
        return EXIT_FAILURE;
      if((dp = nextElement_Ops1) == NULL) {
         fprintf(stderr, "enumeration failed\n");
         return EXIT_FAILURE;
      }
      *dp = d;
   }

    /* show all values using an enumeration */
   reset_Enum();
   while(hasMoreElements_Enum())
       printf("%f\n", *(nextElement_Ops1));
```

```
/* sort */
sort_Ops1();

 /* show again all values using an enumeration */
reset_Enum();
while(hasMoreElements_Enum())
   printf("%f\n", *(nextElement_Ops1));

if(destruct_Ops1() == 0)
   return EXIT_FAILURE;

 return EXIT_SUCCESS;
}
```

The implementation of the module Ops1 will not be discussed (see file ex8-13-ops1.c) because it is very similar to the previous implementation (of the module Ops). For a change, the local sort routine uses shell sort (see [Aho83]). Note how easy it is to sort once you know the type of each object, since you do not have to adjust pointer types anymore.

How reusable is the above design? The client can use it to create collections of objects of any primitive data types, such as int or double. Is it possible to create a collection of pointers to double? The answer is no. It does not make sense to read pointer values from a file (as mentioned earlier). I will not try to fix this problem here, but I will consider another kind of module in Section 14.3.2, which will handle data types other than just primitive data types. For the time being, the reader should be left with a warning: generic modules cannot always be instantiated to concrete types.

8.18.5 ◆ Heterogeneous Data Structures

Heterogeneous data structures are much harder to implement than homogenous data structures. Try to imagine how you go about implementing a collection of objects if you could not assume that all the objects were of the same type. In order to perform any traversal or operations on the collection, the module storing it now needs a lot of additional information. The first problem is that you can no longer assume that each object occupies the same amount of memory—what if the collection stored both integers and doubles? Consequently, the module must store information that allows it to determine each object's size. The next problem is the module interface. How will the client get information about the *type* of the current object in the collection? This information is vital to allow retrieval of the value stored in the object. (Recall that the collection uses generic pointers, which have to be cast before they may be dereferenced). As I already mentioned, C does not support type reflection.

To find a solution, I will first think about the functionality required by the client:

- the ability to add various objects, such as a `double` or an `int` to the collection
- the ability to traverse the collection and print all elements

How would you go about modifying the code in Section 8.18.2 to allow the collection to store heterogeneous objects? First of all, in order to print an element from the collection, such as the one returned by `nextElement_Enum()`, the client must know its type so that the proper cast may be applied. Note that the client can not pass the type information to the module and make the module responsible for casting each element in the collection as needed. For example, say you wanted to print an `int`, and so you pass the string "int" to the module. The problem is that there is no way to use this string to perform a cast from a pointer to an element in the collection; C will not allow it. The actual solution does involve requiring that the client pass the type information to the module. However, in order to have the code work properly, the module has to store that information along with each object. Whenever the client requests an object from the collection, the module must pass back the type information with the object.

To add a new element to the collection, for example a `double`, the client has to use some version of the following code:

```
double d = 2;
add(&d, sizeof(double), "double");
```

In order to print the entire collection, the client has to use a new function `show()` :

```
reset_Enum();
while(hasMoreElements_Enum()) {
    show(nextElement_Enum(), typeEnum());
}
```

For this example, `show()` may be coded as follows:

```
void show(void *p, char *type) {
    if type is "double"  output *(double*)p
    etc
}
```

The solution presented here will work but it is rather cumbersome. A better solution involves taking advantage of C's `union` construct, which I will present in Section 12.3.

8.19 List of Common Errors

1. To declare two pointers of the same type, use

```
int *p1, *p2;
```

The declaration

```
int *p1, p2;
```

declares an integer pointer `p1` and an integer `p2`.

In order to avoid this problem, you may want to use `typedef`, for example

```
typedef int* Pint;
```

and then, use this type when declaring pointers. For example

```
Pint p1, p2;
```

defines two integer pointers.

2. Never use uninitialized pointers.

3. To increment a dereferenced pointer, use

```
(*p)++
```

rather than

```
*p++
```

which means first dereference a pointer, and then increment this pointer (and not its value)—for the discussion of pointer incrementation, see Section 8.12.1.

4. You must always avoid *mixing* statically and dynamically allocated memory. For example, the following code:

```
int i;
int *p;
&i = malloc(sizeof(int));
```

is illegal, because you can not allocate memory for non-pointer variables on the heap.

5. Memory deallocation using `free()` should only be used if memory has been previously allocated with `malloc()`. Using the same declarations from the previous example, the code:

```
p = &i;
free(p);
```

is also wrong, because memory belonging to non-pointer variables (such as `i` in this example) can not be deallocated (deallocation is implicitly done by the system).

Both of these examples illustrate that you must always remember where the memory came from: the heap or the stack. It is illegal to get memory from the stack and return it to the heap.

6. The value of a pointer `p` should never be dereferenced after the call to `free(p)`.

7. Do not create "garbage" objects, such as

```
MALLOC(p, int, 1)
MALLOC(p, int, 1)
```

The first object created above is now inaccessible (garbage).

8. Given two pointers, `p` and `q`, the assignment `p = q` does not copy the block of memory pointed to by `q` into a block of memory pointed to by `p`; instead it assigns memory addresses (so that both `p` and `q` point to the same memory location; changing the value of that memory location affects both pointers).

9. Remember that after `p = q`, `p` and `q` share the value; therefore if you call `free(p)` this would also deallocate q, and now you must not call `free(q)`.

10. Do not access memory locations which have not been allocated by your program; in particular if you allocated a block of n objects, do not try to access objects beyond this block (this includes any objects in locations `p+n` and beyond).

11. Given a block of memory of `SIZE` objects pointed to by `p`, you can set `q` to point to the last object in the block using:

```
q+SIZE-1
```

rather than

```
q+SIZE
```
 ('off by one' error).

12. The comparison of two pointers `p` and `q` using `p == q` does not compare the contents of the memory blocks pointed to by `p` and `q`; it merely compares addresses of these blocks.

13. A generic pointer can not be dereferenced. For example

```
int i;
void *p = &i;

*p = 2;
```

is wrong, but

```
*(int*)i = 2;
```

is correct. Similarly, the code

```
void* f() {
    int *ip;
    if((ip = (int*)malloc(sizeof(int))) == NULL)
        error;
    return ip;
}
*f() = 2;
```

is wrong, but

```
*(int*)f() = 2;
```

is OK.

8.20 List of Idioms

GENERIC POINTERS

Data stored in a memory object can be recovered as a value of a specific data type. For example, if I have a generic pointer

```
void *p
```

which points to an object containing a `double` value, I can retrieve this value using the following syntax:

```
*(double*)p
```

MEMORY ALLOCATION FOR n INTEGERS

```
int* p;
if((p = malloc(n*sizeof(int))) == NULL)
    error
```

MEMORY DEALLOCATION

Always follow the call to `free(p)` with `p = NULL`.

THE iTH OBJECT

`p[i]` is like a regular variable representing the *ith object* in a block whose beginning is pointed to by `p`. In particular, `*p` is the same as `p[0]`.

BLOCK TRAVERSAL

```
for(pi = p; pi < p+SIZE; pi++)
  use pi here
```

BLOCK TRAVERSAL WITH A SENTINEL

```
for(pi = p; until sentinel reached; pi++)
    use pi;
```

PASS BY REFERENCE

1. Declare the formal parameter FP as a pointer, for example `int *FP`
2. In the body of the procedure, dereference FP, that is use `*FP`
3. In the call

    if the actual parameter, AP, is a *variable*, use the address of AP; for example

    ```
    f(&AP)
    ```

    if the actual parameter, AP, is a *pointer*, use AP without the address operator; for example

    ```
    f(AP)
    ```

EFFICIENT PASS BY REFERENCE

```
void f(const T* p);
```

OVERRIDE FUNCTION

To override a function, use a pointer to the function.

CALLBACK

The implementation file may get information from the client using a callback function, passed as a parameter of another function in the interface.

TRAVERSING A BLOCK OF OBJECTS

In order to traverse a block of memory consisting of n objects, where each object is of size elSize, use:

```
for(p = block; p < block + n*elSize; p += elSize)
```

ACCESSING THE iTH OBJECT IN A BLOCK OF OBJECTS

Assuming that each object in the block is of size elSize, to access the ith object, use:

```
p = block + i*elSize
```

BLOCK OF POINTERS

For a block b of pointers, use b[i][j] to refer to the j-th object in a block pointed to by b[i].

8.21 List of Programming Style Guidelines

1. The placement of the whitespace around the asterisk in a pointer declaration is just a lexical convention. All of the following are valid declarations of a pointer variable:

int* p;   — implies that p is of type 'pointer to int'

int * p;   — no implication

int *p;   — implies that *p (the value p points to) is of type int

Actual placement is not as important as consistency and I will always use the last alternative.

2. *(p+i) is not readable and whenever possible should be replaced by p[i].

3. As already pointed out, any memory allocation in a function must be documented clearly (so the client knows who is responsible for freeing this memory).

8.22 List of Portability Guidelines

1. Programs that assume a particular architecture (for example, a big endian) are not portable.

2. Always pass sizeof(type) as a parameter to a malloc() call, rather than the absolute value. For example, use malloc(sizeof(int)), instead of malloc(2).

3. When you open binary files, you should always use 'b' in the second argument for fopen() (see Section 5.4); for example, use "wb" rather than "w". While this will not make any difference under Unix, it will make your programs more portable.

8.23 Exercises

All functions should be well documented. For any exercise that asks you to implement a function, include a main program that carefully tests this function.

Exercise 8-1

Write a procedure alter(x,y) which changes the values of x to x-y, and the value of y to 2 (x and y are of type double). Use the "Pass by Reference" idiom.

Exercise 8-2

Use pointers to implement a solution to the following problem (write a complete program):
a) Create a memory block to store 30 doubles (use the modified "Memory allocation for n integers" idiom)
b) Read in up to 30 doubles from the standard input; stop reading when any of the following conditions are satisfied (use the "Block traversal with a Sentinel" idiom):

(i) 30 doubles have been read

(ii) EOF has been encountered

(iii) a negative value has been encountered

c) Find the maximum double value stored in the block.

Exercise 8-3

Correct the documentation of the following four functions so that it conforms to the standard introduced in Chapter 7.

```
double* myAlloc(int n);
/* Allocate a block of memory large enough to store n double values.
 * Return a pointer to the beginning of this block; and a null pointer
 * if the block cannot be allocated or if n <=0.
 */
int get(double block[], int size);
/* Assume that block points to a block of memory large enough to store
 * size double values. Read double values from the standard input and
 * store incoming values in the block of memory passed as the first
 * parameter. Stop reading when either size values have been read, a
 * value that rounds to 1 (one) has been encountered, or an invalid
 * double value has been encountered.
 * Return the number of values read.
 */
void show(double *block, int size);
/* Assume that block points to a block of memory storing size double
 * values. Print these values to the standard output, each value on a
 * separate line.
 */
double max(double *block, int size);
/* Assume that block points to a block of memory storing size double
 * values. Return the maximum value.
 */
```

Implement all these functions; specify which idioms have been used. Then, write a main program in which you will use the above functions to:

a) allocate memory to store 10 double values

b) read at most 10 values

c) print these values

d) output the maximum value.

Exercise 8-4

Write the definition of a function

```
void shrink(float *x)
```

which, every time it is called, shrinks the memory block pointed to by x by 5 elements (unless this operation can not be performed, in which case it does nothing). Initially the size of x is 50. When shrink() is called for the first time, x will be shrunk to 45 elements, the second time to 40 elements, and so on. Note that shrink() must have only one parameter and must not use any global variables. Write a short main program in which a block of memory of size 50 is allocated, initialized (reading values from the keyboard), and then shrink() is called 5 times.

Exercise 8-5

Write a program to read a file containing data in the following format:

integer followed by a number of doubles (values are separated by one or more whitespace characters)

The program reads the first integer value from the file, say n, and then allocates memory to store n double values, and reads these values from the file. Next, it sorts all values, and writes them back to the file. Include full error checking.

Exercise 8-6

Write a menu-driven program, which supports the following commands:

i n	where n is an integer value
r fname	where fname is a filename
w	
s r	where r is a double
d	
h	
q	

The above commands have the following meaning:

- i allocates a block of memory to store n double values; if a block of memory has previously been allocated, that block is deallocated
- r reads double values from the file whose name is fname; it fails if memory has not been allocated. It stops reading if either the number of values read is equal to the current size of the memory block, or no more double values can be read from the file (because the end-of-file has been encountered or a reading error has occurred)
- w shows all values that are currently stored in the memory block
- s searches the block of memory looking for a given value and informs the user whether or not this value is in the block; it fails if the block has not been allocated
- d is only available when the program is compiled using debugging mode. It turns additional debugging messages on/off; i.e. when it is executed for the first time, it turns debugging on, and

then shows additional information about the commands being executed. When the d command is executed for a second time, these messages are not shown anymore. Subsequent commands using the d option toggle debugging on and off

- h shows all available commands

- q quits the program (but first, it closes any files that have been opened, and deallocates any memory that has been allocated)

Exercise 8-7

Write the following two functions:

```
int text2bin(const char *fname1, const char*fname2);
```

reads the text file fname1, and assumes that this file has the following structure:

integer (say n) followed by n double values (values are separated by whitespace)

The function then writes these values to a binary file.

```
int binary2text(const char *fname1, const char*fname2);
```

performs the reverse translation.

Include full error checking and test your functions carefully.

Exercise 8-8

Write a function maxi() which takes three parameters, two double values x and y and a double function f(double), and returns the larger of the two values: f(x) and f(y). Then, write a function maxi1() that has four parameters. This function is similar to maxi() except it returns the value (the larger of the two values: f(x) and f(y)) through the fourth parameter. Test your functions carefully.

Exercise 8-9

Write a function

```
int compareGen(const void *block1, const void *block2, size_t elemSize,
    size_t block1Size,  size_t block2Size,
    int (*compareIt)(const void*, const void*));
```

which performs a lexicographical comparison of the two blocks. Test your program using blocks of doubles and blocks of pointers to doubles.

Exercise 8-10

Write a function

```
void printGen(const void *block, size_t elemSize, size_t blockSize,
    void (*printIt)(const void*));
```

which prints all elements in the block using the callback function printIt(). Use the "Traversing a Block of Objects" idiom. Test your program using a block of doubles, and a block of pointers to doubles.

Exercise 8-11

Implement a generic module Bags that represents an unordered collection (a bag; duplicates allowed). There should be operations to add an element to the bag, and remove it from the bag. Add enumerations over the collection. Test your module with a collection of double objects, and a collection of integer objects.

Exercise 8-12

Implement a generic module Sets that represents an ordered collection (a set, duplicates are not allowed). Use the "Callback" idiom to compare the elements of a bag. There should be operations to add an element to the bag, and remove it from the bag. Add enumerations over the collection. Test your module with a collection of double objects, and a collection of integer objects.

9

STRINGS

9.1 ◆ Preview

In C, unlike in Java, strings are not a predefined data type; instead, they are represented as pointers to characters. In order to operate on strings, C provides a standard library `string.h`. In this section, I will describe functions declared in this library and show various string applications. The discussion of strings will be continued in the next chapter, which introduces arrays. I will begin this chapter with a related topic: functions that process single characters.

9.2 Character Processing Functions

Faced with the task of being asked to process single characters, many C programmers may be tempted to write their own code, instead of using existing functions. For example, to test whether a `char` variable c represents a lowercase letter, you may write:

```
if(c >= 'a' && c <= 'z') ...
```

There is a better, more portable way of doing this using the standard library `ctype.h`. There are two types of character processing functions:

1. A **classification** function whose name starts with "`is`" and that returns a nonzero value if its argument is in the class, and 0 otherwise; for example

   ```
   islower(int c)
   ```

2. A **conversion** function whose name starts with "`to`", and that returns an integer conversion value if successful, and `EOF` otherwise; for example

   ```
   tolower(int c)
   ```

The classification group includes the following functions.
To classify alphanumerics:

`int isalnum(int c)`	is c an alphanumeric (digit, lower or uppercase letter)
`int isalpha(int c)`	is c an alphabetic letter (lower or uppercase letter)
`int islower(int c)`	is c a lowercase letter
`int isupper(int c)`	is c an uppercase letter
`int isdigit(int c)`	is c a digit
`int isxdigit(int c)`	is c a hexadecimal digit (a digit or upper or lower case a, b, c, d, e, f)
`int isodigit(int c)`	is c an octal digit (0–8)

To classify other characters:

`int isprint(int c)`	is c printable (that is, not a control character)
`int isgraph(int c)`	is c printable but not a space
`int ispunct(int c)`	is c printable but neither space nor alphanumeric
`int isspace(int c)`	is c whitespace

The conversion group includes the following functions:

`int tolower(int c)`   if c is uppercase, return lowercase, else return c

`int toupper(int c)`   if c is lowercase, return uppercase, else return c

In the remainder of this chapter, I will show various applications of these functions.

9.3 | Strings in C

C stores a string in a block of memory. The sequence of characters representing the string is terminated by the character that has an ordinal value of 0; this character is denoted by \0, and pronounced "null" (see Figure 9–1).

If a string is not terminated by the null character, or this character is overwritten, all string operations produce undefined results.

9.3.1 ◆ Definitions of Strings and String Constants

Strings are defined as pointers to characters, for example

```
char *s;
```

In this book, I will often say "a string", by which I mean "a pointer to char". Strings are allocated memory just like any other pointers using *dynamic memory*

Hello\0

↑
Null character

Figure 9–1

Representation of a string "Hello"

allocation. For example, to allocate a string that can hold up to 10 characters, you can use the "Memory allocation" idiom:

```
#define SIZE 10
    if((s = malloc((SIZE+1)*sizeof(char))) == NULL) ...
```

Note that `malloc()` allocates one byte more than the maximum number of characters in the string; this is necessary because you need room for the null character. The pointer s is initialized, but the *string* s is not, because there is no guarantee that the block s points to contains the null character. If I add the code:

```
    s[0] = '\0';
```

then s becomes an *initialized string*, which contains no characters (the very first byte is null); such a string is called a **null string**. For string allocation, it is safer to use `calloc()` rather `malloc()`, because `calloc()` initializes the allocated block to null. Note that the **length** of a string is the number of characters before the null character, and this value may *change* during the execution. The length of a string should not be confused with the size of the memory block allocated for a string, which determines the *maximum* length of that string. For example, the string s in the previous example points to the block of 11 characters and its length is 0.

1. When you allocate memory for a string that can have n characters, do not use

   ```
   calloc(length of string, sizeof(char))
   ```

   because you have to allocate memory for the \0 character.

2. Do not use

   ```
   calloc(sizeof(string), sizeof(char))
   ```

   because that call allocates a block of memory to store the number of characters determined by the size of a pointer to character, rather then the required length.

3. Initialized pointers are not necessarily initialized strings. (If an initialized pointer points to a memory block that does not contain the null character, the string is not initialized.)

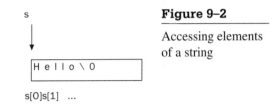

Figure 9–2

Accessing elements of a string

MEMORY ALLOCATION FOR A STRING OF n CHARACTERS:

```
if((s = calloc(n+1, sizeof(char))) == NULL) ...
```

To access the ith character in the string s, you need to dereference s+i, using s[i]. For example,

> s[0] is the first character
>
> s[1] is the second character

and so on, see Figure 9–2.

---

iTH CHARACTER OF A STRING

To refer to the iTH character in the string s, use s[i], where $0 <= i <$ length of s.

The string s in Figure 9–2 has the length 5. Note that s+1 is also a string of length 4, s+2 a string of length 3, etc. s+5 has a length of zero (it is a *null* string). However, s+6 is not well defined, because it points beyond the block of memory allocated to s.

From this description, you can see that it is easy to skip some prefix of a string (consisting of any number of characters) and deal with the remainder of this string, that is its *suffix*; for my example, s+2 points to "llo". This technique is often useful and I designed a special idiom for it.

STRING SUFFIX

If s points to a string, then s+n points to the suffix of this string starting at the n-th position (here, n has to be less than the length of s).

Figure 9–3

String constant

name

Kasia\0

It is not so easy to get the *prefix* of a string, such as the prefix `"He"` in the previous example, because `"He"` is not null-terminated. Sometimes, you can terminate the prefix by modifying the string, specifically by storing `\0` in place of the first letter `"l"`, but this technique is not very elegant.

A string *constant*, which must be enclosed by double quotes, is represented by a *constant* pointer to a block of memory containing the specified characters, followed by the null character. A pointer to a character can be set to point to a string constant, for example

```
char *name = "Kasia";
```

see Figure 9–3.

The block of memory for a string constant may be stored in "read-only" memory, and its contents should not be modified; for example, do not reset any of the characters in the constant string:

```
name[0] = 'B';
```

Double and single quotes that enclose a single character signify different things; for example `"W"` denotes a pointer to a memory block containing two characters; w followed by `\0`. `'W'` denotes the ordinal value of the character w.

9.3.2 ◆ Strings, Parameters, and Return Values

Since C strings are pointers to characters, their use as parameters and return values is subject to the same rules as for any other pointers (see Section 8.15). I will provide various examples, which you can use to verify your understanding of these rules.

Example 9–1

In this example, I will show a function that modifies the first character of the string passed as its parameter by converting it to uppercase. Since this function modifies the value *pointed to* by the pointer rather than the value of this pointer, the parameter can be passed by value:

```
void modify(char *s) {
   s[0] = toupper(s[0]);
}
```

Now, let's look at possible ways of calling this function, given a pointer p:

```
char *p;
```

Clearly, you must not call modify() with p as a parameter:

```
modify(p);
```

because p is not yet an *initialized pointer*. After its initialization,

```
if((p = calloc(10, sizeof(char))) == NULL)
   error
```

p is a *null string*. You can now assign characters to p

```
p[0] = 'h';
p[1] = 'i';
```

p is now initialized, because a string `"hi"` is null-terminated (calloc() clears the entire block, not just the first object). Now, you can call modify():

```
modify(p);
```

and after the call, the value of p will be `"Hi"`.
Note that if you initialized p in a different way, by assigning a *constant to it*:

```
p = "hi";
```

then you can not call modify(p), because you would be modifying a *constant* value.

To avoid this potential error, you may want to rewrite modify() so that it will not modify its argument; instead, it will return a *copy* of the modified string.

Example 9–2

In this example, I will discuss a function:

```
char *modify(const char *s);
```

The parameter is passed as a pointer to a constant because it will not be modified. Since the function must create a copy of its parameter s, it needs to allocate a sufficiently large block of memory, and copy the contents of s to this block. The standard string library supports two operations that are useful for the new function: finding the length of a string and copying a string. Here, I will write my own code to perform both these tasks, but you should consider this code as an *exercise* on pointers and use standard library functions whenever possible.

The function length() uses pointer arithmetic to find the length of the string (see Section 9.6.1 for a library function strlen(), which performs the same operation):

```
int length(const char *s) {
    char *p;

    for(p = s; *p; p++)
        ;
    return p - s;
}
```

Note that above, I broke my rule, and did not use *p != '\0' in the stop condition. Practically all C programmers use this shortcut, and so I decided to follow the crowd. The for statement is often coded as a while loop:

```
    while(*p++)   /* loop until \0 */
        ;
```

The function strdup(), shown below, uses a "Fast Copy" idiom with an additional twist: it includes the copying of \0. This function is *not* a standard C string function, but you can find it on some systems (you should always define your own version to allow for portability):

```
char *strdup(const char *s) {
    char *kopy;        /* copy of s */
    char *ps;          /* used for copying */
    char *pkopy;       /* for copying */

    if((kopy = calloc((length(s)+1),sizeof(char))) == NULL)
        return NULL;

    /* memory allocated, now copy */
    for(ps = s, pkopy = kopy; *ps; ps++, pkopy++)
        *pkopy = *ps;

    *pkopy = *ps; /* do not forget to copy \0 */

    return kopy;
}
```

We are now ready to write the code of the new `modify()` function

```c
char *modify(const char *s) {
   char *news;

   if((news = strdup(s)) == NULL)
      return NULL;

   news[0] = toupper(news[0]);

   return news;
}
```

Using this code, you can now write:

```c
char *p = "michal W.";
char *q = modify(p);
```

or simply

```c
char *q = modify("michal W.");
```

q now points to `"Michal W."` (see Figure 9–4).

You have to remember to *deallocate* the memory block storing this string when you no longer need it

```c
free(q);
q = NULL;
```

Note that you can use the "String Suffix" idiom to modify characters other than the first one, for example

```c
q = modify(p+7);
```

sets the value of q to `"W"`.

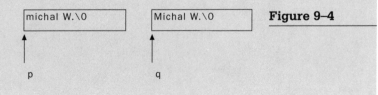

Figure 9–4

TRAVERSING A STRING

```
for(p = s; *p; p++)
    use *p
```

Example 9-3

I will now show how the previous `modify()` function may be rewritten as a procedure (this is one more exercise on pointers) using this prototype:

```
void modify1(const char *s, char **news);
```

Note that the second parameter has to be passed by *reference*, and so I use a pointer to pointer to `char`:

```
void modify1(const char *s, char **news) {
    if(s == NULL)
        return;

    *news = strdup(s);
    (*news)[0] = toupper((*news)[0]);
}
```

Example 9-4

As the last example in this section, I will show a function that takes a string parameter, and returns 1 if this string represents a correct integer number in decimal or hexadecimal; otherwise it returns 0. If I have a string `s` of the form "0xa23", I can use the "String suffix" idiom to skip the prefix of this string, and get the remaining characters. For the `s` = "0xA23" example, `s+2` points to "A23". Therefore, I can traverse this suffix of the string using the following technique:

```
for(s+=2; *s; s++)
    here use *s
```

The code for `isNumber()` follows:

```
int isNumber(const char *s) {

    if(s == NULL || s[0] == '\0') /* null or empty string */
        return 0;

    if(s[0] == '0') { /* check if there is a leading 0 */

        if(s[1] == '\0')  /* just a single 0 */
            return 1;
```

```
        if(s[1] == 'x' || s[1] == 'X') { /* hex ? */

            if(s[2] == '\0')
                return 0; /* just "0x" is not enough */

            /* traverse characters beyond 0x */
            for(s += 2; *s; s++)
                if(!isxdigit(*s))
                    return 0;

            return 1; /* correct hex */

        } /* checking if s[1] is x */
    }
    /* traverse the entire string */
    for(; *s; s++)
        if(!isdigit(*s))
            return 0;

    return 1;
}
```

9.4 Formatted String I/O

The formal control string %s is used to input and output strings. Note that when this format is used in an input function, leading whitespace characters are skipped in a search for the first non-whitespace character, and input stops when a *word* is read. A word is a sequence of characters not containing any whitespace, so the input operation stops when the first whitespace character is encountered. Therefore, scanf() can read at most one word.

In examples that follow, I assume the following declaration and initialization of the string s:

```
const int SIZE = 7;
char *s;
if((s = malloc((SIZE+1)*sizeof(char))) == NULL)
    error
scanf("%s", s);
```

Assuming that the input is

```
Java language
```

the contents of the string s is `"Java"` (the second word is not read). Unfortunately, if the input is

```
language Java
```

the code is wrong, because I allocated memory for at most 7 characters (plus the null character), and the input has 8 characters. The only solution to this problem is to use a *field width specification* in the `scanf()`:

```
scanf("%7s", s);
```

Now, at most 7 characters will be read. Unfortunately, I could *not* use a variable in the field specification,

```
scanf("%SIZEs", s);
```

because macros are not expanded within quoted strings. In Section 9.6.2, I describe a technique that overcomes this limitation.

To input a string:

a) use

```
scanf("%s", s)
```

rather then

```
scanf("%s", &s)
```

because s is a pointer.

b) make sure that s is initialized; i.e. there is some memory allocated for s (for example, using `calloc()`)

c) make sure that there is *enough* memory allocated for s, and consider using the *field width* to avoid overflow.

Since `scanf("%s", ...)` only reads single words, it is not convenient to use it to read multiple words or tokens. There are other functions that will do this job better, and they are described in Sections 9.6.5 and 9.8.

READ A SINGLE WORD (AT MOST 9 CHARACTERS):

```
if(scanf("%10s", s) != 1)
    error
```

The output function `printf("%s", str)` writes all the characters in the block pointed to by `str`, up to the terminating `\0`. Unlike `scanf()`, `printf()` can work with multiple words.

Example.

```
char *s = "C after Java";
printf("%s\n", s);
```

prints

```
C after Java
```

In order to print a suffix of a string, you can use the "String suffix" idiom:

```
printf("%s\n", s + 2);
```

prints

```
after Java
```

The next example shows the application of both `scanf()` and `printf()`.

Example 9–5

```
/*
 * File: ex9-5.c
 * Program that reads a single word of at most 10 characters
 *    and counts the number of lowercase letters
 */
#include <stdio.h>
#include <stdlib.h>
#include <ctype.h>
int main() {
    char *s;            /* to store a word */
    char *p;            /* to traverse */
    int count = 0;      /* number of lowercase letters */

    if((s = calloc(11, sizeof(char))) == NULL)
        return EXIT_FAILURE;
```

```
   if(scanf("%10s", s) != 1)
      return EXIT_FAILURE;

   for(p = s; *p; p++)
     if(islower(*p))
        count++;

   printf("%s contains %d lowercase letters\n", s, count);

   return EXIT_SUCCESS;
}
```

The code traverses a string and stops when it encounters the null character. Some programmers will code this a little differently:

```
p = s;
while(*p++)
    if(islower(*p))
        count++;
```

There are two more useful formatted string I/O operations designed respectively to read from and write to strings. The syntax and semantics of these functions are almost identical to fscanf() and fprintf(), but the first letter in the function name is s, rather than f, to signify string I/O, and the first argument is a string rather than a file:

```
int sscanf(s, "format", arguments)
int sprintf(s, "format", arguments)
```

sprintf() is useful for creating single strings, by concatenating strings with data of various types. The next example shows the concatenation of a string and an integer value.

Example 9-6

```
/*
 * File: ex9-6.c
 * Program that shows output to a string. It reads in an integer
 *   value and outputs a string of characters derived from this value
 */
```

```
#include <stdio.h>
#include <stdlib.h>
int main() {
   int i;
   char *s;

   printf("Enter integer value\n");
   if(scanf("%d", &i) != 1)
      return EXIT_FAILURE;

   if((s = calloc(21,sizeof(char))) == NULL)
      return EXIT_FAILURE;

   sprintf(s, "The input value was %d", i);
   printf("%s\n", s);

   return EXIT_SUCCESS;
}
```

sscanf() is useful for converting strings into numbers.

For example, command line arguments are treated as strings, see Section 9.9, but they may need to be converted to numbers. Suppose you have a program show, which displays the specified number of lines from the input file. It is called with two arguments, as in

```
show 15 filename
```

This execution of show is supposed to display the first 15 lines of the file filename. In order for show to work, the string "15" has to be converted to the integer value 15 within the program.

I will show the code of a similar short program that reads strings representing double values and then converts these strings into doubles:

Example 9–7

```
/*
 * File: ex9-7.c
 * Program that reads two strings representing double value
 *   and outputs the sum of these values.
 */
```

```
#include <stdio.h>
#include <stdlib.h>
int main() {
   char *s;
   char *r;
   double sd;    /* value represented by the first string */
   double sr;    /* value represented by the first string */

   if((s = calloc(21,sizeof(char))) == NULL)
      return EXIT_FAILURE;
   if((r = calloc(21,sizeof(char))) == NULL) {
      free(s);
      return EXIT_FAILURE;
   }

   printf("Enter two strings representing double values, \
      each on a separate line ");
   if(scanf("%s", s) != 1 || scanf("%s", r) != 1)
      return EXIT_FAILURE;
   if(sscanf(s, "%lf", &sd) != 1 || sscanf(r, "%lf", &sr) != 1)
      return EXIT_FAILURE;

   printf("The sum of %f and %f is %f\n", sd, sr, sd + sr);

   return EXIT_SUCCESS;
}
```

Section 9.6.6 will discuss other more versatile functions that perform the same task as `sscanf()` and `sprintf()`.

9.5 Line-Oriented String I/0

There are two functions, declared in `stdio.h`, which are designed to perform line-oriented file I/O:

1. `char* fgets(char *buf, int n, FILE *in);`

   reads a line from the file `in` and stores it in the block pointed to by `buf`. It stops reading when any of the following conditions become true:

- n−1 characters have been read

- end-of-line has been encountered; in this case $\n$ is stored at the end of buf

- end-of-file has been encountered

In any case, buf is always properly terminated, that is $\0$ is stored at the end of it. The function returns buf if successful and NULL if no characters have been read or there has been a reading error.

Often it is useful to rewrite the end-of-line character stored by fgets(), and it can be done as follows:

```
buf[strlen(buf)-1] = '\0';
```

2. `int fputs(const char *s, FILE *out);`

writes the string s, excluding the null character, to the file out; it returns EOF on error, and a nonnegative value otherwise.

READ A LINE (AT MOST n−1 CHARACTERS) FROM A FILE

```
if(fgets(buffer, n, f) == NULL)
    error
```

These functions can also be used to perform line-oriented I/O from the standard input and output, using stdin and stdout respectively. However, the library stdio.h provides two slightly different variants:

```
char* gets(char *buf);
```

differs from fgets(), when reading from stdin, in two respects:

- reading does not stop after a specified number of characters has been read

- if end-of-line has been encountered, it is *not* stored in buf.

Even when reading from the standard input, programmers often use fgets(), because gets() does not provide an option to limit the number of characters read and may result in overflow with respect to the string buf:

```
fgets(buf, n, stdin)
```

The function

```
int puts(const char *buf);
```

is like `fputs()`, but it writes to `stdout` and always appends `\n` to the string `buf`.

The main drawback of line-oriented input functions is that you must assume the input line has some *maximum length*.

The next example shows a procedure that compares two files, line by line. This procedure takes three parameters, representing respectively two file names and the maximum length of the line. Files that differ beyond this maximum length will be considered identical by the procedure. To compare two lines, I will use a standard library function `strcmp()`, which returns 0 only if two strings are identical (see Section 9.6.3).

Example 9-8

```
#include <string.h>
#include <stdlib.h>
#include <stdio.h>
/*
 * File: ex9-8.c
 * Purpose: compare two text files fname1 and fname2, line by line
 * Inputs: fname1, fname2, max (parameters)
 * Returns: 1 if identical, 0 if error or not identical
 * Modifies: nothing
 * Error checking: considers only first max characters in each line
 * Sample call:
 *     if(compText("a.dat", "b.dat", 80)  == 1)  ...
 */
int comptext(const char *fname1, const char *fname2, const int max) {
   char *line1;    /* two buffers */
   char *line2;
   FILE *f1;       /* two file handles */
   FILE *f2;
   int c;

   /* open both files */
   if((f1 = fopen(fname1, "r")) == NULL)
       return 0;
```

```
    if((f2 = fopen(fname2, "r")) == NULL ) {
        fclose(f1);
        return 0;
    }

    /* allocate memory for buffers */
    if((line1 = calloc(max, sizeof(char))) == NULL) {
        fclose(f1);
        fclose(f2);
        return 0;
    }

    if((line2 = calloc(max, sizeof(char))) == NULL) {
        fclose(f1);
        fclose(f2);
        free(line1);
        return 0;
    }

    /* compare lines */
    for(c = 0; fgets(line1, max, f1) != NULL; c++)
        if(fgets(line2, max, f2) == NULL || strcmp(line1, line2) != 0) {
            fclose(f1);
            fclose(f2);
            free(line1);
            free(line2);
            return 0;
        }

    /* free memory and close both files */
    free(line1);
    free(line2);
    if(fclose(f1) == EOF) {
        fclose(f2);
        return 0;
    }
    if(fclose(f2) == EOF)
        return 0;

    return 1;
}
```

For another example of `fgets()`, see Example 9–12.

9.6 C String Operations

ANSI C provides an extensive set of string operations, which you are encouraged to use instead of writing your own functions, because library function are bug-free and also efficient. All string library functions have names starting with `"str"`; they are listed below. For most functions, there is a companion function whose name starts with `"strn"`, and which provides an additional parameter that limits the number of characters used in the string. Note that these functions do not allocate memory, so it is your responsibility to make sure that there is enough memory allocated for actual parameters.

9.6.1 ◆ Length

To compute the length of a string, use:

```
size_t strlen(const char *string);
```

Note that this function returns a value of an *unsigned* type, and so this value should be used with caution. As I explained in Section 3.9.2, the following test

```
if(strlen(x) - strlen(y) >= 0)
```

will always be true. Therefore, to test if the length of one string is greater than some other string, you should use the comparison:

```
if(strlen(x) >= strlen(y))
```

Similarly,

```
if(strlen(x) - SIZE >= 0)
```

will always be false. To correctly perform this test, you can either replace it in the way shown above, or use a cast:

```
if((int)strlen(x) - SIZE >= 0)
```

9.6.2 ◆ Copying

There are two functions designed to copy a string, and two designed to append one string to the end of another string.

```
char *strcpy(char *dest, const char *src);
```

Copy `src` to `dest` and return `dest`.

```
char *strncpy(char *dest, const char *src, size_t n);
```

Copy n characters of `src` to `dest` and return `dest`. If the length of `str` is less than n, then trailing characters are set to `\0`. Note that as a result, `dest` may not be terminated by the null character.

```
char *strcat(char *dest, const char *src);
```

Append (or "catenate") `src` to `dest` and return `dest`.

```
char *strncat(char *dest, const char *src, size_t n);
```

Append (or "catenate") n characters of `src` to `dest` and return `dest`. If the length of `str` is less than n, then trailing characters are set to `\0`. This function always appends the null character.

The functions are usually called as procedures; for example, as in:

```
strcpy(d, s);
```

In some situations, you may want to use the return value of a string function. Nested calls are one such situation, such as a call to `strcat()`, using a nested `strcat()` call:

```
strcat(strcat(dest, "hi"), " are");
```

`strcpy(dest, src)` and `strcat(dest, src)` assume that there is enough memory allocated for the `dest` to perform the required operation.

`strncpy(dest, src)` does have to append the zero character.

Examples

```
char *dest;
#define SIZE 5
```

```
if((dest = malloc(sizeof(char)*SIZE)) == NULL)
    . . .
strcpy(dest, "Hello");
```

The call to `strcpy()` is wrong, because the string `"Hello"` needs 6 bytes rather than 5. The next call is also incorrect:

```
strcat(dest, "Hi");
```

because `dest` is not an initialized string; in order to use it you must first initialize it:

```
dest[0] = '\0';
```

Now you can make the call to `strcat()`. Following the call, the value of `dest` is the string `"Hi"`. What if you tried to further add to the string using:

```
strcat(dest, " are");
```

This is wrong because the string `"Hi are"` requires 7 bytes.

Example 9–9

Using the functions introduced in this section, I can rewrite the function `strdup()` from Example 9–2.

```
char *strdup(const char *s) {
    char *kopy;     /* copy of s */

    if((kopy = calloc(strlen(s)+1, sizeof(char))) == NULL)
        return NULL;
    strcpy(kopy, s);

    return kopy;
}
```

Now I will present another example of a program that finds the longest line in the input file:

Example 9–10

```c
/*
 * File: ex9-10.c
 * Program that reads number of lines from standard input until an
 *   empty line is encountered and then outputs the longest line.
 * I assume that the longest line cannot be longer than 80 characters.
 */
#include <stdio.h>
#include <stdlib.h>
#include <string.h>
int main() {
   const int Max = 81;
   char *longest;    /* buffer to store the longest line */
   char *current;    /* buffer to store the current line */
   int curLen;       /* length of the current line */
   int lonLen;       /* length of the longest line */

   /* allocate memory */
   if((current = calloc(Max, sizeof(char))) == NULL)
      return EXIT_FAILURE;
   if((longest = calloc(Max, sizeof(char))) == NULL) {
      free(current);
      return EXIT_FAILURE;
   }

   if(fgets(longest, Max-1, stdin) == NULL) /* get first line */
      return EXIT_FAILURE;
   lonLen = strlen(longest);

   /* read remaining lines */
   while(fgets(current, Max-1, stdin) != NULL &&
         (curLen = strlen(current)) > 1)
      if(curLen > lonLen) {
         strcpy(longest, current);
         lonLen = curLen;
      }

   /* output the longest line */
   puts(longest);

   return EXIT_SUCCESS;
}
```

For my next example, I would like to return to the problem of limiting the number of characters read by scanf(); for example :

```
scanf("%7s", s);
```

Assume that you have the following declaration:

```
const int SIZE = 7;
```

In order to use the variable SIZE, instead of the literal value 7 in the call to scanf(), you can convert it to a string and concatenate it with the required control format string. To begin, I will declare a string format and allocate memory for it:

```
char *format;
if((format = calloc(sizeof(int)+3, sizeof(char))) == NULL)
    . . .
```

I want to set this string up so that it will look as shown in Figure 9–5.
Now I can use

```
format[0] = '%';
```

to store the leading %, and a call to sprintf() to append the value of SIZE converted to a string:

```
sprintf(format+1, "%d", SIZE);
```

The SIZE value will be stored at format+1, preventing the % from getting overwritten. Finally, I need to store the trailing 's' character:

```
strcat(format, "s");
```

After all these steps, I can now use format as a parameter to scanf():

```
scanf(format, s);
```

Figure 9–5

Format

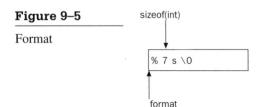

9.6.3 ◆ Comparisons

C provides two functions to compare strings:

```
int strcmp(const char *s1, const char *s2);
```

Performs a lexicographical comparison of s1 and s2; returns a negative value if s1 is less than s2, 0 if the two are equal, and a positive value of s1 is greater than s2.

```
int strncmp(const char *s1, const char *s2, size_t n);
```

As above, but only n characters are compared.

STOP

```
if(strcmp(s1, s2)) ...
```

and

```
if(strcmp(s1, s2) == -1)
```

are both wrong. The first construct is wrong because strcmp() does not return a non-zero value if two strings are equal. The second construct is wrong because strcmp() may return a negative value different from -1.

Example 9-11

This example shows how you can sort strings (I will use an *insertion* sort for this example; see [Aho83]). Strings are read from a file and to facilitate sorting, they are not all stored in a single memory block; instead, the program creates a block of memory that holds *pointers* to the strings. This data structure allows the strings to be sorted by switching the pointer to the string, rather than copying the entire string. The program uses two private variables, respectively, to store a block of strings, and to store the number of lines in the file:

```
static char **block_;
static long lines_;
```

The task of reading strings from a file and storing them in the block of pointers is delegated to the function `input()`. I have two alternatives for dealing with the number of lines in the file:

- assume that the number of lines is not larger than, for example, SIZE = 1000
- compute the number of lines in the file before hand, and use it.

I will use the more flexible second alternative. I am faced with the same two choices when it comes to allocating memory for the length of a line (81); for this example, I will assume a fixed maximum length of each line (and truncate lines bigger than this maximum). See Example 10–3 for an alternative solution.

To count the number of lines, I will use the function `numberOfLines(const char *fname)`, which is similar to the function `lines_fileOps()` introduced in Section 7.4.7.

The code for the function `input()` follows. This function uses a temporary buffer to store a single line, and a variable `current` that stores the length of this line. First, it allocates memory; each element in the block is to hold one pointer to a `char`, and so the block is allocated like this:

```
block_ = calloc(lines_, sizeof(char*));
```

The `for` statement reads lines from the file and stores them in the block; in each step of the loop, a single line is read into the buffer, the end-of-line character is overwritten, and the line is copied from the buffer to the memory allocated in the block. Skipping the error checking, the code for this part looks like this:

```
for(n = 0; n < lines_ && fgets(buffer, LENGTH, f) != NULL; n++) {
    current = strlen(buffer);
    buffer[current-1] = '\0';
    if((block_ñ = calloc(current, sizeof(char))) == NULL) {
        ...
        return 0;
    }
    strcpy(block_ñ, buffer);
}
```

The code for the insertion sort follows (the complete code may be found in file `ex9-11.c`):

```
void insertionSort() {
    int i, j;
    char *aux;

    for (i = 1; i < lines_; i++)
        for (j = i; j > 0 && strcmp(block_[j], block_[j-1]) < 0; j--) {
```

```
        aux = block_[j];
        block_[j] = block_[j-1];
        block_[j-1] = aux;
    }
}
```

1. To compare two strings `str1` and `str2`, do not use

   ```
   str1 < str2
   ```

   which only compares their memory addresses. Instead use

   ```
   strcmp(str1, str2);
   ```

2. To copy a string `str1` to another string `str2`, do not use

   ```
   str1 = str2
   ```

   which only copies the memory address; instead use

   ```
   strcpy(str1, str2);
   ```

9.6.4 ◆ Search

In this section, I will describe various ways of finding characters or substrings in an input string, beginning with a description of two functions that look for an occurrence of a character in a string:

```
char *strchr(const char *str, int c);
```

Search `str` for the *first* occurrence of `c` and return a pointer to this occurrence; return NULL if not found. This function *should* probably be called `strpos()`.

```
char *strrchr(const char *str, int c);
```

As above, except `strrchr()` looks for the last occurrence of `c`.
The third function works with substrings:

```
char *strstr(const char *str, const char *substr);
```

Returns a pointer to the first occurrence of a substring `substr` in the string `str`, `NULL` if not found.
The next example shows applications of some of these functions.

Example 9–12

An *absolute* pathname starts with "/", e.g.

```
/docs/C/archive.old/ex1.c
```

I will show how you can write a function:

```
int pathname(const char *path, char **fileName, char **dirName);
```

which is designed to retrieve the filename (for example, `ex1.c` from the pathname `/docs/C/ archive.old/ex1.c`) *and* a directory containing this file (`archive.old` for my example).

The second and the third parameter of `pathname()` return the required information, and so they are passed by reference. The function `pathname()` takes care of *allocating memory* required for the actual parameters corresponding to the second and the third formal parameter; the caller is responsible for deallocating this memory. For example

```
char *fileName;
char *dirName;

if(pathname("/c/archive.old/ex1.c", &fileName, &dirName) == 0)
    error
/* now fileName points to "ex1.c"
 * dirName points to "archive.old"
 */
free(fileName);
free(dirName);
```

Note that an alternative design would be to make the *caller* responsible for allocating memory for the return values (`fileName` and `dirName`). The problem is that there is no easy way to determine the exact amount of memory required.

To implement this function, it is useful to consider two cases:

case 1) the pathname is of the form

```
/ex1.c
```

where the filename is `ex1.c` and the directory is "/" (root)

case 2) the pathname is of the form

```
/docs/C/archive.old/ex1.c
```

where, as already shown, the filename is `ex1.c` and the directory is `archive.old`

I will refer to these two cases throughout the description of this example.

The function `pathname()` returns 1 if the path is in one of the above forms, (i.e. if the first character in the path is "/", and the last character is not "/", and the entire path does not consist of a single "/"); `pathname()` returns 0 otherwise. All of the required names will be returned through the parameters. Since the implementation of this function is rather complicated, I will now explain some of its details. First, I need to declare a number of auxiliary variables.

```
char *fileP;      /* will point to / just before filename */
char *dirP;       /* will point to / just before directory name */
int fileLength;   /* length of the string filename */
int dirLength;    /* length of the string directory name */
int pathLength = strlen(path);   /* length of the entire path */
```

The meaning of these variables is explained in Figure 9–6.

The constant SEP (for "separator") is declared for readability:

```
const int SEP = '/';
```

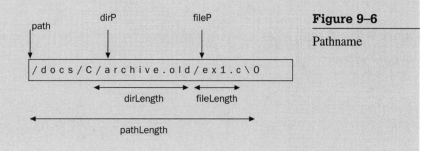

Figure 9–6

Pathname

The code starts with some error checking to ensure that the string starts with "/" and does not consist of a single "/":

```
if(path[0] != SEP)
   return 0;
if(pathLength == 1)
   return 0;
```

`fileP` is now ready to be initialized to the last occurrence of `'/'`:

```
fileP = strrchr(path, SEP);
```

The code performs one more error check to ensure that the path does not end with "/":

```
if(fileP - path == pathLength - 1)
   return 0;
```

To understand the last `if` condition, you have to see that if the pathname string ended with "/", then after its initialization, `fileP` would point to the last character in this string, and the distance between `fileP` and `path` would be equal to the length of the path minus one.

After this error checking, I know that the path is correct and can now initialize the value of `dirP` to point to the *first* occurrence of "/":

```
dirP = strchr(path, SEP);
```

If `fileP` is equal to `dirP`, then we have case 1, and we must allocate memory and copy names (see Figure 9–7) :

```
if(dirP == fileP) {   /* single "/" */
   dirLength = 1;
   fileLength = pathLength -1;

   if((*fileName = calloc(fileLength+1,sizeof(char))) == NULL)
      return 0;
```

Figure 9–7

Pathname with a
single /

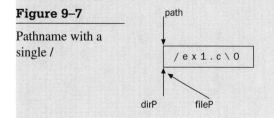

```
   if((*dirName = calloc(dirLength+1, sizeof(char))) == NULL){
      free(*fileName);
      return 0;
   }
   /* copy filename */
   strcpy(*fileName, fileP+1);
   strcpy(*dirName, "/");

   return 1;
}
```

For case 2, I will traverse the path with two pointers: auxP and dirP. auxP will always point to the occurrence of "/" immediately following the one pointed to by dirP. The traversal will stop when auxP reaches fileP, because then dirP (a "predecessor" of auxP) points to the beginning of the directory string :

```
while(1) {
   auxP = strchr(dirP+1, SEP);
   if(auxP == fileP)
      break;
   dirP = auxP;
}
```

I will now discuss how filename and directory name are copied to memory allocated for the pointers *fileName and *dirName. It is easy to copy the filename because it occurs in the suffix of a string:

```
fileLength = strlen(fileP + 1);
dirLength = fileP - dirP - 1;
if((*fileName = calloc(fileLength+1, sizeof(char))) == NULL)
   return 0;
if((*dirName = calloc(dirLength+1, sizeof(char))) == NULL) {
   free(*fileName);
   return 0;
}
/* copy filename */
strcpy(*fileName, fileP + 1);
```

strcpy() can not be used to copy the directory part because it occurs in the middle of the string. I will use the memcpy() function instead, and then append '\0':

```
memcpy(*dirName, dirP + 1, dirLength);
(*dirName)[dirLength] = '\0';
```

The code of `pathname()` follows (the complete code may be found in file `ex9-12.c`):

```c
int pathname(const char *path, char **fileName, char **dirName) {
   const int SEP = '/';
   char *fileP;        /* will point to / just before filename */
   char *dirP;         /* will point to / just before directory name */
   int fileLength;     /* length of the string filename */
   int dirLength;      /* length of the string directory name */
   int pathLength=strlen(path);    /* length of the entire path */
   char *auxP;

   if(path[0] != SEP)  /* doesn't start with '/' */
      return 0;
   if(pathLength == 1) /* the path consists of a single '/' */
      return 0;

   fileP = strrchr(path, SEP);  /* last occurrence of '/' */
   if(fileP - path == pathLength - 1)  /* the path ends with '/' */
      return 0;

   dirP = strchr(path, SEP);  /* first occurrence */

   if(dirP == fileP) {         /* case 1: single "/" */
      dirLength = 1;
      fileLength = pathLength -1;

      /* allocate memory for parameters */
      if((*fileName = calloc(fileLength+1, sizeof(char))) == NULL)
         return 0;
      if((*dirName = calloc(dirLength+1, sizeof(char))) == NULL){
         free(*fileName);
         return 0;
      }
      /* copy filename and dirname */
      strcpy(*fileName, fileP+1);
      strcpy(*dirName, "/");
      return 1;
   }

   /* case 2: pathname with more than one '/' */
   if(strchr(dirP+1, SEP) != fileP)
      while(1) { /* look for the last '/' and the previous one */
         auxP = strchr(dirP+1, SEP);
         if(auxP == fileP)
```

```
            break;
        dirP = auxP;
    }

    /* now, fileP points to last '/' and dirP to the previous */
    fileLength = strlen(fileP + 1);
    dirLength = fileP - dirP - 1;
    /* allocate memory for parameters */
    if((*fileName = calloc(fileLength+1, sizeof(char))) == NULL)
        return 0;
    if((*dirName = calloc(dirLength+1, sizeof(char))) == NULL){
        free(*fileName);
        return 0;
    }
    /* copy filename and directory */
    strcpy(*fileName, fileP + 1);
    memcpy(*dirName, dirP + 1, dirLength);
    (*dirName)[dirLength] = '\0';

    return 1;
}
```

This example was rather difficult to code, but as I will show later, it can be implemented in a simpler way. In any case, it is another good exercise in understanding pointers.

The remaining string library searching functions looks for an occurrence of a character from a set of characters, rather than a single character. The set of characters is passed as a string parameter:

```
size_t strspn(const char *str, const char *set);
```

Search `str` for the first occurrence of any character that does *not* appear in `set`. Return the length of the longest prefix of `str` that has been skipped (or *spanned*).

For example:

`strspn("Java after", "ev")` returns 2.

Two more searching functions are similar to those described above:

```
size_t strcspn(const char *str, const char *set);
```

As above, except searches for characters that do appear in set.

```
char *strpbrk(const char *str, const char *set);
```

As `strcspn()`, except it returns a pointer to the first character.

Example 9–13

In various applications, it is useful to strip an input string of all trailing and leading whitespace characters. The next example shows a more general version of such a function, one that strips all leading and trailing characters from a string, rather than just whitespace.

The function `strip()` has the following prototype:

```
char *strip(const char *s, const char *set);
```

It returns a *copy* of the string s, with trailing and leading characters from the string set removed. It is important to remember that again, it is the caller's responsibility to deallocate memory that has been allocated for the return value. For example:

```
char *str;
str = strip("    hello how    ", " ");
/* Now str points to "hello how" */
free(str);
```

The implementation of `strip()` starts with declaring some local variables:

```
int start = strspn(s, set);   /* number of leading characters */
int length = strlen(s);       /* length of s */
int end;                      /* number of trailing characters */
char *kopy;                   /* copy of s */
```

The function must first check if there are any leading or trailing characters in the string set. If `start` is equal to the length of s, I just have to copy the entire string and return it:

```
if(length == start) {
    if((kopy = calloc(length + 1, sizeof(char))) == NULL)
        return NULL;
    strcpy(kopy, s);
} else { ...
```

At this point, I am faced with the task of finding the trailing characters. To find these, I traverse the string s backwards, and at each step, I examine a single character at the end of the string s:

```
for(end = length; end > 1; end--)
    if(strchr(set, s[end]) == NULL)
        break;
```

The traversal stops when I reach the beginning of the string, or when the examined character is *not* in the string set. (The latter condition means that I have reached the first trailing character that is not in the string set.) Now I calculate how many characters should be copied, use memcpy() to perform the copying, and finally, I enter the terminating '\0' into the new string:

```
length = end - start + 1; /* what is left after strip */
if((kopy = calloc(length + 1, sizeof(char))) == NULL)
    return NULL;

memcpy(kopy, s+start, length);
kopy[length] = '\0';
```

The complete code follows.

```
char *strip(const char *s, const char *set) {
    int start = strspn(s, set);    /* number of leading characters */
    int end;                       /* number of trailing characters */
    char *kopy;
    int length = strlen(s);

    if(length != start)  { /* there are characters not in s */

        for(end = length; end > 1; end--)  /* find trailing */
            if(strchr(set, s[end]) == NULL)
                break;

        length = end - start + 1;
        /* what is left after strip */
        if((kopy = calloc(length + 1, sizeof(char))) == NULL)
            return NULL;

        memcpy(kopy, s+start, length);
        kopy[length] = '\0';

    } else {
```

```
      if((kopy = calloc(length + 1, sizeof(char))) == NULL)
         return NULL;


      strcpy(kopy, s);
   }
   return kopy;
}
```

9.6.5 ◆ Processing Tokens

Example 9–12 showed how to process tokens (a token is a single word). For example, in a pathname

```
/docs/archive.old/ex1.c
```

there are three tokens: docs, archive.old, and ex1.c separated by "/". Token processing can be performed using the following library function:

```
char *strtok(char *str, const char *sep);
```

strtok() separates str into tokens, using characters from sep as separators. The first parameter str may be NULL (but not in the first call). The *first* call to strtok() takes the non-null first parameter and returns a pointer to the first token (skipping over all separators). This call also sets the function's local static internal pointer to the first character of this token. All *subsequent* calls to strtok() take NULL as the first parameter. Each call uses the internal pointer to find and return a pointer to the next token.

If the first call to strtok() does not find any characters in the sep string, the internal pointer is set to NULL and the function returns NULL. There is one more case to consider: if the first parameter str passed to strtok() is NULL, but the internal pointer is not NULL, strtok() will resume search at the internal pointer.

There is one unpleasant property of strtok() that I need to mention, which is that it modifies the string being tokenized. Specifically, it marks the end of the token that has been found by storing the null character. Consequently, if you with to preserve this string, you have to make a copy of it before you call strtok().

The above description looks rather complicated. To help clarify the functionality of strtok(), I will show a simple application; Section 9.7 will show a more general way to tokenize a string based on a similar Java utility.

Example 9–14

The application will re-implement the `pathname()` function from Example 9–12, using `strtok()`:

```
int pathname(const char *path, char **fileName, char **dirName)
```

The implementation performs the same error checking as that in Example 9–12, and then makes a local copy of the path:

```
char *pathCopy;
int pathLength = strlen(path);

if((pathCopy = malloc((pathLength+1)*sizeof(char))) == NULL)
    return 0;
strcpy(pathCopy, path);
```

This local copy will be freed before the function terminates, but in the meantime the function will use it in conjunction with `strtok()`, which avoids modifying the path parameter.

The next step involves breaking the path into tokens, which I accomplish using two pointers: `first` and `second`, where `second` will always point to the token that *follows* the token pointed to by `first`.

```
char *first;
char *second;
char *aux;
char *SEP = "/";
first = NULL;
aux = second = strtok(pathCopy, white);
while(aux != NULL) {
    first = second;
    second = aux;
    aux = strtok(NULL, white);
}
```

The remaining part of the code is similar to that in Example 9–12; the complete implementation is given below.

```
int pathname(const char *path, char **fileName, char **dirName) {
    char *first;
    char *second;
    char *aux;
    char *pathCopy;
    char *white = "/";
    int pathLength = strlen(path); /* length of the entire path */
```

```
    if(path[0] != '/')  /* doesn't start with '/' */
        return 0;
    if(pathLength == 1) /* the path consists of a single '/' */
        return 0;
    if(path[pathLength - 1] == '/')  /* the path ends with '/' */
        return 0;

    /* make a local copy */
    if((pathCopy = malloc((pathLength+1)*sizeof(char)))== NULL)
        return 0;
    strcpy(pathCopy, path);

#define RETURN(i)   {free(pathCopy); return(i); }

    first = NULL;
    aux = second = strtok(pathCopy, white);
    while(aux != NULL) {
        first = second;
        second = aux;
        aux = strtok(NULL, white);
    }

    if(strcmp(first, second) == 0) {   /* single "/" */
        if((*fileName = calloc(strlen(second) + 1, sizeof(char)) == NULL)
            RETURN(0);
        if((*dirName = calloc(2, sizeof(char)) == NULL) {
            free(fileName);
            RETURN(0);
        }

        strcpy(*fileName, second);
        strcpy(*dirName, "/");
        RETURN(1);
    }

    if((*fileName = calloc(strlen(second) + 1, sizeof(char)) == NULL)
        RETURN(0);
    if((*dirName = calloc(strlen(first) + 1, sizeof(char)) == NULL) {
        free(fileName);
        RETURN(0);
    }

    /* copy filename and directory */
    strcpy(*fileName, second);
```

```
    strcpy(*dirName, first);

    RETURN(1);
}
```

9.6.6 ◆ String-to-Number Conversions

Functions described in this section are declared in `stdlib.h`, rather than `string.h`. They are similar to `sscanf()`, but offer more flexibility.

The first three functions convert a string passed as the parameter *to* a number. They have a standard prefix `"str"` followed by `"to"`, followed respectively by `"d"` for doubles, `"l"` for long, and `"ul"` for unsigned long. Each function returns the converted numerical value if successful; otherwise it returns 0. The second parameter `p` is a pointer to pointer to `char`, and is used to return the information as to whether the function was successful. Specifically, if a conversion failed, then `*p` is set to the value of the original string `s`. Otherwise, it is set to point to the first character in the string `s` immediately following the converted part of this string. In addition, in case of an error, the global error variable `errno` (see Section 9.7) is set to `ERANGE`.

```
    double strtod(const char *s, char **p);
    long strtol(const char *s, char **p, int base);
    unsigned long strtoul(const char *s, char **p, int base);
```

The value of `base` determines the base used for the conversion. A default base, signified by 0, is decimal, hexadecimal, or octal, and it is derived from the string. Otherwise, the value of `base` may be any number between 2 (binary) to 36. For bases greater than 10, the string `s` may contain letters A-Z that represent values 10–36. The leading whitespace in the first parameter is skipped.

Example 9–15 in the next section will demonstrate the use of these functions.

The next three functions are defined in ANSI C only to offer compatibility with the older versions of C, and they provide the same power as the above three functions:

```
    double atof(const char *s);
    int atoi(const char *s);
    long atol(const char *s);
```

9.7 Standard Error Handling

Standard library routines use a predefined variable `errno` to indicate errors. Various positive values of `errno` represent implementation-dependent error codes stored in the header file `errno.h`. Library routines should never clear this variable.

Two functions are used in conjunction with `errno`:

- the function `strerror()` found in the standard library `string.h` provides the string representation of an error code:

```
char *strerror(int errnum)
```

- the function `perror()` found in the standard library `stdio.h` prints error messages related to the current value of `errno`:

```
void perror(const char *s)
```

How do you use these facilities? The following technique:

```
errno = 0;
call f()
if(errno)
    error
```

may *not* work. I will use an example provided in [Koe88] to explain why this may be so. Take `fopen()` as a function `f()` above, and assume that `fopen()` does not clear `errno`; it calls another library function that sets this variable if the file does not exist. In this case, `fopen()` may succeed, but still set `errno`! Since all library functions return values that indicate whether or not they were successful, the *correct* technique is:

```
if((ret = f()) == errorCode) /* failed */ {
    examine error, for example
    printf("%s", strerror(errno));
}
```

It should now be evident that `errno` should only be used if you wish to determine the exact source of an error; in other situations, the return value of a function should be checked for possible error.

9.8 Module for String Tokenizing

Files often store data records using a delimited format; each record is stored on a separate line, and fields are separated by delimiters. For example, an appropriate format to store information about employees may look like this:

```
name|salary|id
```

For this example, I will assume that the first field is a string, the second is a double, and the third is a long integer. In addition, I will also assume that each line may have at most 80 characters. Here is a sample set of employees:

```
Mary Smith|2000|185594
John Kowalski|1000|2449488
```

In order to read this data, you need to read one line at a time, extracting the fields from each line.

In this section, I will show a general module designed to tokenize strings, and I will then use this module to perform the task of reading the employee data.

Example 9–15

The module in this example is used to tokenize strings. The interface consists of the following functions:

```
int construct_Token(const char *str, const char *delimiters);
int destruct_Token(void);
int hasMore_Token();
char *next_Token();
int count_Token();
int reset_Token();
```

The user first constructs a "tokenization". A tokenization separates a string into tokens, which may then be extracted using the provided `next_Token()` function. Other functions that operate on the tokenized string are also provided (such as `count_Token()`, used to return the number of remaining tokens contained in an input string). Finally, the user calls a destructor function `destruct_Token()`. The complete code for the interface is in file `ex9-token.h`.

I will now describe the application that reads a file in the format described above. This program assumes that the file `ex9-15.dat` contains data in such a format, for example:

```
Mary Smith|2000|145784875
```

The first field is a string, the second field is a double value, and the third field is a long value. The application program reads the file one line at a time, overwrites the end-of-line character, and then tokenizes the line using the functions provided in `token.h`:

```
const char *delim = "|";
while(fgets(line, SIZE, in) != NULL) {
```

```
    line[strlen(line)-1]= '\0';
    construct_Token(line, delim);
    . . .
}
```

The next step involves extracting the tokens from the tokenized line:

```
char *nameS;
char *salaryS;
char *idS;

if(hasMore_Token())
    nameS = next_Token();
else {
    /* error */
}
if(hasMore_Token())
    salaryS = next_Token();
else {
    /* error */
}
if(hasMore_Token())
    idS = next_Token();
else {
    /* error */
}
```

Finally, the validity of the second and the third tokens is confirmed and these tokens are converted to their values, using functions described in Section 9.6.6:

```
salary = strtod(salaryS, &err);
if(err == salaryS) {
    /* error */
}
id = strtol(idS, &err, 10);
if(err == idS) {
    /* error */
}
```

After the values are printed, the tokenization is destructed:

```
printf("Name: %s, salary %f, id: %ld\n", nameS, salary, id);
destruct_Token();
```

The complete code of the application may be found in file `ex9-15-token-main.c`.

I am finally ready to discuss the *implementation* of the module. The constructor tokenizes the entire string and stores it in a block of pointers to tokens. It is this block of pointers that is used to extract tokens from the string. The module maintains several private variables:

```
static char **block_;           /* stores pointers to tokens */
static int tokenNumber_;         /* total number of tokens */
static int current_;      /* current token number (in enumeration) */
static int initialized_ = 0;   /* was constructor called */
```

The constructor:

```
int construct_Token(const char *str, const char *delimiters);
```

first makes a local copy of the input string argument, which is stored in `copyStr`, and then it tokenizes this string (i.e. divides it into tokens). In order to allocate a block of pointers, it must first count the number of tokens in the input string, and then allocate the memory:

```
for(tokenNumber_ = 0, token = strtok(copyStr, delimiters);
            token != NULL; token = strtok(NULL, delimiters))
   tokenNumber_++;

if((block_ = calloc(sizeof(char*), tokenNumber_)) == NULL) {
   free(copyStr);
   return 0;
}
```

I now need to tokenize the string for the second time, in order to set the pointers in the newly allocated block to the tokens. However, before I can do that, I have to refresh the local copy of the string `str`, because it was modified earlier as a result of tokenizing (recall that `strtok()` modifies the input string):

```
strcpy(copyStr, str);
for(i = 0, token = strtok(copyStr, delimiters);
        token != NULL; i++, token = strtok(NULL, delimiters))
   block_[i] = strdup(token);
```

The destructor function `destruct_Token()` deallocates memory used by the module:

```
int destruct_Token(void) {
   int i;
```

```
    if(!initialized_)
        return 0;

    for(i=0; i < tokenNumber_; i++)
        free(block_[i]);
    initialized_ = 0;
    free(block_);

    return 1;

}
```

The implementation of the remaining functions is simple. For example, next_Token() performs some error checking and returns a pointer to the next token (since the pointers are stored in the block, all the function has to do is return the current pointer):

```
char *next_Token() {
    if(!initialized_ || current_ == tokenNumber_)
        return 0;

    return block_[current_++];
}
```

The complete implementation may be found in file ex9-token.c.

9.9 Main Function's Arguments

As in Java, the function main() has a specific format used for its parameters: they are represented as a block of strings (i.e. pointers to characters):

```
int main(int argc, char **argv);
```

argc is the size of the block (i.e. the number of strings), and argv points to this block (note that you can call these parameters anything you want, but most C programmers use argc and argv). The above declaration is equivalent to

```
int main(int argc, char *argv[]);
```

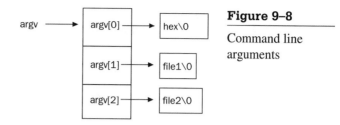

Figure 9–8

Command line arguments

because, as I will explain in Section 10.2.1, an array parameter is the same as a pointer parameter. If a program, for example `hex`, is executed using two arguments:

```
hex file1 file2
```

then `argc` is equal to 3, and `argv` points to the block shown in Figure 9–8

Recall from Section 9.9 that in order to access the first string, you use `argv[0]`, to access the second string, you use `argv[1]`, etc. Similarly, to refer to the first character of the first string, you use `argv[0][0]`.

Example 9–16

The following code may be used to display the number of arguments passed to a program from the command line, along with each argument:

```
int i;

printf("This program has %d arguments\n", argc);
for (i = 0; i < argc; i++)
    printf("%s\n", argv[i]);
```

In many cases, it is useful to have optional arguments to the main program. For example, a program may have a debug flag, which is only activated if the program is executed with a `-d` option.

As another example, consider a program `compare`, which has two mandatory arguments: the two files to be compared. By default, the program compares the two files line by line using a `compareLines()` function, and shows the first line that differs in both files. This version may executed using:

```
compare f1 f2
```

where `f1` and `f2` are the two files to be compared.

The program also provides a `-b` option:

```
compare -b f1 f2
```

which when included, compares the files character by character using a `compareChar()` function and shows the first character where the files differ.

The skeleton of the main function looks like this:

```
int main(int argc, char **argv) {
    char *c;
    int i;

    switch(argc) {
    case 3:
        if((c = compareLine(argv[1], argv[2])) != NULL)
            printf("%s and %s differ at %s\n",
                argv[1], argv[2], c);
        break;

    case 4:
        if(strcmp(argv[1], "-b") != 0) {
            fprintf(stderr, "usage: %s \[-b\] file1 file2\n",
                argv[0]);
            return EXIT_FAILURE;
        }
        if((i = compareChar(argv[2], argv[3])) != 0)
            printf("%s and %s differ at %d\n", argv[1],
                argv[2], i);
        break;

    default:
        fprintf(stderr, "usage: %s \[-b\] file1 file2\n",
            argv[0]);
        return EXIT_FAILURE;
    }
}
```

Note that the program checks the actual *number* of arguments, and decides which version (compare by lines or characters) to use based on that.

COMMAND LINE

```c
int main(int argc, char **argv) {
...
   switch(argc) {
   case ...

   default: fprintf(stderr, "usage: %s ... \n", argv[0]);
           return EXIT_FAILURE;
}
```

This idiom only checks the number of required arguments; it does not check their types or values.

Often you need to pass numerical values on the command line, for example, to a program, which displays up to the first n lines from a file:

```
show -n fname
```

This program can be invoked without the first argument (-n), and in this case it displays up to the first 10 lines (if the file contains fewer than 10 lines, it shows all of them).

Example 9–17

```c
/*
 * File: ex9-17.c
 * Program that displays up to n lines from a file
 */
#include <stdio.h>
#include <stdlib.h>
/*
 * Function: display
 * Purpose: display up to n lines from a file
 *    Lines are truncated to Max characters
 * Inputs: filename, n and Max (parameters)
```

```
 * Returns: 1 if successful, 0 otherwise
 * Modifies: nothing
 * Error checking: fails if the file can not be open
 * Sample call:
 *    if(display("ex9-17.c", 20) == 0)
 *       error
 */
int display(const char *fname, int n, int Max);

#define DEFAULT 10
#define MAX     80

int main(int argc, char **argv) {
    int lines = DEFAULT;

    switch(argc) {
    case 3:
            /* retrieve the number of lines argument */
            if(sscanf(argv[1] + 1, "%d", &lines) != 1 || lines <= 0) {
                fprintf(stderr, "incorrect argument %s\n", argv[1] + 1);
                return EXIT_FAILURE;
            }
            argv++;
            /* no break: retrieve filename */

    case 2:
            if(display(argv[1], lines, MAX) == 0) {
                fprintf(stderr, "incorrect argument %s\n", argv[1]);
                return EXIT_FAILURE;
            }
            break;

    default:
            fprintf(stderr, "usage: %s [-b] file\n", argv[0]);
            return EXIT_FAILURE;
    }

    return EXIT_SUCCESS;
}

int display(const char *fname, int n, int Max) {
    FILE *in;
    char *line;
    int i;
```

```
    if((in = fopen(fname, "r")) == NULL)
        return 0;
    if((line = calloc(Max + 1, sizeof(char))) == NULL) {
        fclose(in);
        return 1;
    }


    /* get n lines */
    for(i = 0; i < n; i++) {
        if(fgets(line, Max, in) == NULL)
            break;
        printf("%s", line);
    }

    free(line);
    if(fclose(in) == EOF)
        return 0;
    return 1;


}
```

I will elaborate on a piece of code from the presented example:

```
switch(argc) {
    case 3:
            /* retrieve the number of lines argument */
            if(sscanf(argv[1] + 1, "%d", &lines) != 1 || lines <= 0) {
                fprintf(stderr, "incorrect argument %s\n", argv[1] + 1);
                return EXIT_FAILURE;
            }
            argv++;
            /* no break: retrieve filename */

    case 2:
            if(display(argv[1], lines, MAX) == 0) {
                fprintf(stderr, "incorrect argument %s\n", argv[1]);
                return EXIT_FAILURE;
            }
            break;

    default:
            fprintf(stderr, "usage: %s [-b] file\n", argv[0]);
            return EXIT_FAILURE;
    }
```

If there are three arguments provided on the command line, as in

```
show -10 fname
```

then the integer value is retrieved from the first argument. This value is stored in a string pointed to by `argv[1]+1`, because `argv[1]` points to '-'. If a conversion of this string to an integer is successful, the switch statement does not invoke a break; instead it increments `argv`, and continues to the next case.

Finally, note that redirection operators > and < are not a part of the command line, for example,

```
program one two < f1 > f2
```

has two command line arguments, rather than six.

Redirection is not a part of the command line of a program.

9.10 List of Common Errors

1. If a string is not terminated by the null character, or this character is overwritten, all string operations produce undefined results.

2. When you allocate memory for a string that can have n characters, do not use

```
calloc(length of string, sizeof(char))
```

because you have to allocate memory for the \0 character.

3. Do not use

```
calloc(sizeof(string), sizeof(char))
```

because that call allocates a block of memory to store the number of characters determined by the size of a pointer to character, rather then the required length.

4. Initialized pointers are not necessarily initialized strings. (If an initialized pointer points to a memory block that does not contain the null character, the string is not initialized).

5. Double and single quotes that enclose a single character signify different things; for example `"W"` denotes a pointer to a memory block containing two characters, `W` followed by `\0`; `'W'` denotes the ordinal value of the character `W`.

6. To input a string:

   a) use

   ```
   scanf("%s", s)
   ```

   rather then

   ```
   scanf("%s", &s)
   ```

   b) make sure that `s` is initialized; i.e. there is *some* memory allocated for `s` (for example, using `calloc()`)

   c) make sure that there is *enough* memory allocated for `s`, and consider using the field width to avoid overflow.

7. `strcpy(dest, src)` and `strcat(dest, src)` assume that there is enough memory allocated for the `dest` to perform the required operation.

   `strncpy(dest, src)` does have to append the zero character.

8. `if(strcmp(s1, s2)) ...`

   and

   `if(strcmp(s1, s2)) == -1)`

   are both wrong.

9. To compare two strings `str1` and `str2`, do not use

   ```
   str1 < str2
   ```

   which only compares their memory addresses. Instead use

   ```
   strcmp(str1, str2);
   ```

10. To copy a string `str1` to another string `str2`, do not use

    ```
    str1 = str2
    ```

    which only copies the memory address; instead use

    ```
    strcpy(str1, str2);
    ```

11. Redirection is not a part of the command line of a program.

9.11 List of Idioms

MEMORY ALLOCATION FOR A STRING OF n CHARACTERS

```
if((s = calloc(n+1, sizeof(char)) == NULL) ...
```

iTH CHARACTER OF A STRING

To refer to the iTH character in the string s, use s[i], where $0 <= i <$ length of s.

STRING SUFFIX

If s points to a string, then s+n points to the suffix of this string starting at the n-th position (here, n has to be less than the length of s).

TRAVERSING A STRING

```
for(p = s; *p; p++)
    use *p
```

READ A SINGLE WORD (AT MOST 9 CHARACTERS)

```
if(scanf("%10s", s) != 1)
    error
```

READ A LINE (AT MOST n-1 CHARACTERS) FROM A FILE

```
if(fgets(buffer, n, f) == NULL)
    error
```

COMMAND LINE

```
int main(int argc, char **argv) {
...
    switch(argc) {
    case ...
```

```
    default: fprintf(stderr, "usage: %s ... \n", argv[0]);
            return EXIT_FAILURE;
    }
```

This idiom only checks the number of required arguments; it does not check their types or values.

9.12 Exercises

All functions should be well documented. For any exxercise that asks you to implement a function, include a main program that carefully tests this function.

Exercise 9-1

Implement an int function charInString() that takes three parameters, a string s, an integer position pos, and an integer value. This function returns 1 if pos is a valid position in the string s, and returns 0 otherwise. If successful, charInString() returns the character at position pos in the string s, through the parameter value. Use the "ith Character of a String" idiom.

Exercise 9-2

Implement a function:

```
int strcmpIgnoreCase(const char *s1, const char *s2);
```

that returns 1 if s1 and s2 differ only in the case of letters, e.g. "abC" and "Abc" are equal in this sense, and 0 otherwise. Use the "Traversing a String" idiom.

Exercise 9-3

Write a void function lowerToUpper() which takes one parameter s representing a zero-terminated string. lowerToUpper() modifies s by replacing every occurrence of a lowercase letter by the corresponding uppercase letter. Use the "Traversing a String" idiom.

Exercise 9-4

Write a procedure

```
void printsubstr(const char s[], int i, int n);
```

that prints n characters of string s, starting with the character s[i]. Use the "String Suffix" idiom.

Exercise 9-5

Write a function

```
void fill(char *p, int n, char pat);
```

to initialize n bytes of memory with the value pat, starting at address p.

Exercise 9-6

Implement the function:

```
strcat(const char* s1, char* s2);
```

Exercise 9-7

Implement the following function:

```
int split(const char* inName, const char* outName1,
          const char* outName2);
/* Read characters from the file inName and output:
 *    all lowercase letters to the file outName1
 *    all uppercase letters to the file outName2
 *    all other characters to the standard output stream.
 * Return 0 if any errors occur
 */
```

Exercise 9-8

Write a program longest so that

```
longest f1 f2 ... fn
```

reads each of the n files named f1, f2, ..., fn in sequence, and writes the length of the longest file to stdout. Use the "Command Line" idiom.

Exercise 9-9

Write a void function sstr() that has the string parameter s and overwrites it with the value "Hello". The function returns the new string through its parameter. Note that sstr() may have to allocate memory. Use the "Memory allocation for a String of n characters" idiom.

Exercise 9-10

Part 1. Write a void function replace() that has the one parameter str representing a zero-terminated string. replace() modifies str by replacing every occurrence of a lowercase letter by the corresponding uppercase letter.

Part 2. In this part, don't use any predefined string function.

Write a function `kill()` that has a single parameter s that represents a string. `kill()` deallocates the string s, sets s to `NULL`, and returns the initial pre-killed length of s.

Exercise 9–11

Write a program that can be executed either with a filename argument, for example,

```
trans x y file.txt
```

or as a filter, for example,

```
trans x y < file.txt
```

In both cases, the program must write to the standard output a copy of `file.txt` in which all occurrences of the character x are replaced by the character y. For example, to convert all 'A' characters in the file `letter.msg` to lowercase (i.e. to 'a'), use

```
trans A a letter.msg
```

or

```
trans A a < letter.msg
```

Check whether the first two arguments (x and y above) are single characters. For example, the execution

```
trans abba baba f1.txt
```

should produce an error message.

Exercise 9–12

Write a program that takes command line arguments. There are two possible number of arguments:

```
program file1 -d
```

or

```
program file1
```

In the first case, this program will display on the standard output the first d lines from the file `file1`. In the second case, it will display up to the first 20 lines from this file. If anything goes wrong (for example, the file `file1` does not exist, or d is not an integer value), an error message should be displayed.

Exercise 9-13

Write a program called `tester`, which prints the sum of all arguments in the command line that are valid integer values. If at least one argument is not an integer value, then `tester` prints 0. For example:

```
tester 1 2       prints 3
tester 1 a2      prints 0
```

Exercise 9-14

Write a program that takes a command line argument representing a number in Roman notation (for example, MXLIV) and outputs this number in standard notation. Consider only values less than 1000.

Exercise 9-15

Write a program that takes any number of filenames on the command line, and displays the contents of all these files on the standard output stream.

Exercise 9-16

Write a program takes any number of filenames followed by an optional -n, where n is an integer, on the command line. This program displays the name of the first file, followed by up to n lines from this file, on the standard output stream, then waits for the user to hit the Enter key, and continues displaying lines from this file (each time up to n lines at a time).The program processes each provided file in this manner. If the value of n is not provided, then the default value of 20 is used. If no files names are specified on the command line, the program reads from the standard input. Your program should handle lines of an unlimited length.

Exercise 9-17

Test Exercise 8–11 with strings. If the implementation of the module from this exercise requires any modifications, rewrite this module.

Exercise 9-18

Test Exercise 8–12 with strings and pointers to strings. If the implementation of the module from this exercise requires any modifications, rewrite this module.

Exercise 9-19

Test Exercise 8–11 with strings and pointers to strings. If the implementation of the module from this exercise requires any modifications, rewrite this module.

Exercise 9-20

Use the tokenizing module from Section 9.8 to implement a menu-driven program that supports the following operations:

```
addInt i1 i2       to display the sum of integer values
addDouble d1 d2    to display the sum of double values
exp n              to display 2 to power n
```

Exercise 9-21

Use the tokenizing module from Section 9.8 to read a single line from the standard input stream and then gather the following statistics:

- number of words of size 1, 2, etc.
- number of vowels
- number of consonants.

Exercise 9-22

Modify the implementation of the module to tokenize strings, from Example 9–15, so that as a result of the constructor call, the module does not store tokens in the array of strings. This modification should not affect the client of the module.

Chapter 10

ARRAYS

10.1 ◆ Preview

In this chapter, I will describe how to declare and use arrays. I will concentrate on single dimensional arrays, and compare them with pointers. Then, I will briefly discuss two-dimensional arrays. Finally, I will present a module that implements dynamic arrays, whose size may be set at run-time. This module will also use assertions to test various preconditions.

10.2 Single-Dimensional Arrays

Like Java, C arrays have a lower bound equal to zero, but unlike Java, they are *static*—their size must be known at compile time.

To define an array, you use the following syntax:

```
type arrayName[size];
```

For example,

```
int id[1000];
char *names[2*50+1];
```

The second declaration uses a size that is a static expression, which can be evaluated by the compiler.

The size of the array can also be defined using a macro or a constant:

```
#define SIZE 10
const int Size = 20;
int id1[SIZE];
int id2[Size];
```

However, the declaration that uses a constant `Size` is legal *only* if it appears in a function; a global declaration is illegal. For example

```
const int S = 10;
/* int id3[S]   -- illegal */
int foo() {
    int id4[S];   /* OK */
    . . .
}
```

The best way to think about a single dimensional array is to see it as a *typed constant* pointer initialized to point to a block of memory that can hold a number of objects. In the above declarations:

id is an int pointer that points to a block of memory that can hold 1000 integer objects

names is a pointer to pointer to char that points to a block of memory that can hold 101 pointers to characters

In order to reference an element in the array, you use the `[]` operator; for example, for the array id, you can use

```
id[0], id[1], ..., id[999]
```

The run-time system of the language does not check if the value of an index expression is less than the upper bound of this array. For example, the use of

```
id[1000]
```

will not necessarily generate a run-time error, but the program's behavior will be undefined (the contents of the memory location is unknown).

1. Given the declaration

    ```
    type arrayName[n];
    ```

    do not use

    ```
    arrayName[n]
    ```

2. Declarations of the form

    ```
    int n = 3;
    double s[n];
    ```

    are illegal, because the size of array s must be a constant.

3. Arrays are not l-values, so

    ```
    int x[2];
    int *pid;
    . . .
    x = pid;
    ```

    is illegal. However, pid = x; is legal.

4. Side-effects may make the result of assignments involving index expressions *implementation dependent;* for example, in the assignment

    ```
    a[i] = i++;
    ```

    i may be incremented before or after it is used as an index expression.

As I mentioned earlier, a declaration of the form

```
int id[1000];
```

defines a *constant pointer* to an integer, which points to a block of memory that can hold up to 1000 integers. On the other hand, the declaration

```
int *pointerId;
```

defines a *variable pointer* to an integer, whose initial value is undefined (no memory has been allocated for `pointerId`). If you declare

```
const int *pointerIdConst;
```

then both `id` and `pointerIdConst` are constants, but there is still no memory allocated for `pointerIdConst`.

There is one more difference between the declarations of `id` and `pointerId`, which shows up when the `sizeof()` function is used:

`sizeof(id)` is `1000*sizeof(int)`—note, size is *not* 1000

`sizeof(pointerId)` is the number of *bytes* used to store a pointer to an int.

You can use the `sizeof()` function to set the pointer `pointerId` to the last element of the array `id`:

```
pointerId = id + sizeof(id)/sizeof(id[0]) - 1;
```

`sizeof(array)` returns the number of objects in the array, not the number of bytes.

One of the consequences of the fact that arrays are pointers is that you have to be careful when comparing and copying arrays. For example, consider:

```
#define SIZE 10
int x[SIZE];
int y[SIZE];
...initialization of x and y ...
```

The equality operator == cannot be used to test if x and y have the same contents

```
x == y
```

For my declarations, the result of the above expression would be 0, because x and y point to two different blocks of memory. To compare the contents of the two arrays, you have to traverse them using, for example, a version of the "Block traversal" idiom:

```
int *px, *py;
for(px = x, py = y; px < x + SIZE; px++, py++)
    if(*px != *py)
        different
```

Note that this code will only work if the two arrays have the same size; if they do not have the same size, then there is no need to perform the traversal because you know the two can not have the same contents. Looking at this piece of code, you may wonder if it is absolutely necessary to use two pointers for the traversal. Given that you know that the size of both arrays is the same, the main reason for doing so is readability. You could have used the px pointer to traverse the array x, and the difference between px and x to access the contents of the array y:

```
for(px = x; px < x + SIZE; px++)
    if(*px != y[px - x])
        different
```

This code should be considered a *test* of your understanding of pointer arithmetic instead of a serious attempt to write readable code. I have saved the simplest solution for last:

```
for(i = 0; i < SIZE; i++)
    if(x[i] != y[i])
        different
```

Similar code can be used to copy arrays. For example, the contents of the array x may be copied to the contents of the array y, using the following code:

```
for(i = 0; i < SIZE; i++)
    x[i] = y[i];
```

Note that I can do this since I know both arrays have the same size. If one array is smaller than the other, care must be taken to copy within the bounds of the smaller array.

COMPARE ARRAYS OF THE SAME SIZE

```
for(i = 0; i < SIZE; i++)
   if(x[i] != y[i])
       different
```

COPY ARRAYS OF THE SAME SIZE

```
for(i = 0; i < SIZE; i++)
   x[i] = y[i];
```

typedef may be used to create a synonym for an array type of a given size using the following syntax:

```
typedef ElemType ArrayType[size];
```

For example

```
typedef int Int10[10];
```

Here, Int10 stands for "an array of 10 integers" and can be used in variable declarations:

```
Int10 x, y;
```

ARRAY TYPE

```
typedef ElemType ArrayType[size];
```

Example 10–1

This example is of a simple calculator program called evaluate, which is invoked on the command line with the expression to be evaluated. A sample call to evaluate looks like this:

```
evaluate 3+7
```

I used several calls to `sscanf()` to read the entire expression. The operator is read correctly because the format string `"%1s"` limits the number of characters read by `scanf()` to a single character. Also note that

```
char oper[2];
```

allocates enough memory for a single character (followed by \0).

```c
/* Note: to enter *, use "*" */
#include <stdio.h>
#include <stdlib.h>
/*
 * File: ex10-1.c
 * A simple version of a calculator program that evaluates expressions
 *   of the form
 *      n blanks op blanks n
 *   passed on the command line.
 * For example
 *   evaluate  10    "*"        5
 */

#include <stdlib.h>
#include <stdio.h>

#define ERROR(mes, fatal) { fprintf(stderr, "%s\n", mes); \
   if(fatal) return EXIT_FAILURE; }

int main(int argc, char **argv) {
   double f, s;
   char oper[2];

#define FATAL 1
#define MILD  0

   if(argc != 4)
      ERROR("usage: %s n blanks op blanks n (for product use \"*\")",
             FATAL)

   if(sscanf(argv[1], "%lf", &f) != 1  ||      /* read first */
         sscanf(argv[2], "%1s", oper) != 1 ||  /* read the operator */
         sscanf(argv[3], "%lf", &s) != 1)      /* read second */
      ERROR("Incorrect input", MILD)
```

```
switch(oper[0]) {

case '+' : f += s;
            break;

case '-' : f -= s;
            break;

case '*' : f *= s;
            break;

case '/' : if(s != 0) {
                f /= s;
                break;
            } else ERROR("Cannot divide by zero", MILD)

default : ERROR("unknown operator", MILD);
}

printf("The result is %f\n", f);

return EXIT_SUCCESS;
}
```

Above, an asterisk has to be "escaped", i.e. it must appear in quotes; otherwise it would have a different meaning, depending on the shell language of the underlying operating system.

10.2.1 ◆ Arrays as Parameters

When arrays are used as function parameters, they are actually treated as pointers. For example, the following two declarations of a function to find the maximum value in a `double` array are equivalent:

```
int maxiA(double arr[], int size);
int maxiP(double *arr, int size);
```

You can use either of these declarations, depending on which one you consider more readable for a specific instance. The second parameter is necessary to specify the size of the incoming array. Unlike Java, you can *not* query C arrays for their size, and you can not use the `sizeof(array-parameter)`, because within the body of the function, the array parameter is treated as a pointer.

Example 10-2

In this example, I will show a function `maxMin()` that returns the largest and the smallest value in a double array:

```
int maxMin(double arr[], int size, double *max, double *min) {
    double *p;

    if(arr == NULL || size <= 0)
        return 0;

    for(*max = *min = arr[0], p = arr + 1; p < arr+size; p++) {
        if(*max < *p)
            *max = *p;
        if(*min > *p)
            *min = *p;
    }
    return 1;
}
```

The main loop of this function uses the "Block traversal" idiom, and initializes the pointers `min` and `max` to store the value at the beginning of the array, and the pointer `p` (used to traverse the array) to the second element of the array. The main function initializes an array of size 5, and the calls `maxMin()` to find the largest and the smallest value:

```
int main() {
    const int SIZE = 5;
    double x[SIZE];
    double max, min;
    int i;

    for(i = 0; i < SIZE; i++) {
        printf("enter a double value:");
        if(scanf("%lf", &x[i]) != 1)
            return EXIT_FAILURE;
    }

    if(maxMin(x, SIZE, &max, &min) == 0) {
        fprintf(stderr, "this could not happen\n");
        return EXIT_FAILURE;
    }
```

```
    printf("maximum = %f, minimum = %f\n", max, min);

    return EXIT_SUCCESS;
}
```

Recall that the above declaration of the array x is legal only because it is a local declaration within a function.

Once you have a function that operates on an array, it is easy to re-use it for operating on a *segment* within the array (see Figure 10–1). For example, to find the largest and the smallest values in a segment of size 2 from the array x, starting at position 2 in x, you can call maxMin() with the following parameters:

```
maxMin(x+2, 2, &max, &min)
```

To limit the segment to the *prefix* of the array x (for example, to the prefix consisting of first three elements), you make a call to maxMin() with the parameters:

```
maxMin(x, 3, &max, &min)
```

The segment can also be limited to the *suffix* of the array x (for example, to the suffix consisting of last three elements) by calling maxMin() with the parameters:

```
maxMin(x+2, SIZE-2, &max, &min)
```

Figure 10–1

Segment of an array

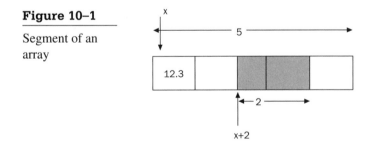

> **PREFIX AND SUFFIX OF AN ARRAY**
>
> For a function `f(T* arr, int n,...)` operating on an array `arr` of size n, call `f(arr+start, segSize)` to operate on the segment of array `arr` of size segSize, starting from position `start` (here, `segSize+start` must be less than or equal to `n`)

```
void f(double b[]) {
    ...sizeof(b) ...
}
```

The call to `sizeof(b)` within the function body returns the size of a pointer, not the size of array b.

10.2.2 ◆ Array Initialization and Storage

Local arrays (declared within functions) are allocated memory from the stack unless they are qualified as static, in which case they are stored in the same fashion as global arrays. Global arrays are declared outside of any function. These arrays, like any other global data, are allocated memory in a special data segment called BSS (Below Stack Segment), and their lifetime is the same as that of the main function.

Arrays can be *initialized* using a list of constant values, enclosed in curly braces:

```
{ v1, v2, ..., vn }
```

For example:

```
int x[2] = { 1, 2 };
```

When an array is initialized in this manner, the programmer has the option of explicitly specifying the size:

- if there is no size specification, the effective size is equal to the number of initializing values; for example

```
int x[] = { 2,3 };    /* has size = 2 */
```

- if the size is specified, and it is greater than the number of initializing values, then the remaining elements of the array are set to a "zero" value (0, 0.0, \0, or NULL)

- if the size is specified, and it is less than the number of initializing values, then the initialization results in a compile-time error

Examples

```
int x[3] = {1, 2, 3};
```
Correct.

```
int x[3] = {1, 2};
```
Correct, x[2] is 0.

```
int x[3] = {1, 2, 3, 4};
```
Error.

Arrays can also be declared as constants, for example

```
const int days[] = {1,2,3,4,5,6,7};
```

and the type of days above is:

```
const int * const
```

(a constant pointer to a constant).

String constants can be used to initialize character and string arrays. For example,

```
char name[] = "John";
char* names[] = {"Mary", "John"};
```

Local arrays may be used within function bodies for many purposes. For example, you may have an integer representation of a code that you wish to translate to a string:

```
/* return string for n-th opcode */
static char* optext(int n) {
    static char* operator[ ] =
      {"lvalue", "rvalue", "push", "+", "-"};

    return operator[n];
};
```

Whenever using local non-static arrays, you must remember that they are allocated on the stack, and you must avoid dangling references. For example, consider the following code:

```
char *setName(int i) {
   char name1[] = "Mary";
   char name2[] = "John";

   if(i == 0)
      return name1;

   return name2;
}


char *p = setName(1);
```

In this example, the pointer p points to memory that has been deallocated from the run-time stack, and is now pointing at invalid memory. The above code should allocate memory on the heap for the name strings.

At this point, I will return to Example 9–11 from the previous chapter, where a program had the task of reading lines from a file, and I was faced with the problem of not knowing how long each line would be. Reading each line twice, once to find its length and a second time to actually read the line into a dynamically allocated buffer, is inefficient. Assuming that the line is no longer than a certain maximum is not always convenient. There are two possible solutions to this problem:

- dynamically allocate memory to store say 80 characters, and read up to 80 characters. If at this point the end of line has not yet been encountered, reallocate the memory as follows: allocate twice as much memory and copy what has been read to the new buffer, then deallocate the previous buffer. Repeat this process until the end of line has been encountered. This technique uses the so-called "dynamic array", which I will implement as a complete module in Section 10.5.

- use recursion and a *single* memory allocation: call a recursive procedure that has a local buffer array of size 80. In the body of the function, read characters into the local array until end of line has been encountered, or 80 characters have been read. If 80 characters have been read, and the end of line has not been encountered, then make a recursive call, which will preserve the previous local array, and create another one in the new instance. When end-of-line is encountered, the total length of the line is known, and a memory block for this line can be allocated in that particular instance of the function. Each instance of the function then returns from the recursion, copying its contents of the buffer into the allocated memory block.

This technique is demonstrated in the next example.

Example 10-3

```
#include <stdio.h>
#include <stdlib.h>
#include <string.h>
/*
 * File: ex10-3.c
 * Function: getLine
 * Purpose: read from file a line of unlimited length using a single
 *    dynamic allocation
 * Inputs: FILE in (parameter)
 * The client is responsible for opening and closing this file.
 * Returns: pointer to the memory block that stores the line
 *    (through parameter)
 *  The client is responsible for deallocating this memory
 *  Through function returns 1 if a line has been read, 0 on error,
 *    and EOF on eof
 * Modifies: file
 * Error checking: returns 0 if fails
 * Sample call:
 *    char *p;
 *    FILE *f;
 *     ... open f ..
 *    if(getLine(f, &p) == 1)
 *       printf("line is %s\n", p);
 *
 */
int getLine(FILE *in, char **result);

/* application of getLine:
 * read lines from a file provided on the command line
 */
int main(int argc, char **argv) {
   FILE *f;
   char *line;
   int count;
   int result;

   if(argc != 2) {
      fprintf(stderr, "usage %s filename\n", argv[0]);
      return EXIT_FAILURE;
   }
```

```
    if((f = fopen(argv[1], "r")) == NULL) {
        fprintf(stderr, "can not open %s\n", argv[1]);
        return EXIT_FAILURE;
    }

    for(count = 1; (result = getLine(f, &line)) != EOF; count++) {
        if(result == 0) {
            fprintf(stderr, "error encountered, terminating\n");
            return EXIT_FAILURE;
        }
        printf("%d\t%s\n", count, line);
        free(line);
    }

    if(fclose(f) == EOF) {
        fprintf(stderr, "could not close %s\n", argv[1]);
        return EXIT_FAILURE;
    }

    return EXIT_SUCCESS;
}

/*
 * Implementation of getLine:
 *    read until the local buffer is full and then recurse
 * Allocate the final buffer based on the number of local
 *    buffers read and as the recursive calls bottom out,
 *    copy them in reverse order into the resulting buffer.
 */
#define BUF_SIZE 80

int getLine(FILE *in, char **result) {
  char buf[BUF_SIZE];
  int c;    /* used to read characters */
  int i;    /* auxiliary variable */
  int base;
  static int size_ = 0; /* used to accumulate the size of the line */

  /* try to read up to BUF_SIZE characters, stop on eoln and eof */
  for (i = 0; i < BUF_SIZE; i++) {

      c = fgetc(in);

      if(c == EOF) {    /* eof or error */
```

```
            if(feof(in)) { /* end-of-file rather than error */
                if(i == 0 && size_ == 0) /* nothing read */
                    return EOF;
                break;
            } else /* error */ {
                size_ = 0;
                return 0;
            }
        }

        if (c == '\n')
            break;

        buf[i] = c;
    } /* end of for loop */

    /* increment the number of bytes */
    size_ += i;

    /* Recurse when the recursion bottoms out
     * allocate the master buffer
     */
    if(c != EOF && c != '\n') {
        if(getLine(in, result) == 0) {
            size_ = 0;
            return 0;
        }
    } else {
        if((*result = malloc((size_+1)*sizeof(char))) == NULL) {
            size_ = 0;
            return 0;
        }
        /* store the terminating \0 */
        (*result)[size_] = '\0';
    }

    /* Copy buf into the appropriate location */
    base = size_ - i ;
    memcpy(*result + base, buf, i);
    size_ -= i;

    return 1;
}
```

I will explain the above program assuming that the input line has 162 characters. Since the client of getLine() is responsible for opening the input stream passed to this function, the implementation provides extra checks for possible errors. The library function fgetc() returns EOF if an end-of-file has been encountered, or if an error has occurred. In order to catch the first case, I used another library function feof(f), which returns a non-zero value only if it has detected an end-of-file.

Consider the first call of the function getLine() at the point just before the comment /* Recurse ... */ (see Figure 10–2). This figure shows the run-time stack, growing towards the top of the page, and on the top of the stack, the instance of the function getLine(). A local variable in this instance, buf, is an array allocated on the stack, and currently holds the first 80 characters from the input line. Another local variable, i, holds the number of characters read, that is 80. The *static* local variable size_, whose value is currently 80, is shown outside of the stack, because memory for this variable is allocated in BSS rather than on the stack.

Now, consider the state of the execution when getLine() has been called for the second time, and its execution has reached the point just before the comment /* Recurse... */ (see Figure 10–3).

In the first instance of the function, the array buf holds the first 80 characters of the input line; in the second instance, it holds the *next* 80 characters. Since end of line still has not been encountered, getLine() gets called for the third time. In that instance, the for statement terminates for i=3, the value of size_ gets updated, and memory for result is allocated (see Figure 10–4).

This figure also shows how memory from the run-time stack is copied to the block pointed to by *result. In the current third call to getLine() I want to copy i characters from buf into the top i characters of the result block, that is, starting at position

```
base = size_ - i;
```

This copy is performed using memcpy().

The key to understanding this function is realizing that dynamic memory (created using malloc()) is allocated only once: in the third instance of getline(), at the point when the length of the line is known. Figure 10–5 shows the state of execution when the third call to getLine() has terminated, and we are back to the second call. Specifically, the execution resumes at the assignment,

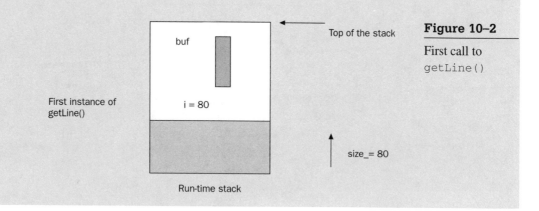

First instance of getLine()

buf

i = 80

Run-time stack

Top of the stack

size_= 80

Figure 10–2

First call to getLine()

Figure 10–3

Second call to
`getLine()`

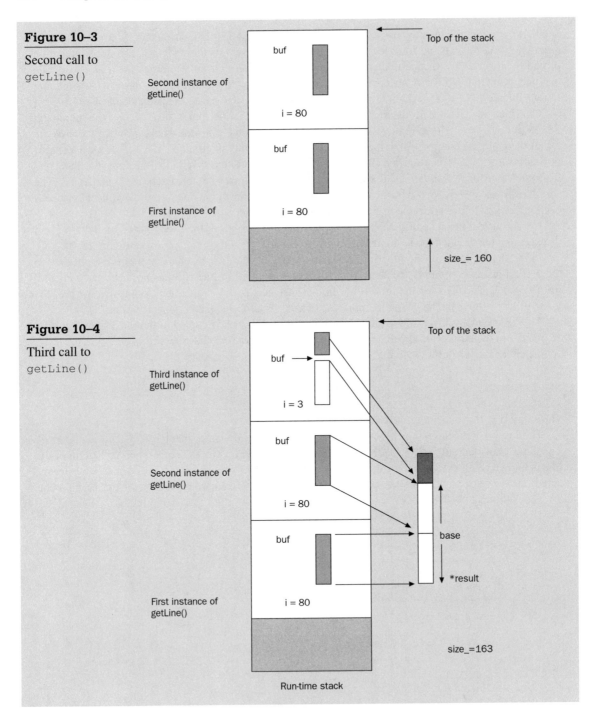

Second instance of
getLine()

buf

i = 80

First instance of
getLine()

buf

i = 80

Top of the stack

size_= 160

Figure 10–4

Third call to
`getLine()`

Third instance of
getLine()

buf

i = 3

Second instance of
getLine()

buf

i = 80

First instance of
getLine()

buf

i = 80

Top of the stack

base

*result

size_=163

Run-time stack

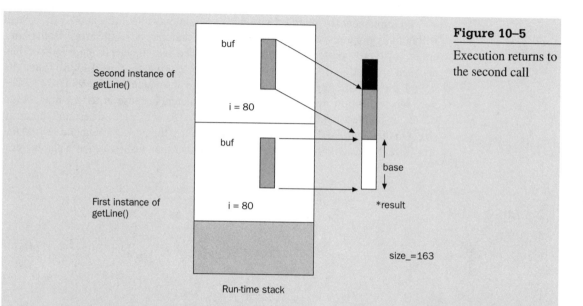

Figure 10–5

Execution returns to
the second call

which sets the value of base. The memcpy() call copies i characters from buf into *result, start-ing at position base. I recommend that you complete tracing the remaining part of the execution yourself.

By using the static variable size_, I avoided making it a parameter of the function getLine():

```
getLine(FILE *f, char **result, int size)
```

This would be correct, but would rely on the client to make the call

```
getLine(f, &p, 0)
```

to properly initialize the value of size.

I will now show an example using a binary search for a string key in a sorted array names of strings, of size s, using the function

```
search(char *key, char *names[], int s);
```

Note that it would be equivalent to specify the second parameter names as

```
char **names;
```

To implement the search, I will use two pointers called `low` and `high`, which will initially point respectively to the beginning and the end of the array. Both pointers are of type "pointer to pointer to `char`". The search selects the middle value, between `low` and `high`, using another pointer `mid`. To determine if I have found the key, I use the `strcmp()` function to compare the value of `key` and `*mid`. The `search()` function must have the third parameter, because array parameters are treated as pointers, and I can not use `sizeof(parameter)` to determine the array size. On the other hand, the main program does use the `sizeof` function to find the array size, because this array is defined here, rather than just passed as a parameter.

Example 10–4

```
#include <stdio.h>
#include <stdlib.h>
#include <string.h>
/*
 * File: ex10-4.c
 * Function: search
 * Purpose: search an array of sorted strings looking for a key value
 * Inputs: string key, array names, and its size (parameters)
 * Returns:  1 if key found 0 otherwise
 * Modifies: nothing
 * Error checking: fails if array is not sorted
 * Sample call:
 *      char *n[] = {"abc", "def" );
 *      if(search("ab", n, 2)) ...
 *
 */
int search(char *key, char *names[], int size) {
    char **low = names;
    char **high = names + size - 1;
    char **mid;
    int c;

    while(low <= high) {

        mid = low + (high - low)/2;
        if((c = strcmp(*mid, key)) == 0)
            return 1;

        if (c < 0)
            low = mid + 1;
        else
```

```
            high = mid - 1;
      }

   return 0;
}


/*
 * Application of the search function
 * Search an array of keywords
 */
char *reservedWords[] = {    /* note the words are sorted. */
   "case", "const", "do", "if", "then", "while", NULL
};

int main() {
   char key[20];
   char **p;
   int size = sizeof(reservedWords)/sizeof(char*);

   /* show all keywords and then ask the user to search for one */
   printf("There are %d reserved words; the list of them follows.\n",
         size);
   for(p = reservedWords; *p != NULL; p++)
      printf("%s\n", *p);

   printf("Enter a word to look for:");
   if(scanf("%19s", key) != 1)
      return EXIT_FAILURE;

   printf("%s has %s been found\n", key,
         search(key, reservedWords, size) ? "" : "not");

   return EXIT_SUCCESS;
}
```

10.3 Declarators: Part 2

Square brackets [] have higher precedence than *, so for

```
double *f[];
```

f is an array of pointers to double. Now, consider

```
double (*f2[])();
```

f2 is an array of pointers to functions returning double
Two more examples:

```
double (*f3()))[]
```

f3 is a function returning pointer to array of double

```
double *(f4[])()
```

this construct is illegal; you can not have an array of functions, only pointers to functions.

10.4 Multi-Dimensional Arrays

C supports multidimensional arrays, and in this section, I will discuss two-dimensional arrays. (I will not discuss arrays in higher dimensions because their syntax and semantics are virtually the same.)

To declare a two-dimensional array, use the following syntax:

```
type arr[s1][s2];
```

For example:

```
int x[2][3];
```

x now has two rows and three columns (see Figure 10–6). Here, x[0] refers to the first row, and x[1] refers to the second row.

Figure 10–6

Two dimensional
array x

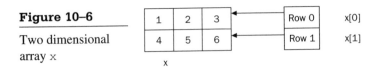

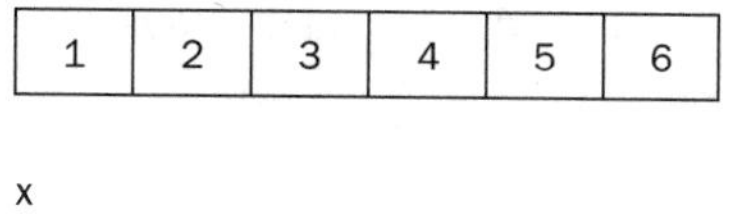

| 1 | 2 | 3 | 4 | 5 | 6 |

x

Figure 10–7

Memory representation of a two dimensional array x

Index expressions can be used as in Java; for example, to print all of the values in the array x, you can use the following code:

```
for(i = 0; i < 2; i++) { /* for each row */
   for(j = 0; j < 3; j++)  /* for each column */
      printf("x[%d][%d] = %d\t", i, j, x[i][j]);
   putchar('\n');
}
```

A two-dimensional array is stored in a single memory block, one row after another. The array x, declared above, is actually stored as shown in Figure 10–7.

Two-dimensional arrays may be passed as function parameters. When declaring the formal parameters, the size of the *first* dimension is not needed, however the second is required and must be a constant expression. Just like one-dimensional arrays, two-dimensional arrays are converted to a pointer type when passed as function parameters. This time, the array becomes converted to a pointer to a row.

Example 10–5

For this example, I will create a function that returns the largest value in a two dimensional array. Since the size in the first dimension is not supplied, the function needs another parameter to get this value.

```
double find(double x[][SIZE], int n) {
   int i, j;
   double max = x[0][0];

   for (i = 0; i < n; i++)
      for(j = 0; j < SIZE; j++)
         if(max < x[i][j])
            max = x[i][j];

   return max;
}
```

Two-dimensional arrays can be initialized in a manner similar to one-dimensional arrays, by using either single braces or nested braces. For example

```
double f[][2] = {
    {1.2, 2.8},
    {3.4, 8.99},
    {61.2, 2.82}
};
```

The second dimension (number of columns) must always be provided, but the braces do not have to be nested if the first dimension is provided:

```
double f[3][2] = {
    1.2, 2.8,
    3.4, 8.99,
    61.2, 2.82
};
```

```
void f(double x[][]);
```

The number of columns must always be provided when declaring two-dimensional arrays as function parameters.

To make code more readable, always use nested braces when initializing two-dimensional arrays.

10.5 Dynamic Array Module (with Preconditions)

In this section, I will provide a longer example of a singleton module called `Arr`, which supports operations on a single dimensional array. I will use the technique introduced in Section 8.18.4 to implement a homogenous module in which the element type is known to the implementation, and will use a `char` type.

As I described earlier in this chapter, C arrays are static. The module `Arr` implements a dynamic array; i.e. its size will be defined at run-time through a call to the constructor of the module. In addition, this module provides a function `set(v, i)`, which will expand the array if the value of `i` is greater than the current array size. This removes the client from the responsibility of having to worry about there being enough memory allocated for the array. The module will also provide additional error checking to ensure that the index expressions used on the array are within the current array bounds. In order to perform some of the error checking, I will introduce yet another standard C library, `assert.h`.

10.5.1 ◆ Testing Preconditions

A **precondition** is a necessary condition that must hold in order for an operation to be performed; for example

`i >= 0` is a precondition to computing the `sqrt(i)`

`b*b - 4*a*c >= 0` is a precondition to finding the real roots of a quadratic equation of the form $ax^2 + bx + c = 0$

`0 <= i < size` is a precondition to using the index expression `x[i]`, for an array `x` declared as `x[size]`

The standard library `assert.h` provides the macro

```
assert(int e)
```

which is used to print a message and stop program execution if a precondition is not satisfied. In the context of this function, a precondition is represented by the argument of `assert()`, for example:

```
assert(i>=0)
assert(b*b - 4*a*c >= 0)
assert(0 <= i && i < size)
```

Using `assert()` may introduce some overhead which reduces program execution speed. To offer the programmer the choice of toggling between using and not using `assert()`, the function is used together with a macro; when this macro is defined, `assert()` does nothing.

Specifically, the meaning of this macro depends on another macro called NDE-BUG:

- if NDEBUG is *not* defined **and** the actual parameter of `assert()` evaluates to 0, then the error message is displayed and the execution of the program is aborted. The contents of the error message include the text of the actual parameter, and two pre-defined macros: __FILE__ and __LINE__ (see Section 6.3.2). To abort program execution, a predefined function abort(void) is called.

- if NDEBUG is *not* defined **and** the actual parameter of assert() evaluates to a value different from 0, or NDEBUG is defined, then the result of calling assert() is void.

Note that *by default* assert() is "enabled", and you have to explicitly undefine NDEBUG to disable it.

The macro NDEBUG may be defined and undefined on the compiler's command line, without modifying the source code (see Section 6.6.1).

10.5.2 ◆ Interface

The interface of the dynamic array module provides a constructor to initialize a "small" block of memory, and two functions respectively called get(i) and set(v, i), which are used to replace indexed expressions, such as x[i]. However, set(v, i) has a special feature, which is transparent to the client. If the value of i is greater than the current length of the block, then this block is automatically expanded. For example, if set() was placed within the body of a loop,

```
for(i = 0; ;i++)
    set(v,i);
```

then the array would continue growing until the system ran out of memory (my implementation does not provide any facility to shrink the array).

The operations in the module test their respective pre-conditions; for example:

0 <= i < length   for get(i) (here, length is the size of the array)
0 <= i   for set(v,i)

As I mentioned in Section 10.5, the element type is known to the implementation, and here is a char:

```
typedef char Element_Arr;
```

The functions provided in the interface include:

```
int construct_Arr(int initSize);
Element_Arr get_Arr(int i);
void set_Arr(Element_Arr value, int i);
```

```
int length_Arr();
void destruct_Arr(void);
```

The meaning of these functions is obvious, and so below, I provided the documentation for only one function:

```
/*
 * Function: set_Arr
 * Purpose: modify the value of the ith element
 * Inputs: the value and the index of the ith element
 *      (parameters)
 * Returns: nothing
 * Modifies: iTH element
 * Error checking: If the index is negative, assert() is
 *     called, and then the result depends on whether or not
 *     NDEBUG is defined. If it is defined, then set does not
 *     do anything. If the index is positive, and larger than
 *     the current length of the array, then the array is
 *     extended.
 * Sample call:
 *   Element_Arr x;
 *   set_Arr(x, 2);
 */
void set_Arr(Element_Arr value, int i);
```

The complete code for the interface may be found in file `ex-10-6-Arr.h`.

10.5.3 ◆ Application

In this section, I will discuss an application of the dynamic array module to solve the previously described problem of reading a line of an unlimited length. The client of the module initializes the array to hold 80 elements:

```
construct_Arr(80);
```

Note that the initial size of the array does not have to be a static value; instead, it can be initialized dynamically, for example, by having the program prompt the user for it. The client uses the module-provided functions to read a single line from a file one character at a time, and store these characters in a dynamic array. The module deals with expanding the array when needed—this action is transparent to the client:

```
for(i = 0; (c = fgetc(f)) != '\n'; i++)
    set_Arr(c, i);
```

Then, to show this line:

```
printf("The line is: ");
for(i = 0; i < length_Arr(); i++)
    putchar(get_Arr(i));
printf("\nbye\n");
```

Finally, the array is destructed:

```
destruct_Arr();
```

The complete code for this implementation may be found in file ex10-6-Arr-main.c.

10.5.4 ◆ Implementation

I will now discuss the implementation of the dynamic array module. It maintains four private variables:

```
static Element_Arr *block_;          /* used to store data */
static int size_;                    /* size of the block  */
static const int increment_ = 10;    /* memory increment */
static int init_ = 0;                /* initialization flag */
```

A private function expand_() takes care of expanding the array as needed. This function is called if set_Arr(v, i) is called and i is larger the current length of the array. expand_() allocates a block of memory, which is of size equal to the previous block length plus an *increment* (for example, the previous size plus 10). This prevents the block of memory from having to be reallocated every time i is incremented by one:

```
static int expand_(int size) {
    Element_Arr *new;
    int i;

    if((new = calloc(size, sizeof(Element_Arr))) == NULL)
        return 0;

    /* now copy the old array */
    for(i = 0; i < size_; i++)
        new[i] = block_[i];
    /* update size_ and block_ */
```

```
      size_ = size;
      free(block_);
      block_ = new;

      return 1;
}
```

To implement `expand_()`, I could have used another library function

```
void* realloc(void *ptr, size_t size);
```

which resizes the memory block pointed to by `ptr`, while preserving its contents:

```
block_ = realloc(block_, size * sizeof(Element_Arr));
```

The constructor simply performs some error checking and then allocates memory for the `block_`:

```
int construct_Arr(int initSize) {
    if(init_)
        return 0;

    init_ = 1;
    size_ = initSize;
    return (block_ = calloc(initSize, sizeof(Element_Arr)))
        != NULL;
}
```

I recommend that you try to extend this implementation by overloading the constructor (for example, using a variable number of parameters) to provide a *second* parameter that allows the client to set the value of the increment.

Now, I will discuss the function used to store a value in the array:

```
void set_Arr(Element_Arr value, int i);
```

The function first tests its preconditions, using a call to the `assert()` function. If the value of NDEBUG is not defined and `assert()` fails, program execution stops. If the value of NDEBUG is defined and so `assert()` is disabled, the function performs the same check and simply returns should the preconditions fail. This may not be the best solution—if the index is negative or the module has not been initialized, then `set_Arr()` does nothing. The idea behind my solution is that if a program using the dynamic array module is in a debugging stage (NDEBUG is not defined), then `assert()` will check preconditions. Once the program is in the production phase (NDEBUG is defined), the precondition should never fail, but things that are "impossible" do happen, and so it is better that set_Arr() does nothing than produce a run-time error:

```
assert(i >= 0 && init_);
if(i < 0 || !init_)
    return;
```

If the value of the index i is larger than the current size of the array, then the array is expanded:

```
if(i >= size_) {
    res = expand_(i + increment_);
    assert(res);
    if(res == 0)
        return;
}
```

Finally, the value is ready to be stored in the array:

```
block_[i] = value;
```

The complete code may be found in file ex10-6-Arr.c.

10.6 List of Common Errors

1. Given the declaration

   ```
   type arrayName[n];
   ```

   do not use

   ```
   arrayName[n]
   ```

2. Declarations of the form

   ```
   int n = 3;
   double s[n];
   ```

   are illegal, because the size of array s must be a constant.

3. Arrays are not l-values, so

```
int x[2];
int *pid;
. . .
x = pid
```

is illegal. However, `pid = x` is legal.

4. Side-effects may make the result of assignments involving index expressions *implementation dependent;* for example, in the assignment

```
a[i] = i++;
```

i may be incremented before or after it is used as an index expression.

5. `sizeof(array)` returns the number of objects in the array, not the number of bytes.

6. ```
void f(double b[]) {
    ...sizeof(b) ...
}
```

The call to `sizeof(b)` within the function body returns the size of a pointer, not the size of array b.

7. ```
void f(double x[][]);
```

The number of columns must always be provided when declaring two-dimensional arrays as function parameters.

10.7 List of Idioms

COMPARE ARRAYS OF THE SAME SIZE

```
for(i = 0; i < SIZE; i++)
   if(x[i] != y[i])
      different
```

COPY ARRAYS OF THE SAME SIZE

```
for(i = 0; i < SIZE; i++)
    x[i] = y[i];
```

ARRAY TYPE

```
typedef ElemType ArrayType[size];
```

PREFIX AND SUFFIX OF AN ARRAY

For a function `f(T* arr, int n,...)` operating on an array `arr` of size n, call `f(arr+start, segSize)` to operate on the segment of array `arr` of size `segSize`, starting from position `start` (here, `segSize+start` must be less than or equal to n)

10.8 List of Programming Style Guidelines

To make code more readable, always use nested braces when initializing two-dimensional arrays.

10.9 Exercises

All functions should be well documented. For any exercise that asks you to implement a function, include a program that carefully tests this function.

Exercise 10-1

Consider the following specification and declaration:

```
/* maxi returns the largest element in an array A of size S  */
int  maxi(int A[], int S) {
    int i;
    int m = 0;

    for(i = 0; i < S; i++) {
        if(A[i] > m)
            m = A[i];
    }
```

```
      return m;
}
```

Give one example of actual parameters for which this function will return an incorrect result.

Exercise 10-2

Write a function, which returns the average of all the double values stored in an integer array `Arr` of size `n`.

Exercise 10-3

Write a function `reverse()` that reverses an array (the first element becomes the last element, the second element becomes the first from the last, etc.) and returns the reversed array through the second parameter.

Then, write a function, `reverseMyself()`, which modifies the array passed as a parameter by reversing it.

Exercise 10-4

Write a function

```
int allzeros(int arr[], int n)
```

to determine if all elements of a single-dimensional integer array `arr` have the value 0. `allzeros()` returns –1 if all elements are 0, otherwise it returns the index of the first non-zero element.

Exercise 10-5

Write the definition of a procedure `create()`, which has three parameters:

- the first integer parameter specifies the size of an array;
- the second double parameter specifies the array;
- the third integer parameter is used to return the value 1 if the procedure is successful and 0 otherwise.

`create()` creates a "dynamic array" of size double values. All elements of this array should be initialized to 0.

Exercise 10-6

Consider an array of pointers to doubles, using the following definition of the type `DoubT`:

```
typedef double* DoubT;
```

Write the function:

```
double sum(DoubT storage[], int numptrs);
```

This function assumes that `numptrs` pointers are stored in the array storage, and it returns the sum of all double values pointed to by elements of the array. Note that some of pointers in the array storage may be `NULL`.

Exercise 10-7

Consider the following definition:

```
typedef char* CharT;
```

Write the functions described below:

```
int init(CharT storage[], int max);
```

Reads characters from the keyboard and stores them in memory fields pointed to by the successive elements of the array `storage` (use `malloc()` to create these fields). Reading terminates when an end-of-line is encountered or max characters have been read, at which point `init()` returns the number of characters read (excluding an end-of-line). If an end-of-file is encountered before an end-of-line, or `malloc()` fails, `init()` returns the value `EOF`.

```
int condense(CharT storage[], CharT *new[], int size);
```

This function assumes that `"size"` pointers are stored in the array `"storage"`, and it first traverses this array, freeing all of the pointers that point to whitespace characters; the function keeps track of how many characters are left. Then, `condense()` creates another array "new" of characters (this is why `"new"` is passed as `CharT*`), traverses the array `"storage"` for the second time, and copies the remaining characters to the array `"new"`. If `malloc()` fails, `condense()` returns `EOF`; otherwise it returns the number of characters stored in `"new"`.

Finally, write a main function (with all necessary definitions) in which first `init()` is called to initialize the array `storage` of size 20, then (if everything goes OK) `condense()` is called to store non-whitespace characters in the variable `new`, and eventually all characters from `new` are displayed.

Exercise 10-8

Write a complete program, which consists of two functions and the main program. A function

```
init(x, N)
```

should read in N real (double) values and store them in a two-dimensional array x of real values which has 5 columns (the number of rows is not known here). A function

```
find(x, f, i, j)
```

returns through i and j the row index and the column index of the occurrence of the real value f in the two-dimensional real array x , or the value –1 if f does not occur in x. Here, assume that x has 4 rows and 5 columns. If f occurs more than once in x, the function find() should find its *last* occurrence.

In the main program:

-   declare a two dimensional array y (4 rows and 5 columns),
-   call init() to read in 20 real values,
-   call find() to search for the value 1.99,
-   and eventually output the position (row and column index) of where this value was found, or a message if the value 1.99 was not found in x.

Exercise 10–9

The module Arr from Section 10.5 does not shrink the memory allocated for the array even if only a small part of this block is being used. Modify the interface and the implementation so that memory can be shrunk.

Exercise 10–10

Implement a singleton, concrete module Arrays, which provides the following operations on single-dimensional arrays of long values:

- a constructor, to set the size of the array (this operation can not be performed while operating on the array)
- enumeration functions, as described in Section 8.18.3
- error functions, as in Example 7–5, Section 7.4.7 (test preconditions, described in Section 10.5.1)

Exercise 10–11

Add conditional compilation to Example 10–3, so that in debugging mode, the function getLine() returning from recursion outputs the contents of a local buffer, and when memory for the final buffer is allocated, it also outputs its contents.

Exercise 10–12

Implement a singleton, concrete module Words, which provides the following operations:

- a constructor that takes a filename and opens this file
- a destructor that closes the file
- show(i) that shows the ith line in the file
- search(word, i) that determines whether the given word occurs in the ith line
- searchGlobal(word) that determines whether the given word occurs in the file.

Exercise 10-13

Re-implement the module Words from Exercise 10–12 such that:

- the constructor reads the first 100 lines and stores (caches) them in internal memory
- show(i) caches the 100 lines around i (50 below the ith line and 50 above)
- search() and searchGlobal() try to use the cached values (if the word can not be found in the cached data, the functions look in the un-cached part of the file). This change should not affect the client of the module.

Exercise 10-14

Re-implement the module Words from Exercise 10–13:

- each line in the cache is broken into words, these words are stored in an array of strings, and this array is kept sorted
- search routines use binary search, which operates on lines

This change should not affect the client of the module.

Chapter 11

STRUCTURES AND THEIR APPLICATIONS

11.1 ◆ Preview

In this chapter, I will introduce structures, which are user-defined complex types designed to package data (in some languages, structures are known as *records*). I will compare structures and Java classes, and provide some technical details, such as how to declare structures and how to combine structures and pointers, arrays, etc. I will conclude this chapter with a continuation of the discussion of module-based programming in C, and explain how structures can be used to design modules for which the user can create *multiple* instances.

11.2 Structures and Classes

C does not provide any constructs that are as powerful as Java classes. The closest construct is the structure—it can be compared to a class as follows:

- a structure has only *data* members (no functions)
- all its members are *public*

While the lack of function members can be overcome by using pointers to functions as structure data, the second limitation is an *insurmountable* obstacle to the process of hiding information from the client. Although a pointer to a constructor function may have been provided in a structure for the purpose of data initialization, there is nothing to make the client call this constructor; furthermore, the client can always change the implementation of the constructor. As a result, structures can not be designed and implemented in the same way as Java classes. For example, consider a Java class Fractions with a member method called Add(Fraction). This method has a single parameter, because when it is called, x.Add(y), it involves two objects: "this" object (here x) and the object passed as a parameter (here y). In C, functions that emulate methods need an extra parameter to represent "this" object. On the bright side, C does support incomplete declaration of pointers to structures, which can be used to hide some of the implementation details from the client (see Section 11.5.1).

11.3 Declaring and Using Structures

Structures are user-defined data types which represent *heterogeneous* collections of data. Therefore, structures differ from arrays, which are homogenous collections. (Structures may contain data of various types, while arrays contain data of one type only.)

In order to declare and use a structure, the keyword struct must be used. The declaration of a *structure data type* follows this syntax:

```
struct id {
    declarations of data members separated by ;
};
```

For example

```
struct info {
    char firstName[20];
    char lastName[20];
    int age;
};
```

defines a new data type called `info` that has three members: `firstName`, `lastName`, and `age`.

The declarations of *variables* of a structure data type follow the same syntax as declarations of other variables; for example

```
struct info i1, i2;
```

defines two variables of type "`struct info`". You must use

```
struct info
```

rather than

```
info
```

Using Java terminology, you can say that structure types *represent* classes, and structure type variables *represent* "objects". I will use this terminology throughout the remainder of the book; for example, I will say that a variable *is* an object of a structure type, or simply that it is a *structure*. For example, `i1` defined above *is* an object of type "`struct info`", or it is a structure of type "`struct info`".

There is an important difference between Java variables of a class type and C variables of a structure type. Java variables are references to objects, which means they are actually *pointers to objects*, which have been allocated memory on the *heap*. In particular, it is possible for two reference variables to refer to the *same* object. In C, structure variables are not pointers; instead they represent structures, for which memory has been allocated in either BSS (for global variables) or on the run-time stack (for local variables).

The declaration of a structure type can declare one or *more* variables of this type at the same time. For example

```
struct info {
    char firstName[20];
    char lastName[20];
    int age;
} i1, i2;
```

declares two variables, `i1` and `i2`. You can use `typedef` to avoid having to use the keyword `struct` in variable declarations. For example

```
typedef struct info {
    char firstName[20];
    char lastName[20];
    int age;
} InfoT;
```

defines a synonym `InfoT` for "`struct info`". You can even omit the identifier `info`:

```
typedef struct {
   char firstName[20];
   char lastName[20];
   int age;
} InfoT;
```

It is syntactically correct to use the same name for a structure and for the `typedef`:

```
typedef struct InfoT {
   char firstName[20];
   char lastName[20];
   int age;
} InfoT;
```

Since `InfoT` is a synonym for "`struct info`," variables of this type can now be declared without the keyword "`struct`," for example

```
InfoT p1;
```

In order to *access* members of a structure, you use the familiar "dot" notation, for example:

```
InfoT p1;
p1.age = 18;
```

It is also possible to define "anonymous" structures, ones that do not have a type name; however, this is rarely useful. For example:

```
struct {
   int i;
   double d;
} x, y;
```

Names of structures defined with `typedef` start with an uppercase letter and end with the uppercase T.

```
struct example {  ...  };
example e;
```

Should be:

```
struct example e;
```

The following declaration is also wrong:

```
struct example {  ...  }
```

The missing semicolon will produce a long list of compiler errors.

11.3.1 ◆ Nested Structures and Incomplete Definitions

Structures can be *nested*, meaning that one structure can be defined within another structure. For example, one could use the previous definition of InfoT in order to define a second structure type:

```
typedef struct {
   InfoT info;
   double salary;
} EmployeeT;
```

In order to access members of a nested structure, you will use multiple dots; for example:

```
EmployeeT e1;
e1.info.age = 21;
```

In general, you have to define a structure type *before* you can use it, either for declaring variables of this type, or for defining another structure type (pointers to structures are treated in a different way, see Section 11.4.1). However, in some cases it is impossible to do so. For example, consider an (invalid) example of "recursive" nesting, such as a section structure that has a sub-section:

```
struct section {
   int hasSubSection;
        /* flag: 1 iff has sub-section */
   char contents[100];
```

```
            struct section subSection;
                           /* nested section */
    };
```

This declaration is *illegal*, because the declaration of subSection uses the struct section type, which at this point has not yet been defined. C deals with this problem by providing an **incomplete type definition**, sometimes referred to as a forward declaration. For example,

```
    struct section;
```

is an incomplete definition to tell the compiler that the type can be used, and will be defined elsewhere. A complete definition must be present in the same scope as the forward declaration:

```
struct section;
struct section {
    int hasSubSection;
    char contents[100];
    struct section subSection;
};
...
struct section {
...
};
```

The above declaration is still wrong. The size of the structure can not be computed; what we could have done is have a pointer to the structure (i.e. a structure can have a field that is a pointer to itself, since the size of a pointer is known; this is useful for lists, trees, etc.).

11.3.2 ◆ Assigning and Comparing Structures

A structure variable can be assigned to another structure variable, for example

```
    InfoT i1, i2;

    i1 = i2;
```

This assignment copies the contents of the memory allocated for i2 into the block allocated for i1. This is a bitwise assignment, which only performs a *shallow* copy. However, structure variables can not be compared; for example

```
    i1 == i2
```

is illegal. If you need to compare two structures, you have to compare members individually.

There is no generic way to compare structures; that is, the way you compare them depends on their members.

For example, to compare i1 and i2, you would use:

```
strcmp(i1.firstName, i2.firstName) == 0 &&
    strcmp(i1.lastName, i2.lastName) == 0 &&
        i1.age == i2.age
```

11.4 Structures and Other Constructs

In this section, I will explain how you use structures with pointers, functions, and arrays.

11.4.1 ◆ Structures and Pointers

The following declaration:

```
struct pair {
    double x;
    double y;
} w, *p;
```

defines a structure w and a pointer p. Alternatively, typedef allows you to define a synonym PairT for "struct pair" and another synonym PairTP for "struct pair *", using

```
typedef struct pair {
    double x;
    double y;
} PairT, *PairTP;
```

Now, when you declare

```
PairTP p;
```

p is a pointer to struct pair.

Type names representing pointers to structures have names ending with TP.

Memory for pointers to structures must be initialized in the same way as memory for other pointers, either by:

- using the address of another structure
- or by using dynamic memory allocation, that is, allocating memory on the heap

I will now provide an example for the first possibility.

```
typedef struct {
    double x;
    double y;
} PairT;

PairT w;
PairTP p = &w;
```

p now points to the structure w (see Figure 11–1).

The members of the structure w can be accessed through the pointer p, but this is a bit tricky. The expected syntax:

```
*p.w
```

is wrong, because * has lower precedence than . and so the above expression is equivalent to

```
* (p.w)
```

The correct syntax for using a pointer to access a structure's data is:

```
(*p) .w
```

C provides a simpler way of doing this, by using the -> operator:

```
p->w
```

Figure 11–1

Pointers to
structures

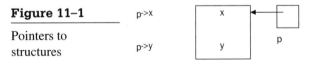

MEMBER ACCESS THROUGH POINTER

If p is a pointer to a structure that has a member w, then p->w gives access to w.

I will now describe dynamic memory allocation for structures. Consider again types PairT and PairTP and a pointer p:

```
PairTP p;
```

In order to allocate memory for p, you have to determine the amount of memory needed for the structure, which can be done using the sizeof() operator:

```
if((p = malloc(sizeof(struct pair))) == NULL) ...
```

or

```
if((p = malloc(sizeof(PairT))) == NULL) ...
```

MEMORY ALLOCATION FOR A STRUCTURE

For a structure s and a pointer p to this structure, use:

```
if((p = malloc(sizeof(struct s)) == NULL) ...
```

Types representing pointers to structures get special treatment. The compiler allows these types to be used prior to the definition of the corresponding structure type, as long as there are no references to members of the structure. (A forward declaration is not needed for pointers to the corresponding data type.) For example,

> You can not assume that the size of a structure is the same as the sum of the sizes of all its members, because the compiler may use padding to satisfy memory alignment requirements. Any program that makes such an assumption is not portable.

```
struct node {
    struct node *next;
    int i;
};
```

The `next` pointer is of the type `struct node *`, which at this point has an *incomplete definition*. Note that the following declaration

```
typedef struct node {
    NodeTP next;
     int i;
} NodeT, *NodeTP;
```

is illegal, because the declaration of `next` uses the *type identifier* `NodeTP`, which at that point is not defined.

Assume now that the structure `hidden` has not been defined yet, and consider the following definition of the type `Visible`:

```
typedef struct hidden *Visible;
```

The above gives an incomplete definition of the structure `hidden`, and allows you to use the type `Visible` as a synonym for "`struct hidden *`". I will use this technique later in Section 11.5.1 to implement opaque types.

11.4.2 ◆ Structures and Functions

Structures can be used as parameters for functions or as return values.

For example, I can declare a structure `pair`:

```
typedef struct pair {
    double x;
    double y;
} PairT, PairTP;
```

and create a *constructor* function which returns an initialized `pair` structure:

```
PairT constructorFunc(double x, double y) {
    PairT p;

    p.x = x;
    p.y = y;

    return p;
}
```

This function can now be called as follows:

```
PairT w = constructorFunc(1, 2.2);
```

The `constructorFunc()` function uses a local variable `p`, memory for which comes from the run-time stack. When the function terminates, the memory used by `p` is popped from the stack, but this does not create a dangling reference because as a rule, the return value is copied. Therefore, the contents of `p` is copied to `w`, even though the memory for `p` has already been popped from the stack. This example demonstrates another characteristic of returning structures as values of functions: the process is *inefficient* because structures have to be copied. The same problem occurs when you pass structures by value as function parameters. For example, the following function uses two structure parameters that are passed by value:

```
int compare(PairT p, PairT q) {   /* compares two structures */
    return p.x == q.x && p.y == q.y;
}
```

Now, consider the following code:

```
PairT w1 = constructorFunc(1, 2);
PairT w2 = constructorFunc(1, 3);
int i = compare(w1, w2);
```

As a result of the third call, `w1` is copied into `p` and `w2` is copied into `q` (`p` and `q` are parameters of `compare()`). To avoid this inefficiency, you can use the "Call by reference" idiom and the "Efficient call by reference" idiom to modify the constructor:

```
void constructorProc(PairTP this, double x, double y){
    this->x = x;
    this->y = y;
}
```

Note that the first parameter is needed because C does not provide a built-in "`this`". This constructor can be called as follows:

```
PairT w;
constructorProc(&w, 1, 2);
```

The function `compare()` can be rewritten as follows:

```
int compare(const PairTP p, const PairTP q) {
    return p->x == q->x && p->y == q->y;
}
```

The above constructor does *not* allocate memory. As a result, the following code is incorrect:

```
PairTP p;
constructorProc(p, 1, 2);
```

However, after a call to `malloc()`

```
PairTP p = malloc(...)
```

the above call to `constructorProc()` would be correct.

A version that performs memory allocation is best implemented as a function (below, I am using the "Memory allocation for structure" idiom):

```
PairTP constructor(double x, double y) {
   PairTP p;

   if((p = malloc(sizeof(PairT))) == NULL)
      return NULL;

   p->x = x;
   p->y = y;

   return p;
}
```

To allocate memory for a structure, do not use

```
   malloc(sizeof(struct *))
```

because this call will allocate a block large enough to store only a pointer to a structure, not the whole structure.

Using the new constructor function, you can construct a pair as follows:

```
PairTP p = constructor(1,2);
```

but then you have to remember to free it.

I should mention that you can *not* use an incomplete structure definition in a function declaration:

```
void f(struct elem*);
```

before declaring the incomplete type:

```
struct elem;
void f(struct elem *); /* OK */
```

11.4.3 ◆ Blocks of Structures and Pointers to Structures

Blocks of memory capable of storing a number of structures can be allocated using a variant of the "Memory allocation for n integers" idiom. For example, in order to represent a *rectangle*, you need a block that can store four pairs:

```
PairTP rectangle;
if((rectangle = malloc(4*sizeof(PairT))) == NULL) ...
```

In order to initialize this *block,* you need to traverse it, which can be done using a version of the "Block traversal" idiom. The constructorFunc() function, defined in the previous section, can be used for the initialization of each pair:

```
PairTP aux;
double x, y;

for(aux = rectangle; aux < rectangle + 4; aux++) {
   printf("Enter two double values:");
   if(scanf("%lf%lf", &x, &y) != 2) /* error */
      break;

   *aux = constructorFunc(x, y);
}
```

This version is correct, but also inefficient due to the use of the constructorFunc() function. To make it more efficient, I can rewrite it using the constructorProc() function defined in Section 11.4.2:

```
for(aux = rectangle; aux < rectangle + 4; aux++) {
   printf("Enter two double values:");
   if(scanf("%lf%lf", &x, &y) != 2) /* error */
      break;

   constructorProc(aux, x, y);
}
```

The rectangle represented by the block of data is now initialized, and I can output all of the coordinates of this rectangle:

```
int i;
for(i = 0; i < 4; i++)
    printf("vertex %d = (%f %f)\n",
        i, rectangle[i].x, rectangle[i].y);
```

Note that `rectangle[i]` represents a `pair`, with an x and a y component. In some situations you may actually want to have a block of pointers, and this can be accomplished using the "block of pointers" idiom (see Figure 11–2).

I will use the `constructor()` function from the previous section (which uses the "Block of pointers" idiom to initialize each vertex) and then print each pair:

```
int i;
for(i = 0; i < 4; i++) {
    printf("Enter two double values:");
    if(scanf("%lf%lf", &x, &y) != 2) /* error */
        error;

    if((prectangle[i] = constructor(x, y)) == NULL)
        error;
}
for(i = 0; i < 4; i++)
    printf("vertex %d = (%f %f)\n", i,
            prectangle[i][0].x, prectangle[i][0].y);
```

In the code, `prectangle[i]` is a pointer to the ith pair (see Figure 11–2); `prectangle[i][0]` is the ith pair, and so I can use `prectangle[i][0].x` to retrieve its x member.

11.4.4 ◆ Structures and Arrays

Arrays and structures can be arbitrarily combined in order to create arrays of structures, structures containing arrays, etc. For example, in order to represent named rectangles, I can create a structure with two members (see Figure 11–3):

Figure 11–2

Block rectangle of four pairs, and block prectangle of four pointers to rectangle.

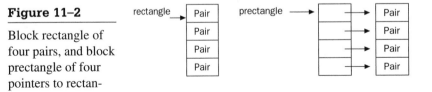

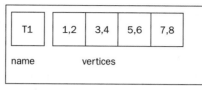

Figure 11–3

A rectangle repre-
sented by arrays and
structures

name represented as an array of characters

vertices represented as an array of four pair structures

```
#define MAX 20
typedef struct {
   char name[MAX+1];
   PairT vertices[4];
} RectangleT, *RectangleTP;
```

I will now show a function that can be used to initialize the rectangle structure, using a string name and four vertex pairs:

```
void constructRectangle(RectangleTP this, const char *name,
   const PairTP s1, const PairTP s2, const PairTP s3,
   const PairTP s4) {

   strncpy(this->name, name, MAX);
   this->vertices[0] = *s1;
   this->vertices[1] = *s2;
   this->vertices[2] = *s3;
   this->vertices[3] = *s4;
}
```

Note that in order to initialize the iTH element of the vertices array, I had to dereference the incoming pointer; for example,

```
vertices[0] = *s1
```

An alternate implementation of the function does not use any structures in the parameters list:

```
void constructRectangle(RectangleTP s, const char *name,
        double x1, double y1, double y1, double y2,
        double w1, double w2, double z1, double z2);
```

Some programmers prefer to avoid this style, since it generally results in very long lists of parameters, which in turn reduces the readability and usability of the code.

I want to look at one more function operating on my rectangle; the function `Show()`, which prints information about the rectangle. In order to implement it, I will use the "Efficient Call by Reference" idiom. Here is the code:

```
void Show(const RectangleTP s) {
   int i;
   printf("Rectangle %s\n", s->name);
   for(i = 0; i < 4; i++)
      printf("vertex %d = (%f %f)\n", i,
             s->vertices[i].x, s->vertices[i].y);
}
```

Looking at Figure 11–3, you can see that:

`s->name`	represents the array of characters
`s->vertices`	represents the array of pairs
`s->vertices[i]`	represents the ith pair
`s->vertices[i].x`	represents the x-coordinate of the ith pair

Inspection of the code of `constructRectangle()` reveals that it is inefficient and can be improved if the definition of `RectangleT` is changed as follows:

```
typedef struct {
   char name[Max+1];
   PairTP vertices[4];
} RectangleT, *RectangleTP;
```

As a side note, it is possible to overload the same identifier to be used for both a structure and an array. Specifically, this is only possible if you do not define a structure type using `typedef`; the syntax is

```
struct info {
   . . .
};
struct info info[20];
```

The identifier `info` used with the keyword `struct` refers to the structure; without the keyword `struct`, it refers to the array.

11.4.5 ◆ Initialization of Structures

Structures can be initialized with lists of constants, much like arrays, using braces and constant initializers. For example, given a structure `PairT`:

```
typedef struct {
    double x;
    double y;
} PairT;
```

it may be initialized as follows:

```
PairT p = {1, 2};
PairT q = {2.3, 4};
```

As a second example, given a definition of the structure `RectangleT`:

```
typedef struct {
    char name[Max+1];
    PairT vertices[4];
} RectangleT;
```

it may be initialized as follows:

```
RectangleT s = { "first",
            {
                {0, 1},
                {2, 3},
                {4, 5},
                {1, 2}
            }
        };
```

The nesting of braces is not required—the above initialization can be written as follows:

```
RectangleT s = { "first", 0, 1, 2, 3, 4, 5, 1, 2};
```

For the sake of clarity, when appropriate always use nested braces.

The rules for the number of initializing constants are the same for structures as for arrays. The actual number of initializers may be *less* than the number of members, in which case the trailing members are set to zero. It is illegal to provide *too many* initializers.

11.4.6 ◆ Structures and Pointers to Functions

As I mentioned earlier, structures have only *data* members. In an object-oriented paradigm, the programmer can group both data and functions together in a class, which has many advantages. In C, the only way to incorporate functions into a structure is by using pointers to functions (see Section 8.15). For example, in order to add a constructor function to the structure `pair` from Section 11.4.5, you can use the following code:

```
struct pair;
typedef struct pair {
    void (*constructor)(struct pair*, double, double);
    double x;
    double y;
} PairT, *PairTP;
```

We now have the classical "chicken and egg" problem, because the constructor is supposed to initialize the structure, but in order to use it, you first have to initialize the constructor pointer, as in:

```
void constructorProc(PairTP p, double x, double y);
PairT w;
w.constructor = constructorProc;
w.constructor(&w, 10, 2);
```

A partial solution to this problem is to use a global function which initializes the constructor:

```
void setConstructor(PairTP p,
            void (*constructor)(PairTP, double, double)) {
    p->constructor = constructor;
}
```

This addition means that there are now two steps required to initialize a structure. First, the pointer to the function must be initialized, using `setConstructor()`, and then the data members must be initialized. This example may cast doubt as to the usefulness of function pointers in structures. While structure members that are pointers to functions may not be so effective in the role as constructors, they do have various useful applications. For example, they may be used to set up *device drivers* for operating systems. Typically, device drivers use structures containing pointers to functions, like this:

```
struct device {
. . .
  int (*open)(struct device *dev);
  int (*stop)(struct device *dev);
. . .
}
```

These structures, in particular functions such as `open()` and `stop()`, can be initialized by code generated by operating system initialization routines, which are of the form:

```
struct device x = {
  . . .
  open,
  stop,
  . . .
}
```

The same technique can be used to initialize arrays of structures.

11.4.7 ◆ Structures and Header Files

In order to use structures in an interface, you can store their definitions in a header file representing this interface. If the same structure needs to be used in several source files, you have to store this structure in all of these files (they have internal linking; see Section 7.4.3). To avoid this code duplication, in such cases you should store structure definitions in a separate header file and include this file wherever it is needed. I will use this technique in Section 14.3.2.

11.4.8 ◆ Binary Files: Part 2

In this section, I will show one more example of binary files, this time applied to structures.

Example 11–1

Consider the problem of storing information about students; there are up to 100 students, and for every student we want to store her or his name (up to NAMELENN in size), up to 10 grades, the actual number of grades stored, and finally the GPA (grade point average). To implement a solution, I will use the following data structures:

```
#define STUDENTSN      100
#define MARKSN         10
#define NAMELENN       20
typedef struct {
    char name[NAMELENN+1];
    int marksNumber;
    double marks[MARKSN];
    double gpa;
} StudentT;
StudentT info[STUDENTSN];
```

I will consider the problem of writing the contents of the array `info` to a binary file, and processing information in this file. Let's start with saving the array. The function

```
int saveStudent(const char *fname, StudentT info[], int number);
```

will write `number` structures, contained in the array `info`, to the file `fname`. The implementation of this function is simple; it requires a single call to `fwrite()` (below, I omitted *any* error checking):

```
FILE *out;
out = fopen(fname, "wb");
fwrite(info, sizeof(StudentT), number, out);
```

Now, consider a function to process the information stored in a file without fetching it to the internal memory:

```
int gpaStudent(const char *fname, const char *studentName, double *gpa);
```

returns 0 if it fails, and 1 if it succeeds. In the latter case, it returns through the third parameter the `gpa` of the student whose name is `studentName`. Note that this function is not hard to implement because it is an accessor function, that is, it does not modify the file. I will keep reading structures from the file, one at a time, searching for the one that stores `studentName`; if I find it, I will retrieve the corresponding `gpa`:

```
FILE *in;
StudentT buffer;

if((in = fopen(fname, "rb")) == NULL)
    return 0;
```

```
while(fread(&buffer, sizeof(StudentT), 1, in) != 0)
    if(strncmp(buffer.name, studentName, NAMELENN) == 0) {
        *gpa = buffer.gpa;
        if(fclose(in) == EOF)
            return 0;

        return 1;
    }

fclose(in);
return 0;
```

Above, the while loop terminates when the required student has been found, the end-of-file has been encountered, or an error has occurred. I could have called `feof()` to determine what has actually happened, but in this case, it does not make any difference. As the next example, consider an example of *updating* the file, specifically initializing all of the `gpa` fields:

```
int updateGpa(const char *fname);
```

This function returns 0 if it fails, and 1 if succeeds. The file is opened for both input and output. In the main loop, I keep reading structures; for each structure, I calculate the corresponding gpa. The next step after the gpa calculation is to write the structure back to the file. To do so, I use `fseek()` to move the current file position back (after `fread()` was called, the current file position points to the position *following* the current structure). Finally, I use `fwrite()` to write the structure back to the file:

```
FILE *inOut;
StudentT buffer;
int i;

if((inOut = fopen(fname, "r+b")) == NULL)
    return 0;

while(fread(&buffer, sizeof(StudentT), 1, inOut) != 0) {

    for(i = 0, buffer.gpa = 0.0; i < buffer.marksNumber; i++)
        buffer.gpa += buffer.marks[i];

    if(buffer.marksNumber != 0)
        buffer.gpa /= buffer.marksNumber;

    if(fseek(inOut, -sizeof(StudentT), SEEK_CUR) != 0) {
        fclose(inOut);
        return 0;
    }
```

```
    if(fwrite(&buffer, sizeof(StudentT), 1, inOut) == 0) {
        fclose(inOut);
        return 0;
    }
}

if(!feof(inOut)) {
    fclose(inOut);
    return 0;
}
if(fclose(inOut) == EOF)
    return 0;
return 1;
```

Note that when the while loop terminates, either the end-of-file has been encountered or an error has occurred; therefore I use `feof()`. The complete code for this example may be found in the file `ex11-01.c`.

11.4.9 ◆ Introduction to Linked Lists

In this section, I will start discussing the application of structures to creating lists. I will show only the most basic examples and continue this discussion in Section 11.5.4, in which I will present the complete code for the module `Lists`.

A *list* is a collection of elements; each element contains data. Some typical operations for lists include the insertion or deletion of the first or the last object in the list, obtaining the length of the list, etc. Lists are typically unbounded, that is they can grow indefinitely, and therefore dynamic memory allocation is the most suitable method for providing memory for its objects.

I am now ready to present some of the data definitions and declarations for the module. Before I define the list elements, I will improve the maintainability of the code by defining the type of *data* stored in each object:

```
typedef double DataType;
```

This makes it easy for the programmer to change the type of data by changing one line of code. Each list element will be stored in a structure with two members: `value` and a pointer `next`, whose value will be `NULL` if there is no next element, otherwise it will be a structure representing the next element:

```
typedef struct elem {
    DataType value;
    struct elem *next;
} ElemT, *ElemTP;
```

I now need to define the type that will represent my list; it will be a structure with a pointer member whose value is the first element of the list, or NULL if the list is empty:

```
typedef struct {
    ElemTP first;
} ListT, *ListTP;
```

Armed with these definitions, I now know what the structure of the list is. An example of such a list p, containing two values 2 and 3.5, is shown in Figure 11–4.

Lists need to be constructed (that is initialized) and destructed (cleaned up). To construct a list, I will implement a function that returns an *initialized* list object; it returns NULL if memory could not be allocated:

```
ListTP construct(void) {
    ListTP p;

    if((p = malloc(sizeof(ListT))) == NULL)
        return NULL;
    p->first = NULL;

    return p;
}
```

The code to destruct a list is more complicated. First, the list parameter must be passed by *reference,* and secondly, the list must be *emptied* before it is destroyed. I will assume that I already have the function clear(), which removes all of the list elements (this function is declared later in this section):

```
void destruct(ListTP *this) {
    clear(*this);
    free(*this);
    *this = NULL;
}
```

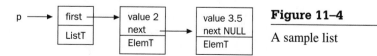

Figure 11–4

A sample list

Above, I used a "Memory deallocation" idiom. Elements of a list may be operated on by functions that perform:

- traversals, for example print all elements in the list
- modifications, for example insert or delete an element

For *traversals*, you do not need to use memory management functions, but for *modifications* you do; respectively `malloc()` to insert a new element and `free()` to remove the existing element. Often, modifications use traversals. For example, to delete the last list element, you have to first traverse the list to get to this element.

In my design, all list operations must preserve the following list *invariants*:

- for an empty list p, `p->first` is NULL
- for a non-empty list p, the value of `next` belonging to the last element is NULL.

I will first discuss traversals. The basic rule of traversing a list is remembering to stop when the end of the list is encountered (this may sound silly, but it's amazing how often this rule is forgotten). Keeping Figure 11–4 in mind, I will design a function that prints all of the elements in the list:

```
void printAll(const ListTP this);
```

The parameter `this` is passed using the "Efficient call by value" idiom, and the `const` keyword to indicate that this function does not modify the list. In order to traverse the list, I will use an auxiliary pointer `aux`, which will be initially set to point to the first element, using

```
aux = this->first;
```

At each point in the traversal, `aux` will be moved to point to the next element, using

```
aux = aux->next;
```

See Figure 11–5.

The complete code for `printAll()` follows:

```
ElemTP aux;
for(aux = this->first; aux != NULL; aux = aux->next)
    printf("%f\n", aux->value);
```

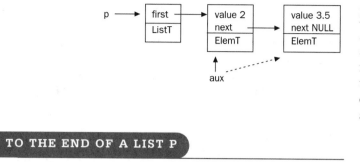

Figure 11–5

Auxiliary pointer aux points to the first element, and then to the second element (dotted arrow).

TRAVERSAL TO THE END OF A LIST P

```
for(aux = p->first; aux != NULL; aux = aux->next)
```

In order to insert a new element in front of a list, you must save the current state of the list, allocate and initialize memory for a new element, and then reconnect the list:

```
int insertFront(ListTP this, DataType d) {
    ElemTP aux;

    if((aux = malloc(sizeof(ElemT))) == NULL)
        return 0;

    aux->next = this->first;    /* save the state */
    aux->value = d;
    this->first = aux;

    return 1;
}
```

As I mentioned before, it is important to check that the code works not only for the "usual" circumstances but also for the boundary conditions (or special cases). In the case of the list traversal, there are two special cases I must think about: memory allocation for a new element may fail, and the list may be initially empty. Considering the second case:

- if the list is initially empty, then `this->first` is NULL. After `aux` was allocated memory, `aux->next` was therefore set to NULL, and then `first` is set to the new element
- if the list is not empty, the value of `aux->next` is set to what was the first element, and then `this->first` is set to the new first element

The list parameter `this` is passed by value, because `this` itself does not get modified; instead, the *contents* of `this` does.

I now need a function that deletes the *last* element from the list. I have three special cases to consider. First, the list may be empty. Second, if the list has only one element, then I have to modify `this->first`. Third, in order to delete the last element, I have to traverse the list, and stop when I reach the *predecessor* of the last element, because I will have to set this element's `next` pointer—specifically, set it to NULL. For example, looking at Figure 11–4, you can see that in order to delete the last element, you need a pointer to the element containing the value 2, so that the member `next` of this element may be updated.

The implementation provided for the `deleteLast()` function returns the data from the last element *through* the `value` parameter; it returns 1 through the function value if successful, and 0 otherwise:

```
int deleteLast(ListTP this, DataType *value) {
    ElemTP aux;

    if(this->first == NULL)   /* empty list */
        return 0;

    if(this->first->next == NULL) { /* single element */
        *value = this->first->value;
        free(this->first);
        this->first = NULL;
        return 1;
    }
    for(aux = this->first; aux->next->next != NULL;
        aux = aux->next)
        ;     /* get to the last element */

    *value = aux->next->value;
    free(aux->next);
    aux->next = NULL;

    return 1;
}
```

The stop condition in the `for` statement uses `aux->next`, which is well defined only if `aux != NULL`. However, this is always the case, because:

■ initially, `aux` is equal to `this->first`, and the first `if` statement checks if this value is not NULL

■ in each step of the loop, `aux` is modified only if `aux->next` is not NULL

Note that the value stored in the last element must be retrieved *before* this element is deallocated.

TRAVERSAL TO THE PREDECESSOR OF THE LAST OBJECT IN A LIST

Assuming the list is not empty and has more than one element

```
for(aux = p->first; aux->next != NULL; aux = aux->next)
```

The last function I will implement is the function `clear()`, responsible for removing all of the elements from the list. It does not destroy the actual list. This code is similar to the function that deletes the *first* element from the list, so I will first implement this `deleteFirst()` function:

```
int deleteFirst(ListTP this) {
    ElemTP aux = this->first;

    if(aux == NULL)     /* empty list */
        return 0;

    this->first = aux->next;  /* removed first element */
    free(aux);

    return 1;
}
```

I am now ready to write the code for `clear()`:

```
void clear(ListTP this) {
    while(deleteFirst(this))
        ;
    this->first = NULL;
}
```

I will continue the discussion of lists in Section 11.5.4 and in Chapter 14.

11.5 Module-Based Programming: Part 3

In this section, I will describe the implementation of opaque types, and how they may be used to design modules. I will also explain how to create multiple-instance modules.

11.5.1 ◆ Implementation of Opaque Types

Recall from Section 11.3.1 that an *incomplete* pointer type does not require that the full definition be provided in the file in which it appears, as long as it is eventually provided. This makes incomplete definitions of pointers particularly suitable for representing opaque types—the client never sees the full type definition, only the incomplete type provided in the header file.

For example, consider a module `Mod` (see Section 7.4.7) that exports a data type called `Abstract` to the client. This data type is called **opaque** because the client can not access its full representation—all the client knows is that it is represented by another data type, but he or she does not know what that data type is (for my example, I will call this type `Concrete`).

An opaque type can be implemented using the technique described below:

The header file `Mod.h` defines a type `Abstract` as a pointer to a structure type called `Concrete`; there is no definition of `Concrete` in this file (see Figure 11–6).

```
typedef struct Concrete *Abstract;
```

The type `Concrete` is defined in the implementation file. The type `Abstract` can be used in the header file provided there are no attempts to dereference values of this type. For example

```
void f(Abstract p);
```

is legal, but

```
Abstract p;
p->x
```

Figure 11–6

Representation of an opaque type

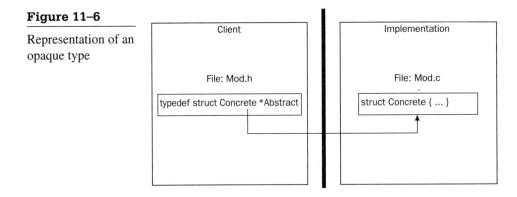

is illegal, because the type `Abstract` represents a pointer to the type `Concrete`, and the compiler has no information about this type. This limitation is not a problem when designing interfaces stored in header files, because these files do not provide the code; they only provide function declarations. Specifically, the interface of the module will consist of functions that reference only the `Abstract` type.

The header file can be included by another file and that file can be separately compiled. However, in order to create executable code, the implementation file containing the full definition of the type `Concrete` must also be linked.

OPAQUE

In order to represent an opaque type `Abstract`, use the definition of the form

```
typedef struct Concrete *Abstract
```

in the header file. Define the structure `Concrete` in the implementation file.

11.5.2 ◆ Enumerations

Section 8.18.3 showed one application of an enumeration. The specific implementation had a serious limitation, namely it was a *singleton* module, which meant that the client could have only one enumeration running at any given point in time. In Java, it is possible to have multiple enumerations, using the `elements()` method. Specifically, collection classes, such as HashTable, have a method called `elements()` that returns a specialized Enumeration, which is an implementation of the Enumeration interface. Using this method, the client can obtain references to multiple enumerations and run them independently.

I will now redesign the module `Enum` described in Section 8.18.3 so that the client can create multiple enumerations. The design uses the "Opaque" idiom for the `Abstract` and `Concrete` enumeration types (see Figure 11–7):

```
typedef struct Concrete_Enumeration *Abstract_Enumeration;
```

I need a constructor function that will associate an enumeration with the data structure, which will be enumerated. Since the enumeration is generic, the function `create_Enumeration()` has a parameter of type `void*`:

```
Abstract_Enumeration create_Enumeration(void *);
```

Figure 11–7

Design of Abstract
Enumeration

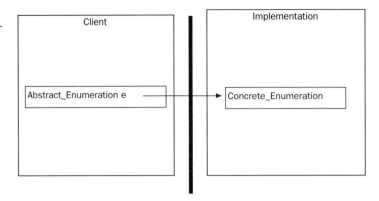

In an implementation using a specific data type, the appropriate cast will be used for this parameter when the function is called. To avoid having to cast objects each time, the interface defines an auxiliary macro:

```
#define nextElementTyped_Enumeration(type, p) \
    ((type)nextElement_Enumeration(p))
```

Two other enumeration functions look like this:

```
int hasMoreElements_Enumeration(Abstract_Enumeration);
void* nextElement_Enumeration(Abstract_Enumeration);
```

The function to destruct the enumeration is missing, because the client can simply use the `free()` function to perform this task.

The complete code for the interface is in file `ex11-enum.h`.

11.5.3 ◆ Generic Dynamic Array Module with Enumerations

In this section, I will show a modified version of the concrete module representing dynamic arrays, introduced in Section 10.5. The new version provides a generic module that can be used to create dynamic arrays of *any* data type. In addition, it allows the client to create multiple enumerations used to traverse the array (see Figure 11–8). The only limitation is that while the enumeration is in progress, the client should not call the provided `set()` function, because this call may result in expanding memory for the array, thus invalidating the enumeration (which would continue to try and operate on the old memory). This module also allows the client to create an arbitrary number of *instances,* specifically dynamic arrays.

One can argue that enumerations are not needed for the array because arrays support random access operations, here called `get()` and `set()`. However, I believe that enumerations are useful for every data structure, and therefore provide them here.

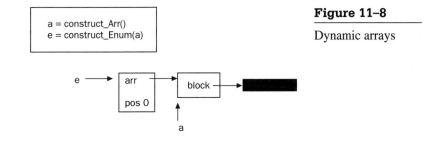

Figure 11–8

Dynamic arrays

Interface

The interface uses the "Opaque" idiom to create an abstract data type:

```
typedef struct Concrete_Arr *Abstract_Arr;
```

Remaining operations are similar to those described in Section 10.5, except that they require an additional parameter representing an array:

```
Abstract_Arr construct_Arr(size_t elSize, int initSize);
void *get_Arr(const Abstract_Arr this, int i);
void set_Arr(Abstract_Arr this, void *value, int i);
int length_Arr(const Abstract_Arr this);
void destruct_Arr(Abstract_Arr *this);
```

The complete code may be found in file ex11-1-Arr.h.

Application

In this section, I will show an application of the array module, which will read a line of *unlimited* length from a file. First, an array is created, initially of size 80:

```
a1 = construct_Arr(sizeof(char), 80))
```

This array will automatically grow when set() is called, and there is not enough memory allocated for it, which frees the client from having to worry about array overflow:

```
for(i = 0; (c = fgetc(f)) != '\n'; i++) {
   if(c == EOF) {
      fprintf(stderr, "could not read first line\n");
      destruct_Arr(&a1);
      return EXIT_FAILURE;
   }
   set_Arr(a1, &c, i);
}
```

Next, an enumeration associated with this array is created, and used to traverse and print the line:

```
e1 = construct_Enumeration(a1);
while(hasMoreElements_Enumeration(e1))
    putchar(nextElementTyped_Enumeration(char, e1));
```

The call to `putchar()` uses the macro `nextElementTyped_Enumeration` supplied in the enumeration interface, which performs a cast to the *type* passed as a parameter of this macro; here `char`.

The array is destroyed using a provided destructor, and the enumeration is freed:

```
destruct_Arr(&a1);
free(e1);
```

The complete code may be found in file `ex11-1-Arr-main.c`.

Implementation

I will now discuss the implementation of the module `Arr`. Since it implements both arrays and enumerations, the implementation provides *two* concrete data types, respectively, for the array and for the enumeration. The concrete data type for the array looks like this:

```
struct Concrete_Arr {
    void *block_;
    int size_;
    size_t elSize_;
    int init_;
};
```

The member `block_` points to the block of memory allocated for the array, `size_` is the size of this block, `elSize_` is the size of each element of the array, and `init_` is a flag used to indicate whether or not the array has been initialized. The constructor creates a "new" array by allocating memory for the structure `Concrete_Arr`, initializing this structure using its parameters, and returning a pointer to it:

```
Abstract_Arr construct_Arr(size_t elSize, int initSize) {
    Abstract_Arr arr;

    if((arr = malloc(sizeof(struct Concrete_Arr))) == NULL)
        return NULL;
```

```
    arr->init_ = 1;
    arr->elSize_ = elSize;
    if((arr->block_ = calloc(initSize, elSize)) == NULL) {
        free(arr);
        return NULL;
    }

    arr->size_ = initSize;
    return arr;
}
```

Note that the constructor also initializes memory for the `block_` variable; should this initialization fail, the previously allocated memory for the structure is deallocated.

The destructor deallocates both blocks allocated by the constructor:

```
void destruct_Arr(Abstract_Arr *this) {
    if(!(*this)->init_)
        return;

    free((*this)->block_);
    free(*this);
    *this = NULL;
}
```

Function `get_Arr()` returns a pointer to the ith element of the array:

```
void* get_Arr(const Abstract_Arr this, int i) {
    assert(this->init_ && i >= 0 && i < this->size_);

    if(this->init_ && i >= 0 && i < this->size_)
        return this->block_ + i*this->elSize_;

    return NULL;
}
```

This function first checks its preconditions: has the array been initialized, and is the index `i` correct. If both of these check out, it returns the ith object in the `block_`.

The function `set_Arr()` uses a local function `expand_()`, which is responsible for reallocating memory:

```
static int expand_(Abstract_Arr this, int size) {
    void *new;
```

```
      if((new = calloc(size, this->elSize_)) == NULL)
         return 0;


      memcpy(new, this->block_, this->size_);
      /* copy the old array */
      this->size_ = size;
      /* update size_ and block_ */
      free(this->block_);
      this->block_ = new;

      return 1;
   }
```

The function `set_Arr()` checks if memory should be expanded, and if so, calls `expand_()`. To avoid too many calls to `expand_()`, the block of memory is increased by the value of `increment_`, a private variable in the module:

```
void set_Arr(Abstract_Arr this, void *value, int i) {
   int res;

   assert(i >= 0 && this->init_);
   if(i < 0 || !this->init_)
      return;

   if(i >= this->size_) { /* expand */
      res = expand_(this, i + increment_);
      assert(this);
      if(res == 0)
         return;
   }
   memcpy(this->block_ + i*this->elSize_, value,
         this->elSize_);
}
```

I am now ready to describe the implementation of an enumeration. The concrete type used for an enumeration is:

```
struct Concrete_Enumeration {
   int pos;
   Abstract_Arr arr;
};
```

where `arr` is the array being enumerated and `pos` is the current position in this array. The constructor of the enumeration allocates memory for the concrete enumeration and then associates an array with the enumeration.

```
Abstract_Enumeration construct_Enumeration(void *p) {
    Abstract_Enumeration e;

    if((e = calloc(1, sizeof(struct Concrete_Enumeration)))
            == NULL)
        return NULL;

    e->arr = (Abstract_Arr)p;
    e->pos = 0;

    return e;
}
```

The implementation of the `nextElement_Enumeration()` increments the current position, and returns the object associated with the *previous* current position:

```
void* nextElement_Enumeration(Abstract_Enumeration e) {
    void *aux;

    assert(e->arr->init_);
    if(e->pos == e->arr->size_)
        return NULL;

    aux = e->arr->block_ + e->pos*e->arr->elSize_;
    e->pos++;

    return aux;
}
```

The complete code may be found in file `ex11-1-Arr.c`.

At this point, I would like to re-examine the design to determine what the client can and can not do. The implementation does not know the actual type of each element, therefore the client can choose to use any data type and create a dynamic array consisting of elements of this type. For example, the client can create an array X of `double` values with an initial size 10 by the constructor call:

```
X = construct_Arr(sizeof(double), 10);
```

The client is responsible for using doubles with X; the compiler is not capable of detecting if a value of a *different* data type is used. It is also possible to create another array Y that has elements of a different data type; for example int, using

```
Y = construct_Arr(sizeof(int), 10);
```

In other words, the above module supports the creation of multiple arrays, possibly consisting of different data types (but each array is homogenous, meaning that it has elements of the same type).

As I described in previous chapters, testing programs should involve looking at the boundary conditions. For generic modules, a good test involves using *pointers*. For example, let's consider a dynamic array S of strings, created using:

```
S = construct_Arr(sizeof(char*), 2);
```

and let's store the string constant "first" in the array S at position 0. You can do so using set_Arr():

```
set_Arr(S, &"first", 0);
```

The state of memory is shown in Figure 11–9.
Therefore

```
printf("%s", (char*)get_Arr(S, 0));
```

will print "first". However, the user of the module Arr should be aware of the fact that this module does not perform *deep copying* of its arguments. As a result, pointers from the array may share values with pointers from other parts of the code, and if that code ever deallocates memory, the dynamic array will end up storing dangling references. In Section 14.3, I will describe techniques that can be used to implement deep copying, but for now, I will add that using fixed-sized strings stored in *arrays* is safe. For example, consider the type String10 that represents an array of 10 characters:

```
typedef char String10[11];
```

Figure 11–9

The state of dynamic array S

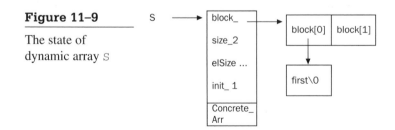

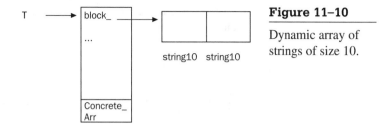

Figure 11–10

Dynamic array of strings of size 10.

When you create a dynamic array of elements of this type:

```
T = construct_Arr(sizeof(String10), 2);
```

`block_` does not contain pointers; instead it contains objects of type `String10` (see Figure 11–10).

The client of the array module can create any number of instances. In some situations, you may want to limit the number of instances, say to n instances. To do so, the function `construct_Arr()`, which returns a new instance, will check if there are already n instances created, and if so, will return `NULL`; otherwise, it will return the new instance.

11.5.4 ◆ List Module

In this section, I will describe the module `LIST`, whose design is based on the following assumptions:

1. the type `DataType` of the data stored in list elements is *known to the implementation*

2. any number of lists can be created; all lists must have elements of the *same* type, namely `DataType`

3. the module supports enumerations

4. the module does *not* support persistence, that is lists can not be saved and later retrieved

5. the representation of the list and list elements are not made visible to the client

This particular version of `List` will operate on a list of strings, which will give us a chance to discuss *shallow and deep copying*. The list and list element type should not be confused with `DataType`, which for this example will be `char *`.

Insertions and deletions of list elements require very careful consideration. When you insert a new element d into the list, you typically write something like this:

```
aux->value = d;
```

Unfortunately, if d and aux->value are pointers, this assignment results in a *shallow* copy, which means that the value from the client and the value within the list will be shared. This is fine until the client deallocates the variable d, rendering the aux->value a dangling reference.

A safe solution is to use a *deep* copy—copy the value pointed to by the pointer over to the list element. (Note that in Java this function is represented by a clone() method.) The implementation of the copy operation depends on the data type being copied, and since the implementation should not be modified every time the DataType is modified, I will use a callback function called copyData_List().

In general, it is sufficient to have a *single* callback function, which is declared in the header file and defined (that is implemented) in the implementation file. If you need different callback functions for various instances of the module, then one of the parameters of the constructor must represent the callback function. Since in my design, I assumed that there would always be a single DataType, a single callback function will be satisfactory. I will show two sample implementations of this function; the first one is used to copy strings (for the implementation of the function strdup(), see Example 9–2):

```
DataType copyData_List(const DataType v) {
   return strdup(v);
}
```

The second callback, used to copy doubles, is trivial:

```
DataType copyData_List(const DataType v) {
   return v;
}
```

There is another issue related to my design decision with respect to the *implementation code* dealing with the copying of the data to be inserted. When a list element is to be deleted, the data in this element must be deallocated by the implementation code, rather than by the client, in order to avoid memory leaks. To support this deallocation, I need another *callback* function, freeData_List(). This function may be implemented for a string as follows:

```
void freeData_List(DataType v) {
   free(v);
}
```

For double values, this function will do nothing:

```
void freeData_List(DataType v) {
}
```

Other extensions and variants of the shallow and deep interfaces will be discussed in Section 14.3.

Interface

Since the implementation knows the data type, the interface will contain a declaration of the type:

```
typedef char* DataType;
```

To support the fifth assumption, I will use the "Opaque" idiom and define:

```
typedef struct Concrete_List *Abstract_List;
```

The type representing the list *element* will not be made visible to the client, even in its abstract form.

The following functions are declared in the interface:

```
DataType copyData_List(const DataType v);
void freeData_List(DataType v);
Abstract_List construct_List(void);
int insert_List(Abstract_List this, int pos, DataType value);
int delete_List(Abstract_List this, int pos, DataType *value);
int length_List(const Abstract_List this);
void destruct_List(Abstract_List *this);
```

The first two functions are callback functions, the implementation of which must be provided by the client. They are declared in the header file so that the implementation code can call them.

In order to initialize a list, the client declares a list variable and uses a constructor:

```
Abstract_List myList;
if((myList = construct_List) == 0) error
```

Delete and insert operations take an additional integer parameter pos, which represents the position of the element to be deleted, or the position at which the element is to be inserted. (Inserting at position 0 means inserting in front of the list, inserting at position 1 means inserting after the first element, etc.):

```
int insert_List(Abstract_List this, int pos, DataType value);
int delete_List(Abstract_List this, int pos, DataType *value);
```

I can use these functions to build a list consisting of {"one", "two"}:

```
if(insert_List(myList, 0, "one") == 0) error
if(insert_List(myList, 1, "two") == 0) error
```

A list should be removed when it is not needed anymore, by using a destructor:
```
destruct_List(&myList);
```
This function first removes all elements from the list, and then deallocates memory that has been allocated for this list. To support the third assumption, the interface includes enumeration functions (see Section 11.5.2); here I will use a deep copy implementation of this interface. The complete code for the interface may be found in file ex11-2-list.h.

Application

In this section, I will show an application using the List module, which reads words from a file and stores them in a list. For this example, I made the assumption that a *word* consists of at most 80 non-whitespace characters, and the list will store string data (pointers to char). As a result, the application will have to implement the copyData() and freeData() functions, which I illustrated earlier.

In the main program, the list is constructed and initialized by words which are read from a file using fscanf() and inserted in front of the list:

```
if((a1 = construct_List()) == NULL) {
   error
}

while(fscanf(f, "%80s", buffer) == 1)
   if(insert_List(a1, 0, buffer) == 0) {
      error
   }
```

After all of the words have been read, they are printed using an enumeration:

```
e1 = construct_Enumeration(a1);
printf("words backward are:\n");
while(hasMoreElements_Enumeration(e1)) {
   aux = nextElementTyped_Enumeration(char*, e1);
```

```
      printf("%s\n", aux);
      free(aux);
   }
   free(el);
   destruct_List(&a1);
```

The client must remember to free memory allocated by the enumeration function; otherwise the code creates memory leaks (this is why `free(aux)` is needed in each step of the loop). In this example, there is really no need for using a deep copy for *enumerations*; a shallow copy would be sufficient. For now, I will not change the code to use a shallow copy. In Chapter 14, I will discuss both shallow and deep interfaces.

The complete code may be found in file `ex11-2-list-main.c`.

Implementation

The implementation of the list uses two concrete data types. The first type represents a list element, and is not visible to the client:

```
typedef struct elem {
   DataType value;
   struct elem *next;
} ElemT, *ElemTP;
```

The second type represents a list, and is the representation of the abstract type `Abstract_List` used by the client:

Interface:
```
typedef struct Concrete_List
      *Abstract_List;
```

Implementation:
```
struct Concrete_List {
   ElemTP first;
};
```

The list is initialized using a constructor, which allocates memory and sets the pointer `first` to NULL:

```
Abstract_List construct_List(void) {
   Abstract_List p;

   if((p = malloc(sizeof(struct Concrete_List))) == NULL)
      return NULL;

   p->first = NULL;

   return p;
}
```

I will now discuss the implementation of:

```
int insert_List(Abstract_List this, int pos, DataType value);
```

First, this function checks whether pos is less than the length of the list. There are two cases to consider when thinking about the correctness of this function: inserting at the front of the list (pos == 0), and inserting after the pos-th element. In the first case, the code allocates memory for the new element and uses the call-back function to copy the value into this element; it then connects this new element with the list:

```
/* insert in front */
if((auxm = malloc(sizeof(ElemT))) == NULL)
    return 0;

auxm->value = copyData_List(value);
auxm->next = this->first;
this->first = auxm;
```

In the second case, the list has to be traversed in order to find the pos-th element:

```
ElemTP auxp;
for(i = 1, auxp = this->first; i < pos; i++,
   auxp = auxp->next)
   ;
```

Note that i is initialized to 1, rather than to 0. If pos is equal to 1, we are inserting after the first element, and so we need a pointer to this element. In this case the above loop will not execute, and so auxp will be left pointing to the first element. For example, consider a list consisting of two elements, and assume that pos is equal to 2 (we are inserting after the last element). In this case, the loop will execute once, leaving auxp pointing to the last element.

Once the required list element has been found, it is easy to insert a new element after this element:

```
if((auxm = malloc(sizeof(ElemT))) == NULL)
    return 0;
auxm->value = copyData_List(value);
auxm->next = auxp->next;
auxp->next = auxm;
```

I will now move on to the delete function. The implementation of this function has to consider two boundary cases: deletion of the first element, and deletion of the pos-th element, where pos>1. The `first` pointer has to be modified only if the first element is deleted (in particular, as a result of deleting the first element, the list may become empty). Error checking is the same for deleting as for inserting; that is, testing with a negative value of `pos`, and with a `pos` that is greater than the length of the list.

The first case is implemented by saving a pointer to the first element in an auxiliary variable, reconnecting the list to remove the first element, retrieving the value stored in the element being removed (using the `copyData_List()` callback function), and finally deallocating memory. Memory for the data is deallocated using the `freeData_List()` callback function:

```
if(pos == 1) { /* delete first */
   auxp = this->first;
   this->first = this->first->next;
   *value = copyData_List(auxp->value);
   freeData_List(auxp->value);
   free(auxp);
}
```

The second case is slightly more complicated, because I have to find the predecessor of the `pos`-th element, and so I will try the modified "Traversal to the predecessor of the end of list" idiom:

```
for(i = 1, auxp = this->first; i < pos; i++,
    auxp = auxp->next)
   ;
```

Since I have already considered the case where `pos` is equal to 1, and I know that `pos` is not greater that the length of the list, I only have to make sure that `auxp` points to the predecessor of the `pos`-th element. For example, if `pos` is equal to 2, the loop will be executed once, leaving `auxp` pointing to the second element of the list—therefore the code is **wrong**. My loop should have looked like this:

```
for(i = 1, auxp = this->first; i < pos-1; i++,
    auxp = auxp->next)
   ;
```

Now for `pos == 2`, the loop terminates, leaving `auxp` pointing to the first element. (You may wish to think about another boundary case where `pos` is equal to the length of the list.) The rest of the code is now simple:

```
auxm = auxp->next;
auxp->next = auxp->next->next;
```

```
*value = copyData_List(auxm->value);
freeData_List(auxm->value);
free(auxm);
```

Finally, I will discuss the implementation of enumerations. The concrete data type used by the implementation is:

```
struct Concrete_Enumeration {
    ElemTP pos;
}
```

Therefore, each enumeration will have a pointer `pos` pointing to the current element of the list being enumerated. An enumeration is created by allocating memory and setting `pos` to point to the first element of the list:

```
Abstract_Enumeration construct_Enumeration(void *p) {
    Abstract_Enumeration e;

    if((e = calloc(1, sizeof(struct Concrete_Enumeration)))
        == NULL)
      return NULL;

    e->pos = ((Abstract_List)p)->first;

    return e;
}
```

The enumeration function that returns a pointer to the data stored in the *next* element looks like this:

```
void* nextElement_Enumeration(Abstract_Enumeration e) {
    DataType aux;

    if(e->pos == NULL)
        return NULL;

    aux = copyData_List(e->pos->value);
    e->pos = e->pos->next;

    return aux;
}
```

This function uses the callback function to return a copy of the data to the client. The client of this module must remember that it is her or his responsibility to deallocate memory for this copy.

The complete code for the implementation may be found in the file `ex11-2-list.c`.

11.6 List of Common Errors

1. ```
   struct example { ... };

   example e;
   ```

   Should be:

   ```
   struct example e;
   ```

   The following declaration is also wrong:

   ```
   struct example {  ...  }
   ```

   The missing semicolon will produce a long list of compiler errors.

2. To allocate memory for a structure, do not use

   ```
   malloc(sizeof(struct *))
   ```

   because this call will allocate a block large enough to store only a pointer to a structure, not the whole structure.

11.7 List of Idioms

MEMBER ACCESS THROUGH POINTER

If p is a pointer to a structure that has a member w, then p->w gives access to w.

MEMORY ALLOCATION FOR A STRUCTURE

For a structure s and a pointer p to this structure, use:

```
if((p = malloc(sizeof(struct s)) == NULL) ...
```

TRAVERSAL TO THE END OF A LIST P

```
for(aux = p->first; aux != NULL; aux = aux->next)
```
```

TRAVERSAL TO THE PREDECESSOR OF THE LAST OBJECT IN A LIST

Assuming the list is not empty, and has more than one element:

```
for(aux = p->first; aux->next != NULL; aux = aux->next)
```

OPAQUE

In order to represent an opaque type `Abstract`, use the definition of the form

```
typedef struct Concrete *Abstract
```

in the header file. Define the structure `Concrete` in the implementation file.

11.8 List of Programming Style Guidelines

1. Names of structures defined with `typedef` start with an uppercase letter and end with the uppercase T.
2. Type names representing pointers to structures have names ending with TP.
3. For the sake of clarity, when appropriate always use nested braces.

11.9 List of Portability Guidelines

You can not assume that the size of a structure is the same as the sum of the sizes of all its members, because the compiler may use padding to satisfy memory alignment requirements. Any program that makes such an assumption is not portable.

11.10 Exercises

All functions should be well documented. For any exercise that asks you to implement a function, include a main program that carefully tests this function.

Exercise 11-1

Assume the following definition for this exercise:

```
typedef struct {
    double something;
```

```
        char* name;
    } ElemT;
    #define MAX 100
```

Write the definition of a function `Show()`, which takes as one of its parameters an array of structures `ElemT` (there are 100 structures in this array) and returns through another parameter the number of names which are equal to `"Mary"`. Note that for some structures, the value of `name` may be equal to `NULL`.

Exercise 11-2

Consider the following two parallel arrays used to store information about books:

```
#define M 1000          /* maximum number of books */
int bookId[M];          /* book IDs */
char *bookName[M];      /* book names */
```

Each book has a unique id, but there may be several books with the same name. An integer variable

```
  int size;
```

specifies how many books are stored in the array. Assume that the "effective size" of both arrays satisfies this condition:

```
0 <= size < M
```

and books are never removed from the arrays.

Modify the above definitions and use *structures* and a single array of structures. Then, write definitions of the following functions:

```
void printIds(const char *name);
/* prints IDs of all books with this name */
void printAll(const char *fname);
/* writes to the text file fname lines of the form:
 * book name tab book id
 * In case of any errors, write to the standard output
 */
char *myId(int id);
/* returns the name of the book with this id;
 * or NULL if this book is not in the array
 */
int addBook(const char *name, int id);
/* adds a book with the given name and id, and returns 1;
 * returns 0 if fails (the array is full)
 */
```

Write a menu-driven main program to test all these functions.

Exercise 11-3

Design the data structures for a collection of exactly 100 tickets; each ticket has a long ID, a double price, and a string name (use an array of 20 characters). Then, write definitions of the following functions (for these functions, your data structures are global, i.e. are not passed by parameters):

```
int myTicket(double* price, const char* name, long ID);
/* Returns 0 if the collection does not contain a ticket with the given
 * name and ID. Otherwise, returns 1, and returns  the price of this
 * ticket through the parameter price.
 * Assumes that there is at most one ticket with the given name and ID.
 */
double leastExpensive();
/* return the price of the least expensive ticket */
int initialize(const char *fname);
/* reads a text file fname in which every line is of the form:
 *  id one-or-more spaces price one-or-more spaces name
 * and stores this information in the data structure;
 * returns 1 if successful and 0 otherwise
 */
```

Exercise 11-4

Consider the following definition:

```
typedef struct {
    int data[100];
    int size;
} *DataTP;
```

where `size` is interpreted as the number of elements in the array `data` (i.e. `0 <= size < 100`). Write a function `initialize(const char *fname)` that reads integer values from the text file and stores them in the above data structure.

Then, write a function `divisible()`, which returns the number of elements in `d` which are divisible by `factor`:

```
int divisible(const DataTP d, int factor);
```

Exercise 11-5

Consider the following modification of the data structure from Exercise 11-4:

```
typedef struct {
    int *data;
    int size;
} *DataTP;
```

size is interpreted as the number of elements in the block pointed to by data. Implement both of the functions described in Exercise 11–4 (note that the function initialize() determines the number of integer values present and allocates memory for data).

Exercise 11–6

Write a void function input() which has two parameters: fname which represents the name of a text file, and storage which represents an array of pointers to characters:

```
#define MAX 100
char* storage[MAX];
```

input() reads the file fname and stores storage lines from this file in the array. Do not make any assumptions about the length of input lines (use a function getLine() from Example 10–3). The function input() should then remove all lines that are empty (contain only the end-of-line character, possibly preceded by whitespace characters) from this array, and report the number of lines that have been removed. Then, write the main function which calls input(), and then outputs the contents of the array storage to the standard output stream.

Exercise 11–7

Consider the type StudentT, representing a student name and id and defined by

```
typedef struct {
   char *name;
   int id ;
} StudentT;
```

A global array table (only the first tabsize elements of the array are used) is also declared:

```
StudentT table[100];
int tabsize = 0; /* 0 <= tabsize <= 100 */
```

Write a function add(), which adds a student to the table using the following prototype:

```
int add(const char *sName, int sId);
```

where sName and sId are the name and id of the student to add. Duplicates are not allowed, and id is a key. The function must return the index of the array element where the student record is added or −1 if the student record is not added.

Now suppose that the table is redefined to be an array of pointers to StudentT structures:

```
StudentT *tabp[100];
int tabsize = 0; /* 0 <= tabsize <= 100 */
```

Write a new version of the `add()` function to update `tabp` rather than `tab`.

Exercise 11-8

We can store information about a text line using a structure. The first field of this structure stores the length of the text line (all characters excluding the end-of-line), and the second field stores all of the characters in that line (excluding the end-of-line). We will assume that there are at most 80 characters in the line. Write an int function `getLine()`, which reads a single line from the input stream, stores this line in the structure using the format described above, and returns the line through a parameter. This function returns the number of characters in the input line, or −1 if end-of-file was encountered before the end-of-line character.

Exercise 11-9

Consider the following data structures::

```
const int Max = 100;
typedef int IntType[Max];
typedef struct {
    IntType integers;  /* up to 100 integers */
    int counter;  /* the actual number of integers */
} IntegersT;
```

Write a procedure `KillOdds()` which removes all odd numbers from the integer array and updates the counter field of the structure.

Exercise 11-10

The following definition can be used to represent a list of double values:

```
typedef struct node {
    struct node *next;
    double value;
} NodeT, *NodeTP;
```

Write the following functions:

■ `NodeTP dupNode(const NodeTP *p)` that returns a copy of p

■ `deleteNode(p)` that recovers the storage used by the node p that is no longer needed and sets the value of p to NULL

■ `int maxi(firstEle, largestEle)`, where `firstEle` is a pointer to the first element of the list. The second parameter `largestEle` is used to return the largest element in the list, if the list is non-empty; otherwise, −1 is returned. `maxi()` returns 1 if the list is non-empty and 0 if the list is empty.

- ▪ `int insert(firstEle, value)`, where `firstEle` is a pointer to the first element of the list and `value` is an integer value; it assumes that the list is sorted in ascending order, and inserts `value` so that the list remains sorted

- ▪ `int kill(firstEle)`, where `firstEle` is a pointer to the first element of the list. `kill()` deletes the 5 last elements of the list (if the list has less than 5 elements, all these elements should be deleted)

- ▪ `int print(List)`, which prints all of the elements in the list (write a recursive implementation)

Finally, write a menu-driven program to test all of these.

Exercise 11-11

Rewrite Exercise 11–4 using a binary file of integers.

Exercise 11-12

In this exercise, we use a binary file "fname" storing information about employees. For each employee, store the name, the identification number, and a salary:

```
struct employee {
    long id;
    char name[50];
    double salary;
};
```

Write the following functions:

- ▪ `int add(fname, empId, stringName, salary)` where fname is a string representing a binary file, `empId` is an integer, `stringName` is a string, and a `salary` is a double. This function appends a new employee to the binary file (an `empId` is a key and uniquely identifies an employee; therefore this function may fail)

- ▪ `void moreDollars(fname, empId, incr)` with three parameters: a string fname, an integer `empId`, and a double `incr`. This function operates on a binary file fname, and it increases by `incr` the salary of every employee whose id is greater than or equal to `empId`. This function should operate on a binary file, that is, it should not read *all* the data in internal memory at once; instead it should read one structure at a time.

- ▪ `void show(const char *fname)` that shows all information stored in the binary file fname

Exercise 11-13

Consider the following declarations:

```
#define MAXI 20
  typedef struct {
```

```
    char title[MAXI];       /* book title */
    char author[MAXI];      /* book author */
    long callNo;            /* call number */
    int copies;
    /* number of copies currently available in the library */
} BookT;
```

The above declarations can be used to maintain information about books borrowed from the library. This information will be stored in a binary file called `library.inf`, containing structures `BookT`. The call number is a unique key. Write a function

```
int (long callNo, char **name);
```

that searches the file `library.inf` looking for the book with the given call number. If the number is not found, or any other error occurred, the function returns the value 1. If the number is found, but the number of available copies is 0, the function returns the value 2. Otherwise, the function returns the value 0, and it decrements the number of available copies by one, updates the file, and returns the name of the author of the given book through the parameter `name`.

Exercise 11-14

Consider a text file in which each line is of the form

```
integer spaces string (1 or more words)
```

and so it can be represented by a structure

```
struct {
    int value;
    char str[101];
};
```

Write a function

```
int to_bin(const char *fname, const char *bname);
```

that reads the text file `fname` of the above form, and for each input line, writes the corresponding structure to the binary file `bname`. The function terminates when either end-of-file of `fname` is encountered (and in this case it returns 1), or an error occurred (returns 0).

Then, write a function

```
int sum(const char *bname)
```

that returns the sum of all of the integer values from the binary file `bname`.

Finally, write a function

```
int mem(const char *bname, const char *sname)
```

which returns 1 if `sname` is present in the binary file `bname`, and 0 otherwise.

Exercise 11–15

In Exercise 11–14, the string in each line was limited to at most 100 characters. Modify the data structures and reimplement functions described in this assignment so that this string could be of any length.

Exercise 11–16

For this exercise, you have to write two related programs. Your program for part (b) must be able to use the binary file created by your program for part (a); remember this as you design the structure of the file. Assume that all file operations succeed and that the input data is valid.

(a) Write a program to build a binary file of records representing student grades from data read from standard input. The program reads the student names from the standard input, which has the following form: there is one input line for each student, containing 2 fields, the student's id and the student's full name. The `id` is a non-negative integer followed by one space character. The name has up to 60 characters, possibly including spaces and punctuation.

Sample input is:

```
9654 Bombardier, Jean-Michel
9608 Menzies, Michelle
```

The name of the output (binary) file should be provided in the command line. For each student, write one record consisting of 3 fields: the student's name, id, and mark to the binary file. The marks are all 0.

(b) Write a program to display the contents of a binary file of student mark records on standard output. This program will be executed after the marks have been updated (by another procedure not defined in this exercise). Obtain the name of the input (binary) file from the command line. For each student, read one record of the format written by your program for part (a) and write a line showing the student's name and letter grade. Use the grade scale: A is 80–100, B is 70–79, C is 60–69, D is 50–59 and F is 0–49. For example:

```
Menzies, Michelle B
```

Exercise 11–17

Modify the module from Section 11.5.3 to shrink the memory block when it has more than 10 free blocks.

Exercise 11-18

Use a generic module from Exercise 11–17 to implement a simple line editor. Your editor should support the following operations:

- show the current line
- change the current line
- show lines from line n to line m
- change the contents of the current line

Exercise 11-19

Modify the module List from Section 11.5.4 and add persistence, that is, functions to save the list in the file and restore the list from the file.

Exercise 11-20

Use a generic module from Exercise 11–19 to implement a simple line editor. Your editor should support the operations described in Exercise 11–18, and additionally, it should support the operations of saving to a file and reading from a file.

Exercise 11-21

A list is a collection of homogenous objects, such as integers, characters, etc. An array may be used to store a list. In this exercise, you are to use an array of integers to implement a list, where each element of the list consists of three integers. For example, take an array of size 9, containing 9 integers. The integers at array locations 1, 2, and 3 make up the first element of the list, the next three integers at array locations 4, 5, and 6 make up the second element of the list, and finally the last three integers in the array make up the final element of the list. More specifically, consider an array containing the following integers: 2 1 4 6 3 7 9 10 23. The list representing this array consists of three elements, the first being 2, 1, 4; the second being 6, 3, 7; and the third being 9, 10, 23.

Given an array of integers of size 99, the iTH element of the list (which consists of three integers) may be found at array locations

```
3*(i-1)  +1, 3*(i-1) + 2,  3*(i-1)  + 3,
```

where i may be any integer from 1 to 33.
Write a concrete module List3, which supports the following operations:

- a constructor, which sets the maximum number of integers
- the reading of integers which are stored in a file
- the writing of the contents of the list to a file
- the appending of a new integer to the end of the list
- the removing of the first element from the list

- the displaying of the ith element or a message "no such element" if there is no ith element
- a destructor

Also write a menu-driven program that tests all operations in this module.

Exercise 11-22

Write a module `Points` that supports the following operations on points on a plane:

- a constructor, to create a point
- accessor functions to obtain values of coordinates of a given point
- a modifier function, to set the value of the first or second coordinate of a given point
- a function that returns 1 if two points are equal, and returns 0 otherwise
- a destructor

Exercise 11-23

Implement a concrete module `Arrays`, which provides the following operations on single-dimensional arrays of long values:

- a constructor, to set the size of the array (this change can not be changed while operating on the array)
- an accessor, to get the ith element of the array
- a modifier, to set the ith element of the array
- a function to add two arrays together, resulting in a single array (of the same size)
- a function to multiply two arrays together, resulting in a single array (of the same size)
- a function to compare two arrays to determine if they are identical (of the same size)
- error functions, as in Example 7–5, Section 7.4.7

Exercise 11-24

This exercise is similar to Exercise 11–23, except you should implement a generic module and then show how it can be used with a long values.

12

ENUMERATED TYPES AND UNIONS

12.1 ◆ Preview

This short chapter covers two additional C structured data types: enumerated types and unions. Both these types are new to Java programmers. Enumerated types are *not* related to Java enumerations, instead they define a collections of names. Unions are similar to structures and provide a memory-efficient representation of heterogeneous collections.

12.2 Enumerated Types

Enumerated types are ordered collections of named constants. They provide a more readable solution than macros to naming integer constants. The syntax is almost identical to the syntax used for structures, except that the keyword enum is required. For example

```
enum opcodes {
    lvalue, rvalue, push, plus
};
```

or

```
typedef enum opcodes {
    lvalue, rvalue, push, plus
} OpcodesT;

enum opcodes e;
OpcodesT f;
```

The definition of the type enum opcodes introduces four constants: lvalue, rvalue, push, and plus; all are of type int. C assigns integer values to enumerated types—by default, the first enumerated type constant receives the value 0, and subsequent constants receive a value one greater than the value of the previous constant. For the above example:

lvalue	represents the integer value	0
rvalue	represents the integer value	1

and so on.

A declaration of an enumerated type may also explicitly define integer values associated with enumerated constants. For example:

```
enum opcodes {
    lvalue = 1, rvalue, push, plus
}
```

Enumerated type variables can be assigned enumerated type values, for example

```
e = lvalue;
```

They can also be compared for equality, for example

```
if(e == push) ...
```

Enumerated type values may be converted to integer values, but if you do so, you must remember to use a cast, otherwise the conversion results in potentially non-portable code. For example, the value of the variable

```
OpcodesT e;
```

may be converted to int, using the cast

```
int i = (int)e;
```

As I mentioned earlier, the main use of enumerated types is to increase readability. Compare the definition of opcodes with the following set of macros:

```
#define LVALUE    0
#define RVALUE    1
#define PUSH      2
#define PLUS      3
```

The enumerated type code is much more readable because it groups identifiers representing constant values under a named type.

Another application of enumerated types is to represent function return codes. For example, if you have a function where the return value depends on the following conditions

failure because a file can not be opened

failure because a file can not be closed

success

then you can define an enumerated type to represent these conditions:

```
typedef enum {
    FOPEN, FCLOSE, FOK
} FoperT;
```

In order to convert an FoperT value to an integer, I will define the following macro:

```
#define TOINT(f)    ((int)(f))
```

For example, TOINT(FOPEN) is equal to 0.

Note that enumerated type values are *not* strings. For example, if you have a function

```
FoperT process();
```

and you want to output the result of calling this function as a string, then you have to explicitly create the appropriate strings:

```c
char *Messages[] = {
      "File can not be opened",
      "File can not be closed",
      "Successful operation",
      "This can not happen"
};
char *result;

switch(process()) {

case FOPEN:  result = Messages[0];
             break;

case FCLOSE: result = Messages[1];
             break;

case FOK:    result = Messages[2];
             break;

default:     result = Messages[3];
             break;
}
printf("result of calling process() is %s\n", result);
```

I added an extra message using the default tag to take into account an "impossible case". This style of defensive programming is a very good idea. Alternatively, instead of using the switch statement, you can use the macro TOINT to output the enumerated type:

```c
printf("result of calling process() is %s\n",
   Messages[TOINT(process())];
```

CONVERSION OF ENUMERATED TYPE VALUES TO STRINGS

Define an array Arr of strings (one string for each value) and a macro TOINT to convert these values into integers. Then a value V can be converted into a string using Arr[TOINT(V)]

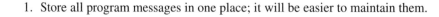

1. Store all program messages in one place; it will be easier to maintain them.

2. When you consider various cases, do not forget to account for the "impossible" cases; they do happen.

12.3 Unions

The syntax for unions is almost identical to the syntax used for structures, except that the keyword union is used. For example

```
union intOrDouble {
    int i;
    double d;
};
```

or

```
typedef union intOrDouble {
    int i;
    double d;
} IntOrDoubleT;

union intOrDouble x, y;
IntOrDoubleT z;
```

The basic difference between structures and unions is that the memory allocated for the structure is large enough to store all of its components, while the memory allocated for the union is only large enough to store the *largest* component. In order to compare the union intOrDouble with the structure intAndDouble defined as follows

```
struct intAndDouble {
    int i;
    double d;
}
```

see Figure 12–1, in which I assumed that the size of double is larger than the size of int.

In other words, you can think of the union

```
    IntOrDoubleT z;
```

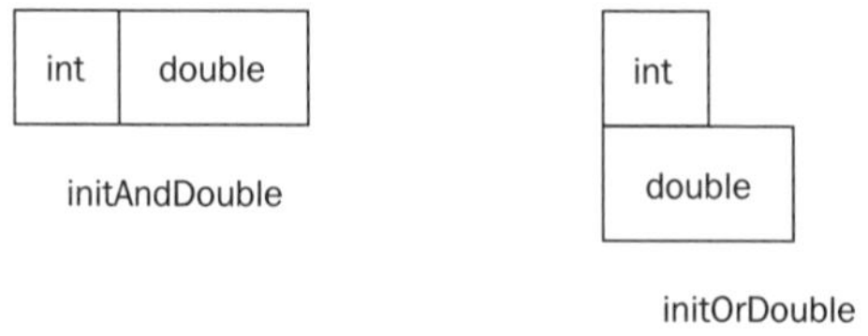

Figure 12–1

Unions and structures

as having only one member. You can *not* store both an int and a double in IntOrDouble at the same time; however, you can toggle between them throughout program execution. The run-time system of C *interprets* the contents of the memory allocated for the union, depending on the type of the member:

- for the z.d member, the type is double, therefore the first sizeof (double) bytes for memory allocated for z will be interpreted as a double object
- for the z.i member, the type is int, therefore the first sizeof(int) bytes for memory allocated for z will be interpreted as an int object

You can access either member, using the familiar notation:

z.d represents a double

z.i represents an int

It is important to remember that while C allows you to access both members, the result will only be well defined if you access the member that is currently being stored in the union. In other words, the union does not store the information that specifies what value is currently stored in it. For example, if you say

```
z.d = 1.2;
```

and then use the i member:

```
printf("%d", z.i);
```

then the result is undefined. Consequently, it is useful to add a **tag field**, whose value determines the current interpretation of the union value. This tag field may be of an enumerated type that will represent all of the possible value types that the union can store. In order to add the tag field, you nest a union in a structure, for example:

```
typedef enum {
    integer, real
```

```
} TagTypeT;

typedef union {
    int i;
    double d;
} IntOrDoubleT;

typedef struct {
    TagTypeT tag;
    IntOrDoubleT value;
} TaggedValueT;
```

If the type `IntOrDoubleT` is not needed, then the last two definitions can be combined into one:

```
typedef struct {
    TagTypeT tag;
    union {
        int i;
        double d;
    } value;
} TaggedValueT;
```

The value of the tag can now be used to check the type of the union member:

```
TaggedValueT v;
...
if(v.tag == integer)
    ...v.value.i...;
else
    ...v.value.d...;
```

Example 12-1

In this example, I will use an array that stores strings or double values, so the data structures are similar to those shown above:

```
typedef enum {
    real, string
} TagTypeT;
```

```
#define MAXSTR 80      /* maximum size of a string */

typedef union {
   double d;
   char s[MAXSTR+1];
} DoubleOrStringT;

typedef struct {
   TagTypeT tag;
   DoubleOrStringT value;
} TaggedValueT;
```

The program reads a text file. For each read operation, it attempts to first read a double—if the read operation succeeds, the double is stored in the array. If the read operation for a double fails, the program reads a string from the input file and stores it in the array. The program will then output all the double values and all strings read from the file. The entire program consists of four functions

```
int readFile(const char *fname, TaggedValue storage[]);
void showDoubles(TaggedValue storage[], int size);
void showStrings(TaggedValue storage[], int size);
```

and the main function. The first function reads the file and stores values in the array, the second and the third function respectively output double values and strings. I will now briefly discuss the implementation of this function. Its main loop tries to read a double; if it fails it reads a string, otherwise it stores the double value and sets the tag:

```
while(1)
   if(fscanf(in, "%lf", &aux) == 1) {
      storage[size].tag = real;
      storage[size].value.d = aux;
      size++;
   } else {
      if(fscanf(in, "%80s", buffer) == 1) {
         storage[size].tag = string;
         strcpy(storage[size].value.s, buffer);
         size++;
      }
   ...
}
```

The complete code follows.

```
/*
 * File: ex12-1.c
 */
```

```
typedef enum {
   real, string
} TagTypeT;

#define MAXSTR 80 /* maximum size of a string */
typedef union {
   double d;
   char s[MAXSTR+1];
} DoubleOrStringT;

typedef struct {
   TagTypeT tag;
   DoubleOrStringT value;
} TaggedValueT;

const int Max = 100;   /* maximum number of items */

/*
 * Read a text file and store double values and strings in the array of
 *   unions. At most Max items are read, and each string has at most
 *   MAXSTR characters
 * Inputs: filename, and storage - an array of TaggedValues
 * Returns: number of items read, EOF if can not open a file
 * Modifies: the array
 * Error checking: stops reading on error, and returns what has been
 *   read. Doesn't report an error if the file can not be closed
 * Sample call:
 *    if((i = readFile("a.dat", storage)) == EOF)
 *       error
 */
int readFile(const char *fname, TaggedValueT storage[]);

/*
 * Output all double values from the array of unions, 5 doubles per line
 * Inputs: storage - an array of TaggedValues, and size - number of
 *   elements in storage
 * Returns: nothing
 * Modifies: nothing
 * Error checking: none
 * Sample call:
 *    showDoubles(storage, 10);
 */
void showDoubles(TaggedValueT storage[], int size);
```

```
/*
 * Output all strings from the array of unions, each string on a
 *     separate line
 * Inputs: storage - an array of TaggedValues, and size - number of
 *     elements in storage
 * Returns: nothing
 * Modifies: nothing
 * Error checking: none
 * Sample call:
 *     showStrings(storage, 10);
 */
void showStrings(TaggedValueT storage[], int size);

/*
 * Application of the above functions
 * The name of the input file is passed on the command line
 */
#include <stdio.h>
#include <stdlib.h>
#include <string.h>
int main(int argc, char **argv) {
    int size;
    TaggedValueT storage[Max];

    if(argc != 2)
        return EXIT_FAILURE;
    if((size = readFile(argv[1], storage)) == EOF)
        return EXIT_FAILURE;

    printf("Double values:\n");
    showDoubles(storage, size);
    printf("Strings:\n");
    showStrings(storage, size);

    return EXIT_SUCCESS;
}

int readFile(const char *fname, TaggedValueT storage[]) {
    FILE *in;
    char buffer[MAXSTR+1];
    double aux;
    int size = 0;
```

```
    if((in = fopen(fname, "r")) == NULL)
        return EOF;

    /* start reading */
    while(1)
        /* first try to read a double */
        if(fscanf(in, "%lf", &aux) == 1) { /* store it */
            storage[size].tag = real;
            storage[size].value.d = aux;
            size++;
        } else { /* try to read a string */
            if(fscanf(in, "%80s", buffer) == 1) { /* store */
                storage[size].tag = string;
                strcpy(storage[size].value.s, buffer);
                size++;
            } else /* can't read anything
                    * stop no matter whether it is eof or error
                    */
                break;
        }

    fclose(in);
    return size;
}

void showDoubles(TaggedValueT storage[], int size) {
    int i;
    int count = 0;
    const int numPerLine = 5;

    for(i = 0; i < size; i++) {
        if(count == numPerLine) {
            putchar('\n');
            count = 0;
        }
        count++;
        if(storage[i].tag == real)
            printf("%f\n", storage[i].value.d);
    }
}

void showStrings(TaggedValueT storage[], int size) {
    int i;
```

```
    for(i = 0; i < size; i++)
        if(storage[i].tag == string)
            printf("%s\n", storage[i].value.s);
}
```

As you can see from the presented examples, if you know you will only have one of several possible values, unions are useful because they conserve *memory*. For example, assuming that the `sizeof(double)` is 8, for the array `storage`, the memory block will be of the following size:

size of array * size of each element = 100 * 81 = 8100 bytes

If you used structures rather than unions, then the amount of memory created would be:

size of array * size of each element = 100 * (81+8) = 8900 bytes

(in both cases, the exact amount of memory may be slightly different because of system-dependent memory alignment).

12.4 List of Idioms

CONVERSION OF ENUMERATED TYPE VALUES TO STRINGS

Define an array `Arr` of strings (one string for each value) and a macro `TOINT` to convert these values into integers. Then a value `V` can be converted into a string using `Arr[TOINT(V)]`

12.5 List of Programming Style Guidelines

1. Store all program messages in one place; it will be easier to maintain them.
2. When you consider various cases, do not forget to account for the "impossible" cases; they do happen.

12.6 Exercises

Exercise 12-1

Write the definition of an enumerated data type DAYS that represents all days of the week. Then, write a procedure that has a parameter of type DAYS and prints the name of this day.

Exercise 12-2

Consider the following interface for a SET:

File set.h:

```
#ifndef SET_H
#define SET_H

typedef enum { OK, FULL, FAIL } result;

result insert(double n);
/* return FULL if the set is full, FAIL if n is in the set,
 * OK otherwise; n is actually inserted into the set only in
 * the last case.
 */

result member(double n);
/* returns OK if n is in the set, and FAIL otherwise */

#endif
```

Implement a module to represent these sets using an array (of size 100).

Exercise 12-3

Write data type Elem to store either an integer or a character (but not both). Then, write a program which reads values from standard input and when it finds integers, stores them in the array of Elem's. Should the reading of an integer fail, the program will read a single character, store it, and continue processing. Reading should terminate when either end-of-file has been encountered, or 100 items have been read. Your program should output in reverse order all integers which have been stored.

For the input

```
12 b3 6g
```

the array will store

```
12
b
```

```
3
6
g
```

and the output will be: `6  3  12`

Exercise 12-4

Assume that a program includes the following type declaration:

```
enum Days {
    Monday, Tuesday, Wednesday, Thursday, Friday, Saturday, Sunday
}
```

Write a function called `convert()` that has two parameters, `d` of type `Days` and an integer `numericDay`. The function returns the value 3 if `d` is `Monday`, `Wednesday`, or `Friday` and returns the value 2 if `d` is `Tuesday`, or `Thursday`, through the parameter `numericDay`. If `d` is either `Saturday` or `Sunday`, then `convert()` returns the value 0, through `numericDay`.

BITWISE OPERATIONS AND BIT FIELDS

13.1 ◆ Preview

This chapter discusses bitwise operations on individual bits. These operations are useful for some specialized applications, for example for image compression. I also introduce the concept of a bit field.

13.2 Bitwise Operations

C provides the following operations that access individual bits in a memory word:

    &   bitwise and

    | bitwise or

    ^   bitwise xor, also called exclusive or

    <<   left shift

    >>   right shift

    ~   one's complement

All these operations take integer arguments and have similar meaning to the corresponding Java operators. However, in Java, bitwise operators &, |, and ^ applied to Boolean values return the same values as logical operators; in C, there is no Boolean type and bitwise operators have always the "bitwise" semantics. For the sake of completeness, I will describe them in detail below. In order to simplify the description, I will use the following notation:

$(z)_i$ denotes the ith bit in z

In this chapter, "to clear" means to set to 0; and "to set" means to set to 1.

Bitwise and: `x & y`

if $(x)_i == 1$ *and* $(y)_i == 1$ then $(x \& y)_i == 1$

                                           otherwise $(x \& y)_i == 0$

For example:

```
int i;
```

`i & 1` is 1 only if `i` is odd. This operation is useful and I will define a macro for it:

```
#define ISODD(n)        (1&(n))
```

Bitwise *and* is often used to *clear* bits or bytes. For example:

```
x & 0xff
```

clears all bytes but the low-order byte, see Figure 13–1.

Bitwise or: `x | y`

if $(x)_i == 1$ *or* $(y)_i == 1$ then $(x | y)_i == 1$

                                           otherwise $(x | y)_i == 0$

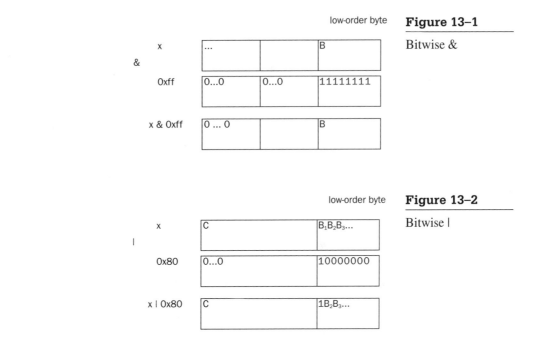

Figure 13–1

Bitwise &

Figure 13–2

Bitwise |

This operation is often used to *set* bits. For example to set the high order bit of the low order byte of x, use

$x \; | \; 0x80$, see Figure 13–2.

Bitwise xor: $x \; \hat{} \; y$

if $(x)_i \; == \; (y)_i$ then $(x \; \hat{} \; y)_i \; == \; 0$

                            otherwise $(x \; \hat{} \; y)_i \; == \; 1$

In other words, bitwise *xor* clears those bits that are the same in both arguments, and sets the other bits. This operation can be used to test if two words are equal, for example

$x \; \hat{} \; y$

returns 0 if x and y are equal.

Bitwise complement: $\sim x$

$(\; \sim x \;)_i \; == \; 1 \; - \; (x)_i$

clear any bits that are 1, and set those that are 0. This operation is useful to set up specific values in a portable way. For example, assume that you want to clear the 3 low-order bits of x, and use a value that has 1's in all the other bits. The value I just described translates to the value `0xff8` in hexadecimal:

```
x & 0xff8
```

Unfortunately, my solution is not entirely correct, since it only works with 16-bit words. A fully portable solution requires that I find a value that has 1's in the 3 low-order bits, and then complement it:

```
x & ~7
```

(If you consider the binary representation of 7, you will see that it fits this description.)

Similarly, to set a value (i.e. all bits equal to 1), use

```
~0
```

Left shift: `i << j`

The resulting word will have all bits shifted to the left by `j` positions; for every bit that is shifted off the left end of the word, there is a zero bit added at the right end. The result is the same for both signed and unsigned right arguments. A simple application of this operation is to perform multiplication:

```
x <<= 1
```

is equivalent to x `*= 2`, and

```
x <<= 2
```

is equivalent to x `*= 4`.

Right shift: `i >> j`

The resulting word will have all bits shifted to the right by j positions; if `j` is unsigned, then for every bit that is shifted off the right end of the word, there is a zero bit added at the left end. If `j` is signed, then the result is implementation dependant. A simple application of this operation is to perform division:

```
x >>= 1
```

is equivalent to x `/= 2`, and

```
x >>= 2
```

is equivalent to x `/= 4`.

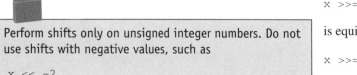

Perform shifts only on unsigned integer numbers. Do not use shifts with negative values, such as

```
x << -2
```

Example 13–1

In the following example, I will show two functions that operate on the jth bits of a word. These function will use a word representing the jth position, obtained by left-shifting the value 1 by j (see Figure 13–3):

```
#define MASK(j)    (1 << j)
```

The first function, getBit(), returns the ith bit in w and uses a bitwise and of its first argument and MASK(j):

```
int getBit(int w, unsigned j) {
   return ((w & MASK(j)) == 0) ? 0 : 1;
}
```

The second function:

```
int setBit(int w, unsigned j, short value)
```

sets the ith bit in w to value, which is 0 or 1; therefore, its code uses a bitwise or for the value equal to 1, and a bitwise and for the value equal to 0:

```
int setBit(int w, unsigned j, short value) {

   switch(value) {

   case 0:   return w & MASK(j);

   case 1:   return w | MASK(j);

   default:  return w;   /* unchanged */
   }
}
```

j-th position

Figure 13–3

Shifting 1 to left by j

13.3 Bit Fields

Bit fields provide a *non-portable* way to pack integer components into a memory block that is smaller than typically allocated. They are declared using a modified version of the syntax for a structure. For example

```
struct {
    unsigned leading : 3;
    unsigned FLAG1: 1;
    unsigned FLAG2: 1;
    trailing: 11;
}
```

defines five components that occupy respectively three, one, one, and eleven bits. Each component can represent values in the range from 0 to $2^n - 1$ for unsigned components (such as leading above), and values in the range from -2^{n-1} to $2^{n-1} - 1$ for signed integers (such as trailing above).

13.4 List of Portability Guidelines

Perform shifts only on unsigned integer numbers. Do not use shifts with negative values, such as

```
x << -2
```

13.5 Exercises

Exercise 13-1

Write a function that reverses the bits in a byte.

Exercise 13-2

Write a procedure octal(i) that prints a base–8 representation of the integer i using shift operators.

Exercise 13-3

Write a procedure

```
void compress(char *str, char mask)
```

that compresses the string str according to the specified 8-bit mask. For example, if str is

```
The quick red fox jumped
```

and the binary representation of mask is

```
10110011
```

the resulting value of `str` would be

```
Te ickrefoxjued
```

This result is determined by duplicating the mask for every group of eight characters and eliminating characters masked by a 0 bit:

```
The quick red fox jumped
101100111010011101110110011
```

Note: The string being compressed might not be a multiple of eight characters in length, as it is in this example.

Exercise 13-4

Write a procedure `hexi(i)` that outputs the 32-bit integer `i` as eight hexadecimal digits using bit fields.

Exercise 13-5

Consider a character `c`. For any character `d`, applying the xor operation twice, `(c ^ d) ^ c`, returns the original character `c`. Therefore, you can use this technique to encrypt files. Implement a singleton module `Encrypt` that provides two functions:

- `encrypt(const char *fileIn, const char *fileOut, const char *key)`, which reads the text file `fileIn` and writes the contents of `fileIn` to the binary file `fileOut`. The contents should be encrypted by successfully applying the xor operation to each character in the input file, using characters in the key (for example, if the `key` is `"ab"`, then for every character `c`, you would use `c^'a'^'b'`)
- `decrypt(const char *fileIn, const char *fileOut, const char *key)`, which reads the binary file `fileIn` and writes the contents of `fileIn` to the text file `fileOut`. The contents should be decrypted by reversing the algorithm described above (for the above example, for each input character `c`, use `c^'b'^'a'`).

MODULE-BASED PROGRAMMING: FINALE

14.1 ◆ Preview

In the last chapter of this book, I will cover the following topics:

- continuation of the discussion of error handling
- characterization of the various kinds of modules
- shallow and deep interfaces

I will also comment on the implementation of other data structures.

14.2 Error Handling

I will begin this section by summarizing the previous discussion of error handling:

1. Section 7.4.7 gave an example of a module with user-defined error handling, which had the following interface:

   `isError_IO()` to test whether or not the error has occurred

   `clearError_IO()` to clear any error indication

   `printError_IO()` to print a description of the error on the standard error stream

2. Section 7.4.7 explained how to modify the above interface, specifically by removing the function `clearError_IO()` and passing the task of clearing errors to the other I/O functions.

3. Section 9.7 provided a description of error handling provided by C, `errno`, and two functions: `strerror()` and `perror()`.

4. Section 10.5 introduced the testing of preconditions.

The main problem with these methods is that they all, in one way or another, require that an error state be checked after the function terminates, whether this involves testing a Boolean flag or the return value of a function.

This technique is particularly cumbersome for longer chains of calls. For example, consider a calculator program that uses a recursive descent parser, extended with semantic actions that calculate values of arithmetic expressions. Furthermore, assume that the user of this program may enter several expressions, separated by a semicolon, and expects to see a value for each expression. A further requirement is that each invalid expression (for example, one that uses invalid numbers), should be skipped, and the next expression should be evaluated. As a result, each of the functions in a recursive descent parser has to test whether the function it calls has succeeded, and in the case of a failure, it must propagate this failure; for example:

```
int term() {
...
    if(!factor())
        return 0;
...
}
```

As you can see, the result easily becomes a tangle of `if` statements. The source code of famous operating systems, such as Unix, is similarly obscured with `if` statements. The model of exception handling used by Java makes the code much clearer, but unfortunately, C does not support such a model. The following section describes a rather limited form of exception handling, using jumps.

14.2.1 ◆ Long Jumps

Suppose I have a function f() called by a function g(). If f() fails and terminates, g() has to decide to either handle this failure, or propagate it to its caller. In Java, g() could handle the failure by calling f() in a try block, or propagate it to its caller by specifying the exception in its signature.

In the absence of the Java exception handling mechanism, the alternative solution for this situation is to use some kind of an error flag or a Boolean return value, and test for this value each time a function is called. This is rather cumbersome (and inefficient) because it requires a check for each call. In run-time terms, each time a function is called, its instance is pushed on to a run-time stack; each time a function terminates or fails, its instance is popped off the stack. For example, suppose function a() calls b(), which calls c(). Given this sequence of calls, there are now three function instances on the stack. If the function c() fails, it must be popped off the stack, and control is returned to b(). In some situations, the programmer may want to control the exception handling; for example, he or she may want to return control to the function a(), not b(), should c() fail. This may be accomplished by using many if statements, but C provides a better way through two functions: setjmp() and longjmp().

A call to setjmp() saves the current run-time stack, while a call to longjmp() restores that saved stack. To use these functions, you include the standard header file setjmp.h, which also defines the type jmp_buf, used to describe the type responsible for saving the state of the stack.

For a variable env of type jmp_buf, the call

```
setjmp(env)
```

saves the current state of the run-time stack in env, and returns 0 to the caller. A subsequent call to

```
longjmp(env, val)
```

restores program execution at the point saved by setjmp(). It does so by returning control to setjmp(env), which returns the value val. This is easier to understand if you think of it in terms of the program counter and run-time stack. The program counter may be thought of as an index into an array where all of the program instructions are stored. When setjmp() is called, the program counter set to the index right before setjmp()'s return statement is saved. Calling longjmp() restores program execution at the instruction pointed to by the saved program counter. As a result, setjmp() returns twice: the first return occurs when setjmp() is called explicitly by the programmer and the second return occurs implicitly when longjmp() is called. A typical calling sequence may look like this:

```
i = setjmp(env);
if(i != 0)
    ...use i ...
...
longjmp(env, i)
```

When setjmp(env) is called explicitly, it returns 0. When longjmp(env, i) is called, setjmp() returns again, this time with the value i.

I will provide two examples of applications using these functions. The first example is a bit artificial and is meant to exercise your understanding of the two functions; it shows how a recursive factorial function can terminate when it "bottoms out".

```
void fact(int n, int i) {

    if(n <= 1)
        longjmp(env, i);

    fact(n - 1, i * n);
}
```

Within this function, i is used to accumulate the value of factorial.

Here is the code to call fact():

```
jmp_buf env;
int k = 4;
int i;

if((i = setjmp(env)) == 0)
    fact(k, 1);
else printf("factorial of %d is %d\n", k, i);
```

When setjmp() returns for the first time, it returns the value 0, and the function fact() is called. After four recursive calls, the condition n <= 1 becomes true and longjmp() is called, and returns the value of i (24 above). As pointed out earlier, the call to longjmp() results in setjmp() returning for the *second* time, this time with the value 24. The main difference between this implementation and a typical recursive one is that fact() terminates by executing a single jump, while in a typical recursive implementation, its execution completes through a chain of returns from recursive calls (see Figure 14–1).

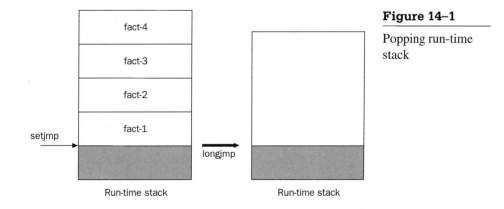

Figure 14–1

Popping run-time stack

longjmp() has to be used with caution; according to the ANSI C standard, in the following two cases the behavior is undefined:

- longjmp(env, val) is called before setjmp(env) has been called
- the function containing setjmp() terminated before longjmp() was called

14.2.2 ◆ Exception Handling

I will now focus on the use of jumps to simulate exception handling. Consider a function add(), which tries to add two integer values, and will raise "exceptions" in case of overflow or underflow. For the time being, I will assume that exceptions are identified by integer values. The code for the function add() follows:

```
#include <limits.h>
#define OVERFLOW 1
#define UNDERFLOW 2
int add(int x, int y) {

    if(x > 0 && y > 0 && x > INT_MAX - y)
        longjmp(env, 1);

    if(x < 0 && y < 0 && x > INT_MIN + y)
        longjmp(env, 2);

    return x + y;
}
```

Note that the function `add()` may terminate in one of two ways: normal termination, through a return, or exceptional termination, through a `longjmp()`. The caller of `add()` may handle the different cases as follows:

```
int sum;
switch(setjmp(env)) {

case 0:        sum = add(100000, 22478474);
               break;

case OVERFLOW:  ... process error1

case UNDERFLOW: ... process error2

}
here sum is well-defined
```

There are several problems with my solution:

- the variable `env` has to be a *global* variable, visible in the function `add()` and to the caller of this function
- exceptions are identified by integer numbers, which makes them less readable
- nested handlers will not work

Addressing the second issue of readability is awkward: `setjmp()` can not be encapsulated in a function (see the end of the previous section), and so the only solution is to use macros. I will begin my improvements to the code by implementing my own exception type:

```
typedef struct {
   char *reason;
   jmp_buf env;
} ExceptionT;
```

An exception is identified by a variable of type `ExceptionT`. The following macros are used to set up an exception (it is like setting up a try block):

```
#define TRY(exc)        setjmp(exc.env)
#define SHOW(exc)       exc.reason
```

The function that raises the exception will use this macro:

```
#define RAISE(exc, str)    {\
```

```
        exc.reason = strdup(str); \
        longjmp(exc.env, 1); \
    }
```

For example, the function `add()` may be re-implemented like this:

```
ExceptionT e;
/* global variable that specifies the exception */

int add(int x, int y) {

    if(x > 0 && y > 0 && x > INT_MAX - y)
        RAISE(e, "Overflow")
    if(x < 0 && y < 0 && x > INT_MIN + y)
        RAISE(e, "Underflow")

    return x + y;
}
```

The caller of `add()` will return a NULL pointer if successful, and in this case will also return the sum of x and y through res; it will return a string representing an error if it fails:

```
char *catch(int x, int y, int *res) {
    if(TRY(e))
        return SHOW(e);
    *res = add(x, y);
    return NULL;
}
```

If the function that directly catches exceptions calls the function that raises exceptions (in my example, `catch()` calls `add()` and catches its exceptions), then the `setjmp/longjmp` technique is not much better than using one of the standard C error techniques. The advantage of using jumps is clear when you consider *indirect* calls. For example, `catch()` may call another function, say `f()`, which calls yet another function, etc., and eventually `add()` gets called. All intermediate functions propagate the exception, and then `catch()` handles it. As another example, consider an editor program, where if one of the commands fails, control is returned to a central error handler, which dispatches the error and returns to the editor command level to accept the next command.

As I mentioned earlier, the "jump" technique in my example does not properly handle nested exceptions. There is a solution to this problem, but it is beyond the scope of this book and I refer the interested reader to [Han97] for more details.

14.3 Characterization of Modules

I will begin this section with a review of the various modules that were discussed in the previous chapters, and use this opportunity to introduce some useful terminology. I will not re-visit the stateless modules discussed in Section 7.4.7, and will only deal with the modules introduced in Chapters 8, 10, and 11:

1. The singleton module introduced in Section 8.18.2 represented a homogenous collection of elements of the same data type. The implementation did *not* know the type of data stored in the collection. Since operations on the collection included the ability to search for a given value, the implementation used a *callback* function to compare two elements.

2. The singleton module introduced in Section 8.18.4 represented a homogenous sorted collection and assumed that the element type was *known* to the implementation.

3. The module introduced in Section 11.5.3 represented a homogenous array, consisting of elements of the same data type that is *not known* to the implementation, and provided only *shallow* copying of elements.

4. The module introduced in Section 11.5.4 represented a homogenous list, and assumed that the element type was *known* to the implementation. The module presented did provide *deep* copying, but did not support *persistence*.

From this list, you can see that one or more of the following properties can characterize a module:

Multiplicity:
Singleton (at most one of instance can be created)
Ordinary (any number of instances can be created)

Generocity:
Generic (the element type is *not* known to the implementation)
Concrete (the element type is known to the implementation)

Containment:
Shallow (elements are copied from the client to the implementation using the standard assignment operator)
Deep (elements are copied from the client to the implementation using the clone function supplied by the client as a callback function)

Persistence:

Transient (exist only in the internal memory)

Persistent (can be saved in the external memory and restored when needed)

For example, the Dynamic array module from Section 11.5.3 is a generic, shallow, transient module; the List module introduced in Section 11.5.4 is a concrete, deep, transient module.

In this section, I will elaborate further on the last property of modules, beginning with a brief description of the use of internal and external memory. All of the data structures discussed in this book were stored in internal memory. Sometimes, this is not possible—for example, if you are working with very large collections, which can not all be loaded into internal memory at once. This may be a rare case, because virtual memory gives the programmer a very large address space, but it is still worthwhile considering it. Collections of data that are stored in external memory are referred to as **external** collections. There are two methods for handling external collections. Collections can be *structured* in a fashion similar to internal collections, for example, lists. However, pointers are meaningless in the context of external memory, and an alternative implementation of a list has to be used, one that uses integer numbers (cursors) to link list elements. For example, a file may be treated as an open-ended array of structures representing list elements; each element stores data and the cursor to the next element of the list. This cursor is an index (or position) of the element. Alternatively, in order to increase efficiency, a portion of the external collection may be stored in an internal cache. I will now move on to the characteristic of *persistence*, which refers to preserving the data in the collection after the program has terminated. Adding persistence to collections that support enumerations is straightforward and usually accomplished by saving data to files. In order to save a collection to a file, the collection is enumerated and each element is written to the file. Loading a collection from a file is similarly simple. The only question remaining is what kind of file should you choose: text or binary? For concrete modules, you do have a choice, but for generic modules, the implementation has to use a binary file because it does not know the type of the collection's element. When you do have a choice and are trying to decide which type of file to use, remember that text files are fully portable, while binary files may require additional processing when moved to another architecture (see Section 8.14).

Now I will discuss problems related to shallow and deep copying of elements.

14.3.1 ◆ Shallow and Deep Interfaces

In some cases (typically when data involves the use of pointers), a shallow copy of a data element is not sufficient, and a deep copy must be performed (which in Java would be accomplished by cloning the data). For example, a list of strings (pointers to char) that supports only a shallow copy of its data (strings) may be tricky to use, because the user must remember not to create dangling references in the list by de-allocating memory for the strings which belong to the client, but are shared by the list.

In this section, I will use an Enumeration to illustrate the issue of shallow and deep copying. I will describe the design of two Enumeration interfaces, providing access respectively to a shallow and deep copy (I will refer to them as a *shallow interface* and a *deep interface*). In the next section, I will show the implementations of these interfaces. The enumeration interface consists of three functions:

```
int hasMoreElements_Enumeration(Abstract_Enumeration);
Abstract_Enumeration construct_Enumeration(void *);
void *nextElement_Enumeration(Abstract_Enumeration);
```

(see Section 8.18.3). The first two functions have the same semantics for both a shallow and a deep interface. The third function:

```
void* nextElement_Enumeration(Abstract_Enumeration e)
```

is responsible for returning a pointer to the data stored in the next element of the data structure being enumerated. The semantics of this function depend on the kind of copy performed. In the explanation provided below, I will assume that we enumerate over a list of strings (pointers to char), and I will consider the call:

```
char *p = nextElement_Enumeration(e);
```

The returned element may be provided using one of the following two methods:

1. Shallow copy

   In this case, the string in the current list element (i.e. the element being enumerated) is shared with the pointer p. Thus the client can freely *access* the value of p, for example, to print it:

   ```
   printf("%s", p);
   ```

   but must *avoid* modifying the value of p; for example

   ```
   free(p);
   ```

   creates a dangling reference for the pointer in the current list element. If the client wishes to modify the data, then she or he should *copy* this data, for example:

   ```
   aux = strdup(p);
   ```

2. Deep copy

In this case, the client has access to a *copy* of the data contained in the list, and can freely use it, but is responsible for deallocating this copy when appropriate. For example:

```
char *p = nextElement_Enumeration(e);
printf("%s", p);
/* modifications of p do not affect the list */
free(p);
```

Therefore, the two versions of the Enumeration interface will differ in the semantics of the function `nextElement_Enumeration()`. Depending on which version is used, the client is responsible for either not modifying the value returned by this function (for the shallow copy), or for deallocating the copy when it is no longer needed (for the deep copy).

How many header files should I have for these two Enumeration interfaces? At first, it may appear that there should be two header files; one for the shallow interface and one for the deep interface. The problem with this solution is that these two files would contain some common code, specifically the declarations of the first two functions:

`hasMoreElements_Enumeration()` and `construct_Enumeration()`.

A general rule for designing larger modules is that any code that is *common* to several files should be placed in a single file, included by other files. This is essential for maintainability of the software—having more than one copy of identical code means that any changes made to one copy must be made to all the other copies, which is at the very least inconvenient and usually error-prone. Applying this technique to the above example, you can see that one should create an additional header file, which stores all the common code, and have it included by the other header files.

The header file `ex14-enum.h` provides declarations of two functions that are common to both kinds of enumerations: `hasMoreElements_Enumeration()` and `construct_Enumeration()`. The above header file is not useful to the client; instead, it is used by other header files.

Two files are needed (see Figure 14–2):

- `ex14-enumDeep.h` includes the file `ex14-enum.h` and declares the function `nextElement_EnumerationDeep()`;

- `ex14-enumShallow.h` includes the file `ex14-enum.h` and declares the function `nextElement_EnumerationShallow()`.

Figure 14–2

Header files for
shallow and deep
enumerations.

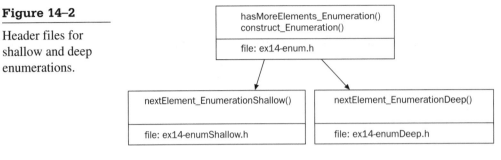

The *client* can use either or both enumerations:

- to use a deep enumeration, the client includes `ex14-enumDeep.h`
- to use a shallow enumeration, the client includes `ex14-enumShallow.h`
- to use both enumerations, the client includes both header files

Above, I had to use two different functions names, respectively

```
nextElement_EnumerationShallow()
```

for performing a shallow copy, and

```
nextElement_EnumerationDeep()
```

for performing a deep copy; otherwise there would have a name conflict if both interfaces are used.

The next section will show examples of the implementations of both interfaces.

14.3.2 ◆ Lists

In this section, I will provide the last example of a module in this book: a generic module `Lists`, with two interfaces respectively for shallow and deep copying. The data in the list is homogenous (I will briefly discuss heterogeneous lists in Section 14.4.2), but it is possible to create two *distinct* lists containing data of different types; for example, a list of strings and a list of integers.

As always, the shallow list interface and the deep list interface differ if pointers are used. In the discussion below, I will consider a list of strings. For example, when a string p

```
char *p = strdup("one");
```

is inserted into the list using the shallow interface, this string is shared by p and by the pointer from the list element. On the other hand, when this string is inserted into the list using the deep interface, a copy of the string is inserted.

Now, consider lists with enumerations. Both the shallow enumeration and the deep enumeration can be used. In the former case, the value returned by the enumeration function nextElement_Enumeration() is shared with the pointer in the list element; in the latter case it is copied. Various combinations of the list interface and the enumeration interface can be used. In this example, I will consider the implementation of the shallow list interface that will also implement the shallow enumeration interface, and the implementation of the deep list interface that will implement *both* the shallow enumeration interface and the deep enumeration interface (you may create other combinations; for instance you may have a shallow list implementation with only a deep enumeration interface). I will continue this discussion in Section 14.3.2, but first I will present the interfaces and implementation for the above example.

List Interfaces and Implementation

The design of two list *interfaces* is similar to the design of the interfaces for enumerations, discussed in the previous section. I define three header files: one "abstract" header file that contains common definitions for all list operations, stored in the file ex14-list.h, and two other header files for specific implementations; the header file ex14-listShallow.h for the shallow interface, and the file ex14-listDeep.h for the deep implementation.

The header file ex14-list.h contains a definition of Abstract_List (I am using the "Opaque" idiom):

```
typedef struct Concrete_List *Abstract_List;
```

and declarations of the following functions:

```
Abstract_List construct_Lists(size_t elSize,
    void* (*copyData)(const void*), void (*freeData(void*));
int length_Lists(const Abstract_List this);
void destruct_Lists(Abstract_List *this);
```

Above, I have provided a constructor to initialize data, a destructor to clean up after a list is no longer needed, and a function to return the length of the list. There is a *single* constructor for both a shallow and a deep implementation. Since the shallow list interface implements only the shallow enumeration interface, callback functions are not needed, and the client of the shallow list interface passes NULL arguments for both callback functions in the constructor call; for example

```
construct_List(sizeof(double), NULL, NULL);
```

Even if the client of shallow implementation did provide callback functions, these functions would be ignored. On the other hand, the client of the *deep* implementation must provide both callback functions. The two remaining header files contain declarations of functions that are specific to a shallow or deep interface.

File `ex14-1-listShallow.h`:

```
int insert_ListsShallow(Abstract_List this, int pos,
    void *value);

int delete_ListsShallow(Abstract_List this, int pos,
    void *value);
```

File `ex14-1-listDeep.h`:

```
int insert_ListsDeep(Abstract_List this, int pos,
    void *value);

int delete_ListsDeep(Abstract_List this, int pos,
    void *value);
```

The complete code for both interfaces is provided in files `ex14-list.h`, `ex14-listShallow.h`, and `ex14-listDeep.h`. I will now discuss the *implementation* of these interfaces. Following the design described in the previous section (a shallow enumeration for the shallow list interface, and two enumeration interfaces for the deep list interface), there will be three implementation files (see Figure 14–3):

- `ex14-list.c` that implements the common code, that is, the interface specified in the file `ex14-list.h` and the common enumeration interface specified in the file `ex14-enum.h`

- `ex14-listShallow.c` that implements the shallow list interface specified in the file `ex14-listShallow.h` and the shallow enumeration interface specified in the file `ex14-enumShallow.h`

- `ex14-listDeep.c` that implements the deep list interface specified in the file `ex14-listDeep.h` and the deep enumeration interface specified in the file `ex14-enumDeep.h`

Note that Figure 14–3 uses two kinds of arrows, respectively representing the inclusion of files and the implementation of the interface. For example,

- the file `ex14-enumShallow.h` includes the file `ex14-enum.h`
- the file `ex14-listShallow.c` implements two interfaces: `ex14-enumShallow.h` and `ex14-listShallow.h`

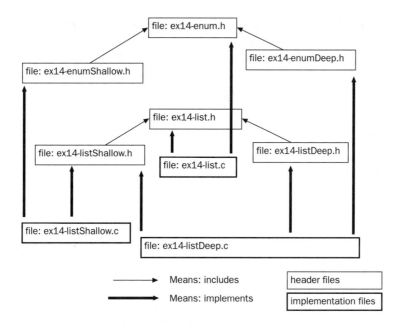

Figure 14–3

Interfaces and implementations of Lists with shallow and deep copying.

Up to this point, all examples of modules had the interface stored in exactly one header file, and the implementation stored in exactly one ".c" file. Here, the situation is different; for example, for the shallow lists:

- the interface is stored in four files: ex14-enum.h, ex14-enumShallow.h, ex14-list.h and ex14-listShallow.h

- the implementation consists of two files: ex14-list.c and ex14-list-Shallow.c.

The reason for splitting the code into more than one file is that it avoids code duplication, which makes maintenance very difficult.

Following the design described in Section 14.3.2, in order to use the shallow list interface, the client needs to follow these steps:

- include the files ex14-listShallow.h and ex14-enumShallow.h

- link the code with the two files: ex14-list.o and ex14-listShallow.o.

(the client does not explicitly include the header file ex14-list.h). In order to use the deep list interface, the client needs to:

- include three header files: ex14-listDeep.h, ex14-enumShallow.h, and ex14-enumDeep.h

- link the code with the two files: ex14-list.o and ex14-listDeep.o.

I will now describe the details of the implementation, starting with the common code, stored in the file `ex14-list-main.c`. The data types used by both implementations include a structure to store a list *element*

```
typedef struct elem {
    void *value;
    struct elem *next;
} ElemT, *ElemTP;
```

and a *concrete* type representing the list:

```
struct Concrete_List {
    ElemTP first;
    size_t elSize;
    void* (*copyData)(const void*);
    void (*freeData)(void*);
};
```

The above structure includes fields for storing the size of each data element and two callback functions (see Figure 14–4). For example, Figure 14–5 shows the memory representation for a list of strings, consisting of a single element `"hello"`.

In addition, this file implements the common code for both enumerations. It stores a concrete type used to represent an enumeration:

```
struct Concrete_Enumeration {
    Abstract_List list;
    ElemTP pos;
};
```

Figure 14–4

Design of a generic list.

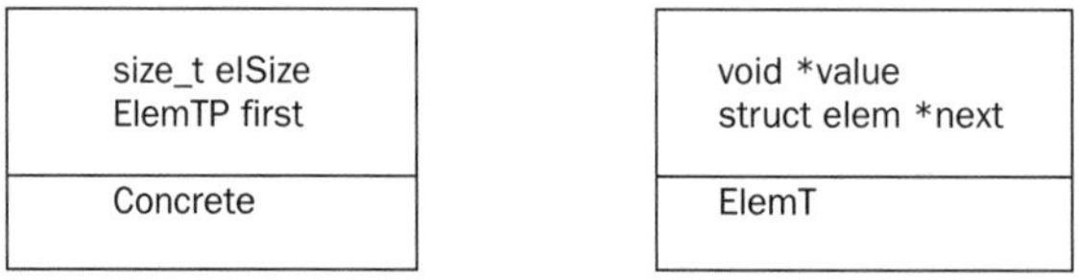

Figure 14–5

Sample list of strings.

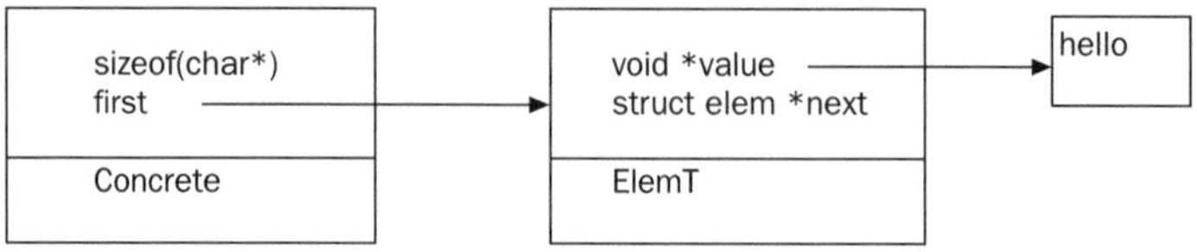

The reason that this structure has two members, rather than just one as in Section 8.18.3, is that the enumeration needs to know which list it is used for so that it could retrieve the callback functions.

The implementation of all of these functions is similar to the implementation of the concrete module List (see Section 11.5.4). The constructor allocates memory for a Concrete_List and initializes its fields:

```
Abstract_List construct_Lists(size_t elSize,
        void* (*copyData)(const void*),
        void (*freeData)(void*)){
    Abstract_List p;

    if((p = malloc(sizeof(struct Concrete_List))) == NULL)
        return NULL;

    p->first = NULL;
    p->elSize = elSize;
    p->freeData = freeData;
    p->copyData = copyData;

    return p;
}
```

The destructor uses a private function clear() to remove all elements from the list:

```
void destruct_Lists(Abstract_List *this) {
    clear(*this);
    free(*this);
    *this = NULL;
}
```

The function clear() removes all the elements from the list. This function is called in the destructor common to both implementations; for the shallow implementation, the freeData() callback function is not provided by the client and a standard deallocation function free() is called; for the deep implementation, the user-provided callback function is called:

```
static void clear(Abstract_List this) {
    ElemTP auxp;

    while(this->first != NULL) {
        auxp = this->first;
```

```
        this->first = this->first->next;

        if(this->freeData == NULL) /* shallow */
            free(auxp->value);
        else (this->freeData)(auxp->value); /* deep */
        free(auxp); /* finally, remove the element */
    }
}
```

The constructor for the *enumeration* associates it with the list, and initializes the pointer `pos` to point to the first element of the list:

```
Abstract_Enumeration construct_Enumeration(void *p) {
    Abstract_Enumeration e;

    if((e = calloc(1, sizeof(struct Concrete_Enumeration)))
            == NULL)
        return NULL;

    e->list = (Abstract_List)p;
    e->pos = e->list->first;

    return e;
}
```

The implementation of the function `hasMoreElements_Enumeration()` is straightforward: each time `nextElement_Enumeration()` is called, the pointer `pos` is moved to point to the next list element. `pos` is NULL when the entire list has been enumerated:

```
int hasMoreElements_Enumeration(Abstract_Enumeration e) {
    return e->pos != NULL;
}
```

Now, I will discuss *some* details of the shallow and the deep interfaces, specifically a function for inserting an element using a shallow implementation, a function to delete an element using a deep implementation, and an enumeration function to get the next element. The complete code is in files `ex14-list.c`, `ex14-list-Shallow.c`, and `ex14-listDeep.c`.

The shallow implementation to insert an element into the list is practically identical to that described in Section 11.5.4:

```
int insert_ListsShallow(Abstract_List this, int pos,
    void *value) {
```

```
    int i;
    ElemTP auxp, auxm;
    int length = length_Lists(this);

    if(pos < 0 || pos > length)
        return 0;

    if(pos == 0) /* in front */ {
        if((auxm = malloc(sizeof(ElemT))) == NULL)
            return 0;

        auxm->value = value;
        auxm->next = this->first;
        /* connect with old list*/
        this->first = auxm;

        return 1;
    }
    if(this->first == NULL) /* empty list */
        return 0;

    /* search */
    for(i = 1, auxp = this->first; i < pos;
        i++, auxp = auxp->next)
        ;

    /* insert after auxp */
    if((auxm = malloc(sizeof(ElemT))) == NULL)
        return 0;

    auxm->value = value;
    auxm->next = auxp->next; /* connect with old list*/
    auxp->next = auxm;

    return 1;
}
```

The enumeration function `nextElement_EnumerationShallow()` for the *shallow* interface does not involve any copying:

```
void* nextElement_EnumerationShallow(Abstract_Enumeration e) {
    void *aux;
```

```
        if(e->pos == NULL)
            return NULL;


        aux = e->pos->value;
        e->pos = e->pos->next;


        return aux;
}
```

Next, I will discuss the implementation of the delete function to be used with lists implementing a *deep* copy:

```
int delete_ListsDeep(Abstract_List this, int pos, void *value) {
    int length = length_Lists(this);
    ElemTP auxp, auxm;
    int i;

    if(this->first == NULL)
        return 0;

    if(pos < 1 || pos > length)
        return 0;

    /* check pos 1 */
    if(pos == 1) { /* delete first */
        auxp = this->first;
        this->first = this->first->next;
        value = (this->copyData)(auxp->value);
        (this->freeData)(auxp->value);
        free(auxp);

        return 1;
    }

    /* search */
    for(i = 1, auxp = this->first; i < pos-1;
        i++, auxp = auxp->next)
        ;

    auxm = auxp->next; /* will be deleted */
    auxp->next = auxp->next->next;
```

```
    value = (this->copyData)(auxm->value);
    (this->freeData)(auxm->value);
    free(auxm);

    return 1;
}
```

I will comment on one part of the code:

```
value = (this->copyData)(auxm->value);
(this->freeData)(auxm->value);
free(auxm);
```

The data is retrieved from the list element being deleted using the provided callback function `copyData()`, and then this data is removed from the list using the other user-provided callback function `freeData()`; finally the element itself is deallocated (for the deep copy implementation, the user must provide both callback functions).

The last function I describe is the enumeration function:

```
void* nextElement_EnumerationDeep(Abstract_Enumeration e) {
    void *aux;

    if(e->pos == NULL)
        return NULL;

    aux = (e->list->copyData)(e->pos->value);
    e->pos = e->pos->next;

    return aux;
}
```

This function retrieves the data from the current element using the callback function `copyData()`.

The three files duplicate some code; specifically, the declarations of types `ElemT`, `ElemTP`, and `Concrete_List`. All three type declarations must be included in the implementation files, otherwise you would not be able to compile them. However, it would be better to store these definitions in an additional header file, say `concreteTypes.h`, and include this file in all three implementation files.

Applications

I will now show a sample application using both of these modules. The code fragment provided below works with a list of strings using both a shallow copy and a deep copy (function `freeData()` and `copyData()` are defined in Section 11.5.4). Below, error checking is omitted. First, I declare two list and two enumeration variables, and two string variables respectively representing strings "one" and "two":

```
Abstract_List deepList;
/* list containing a deep copy of data */
Abstract_List shallowList;
/* list containing a shallow copy of data */
Abstract_Enumeration deepEnum, shallowEnum;
char *pone = strdup("one");
char *ptwo = strdup("two");
```

Then, I construct both lists:

```
shallowList = construct_Lists(sizeof(char*), NULL, NULL);
deepList = construct_Lists(sizeof(char*), copyData, freeData);
```

Now, I insert strings "one" and "two" to both lists:

```
insert_ListsDeep(deepList, 0, pone);
insert_ListsDeep(deepList, 1, ptwo);
insert_ListsShallow(shallowList, 0, pone);
insert_ListsShallow(shallowList, 1, ptwo);
```

The current state of both lists is shown in Figure 14–6. As you can see from this figure, in the shallow list implementation, the pointer pone *shares* its value with the data in the first list element (and the pointer ptwo shares its value with the data in the second list element). On the other hand, in the deep implementation, data are not shared. For example, if you execute

```
free(pone)
```

then your deepList will not be affected, but your shallowList will have a dangling reference; specifically the pointer value from the first element of the list.

I will now construct the enumeration shallowEnum to print the list shallowList:

```
shallowEnum = construct_Enumeration(shallowList);
while(hasMoreElements_Enumeration(shallowEnum))
    printf("%s\n",
        (char*)nextElement_EnumerationShallow(shallowEnum));
free(shallowEnum);
```

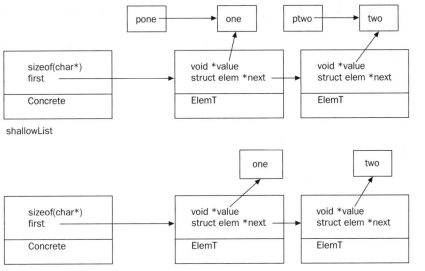

Figure 14–6

Lists of strings with shallow and deep coping

To print the list `deepList`, I can also use the shallow enumeration interface:

```
shallowEnum = construct_Enumeration(deepList);
while(hasMoreElements_Enumeration(shallowEnum))
    printf("%s\n",
        (char*)nextElement_EnumerationShallow(shallowEnum));
free(shallowEnum);
```

To copy the list `deepList` into the local array of strings, I will use the deep enumeration interface:

```
char *store[100];
deepEnum = construct_Enumeration(deepList);
for(i = 0; i < 100 && hasMoreElements_Enumeration(deepEnum);
        i++)
    store[i] = nextElement_EnumerationDeep(deepEnum);
free(deepEnum);
```

Now, I can operate on strings in the array `store`, and these operations will not affect the list.

As a final note, remember that using generic lists means that you have the responsibility for correctly applying all the operations. For example, if you created a list of `long double` values, and then retrieved some of these value as `double` values (assuming the both types are of the same size), then the values retrieved will not be correctly defined. The C compiler helps you with type checking for the basic operations, but once you start using more generic types, you can not rely on the compiler's help.

14.4 Conclusion

I have described many variants of lists in this book; the lack of space prevents me from continuing. Some more interesting possibilities are:

- applications of the exception handling techniques, described above in Section 14.2.2 to the implementation of lists
- alternative implementations of lists:
- doubly linked lists
- lists that manage their own heap
- lists implemented as an array, without using pointers

It is my hope that the reader has gained enough understanding of C and its high-level techniques to be capable of implementing some of these variants on their own.

In Section 8.18.5, I briefly described heterogeneous data structures. At this point, I would like to add that it is *possible* to extend the implementation of the generic List module to handle heterogeneous lists, but there is no "elegant" solution. Since each list element may contain data of different size, the field representing the element size would have to be moved from the list header into each list element. Unfortunately, storing only the size of the data is not sufficient to support all operations, for example, to print the data stored in the element. Lack of type reflection in C means that the only possible solution to this problem is to decide on the set of all allowable data types, and encode them using, for example, enumerated data types (for example, using `enum {chars, integers}`). As you can see, there is no clean solution that would be even remotely similar to the one possible in Java.

This book concentrated on one kind of data structure: lists. However, if you understood all of the presented concepts, then it should be easy to apply them to other data structures. For example, open hash tables used to implement symbol tables and dictionaries are simply arrays of lists—to implement them, you can reuse some of the code for the lists described in this chapter. Another useful application of lists is for an implementation of a line editor, described in the exercises presented at the end of this chapter. Trees are slightly more complicated, but again the basic concepts are the same.

14.5 Exercises

Exercise 14-1

Implement a module that represents a polynomial of degree n. Provide a constructor of the following form:

```
Abstract_Polynomial constructor_Polynomial(int degree, double *p);
```

where p is the polynomial, and n is its degree. Also, provide functions to add, subtract, and multiply polynomials, and functions to show and modify them. Finally, provide an enumeration over polynomials that gives access to the polynomial's coefficients.

Exercise 14-2

Implement a module that represents open hash tables (like in Java), storing strings as keys, and pairs consisting of a double and an integer values and as values.

Exercise 14-3

Implement a concrete transient module Stacks with the following operations on integer values:

- is the stack empty
- push an element on top of the stack
- pop the first element of the stack
- show the first element of the stack

Use this module to evaluate simple arithmetic expressions (in Polish postfix notation, developed by Lukasiewicz), consisting of single digits and two operators: + and *. The program will read an expression (consisting of at most 100 characters) into an array, and then use a stack to evaluate this expression.

For example, if the user enters

235+*

(which using infix notation is: 2 * (3 + 5)), the result will be 16.

The input expression doesn't have to be correct; for example, it is possible that the user enters 23+*. Thus, the main program has to check if the above algorithm can be applied (for example, if there are two elements on the stack that can be popped), and aborts execution upon error.

Exercise 14-4

Implement a generic transient module GenStacks with the following operations:

- is the stack empty
- push an element on top of the stack

- pop an element from the stack
- show the first element of the stack.

Consider the arithmetic expressions, described in Exercise 14–3, but consisting of double values. To evaluate these expressions, you can use a stack that holds a double value. Use your generic stack to evaluate these arithmetic expressions.

Exercise 14–5

Reimplement the module `Stacks` from Exercise 14–3 and make it persistent. Use it for the application described in this exercise, so that during the evaluation of expressions, the state of the stack (the "snapshot") is saved in files. Write a function that reads all snapshots files and shows the history of the computation.

Exercise 14–6

Reimplement the module `Stacks` from Exercise 14–3 and make it generic. Create a concrete stack of integer values and use it in the main program.

Exercise 14–7

Reimplement the module `Fractions` from Exercise 7–30 and allow the client to create multiple fractions.

Exercise 14–8

Reimplement the generic module from Exercise 8–11 and allow the client to create multiple bags. Test your concrete modules with double values and pointers to char.

Exercise 14–9

Modify the implementation of the module to tokenize strings, from Example 9–15, so that the client can work with multiple strings. Provide a shallow and a deep interface for enumerations.

Exercise 14–10

Reimplement the concrete module `Arrays` from Exercise 10–10. Make it a generic module and allow the client to create multiple arrays. Provide a shallow and a deep interface for enumerations. Test your concrete modules with double values and pointers to char.

Exercise 14–11

Implement the concrete, persistent module `BigNumbers`, meant to work with lists of "very large" integer values, called `VERYLONG`. The digits of each such value are stored in an array of 100 integers (right-justified and padded with zeroes on the left). The following operations should be supported:

- read a `VERYLONG` value from the standard input (this value is provided as a string)
- print the `VERYLONG` value to the standard output
- add two `VERYLONG` values

- subtract two VERYLONG values
- multiply two VERYLONG values

(the last three operations should consider a possibility of an overflow).

Exercise 14-12

A simple two-dimensional figure can be represented as an ordered collection of points. The following operations should be supported:

- given a point and a figure, remove this point from the figure
- given a point and a figure, add this point to a figure
- given two figures, determine if these figures are represented by the same set of points (in the same order)
- enumerations on the points

Design and implement a concrete, persistent module Figures to support these operations.

Exercise 14-13

Consider the module Figures from Exercise 14–12. Is it possible to modify this module so that it supports nested figures? (A figure is a simple figure, or a collection of (nested) figures.) If so, design and implement this module; otherwise justify your answer.

Exercise 14-14

Implement a module Database to store information about employees of a small company. For each employee, store his or her name, salary, and the number of years this employee has worked for the company. Names of employees consist of letters only, and are unique, i.e. there are no two employees with the same name. The following operations should be available:

- insert a new employee into the database. If there is already an employee with the same name, do not insert them
- remove the employee from the database. If there is no employee with this name, return a failure code; do not abort program execution
- search for an employee with the given name and return her or his salary and years of employment
- save all employee information to a text file
- retrieve all employee information from a text file
- save all employee information in a binary file
- retrieve all employee information from the binary file
- quit (without saving)

Use the module from Exercise 14–2 to support the first three operations.

PRECEDENCE AND ASSOCIATIVITY TABLES

Precedence determines the order in which operators are evaluated in expressions in the absence of explicit parentheses. The following table lists the operators in order of decreasing precedence; operators with higher precedence are evaluated first in expressions.

If two operators have the same precedence, associativity rules are used to decide the order of evaluation. There are two possible types of associativity rules: *left to right* and *right to left*. For example, in the expression

```
a = b = c
```

the associativity rule must be used to determine the order of evaluation. If the rule is right to left, this expression is equivalent to

```
a = (b = c)
```

In the table, all operators within the same box have the same precedence and associativity rule.

Operator	Meaning	Associativity
() [] . ->	function call indexing dotted access access using pointers	left to right
! ~ - ++ -- & * (type-name) `sizeof`	not one's complement negation increment decrement address dereferencing casting size of an object	right to left
* / %	multiplication division modulo	left to right
+ -	addition subtraction	left to right
<< >>	left shift right shift	left to right
< <= > >=	less than less than or equal to greater than greater than or equal to	left to right
== !=	equality inequality	left to right
&	bitwise and	left to right
^	bitwise exclusive or	left to right
|	bitwise or	left to right
&&	and	left to right
||	or	left to right
?:	conditional expression	right to left
= *= /= %= += -= <<= >>= &= != ^=	assignment	right to left
,	comma expression	left to right

SUMMARY OF
ALL STANDARD
LIBRARY
FUNCTIONS

(Note: locales and time facilities are not described here; for a description, see [Har91])

Function	Header	Description

`void`
`(*signal (int sig,`
` void (*func)(int)))(int)`
	`signal.h`	determine how receipt of signal number `sig` will be treated. If the call succeeds, signal associates the handler `func()` with `sig`, and returns a pointer to the previous handler routine for the specified signal type. If the call fails, signal returns `SIG_ERR` and sets `errno` to `EINVAL`

`constant` `_IOFBF`	`stdio.h`	full buffering, used by `setvbuf()`
`constant` `_IOLBF`	`stdio.h`	use the following buffering when `setvbuf()` is called: flush when newline is written or buffer is full
`constant` `_IONBF`	`stdio.h`	no buffering, used by `setvbuf()`
`void` `abort(void)`	`stdlib.h`	raise `SIGABRT` signal; abnormal program termination even if the signal is ignored
`double` `acos(double x)`	`math.h`	compute arc cosine. Range: $0..\pi$
`double` `asin(double x)`	`math.h`	compute arc sine. Range: $-(\pi/2)..+(\pi/2)$
`void` `assert(int exp)`	`assert.h`	if `exp` is 0 and `NDEBUG` undefined, then print message and call `abort()`; else `void`
`double` `atan(double x)`	`math.h`	compute arc tangent. Range: $(\pi/2)..+(\pi/2)$
`double` `atan2(double y, double x)`	`math.h`	compute arc tangent of y/x. Range: $\pi..+\pi$
`int` `atexit(void (*f)(void))`	`stdlib.h`	register a function `f()` to be called when `exit()` is called or `main()` returns
`double` `atof(const char *s);`	`stdlib.h`	convert string s to a `double`
`long` `atol(const char *s)`	`stdlib.h`	convert string s to a `long`, using a given base

Function	Header	Description
`int` `atoi(const char *s);`	`stdlib.h`	convert string `s` to an `unsigned`

`void *`
`bsearch(`
`  const void *key,`
`  const void *base,`
`  size_t elSize,`
`  int (*compare) (`
`    const void *theKey,`
`    const void *theValue`
`  )`
`);`
	`stdlib.h`	use binary search to look for `key`, in the block `base` (must be sorted in ascending order), consisting of objects of size `elSize`, using the function `compare()` to compare two objects (this function returns a negative value, 0 or a positive value depending on whether the `theKey` is less than, equal, or greater than `theValue`). Return a pointer to an element that matches `key`, or `NULL` if no such element found

`constant` `BUFSIZE`	`stdio.h`	buffer size used for `setbuf()` and `setvbuf()`
`void *calloc(size_t count,` `size_t elSize);`	`stdio.h`	return a pointer to a block of memory of size `count*elSize` or `NULL` if failed
`double` `ceil(double x)`	`math.h`	return as a `double` the smallest `int` not less than `x`
`constant` `CHAR_BIT`	`limits.h`	number of bits in a `char` (>= 8)
`constant` `CHAR_MAX`	`limits.h`	maximum value of `char`
`constant` `CHAR_MIN`	`limits.h`	minimum value of `char`
`void` `clearerr (FILE *fp)`	`stdio.h`	reset `EOF` and `error` indicators to 0 for the file
`double` `cos(double x)`	`math.h`	compute cosine
`double` `cosh( double x)`	`math.h`	compute hyperbolic cosine
`constant` `DBL_DIG`	`float.h`	number of digits of precision in a `double` (>=10)
`constant` `DBL_EPSILON`	`float.h`	minimum positive number such that `1.0+x<>1.0` (>=1E-5)

Function	Header	Description
constant DBL_MANT_DIG	float.h	number of base FLT_RADIX digits in the mantissa
constant DBL_MAX	float.h	maximum value of a double (>=1E+37)
constant DBL_MAX_10_EXP	float.h	maximum value of exponent, base 10; (>=+37)
constant DBL_MAX_EXP	float.h	maximum value of exponent, base FLT_RADIX
constant DBL_MIN	float.h	minimum value of a double (>=1E-37)
constant DBL_MIN_10_EXP	float.h	minimum value of exponent; (base 10) of a double (>=-37)
constant DBL_MIN_EXP	float.h	minimum value of exponent, base FLT_RADIX
constant EDOM	errno.h	an argument does not belong to the domain of a mathematical function
constant EOF	stdio.h	end-of-file
constant ERANGE	errno.h	the result of a mathematical function is out of range
constant errno	errno.h	holds error code
void exit(int status)	stdlib.h	call all functions registered with the atexit() in the reverse order of their registration; flush and close open output streams, remove files created with tmpfile(), and return to the environment with a status value
constant EXIT_FAILURE	stdlib.h	failure return code
constant EXIT_SUCCESS	stdlib.h	successful return code
double exp(double x)	math.h	exponential function

Function	Header	Description
`double` `fabs(double x)`	`math.h`	absolute value
`int` `fclose(FILE *fp)`	`stdio.h`	flush out any buffered data and close the open file. 0 is returned on success, EOF if there are errors
`int` `feof(FILE *fp)`	`stdio.h`	test fp for an EOF indication, returns nonzero if found
`int` `ferror(FILE *fp)`	`stdio.h`	test fp for a read or write error, returns nonzero if error is detected
`int` `fflush(FILE *fp)`	`stdio.h`	write a file's buffer, return 0 if successful
`int` `fgetc(FILE *fp)`	`stdio.h`	read the next character from the file and return it, return EOF if an end of file
`int` `fgetpos(FILE *fp,` `        fpos_t *pos)`	`stdio.h`	store the current file position indicator for fp in area pointed to by pos
`char *` `fgets(char *s, int n,` `        FILE *fp)`	`stdio.h`	read characters into array s (size given by n), until it encounters a newline or until the array s is full
type `FILE`	`stdio.h`	type used for file handles
constant `FILENAME_MAX`	`stdio.h`	maximum length for a file name
`double` `floor(double x)`	`math.h`	return as a `double` the largest `int` not greater than x
constant `FLT_DIG`	`float.h`	number of precision digits in a `float` (>=6)
constant `FLT_EPSILON`	`float.h`	minimum positive number such that $1.0+x<>1.0$ (>=E-5)
constant `FLT_MANT_DIG`	`float.h`	number of base `FLT_RADIX` digits in the mantissa part of a `float`
constant `FLT_MAX`	`float.h`	maximum value of a float (>=1E+37)
constant `FLT_MAX_10_EXP`	`float.h`	maximum value of exponent (base 10) of a `float` (>=+37)

Function	Header	Description
constant FLT_MAX_EXP	float.h	maximum value of exponent, base FLT_RADIX
constant FLT_MIN	float.h	minimum value of a float (>=1E-37)
constant FLT_MIN_10_EXP	float.h	minimum value of exponent (base 10) of a float (>=- 37)
constant FLT_MIN_EXP	float.h	minimum value of exponent, base FLT_RADIX
constant FLT_RADIX	float.h	radix of exponent (>= 2)
constant FLT_ROUNDS	float.h	determines rounding mode: -1 indeterminable; 0 toward 0; 1 to nearest; 2: toward + infinity; 3: toward - infinity
double fmod(double x, double y)	math.h	floating point remainder of x/y
void free(void *p)	stdio.h	deallocate a block of memory pointed to by p
constant FOPEN_MAX	stdio.h	maximum number of streams that can be open at the same time

int
fprintf(FILE *fp,
     const char *fmt,
     arg1, ..., argn)
	stdio.h	perform formatted output to a file with the specified format

int fputc(int c, FILE *fp)	stdio.h	write a character to a file
int fputs(const char *s, FILE *fp);	stdio.h	write an entire line to the file, it does not automatically terminate the line with a newline

size_t
fread(void *ptr,
  size_t elemSize,
  size_t count, FILE *fp)
	stdio.h	read from fp a block of count objects of size elemSize into block ptr

FILE * fopen(const char *filename);	stdio.h	return a file handle to filename NULL if failed

Function	Header	Description

`FILE *`
`freopen(`
`  const char *filename,`
`  const char *mode, FILE *fp)`
	`stdio.h`	reopen `fp` with file `filename` using the specified `mode`

`double` `frexp(double x, int *exp)`	`math.h`	store an exponential value x in `exp`, in the form: normalized fraction, integral power of two

`int`
`fscanf(FILE *fp,`
`      const char *fmt,`
`      arg1, ..., argn)`
	`stdio.h`	formatted input from a file with a specified format

`int`
`fseek(FILE *fp,`
`     long offs, int mode)`
	`stdio.h`	move the internal file pointer to a specified location

`int`
`fsetpos(FILE *fp,`
`       const fpos_t *pos)`
	`stdio.h`	position the file handle to the location in the file, as specified by the value pointed to by `pos`

`long` `ftell(FILE *fp)`	`stdio.h`	return a long value that contains the current `offset`

`int`
`fwrite(char *buf,`
`  unsigned elemSize,`
`  int count, FILE *fp)`
	`stdio.h`	write to a file a block stored at `buf`, and consisting of `count` objects, each of size `elemSize`
		Return the number of objects written

`int` `getc(FILE *fp)`	`stdio.h`	read the next character in the file
`int` `getchar();`	`stdio.h`	read the next character from `stdio`
`char *` `getenv(const char *envName)`	`stdlib.h`	return the value of the environment variable `envName`, `NULL` if there is no such variable
`char *` `gets(char *s)`	`stdio.h`	read one line from the `stdin` and store it in `s`
`constant` `INT_MAX`	`limits.h`	maximum value of an `int` (>= +32767)
`constant` `INT_MIN`	`limits.h`	minimum value of an `int` (>= -32767)

Function	Header	Description
int isalnum(int c)	ctype.h	is c an alphanumeric (digit, lower or uppercase letter)
int isalpha(int c)	ctype.h	is c an alphabetic letter (lower or uppercase letter)
int isdigit(int c)	ctype.h	is c a digit
int isgraph(int c)	ctype.h	is c printable but not a space
int islower(int c)	ctype.h	is c a lowercase letter
int isodigit(int c)	ctype.h	is c an octal digit (0-8)
int isprint(int c)	ctype.h	is c printable, that is not a control character (not in the range 0-37 and 127)
int ispunct(int c)	ctype.h	is c printable but neither space nor alphanumeric
int isspace(int c)	ctype.h	is c whitespace
int isupper(int c)	ctype.h	is c an uppercase letter
int isxdigit(int c)	ctype.h	is c a hexadecimal digit (a digit or upper or lowercase a, b, c, d, e, f)
constant L_tmpname	stdio.h	length of temporary filename; used with tmpnam()
constant LDBL_DIG	float.h	number of precision digits in a long double (>=10)
constant LDBL_EPSILON	float.h	minimum positive number such that $1.0+x<>1.0$ (>=1E-9)
constant LDBL_MANT_DIG	float.h	number of base FLT_RADIX digits in the mantissa
constant LDBL_MAX	float.h	maximum value of a long double (>=1E+37)
constant LDBL_MAX_10_EXP	float.h	maximum value of exponent (base 10) of a long double (>=+37)

Function	Header	Description
constant LDBL_MAX_EXP	float.h	maximum value of exponent, base FLT_RADIX
constant LDBL_MIN	float.h	minimum value of a long double (>=1E- 37)
constant LDBL_MIN_10_EXP	float.h	minimum value of exponent (base 10) of a long double (>=-37)
constant LDBL_MIN_EXP	float.h	minimum value of exponent, base FLT_RADIX
double ldexp(double x, int exp)	math.h	return $x*(2^{exp})$
double log(double x)	math.h	natural log
double log10(double x)	math.h	base 10 log
constant LONG_MAX	limits.h	maximum value of a long int (>=2,147,483,647)
constant LONG_MIN	limits.h	minimum value of a long int (>= -2,147,483,647)
void longjmp(jmp_buf env, int retval)	setjmp.h	use the variable env and return in such a way that setjmp() appears to have returned with the value retval
constant MB_LEN_MAX	limits.h	maximum number of bytes in a multi-byte char (>=1)
void *malloc(size_t elSize);	stdio.h	return a pointer to a block of memory of size elSize or NULL if failed
void * memchr(const void *s, int c, size_t n)	string.h	return a pointer to the first occurrence in the initial n characters of *s of c
int memcmp(const void *s1, const void *s2, size_t n)	string.h	compare first n characters in the objects pointed to by s1 and s2
void * memcpy(void *s1, const void *s2, size_t n)	string.h	copy n bytes from s2 to s1. If objects overlap, the result is undefined

Function	Header	Description

`void *`
`memmove(void *s1,`
`   const void *s2, size_t n)`
	`string.h`	as `memcpy()`, but works for over-lapped objects

`double` `modf(double x, double *p)`	`math.h`	store in the object pointed by `p` the integral part of `x` and return the fractional part of `x`
constant `NULL`	`stddef.h`	null pointer
type `offsetof`	`stddef.h`	offset (in bytes) of a structure member
`void` `perror(const char *s)`	`stdio.h`	output a single-line error message to the `stdout`
`double` `pow(double x, double y)`	`math.h`	return `x` to power `y`

`int`
`printf(char *fmt,`
`      arg1, ..., argn)`
	`stdio.h`	formatted output to `stdout`

type `ptrdiff_t`	`stddef.h`	a type of a difference of two pointers
`int` `putc(int c, FILE *fp)`	`stdio.h`	write a character c to a file
`int` `putchar(int c)`	`stdio.h`	write a character to `stdout`
`int` `puts(char *s)`	`stdio.h`	write string s to `stdout`

`void`
`qsort(const void *base,`
`   size_t count,`
`   size_t elSize,`
`   int (*compare(`
`     const void *el1,`
`     const void *el2`
`   )`
`)`
	`stdlib.h`	sort a block base, consisting of `count` objects, each of size `elSize`, using the function `compare()` to compare two objects (this function returns a negative value, 0 or a positive value depending on whether `el1` is less than, equal, or greater than `el2`)

`int` `raise(int sig)`	`signal.h`	send signal `sig`; return 0 if successful, non-zero otherwise

Function	Header	Description

`void*`
`realloc(void *ptr,`
`        size_t size)`
	`stdlib.h`	changes the size of memory block pointed to by ptr while preserving its contents. If realloc() returns a pointer that is different from `ptr`, it means that the old region has been deallocated and should not be used

`int` `remove(const char *fname)`	`stdio.h`	remove a file

`int`
`rename(const char *old,`
`       const char *new)`
	`stdio.h`	rename a file

`void` `rewind(FILE *fp)`	`stdio.h`	move the internal file pointer to beginning of the file

`int`
`scanf(char *fmt,`
`      arg1, ..., argn)`
	`stdio.h`	formatted input from `stdin`

constant `SCHAR_MAX`	`limits.h`	maximum value of a signed `char` (>= 127)
constant `SCHAR_MIN`	`limits.h`	minimum value of a signed `char` (>= -127)
macro `SEEK_CUR`	`stdio.h`	offset from current position; used in `fseek()`
macro `SEEK_END`	`stdio.h`	offset from end; used in `fseek()`
macro `SEEK_SET`	`stdio.h`	offset from beginning; used in `fseek()`
`void` `setbuf(FILE *fp, char *buf)`	`stdio.h`	control the buffering for an open file `fp`; buffer `buf` is used for buffering I/O
`int` `setjmp(jmp_buf env)`	`setjmp.h`	save the state of the execution in env, and return zero. Must be called before `longjmp()`

`int`
`setvbuf (FILE *fp,`
` char *buf, int bufmode,`
` size_t size)`
	`stdio.h`	as `setbuf()`, but `size` is the size of the buffer, and `bufmode` is one of macros: `_IOFBF`, `_IOLBF`, `_IONBF`

constant `SHRT_MAX`	`limits.h`	maximum value of a `short` (>= +32767)

Function	Header	Description
constant SHRT_MIN	limits.h	minimum value of a short (>= −32767)
constant SIG_DFL	signal.h	default handler, terminate the program
constant SIG_ERR	signal.h	indicates error return from signal
constant SIG_IGN	signal.h	handler; ignore this type signal
constant SIGABRT	signal.h	abnormal termination
constant SIGFPE	signal.h	floating-point exception (e.g. division by 0)
constant SIGILL	signal.h	illegal instruction
constant SIGINT	signal.h	interrupt (e.g. BREAK key is pressed)
constant SIGSEGV	signal.h	invalid memory access (e.g. bad pointer)
constant SIGTERM	signal.h	terminate signal
double sin(double x)	math.h	compute sine
double sinh(double x)	math.h	compute hyperbolic sine
type size_t	stddef.h	a type of sizeof()
int sprintf (char *s, *fmt, arg1, ..., argn)	stdio.h	formatted output to string s
double sqrt(double x)	math.h	return square root
int sscanf (char *s, *fmt, arg1, ..., argn)	stdio.h	formatted read from string s

Function	Header	Description
constant `stderr`	`stdio.h`	predefined constant file handle: the standard error stream
constant `stdin`	`stdio.h`	predefined constant file handle: the standard input stream
constant `stdout`	`stdio.h`	predefined constant file handle: the standard output stream

`char *`
`strcat(char *s1,`
`        const char *s2)`
	`string.h`	append string `s2` to `s1`, overwrites `NULL` at the end of `s1`

`char *` `strchr(const char *s, int c)`	`string.h`	return a pointer to the first occurrence of `c` in `*s`

`int`
`strcmp(const char *s1,`
`       const char *s2)`
	`string.h`	compare two strings

`char *`
`strcpy(char *s1,`
`       const char *s2)`
	`string.h`	copy `s2` into `s1`

`size_t`
`strcspn(const char *s1,`
`        const char *s2)`
	`string.h`	return the length of the initial part of `s1` which contains no characters from `s2`

`char*` `strerror(int errnum)`	`string.h`	return a pointer to a string describing the error number
`size_t` `strlen(const char *s)`	`string.h`	return the length of string `s`

`char*`
`strncat(char *s1,`
`        const char *s2,`
`        size_t n)`
	`string.h`	as `strcat()` with at most `n` characters copied

`int`
`strncmp(const char *s1,`
`        const char s2,`
`        size_t n)`
	`string.h`	as `strcmp()`, but compares at most `n` characters

`char *`
`strncpy(char *s1,`
`        const char *s2,`
`        size_t n)`
	`string.h`	as `strcpy()`, but copies only `n` characters

`char *`
`strpbrk(const char *s1,`
`        const char *s2)`
	`string.h`	return pointer to first char in `s1` which is any in `s2`

Function	Header	Description

`char *`
`strrchr(const char *s,`
`        int c)`
	`string.h`	return pointer to the last occurrence in `s1` of `c`

`size_t`
`strspn(const char *s1,`
`       const char *s2)`
	`string.h`	return length of initial part of `s1` consisting entirely of characters from `s2`

`char *`
`strstr(const char *s1,`
`  const char *s2)`
	`string.h`	return a pointer to first occurrence in `s1` of `s2`

`double`
`strtod(const char *s,`
`       char **p);`
	`string.h`	convert string `s` to a `double`

`char *`
`strtok(const char *s1,`
`       const char *s2)`
	`string.h`	break `s1` into tokens, each delimited by one of the characters from `s2`, return a pointer to first token.

`long`
`strtol(const char *s,`
`  char **p, int base)`
	`string.h`	convert string `s` to a `long`, using a given base

`unsigned long`
`strtoul(const char *s,`
`  char **p, int base)`
	`string.h`	convert string `s` to an `unsigned long`, using a given base

`int` `system(const char *cmd)`	`stdlib.h`	execute `cmd` by the operating system, return status code
`double` `tan(double x)`	`math.h`	compute tangent
`double` `tanh(double x)`	`math.h`	compute hyperbolic tangent
`constant` `TMP_MAX`	`stdio.h`	maximum number of successful successive calls to `tmpnam()`
`FILE *` `tmpfile(void)`	`stdio.h`	use `fopen(., "w+b")` to create a new file, which is automatically deleted when it is closed or the program terminates
`char *` `tmpnam(char *buf)`	`stdio.h`	create a filename that is not in conflict with other filenames currently in use, `buf` points to a block of size at least `L_tmpname`, a new filename is copied into this block
`int` `tolower(int c)`	`ctype.h`	if `c` is uppercase, return lowercase, else return `c`

Function	Header	Description
int toupper(int c)	ctype.h	if c is lowercase, return uppercase, else return c
constant UCHAR_MAX	limits.h	maximum value of an unsigned char (>= 255U)
constant UINT_MAX	limits.h	maximum value of an unsigned int (>=65535U)
constant ULONG_MAX	limits.h	maximum value of an unsigned long (>=4294967295U)
int ungetc(char c, FILE *fp)	stdio.h	push c back onto fp.
constant USHRT_MAX	limits.h	maximum value of a unsigned short (>=65535U)
type va_arg(va_list ap, type)	stdarg.h	each call extracts an expression that has the same type and value as the next argument being passed (type)
void va_end(va_list ap)	stdarg.h	terminates processing of a variable number of arguments
macro va_list	stdarg.h	type to hold a variable argument list
void va_start(va_list ap, lastP)	stdarg.h	set ap to point to the first of the variable arguments being passed to the function; lastP is the name of the rightmost parameter just before ...

int
vfprintf (FILE *fp,
  const char *fmt,
  va_list arg)
	stdio.h	formatted output to a file, but with a variable argument list replaced by arg

int
vfscanf (FILE *fp,
  const char *fmt,
  va_list param)
	stdio.h	formatted input from a file, but with a variable parameter list replaced by param

int vprintf (const char *fmt, va_list param)	stdio.h	as vfprintf() but with output sent to stdout
int vscanf(const char *fmt, va_list param)	stdio.h	as vfscanf(), but with input from stdin

Function	Header	Description

`int`
`vsprintf(char *s,`
`  const char *fmt,`
`  va_list arg)`
	`stdio.h`	formatted output to string s, but with variable argument list replaced by `arg`

`int`
`vsscanf(char *s,`
`  const char *fmt,`
`  va_list param)`
	`stdio.h`	formatted input from a string s, but with a variable parameter list replaced by `param`

type `wchar_t`	`stddef.h`	an integral type that can hold a wide character

B.1 Formatted Input

The format control string contains:

■ Conversion specifications starting with %

■ Whitespace characters

■ Ordinary characters

A % character may be followed by an *optional* * character, which suppresses the conversion (the input data is read, but it is not assigned to the argument; instead it is discarded). The number of conversion specifications that are not suppressed and the number of arguments must be equal. Moreover, the type of an argument must match its corresponding conversion specification.

Example.

```
scanf("%d%*c%d", &i, &j);
```

Input:

```
12a3
```

Result:

```
i is equal to 12 and j is equal to 3
```

An input data is defined as a string of consecutive non-whitespace characters, so it extends to the next whitespace character (whitespace characters, line boundaries in particular, are skipped when an input function is looking for an input field that matches the specification). This may be changed by the specification of the conversion; one of the following:

```
c, n and [
```

The optional maximum field width limits the number of characters read (whitespace skipped does not count).

Example.

```
scanf("%2d%2d", &i, &j);
```

Input:

```
12345c
```

Result:

i is equal to 12 and j is equal to 34

The optional size specifications are:

h to indicate short; used for an integer (for conversions: d, i, n, u, o and x)

l to indicate double; used for an integer (same conversions as above) or for a float (for conversions e, f, and g)

L to indicate long double; used for double (for conversions e, f, and g)

Conversion specifications

d, i	signed decimal
u	unsigned decimal
o	unsigned octal
x, X	unsigned hexadecimal
s	character string (terminates on whitespace, appends NULL)
f, e, g E, G	float number
[ ]	character class enclosed by square brackets. There are three types of character classes (and they can be combined):

    list of characters, e.g., [AbC]
    ASCII range of characters specified with a
    hyphen, e.g. [a-z] complement of a range, with a
    circumflex ^ as the first character; e.g., [^a-z]

c	a single character (including whitespace)

p	read a pointer (`void*`) previously written using `%p` in a `printf()`
n	return as an integer the number of characters read by this call so far.

When looking for an input field, there are two cases for which whitespace characters are not skipped: a character and a character class conversion specification. In the following examples, **b** stands for a blank character, characters from the input that have been processed (read) are in italics, and the following variables are assumed to be defined:

```
int i, j;
double f;
char *s;
```

Call	Input	Comment
`scanf("%d-%d", &i, &j);`	**b***12***b**34c	one value read, `i==12`, `j` is undefined
`scanf("%d-%d", &i, &j);`	**b***12-34*c	two values read, `i==12`, `j==34`
`scanf("%[0-9]", s);`	**b***12-34*c	s is "12" (note: the string is null-terminated)

B.2 Formatted Output

A format control string is of the form:

% flags field-width precision size conversion

(items in italics are optional). Flags specify output justification, numeric signs, decimal points, trailing zeros, octal and hexadecimal prefixes.

Field-width specifies the minimum number of characters to print, padding with blanks or zeros.

Precision specifies the maximum number of characters to print; for integers, minimum number of digits to print.

Length can be used to specify short or long data types.

The number of arguments must be equal to the number of conversion specifications.

Below, I provide a detailed description of all items.

Flags are created by taking zero or more of the following items:

-	left justification (by default, it is right justification)
+	signed integer conversion
space	inserts a leading space if the first character is not a sign
0	pad with leading zeros for the following conversions: i, o, u, x, X, e, E, f, F, G
#	unsigned integer control, inserts a leading 0 or 0x, respectively, to the octal or hexadecimal value displayed.

Field-width

An unsigned integer specifying the minimum field width; the field width will be automatically expanded if necessary. The field width may be specified as an *, in which case an additional argument to printf must be provided to specify the field width to use. By default a value is right justified in the field.

Precision

An unsigned integer preceded by a dot. For real values, it indicates the number of digits in the fractional part; for a string, it indicates the maximum length of the string to be printed. As above, an asterisk (with the next argument) can be used to specify the precision.

Length

There are three specifiers for printing an integral type: h, l, and L, and so this specification may only be used with the following conversions:

%d, %o, %u, %x, %X:

  h specifies short

  l specifies long

  L specifies long double

To output a % character, it must be preceded by another % character.

Conversion

d, i	signed decimal (default precision 1)
u	unsigned decimal (default precision 1)
o	unsigned octal (default precision 1)
x, X	unsigned hexadecimal (default precision 1)
c	unsigned character
s	character string

f, e, E, g, G	floating-point number in the form:
	`f [-] ddd.ddd`
	`e [-] d.ddddde{sign}dd`
	`E [-] d.dddddE{sign}dd`
g	shorter of `f` and `e`
G	shorter of `f` and `E`
	The default precision is 6.
p	Value of a pointer (`void*`)
n	The argument must be in the form `int* p`. Writes the number characters output thus far by this call into `p`

Examples (below **b** stands for a blank character)

Call	Output	Comment
`printf("%-5d", 12);`	12**bbb**	12 left-justi ed in the eld of width 5
`printf("%+05d", 12);`	+0012	Adds leading 0's
`printf("%5.2f", 12.787);`	12.78	Here, precision is the number of digits in the decimal part
`printf("%8.4f", 12.787);`	**b**12.7870	Left-justi ed in the eld of width 8.
`printf("%#x", 12);`	0xc	Adds leading 0 or 0x, converts to hexadecimal
`printf("%3.2", "Java");`	**bbbb**Ja	Here, precision is the number of characters printed
`printf("%f", 12.9876543);`	12.987654	Default precision is 6
`printf("%e", 12.9876543);`	1.298765e+01	Scienti c notation
`printf("%g", 12.9876543);`	12.9877	Shorter out of e and f with only 6 digits (default)
`printf("%E", 12.9876543);`	1.298765E+01	Like the e speci cation b ut in uppercase
`printf("%*.2f", 4, 15.123);`	**bb**15	The value 4 replaces * and is used as a eld width
`printf("%*.*f", 4, 2, 15.123);`	**bb**15	Values 4 and 2 replace *'s
`printf("%d%n", 15, &i);`	15	The value of i is 2 because 2 characters have been printed.

GLOSSARY

actual parameters: parameters appearing in a call to the function.

alphabet: the set of characters that may appear in source files

binary file: file for which processing is not line-oriented

block: enclosed in braces; may contain both definitions and statements.

buffered operations: writing a character does not immediately write it to disk; instead, it places it in an appropriate buffer

byte: a part of a computer word, normally 8 bits

byte-oriented memory architecture: the smallest addressable unit is one byte

concrete data structure: the type of each element is known

conditional compilation: the compiler ignores portions of the code depending on some specified condition

dangling reference: a variable referencing a memory block whose lifetime has expired

declaration of a function: provides the function prototype, but does not say anything about the implementation

definition of a function: includes both the function prototype and the function body, that is its implementation

dereferencing: accessing the contents of the memory location pointed to by a pointer

dynamic memory allocation: a block of memory, requested by some program, is removed from the heap and can be used by the program

dynamic memory deallocation: a program returns a block of memory to the heap

dynamic memory management: the running program is using memory which is not stored on the run-time stack governed by the First-In-First-Out rule. Instead, memory blocks required by the program come from a memory pool called a heap

explicit conversion: a casting conversion performed by the programmer

file handle: pointer to a `FILE`

filters: programs that are designed to read from the standard input stream only and write to the standard output stream only

formal parameters: parameters appearing in a declaration or a definition of a function

format control string: specifies formatting requirements for formatted I/O

generic data structure: the type of each element is not known

heap fragmentation: the heap becomes divided into a large number of small memory blocks

heterogeneous data structure: consists of elements of various types

homogenous data structure: consists of elements of the same type

hosted environments: to create executable code, the object code must be linked with the code of the system routines used in this program

identifier: a sequence of letters, digits, and underscores that does not start with a digit

idiom: code patterns frequently used and reused.

implicit conversion: a conversion performed by the compiler

include directives: the named files are to be included at the points where the directives occur

incomplete type definition: `struct t`; the type `t` is defined elsewhere

initialized pointer: points to a memory block that has been allocated for your program

lazy evaluation: a certain action is delayed until it is absolutely necessary

lexically correctness: correctness according to the lexical structure of the language

line-oriented file processing: assumes that the file contains end-of-line terminators, and uses this assumption to process the file

linker: a program that links the code with the system libraries and creates executable code

linking: combining the object code and possibly some libraries of several files

l-value: an expression that can be interpreted as an address

lifetime of a variable: period of time during which memory is allocated to the variable.

macro substitution: the process of replacement of a macro by the macro replacement

memory leakage: appears when the programmer forgets to deallocate memory

module: consists of the interface (stored in a header file) and one or more implementation files

opaque type: type whose internal representation is hidden from the client

pointer: a variable whose value is a memory address

portable programs: after recompilation, can run on any machine

preprocessing: replacement of certain text in the source file by other text

procedural programming paradigm: functions communicating by passing arguments and returning values

prototype: the "header" of a function; includes the return type, function name, and the list of parameters

run-time stack: the stack used by the run-time system to manage memory for functions

run-time system: support code to manage run-time program requirements

scope of an identifier: the region of the program in which this identifier is visible

sentinel value: the value used to stop the input

separate compilation: one or more source files may be compiled to create object codes

size of a type: the number of bytes occupied by an object of this type

standard input: usually a keyboard, unless it has been redirected, in which case it is a file

standard output: usually the screen, unless it has been redirected, for example to a file or a printer

text file: file for which processing is line-oriented

tokens: characters are collected into lexical units called tokens

traversal of a block: the ability to access each object in the block

trigraph: used to represent the missing symbols using ISO 646–1083

whitespace: spaces, tabs, formfeeds, and newlines

THE COMPLETE LIST OF COMMON ERRORS

Chapter 3

1. In order to check whether the sum of two integers i and j *overflows*, do not use

   ```
   i + j > INT_MAX
   ```

   (INT_MAX is defined in limits.h), because this creates an overflow. Instead, use

   ```
   i > INT_MAX - j
   ```

2. String constants and character constants are very different. One must take care not to use a string constant

   ```
   "a"
   ```

   if a character constant is required

   ```
   'a'
   ```

3. Since < is left associative, the expression

```
a < b < c
```

is interpreted as

```
(a < b) < c
```

and has a different meaning than

```
a < b && b < c
```

4. The code fragment presented will show a common error, related to the placement of brackets (notice the lack of any inner brackets):

```
if(c = getchar() == EOF)
```

Due to the precedence rules, the compiler interprets the code fragment as follows:

```
if(c = (getchar() == EOF))
```

As a result, c gets assigned a Boolean value, and the character read is not stored in c.

5. Always use an integer variable instead of a char variable c to store the result of getchar().

6. The ampersand & preceding the variable i in scanf("%d", &i) is crucial.

7. printf() expects a string, so

```
printf("\n");
```

is correct, but

```
printf('\n');
```

is wrong.

8. To print a double, you use %f, but to read the same double value, you use %lf. Similarly, to print a long integer use %d, and to read it, use %ld.

9. Use correct conversions; for example

```
printf("%d", 3.5);
```

and

```
printf("%g", 4);
```

will both print *garbage*.

10. The number of conversions must be equal to the number of arguments; for example

```
printf("%d%d", i)
```

is incorrect. Remember that with `scanf()` you need to pass the address of the variable, therefore

```
scanf("%d", i);
```

is incorrect.

11. Spurious characters in `scanf()`'s format control string are a source of errors that are very hard to spot. Use them with caution!

Chapter 4

1. Remember that `i = 8` is very different from `i == 8` (assignment vs. equality).

2. Watch for off-by-one errors.

3. Avoid the following errors:

`e1 & e2`	likely should be	`e1 && e2`
`e1	e2`	likely should be	`e1 || e2`
`if(x = 1) ...`	should be	`if(x == 1) ...`

4. Be careful with loops that have empty bodies. It is easy to write

```
while(condition)
     statement
```

when what was really intended was

```
while(condition)
   ;
statement
```

For example, compare

```
while((c = getchar()) != 'a')
 putchar(c);
```

with

```
while((c = getchar()) != 'a')
   ;
putchar(c);
```

In the first case, input characters will be output until 'a' is encountered, but in the second case, only the character 'a' will be output.

Chapter 5

1. To declare more than one FILE variable, the asterisk must be repeated, for example,

```
FILE *f, *g;
```

2. Be very careful of the spelling of file operations; do not use open() or close(). These are low-level file operations that are often accessible from C, but do not have the same functionality.

Chapter 6

1. To define a macro such as PI, do not use:

```
#define PI = 3.14
```

This replacement for PI consists of two tokens, = and 3.14. For example, the code

```
    i = PI;
```

would be replaced by

```
    i = = 3.14;
```

Also, remember to omit the ';' from a macro definition. For example,

```
#define PI 3.14;
```

is incorrect.

2. The preprocessor syntax is not the same as C syntax.

3. There should be no whitespace between the macro name and the opening parenthesis '(' for the parameters; otherwise, the preprocessor will interpret the parameters as part of the text to be included.

4. Enclose the entire macro, as well as each occurrence of a macro argument, in parentheses.

5. Avoid side effects in macro arguments.

6. Make sure that in a header file you use

```
#ifndef
```

rather than

```
#ifdef
```

Chapter 7

1. A function must be declared or defined *before* it can be called (strictly speaking this is not true, and a function may be called even if its prototype has not been seen, but the rules that describe this case are complicated, and the technique often leads to programming errors).

2. Remember that a function declaration is terminated with ; but that in the definition, the function prototype is not terminated with ;, instead the function body is enclosed in braces (this is a very common error when copying code from a header file to an implementation and then forgetting to make the necessary changes).

3. A return statement that returns nothing, such as:

```
return;
```

is meaningful only in a procedure; for a function you need to return an expression:

```
return exp;
```

Chapter 8

1. To declare two pointers of the same type, use

```
int *p1, *p2;
```

The declaration

```
int *p1, p2;
```

declares an integer pointer `p1` and an integer `p2`.

In order to avoid this problem, you may want to use `typedef`, for example

```
typedef int* Pint;
```

and then, use this type when declaring pointers. For example

```
Pint p1, p2;
```

defines two integer pointers.

2. Never use uninitialized pointers.

3. To increment a dereferenced pointer, use

```
(*p)++
```

rather than

```
*p++
```

which means: first dereference a pointer, and then increment this pointer (and not its value). For the discussion of pointer incrementation, see Section 8.12.1.

4. You must always avoid *mixing* statically and dynamically allocated memory. For example, the following code:

```
int i;
int *p;
&i = malloc(sizeof(int));
```

is illegal, because you can not allocate memory for non-pointer variables on the heap.

5. Memory deallocation using `free()` should only be used if memory has been previously allocated with `malloc()`. Using the same declarations from the previous example, the code:

```
p = &i;
free(p);
```

is also wrong, because memory belonging to non-pointer variables (such as `i` in this example) can not be deallocated (deallocation is implicitly done by the system).

Both of these examples illustrate that you must always remember where the memory came from: the heap or the stack. It is illegal to get memory from the stack and return it to the heap.

6. The value of a pointer should never be dereferenced after the call to `free(p)`.

7. Do not create "garbage" objects, such as

```
MALLOC(p, int, 1)
MALLOC(p, int, 1)
```

The first object created above is now inaccessible (garbage).

8. Given two pointers p and q, the assignment p = q does not copy the block of memory pointed to by q into a block of memory pointed to by p; instead it assigns memory addresses (so that both p and q point to the same memory location; changing the value of that memory location affects both pointers).

9. Remember that after p = q, p and q share the value; therefore if you call `free(p)` this would also deallocate q, and now you must not call `free(q)`.

10. Do not access memory locations which have not been allocated by your program; in particular if you allocated a block of n objects, do not try to access objects beyond this block (this includes any objects in locations p+n and beyond).

11. Given a block of memory of SIZE objects, pointed to by p, you can set q to point to the last object in the block using:

```
q+SIZE-1
```

rather than

```
q+SIZE
```
('off by one' error).

12. The comparison of two pointers p and q using p == q does not compare the contents of the memory blocks pointed to by p and q; it merely compares addresses of these blocks.

13. A generic pointer can not be dereferenced. For example

```
int i;
void *p = &i;

*p = 2;
```

is wrong, but

```
*(int*)i = 2;
```

is correct. Similarly, the code

```
void* f() {
    int *ip;
```

```
    if((ip = (int*)malloc(sizeof(int))) == NULL)
        error;
    return ip;
}
*f() = 2;
```

is wrong, but

```
*(int*)f() = 2;
```

is OK.

Chapter 9

1. If a string is not terminated by the null character, or this character is overwritten, all string operations produce undefined results.

2. When you allocate memory for a string that can have n characters, do not use

```
calloc(n, sizeof(char))
```

because you have to allocate memory for the \0 character.

3. Do not use

```
calloc(sizeof(string), sizeof(char))
```

because that call allocates a block of memory to store the number of characters determined by the size of a pointer to character, rather then the required length.

4. Initialized pointers are not necessarily initialized strings. (If an initialized pointer points to a memory block that does not contain the null character, the string is not initialized).

5. Double and single quotes that enclose a single character signify different things; for example "W" denotes a pointer to a memory block containing two characters, W followed by \0; 'W' denotes the ordinal value of the character W.

6. To input a string:

   a) use

   ```
   scanf("%s", s)
   ```

   rather than

   ```
   scanf("%s", &s)
   ```

     b) make sure that s is initialized; i.e. there is *some* memory allocated for s (for example, using `calloc()`)

     c) make sure that there is *enough* memory allocated for s, and consider using the field width to avoid overflow

7. `strcpy(dest, src)` and `strcat(dest, src)` assume that there is enough memory allocated for the `dest` to perform the required operation.

   `strncpy(dest, src)` does have to append the zero character.

8. `if(strcmp(s1, s2)) ...`

   and

   `if(strcmp(s1, s2)) == -1)`

   are both wrong.

9. To compare two strings `str1` and `str2`, do not use

     `str1 < str2`

   which only compares their memory addresses. Instead use

     `strcmp(str1, str2);`

10. To copy a string `str1` to another string `str2`, do not use

     `str1 = str2`

   which only copies the memory address; instead use

     `strcpy(str1, str2);`

11. Redirection is not a part of the command line of a program.

Chapter 10

1. Given the declaration

     `type arrayName[n];`

   do not use

     `arrayName[n]`

2. Declarations of the form

```
int n = 3;
double s[n];
```

are illegal, because the size of array `s` must be a constant.

3. Arrays are not l-values, so

```
int x[2];
int *pid;
. . .
x = pid
```

is illegal. However, `pid = x` is legal.

4. Side-effects may make the result of assignments involving index expressions *implementation dependent;* for example, in the assignment

```
a[i] = i++;
```

`i` may be incremented before or after it is used as an index expression.

5. `sizeof(array)` returns the number of objects in the array, not the number of bytes.

6.
```
void f(double b[]) {
    sizeof(b) . . .
}
```

The call to `sizeof(b)` within the function body returns the size of a pointer, not the size of array `b`.

7. `void f(double x[][]);`

The number of columns must always be provided when declaring two-dimensional arrays as function parameters.

Chapter 11

1.
```
struct example { ... };
example e;
```

Should be:

```
struct example e;
```

The following declaration is also wrong:

```
struct example {  ...  }
```

The missing semicolon will produce a long list of compiler errors.

2. To allocate memory for a structure, do not use

```
malloc(sizeof(struct *))
```

because this call will allocate a block large enough to store only a pointer to a structure, not the whole structure.

THE COMPLETE LIST OF IDIOMS

Chapter 3

Main Function

main() is an integer function, which returns one of two standard return codes: EXIT_FAILURE and EXIT_SUCCESS.

Read Single Character

```
if((c = getchar()) == EOF) ... /* error, else OK */
```

Read Single Integer

```
if(scanf("%d", &i) != 1 ) ...   /* error, else OK */
```

Read Single Integer with Prompt

```
printf("Enter integer: ");
if(scanf("%d", &i) != 1 ) ...   /* error, else OK */
```

Read Two Integers

```
if(scanf("%d%d", &i, &j) != 2 ) ... /* error, else OK */
```

Type Synonym

```
typedef existingType newType
```

Chapter 4

Read Characters Until Sentinel

```
while(1) {
    /* read in a value and check it */
    if((aux = getchar()) == EOF || aux == SENTINEL)
       break;
     /* further processing */
}
```

or:

```
while(1) {
    /* read in a value and check it */
    if((aux = getchar()) == EOF)
       break;
    if(aux == SENTINEL)
       break;
    /* further processing */
}
```

Read Integers Until Sentinel

```
while(1) {
    if(scanf("%d", &i) != 1 || i == SENTINEL)
       break;
      ...
}
```

Repeat N Times

```
for(i = 1, initialization; i <= N; i++, processing)
```
with i as a control variable.

Read Until Condition

```
while(1) {
    printf("enter two integers a and b, a < b:");
    if(scanf("%d%d", &a, &b) == 2)
       break;
    if(a < b)
       break;
      ...
}
```

Chapter 5

Opening a File

```
if((fileHandle = fopen(fname, fmode)) == NULL)
    /* failed */
```

Closing a File
```
if(fclose(fileHandle) == EOF)
   /* failed */
```

Read Single Character from a File
```
if((c = fgetc(fileHandle)) == EOF) /* error */
```

Read Single Integer from a File
```
if(fscanf(fileHandle, "%d", &i) != 1) /* error */
```

Read a Line
```
while((c = getchar()) != '\n')
```

Read a Line from a File
```
while((c = fgetc(fileHandle)) != '\n')
```

Read until end-of-file
```
while((c = getchar()) != EOF)
```

Read from a File until end-of-file
```
while((c = fgetc(fileHandle)) != EOF)
```

Clear until end-of-line
```
while(getchar() != '\n')
    ;
```

Note that this code assumes that end-of-line will eventually be encountered.

Read until Condition, then push back the last character
```
while(condition(c = fgetc(fileHandle)))
    process c
ungetc(c, f)
```

Chapter 6

Include Files

Use

```
#include <filename>
```

for system files, and

```
#include "filename"
```

for user-defined files

Debugging using Conditional Compilation

```
#define DEB        /* empty, but defined */
#ifdef DEB
    /* some debugging statement, for example */
    printf("value of i = %d", i);
#endif
/* code which will be executed when NOT debugging */
```

Header File using Macro

```
#ifndef SCREEN_H
#define SCREEN_H
    /* contents of the header */
#endif
```

Chapter 7

Function Names

Use function names that are relevant to the module in which they appear. I recommend using this convention

```
FunctionName_moduleName
```

Static Identifiers

Any functions and variable definitions that are private to a file (and are not accessible outside of this file) should be qualified as `static`.

Header and Implementation

The implementation file always includes its corresponding header file.

Module Extension

To extend a module `M` to a module `M1`, define the header file `M1.h` and the interface `M1.c`. `M1.h` includes `M.h` and `M1.c` includes `M1.h`. The client of `M1` includes `M1.h` and links the application code with `M.o` and `M1.o`

Module Modification

To define module `M1`, which extends an existing module `M`, follow these steps:

1. Declare the new interface in `M1.h` (`M1.h` does not include `M.h`)
2. `M1.c` includes both `M1.h` and `M.h`
3. The client of `M1` includes `M1.h` and links the application code with `M.o` and `M1.o`

Overload Function

To overload a function, use a variable number of arguments.

Chapter 8

Generic Pointers

Data stored in a memory object can be recovered as a value of a specific data type. For example, if I have a generic pointer

```
void *p
```

that points to an object containing a double value, I can retrieve this value using the following syntax:

```
*(double*)p
```

Memory allocation for n integers

```
int* p;
if((p = malloc(n*sizeof(int))) == NULL)
    error
```

Memory Deallocation

Always follow the call to free(p) with p = NULL.

The iTH Object

p[i] is like a regular variable representing the *iTH object* in a block whose beginning is pointed to by p. In particular, *p is the same as p[0].

Block Traversal

```
for(pi = p; pi < p+SIZE; pi++)
    use pi here
```

Block Traversal with a Sentinel

```
for(pi = p; until sentinel reached; pi++)
    use pi;
```

Pass by Reference

1. Declare the formal parameter FP as a pointer, for example int *FP
2. In the body of the procedure, dereference FP, that is use *FP
3. In the call

if the actual parameter AP is a *variable*, use the address of AP; for example

```
f(&AP)
```

if actual parameter AP is a *pointer*, use AP without the address operator; for example

```
f(AP)
```

Efficient Pass by Reference

```
void f(const T* p);
```

Override Function

To override a function, use a pointer to the function.

Callback

The implementation file may get information from the client using a callback function, passed as a parameter of another function in the interface.

Traversing a Block of Objects

In order to traverse a block of memory consisting of n objects, where each object is of size elSize, use:

```
for(p = block; p < block + n*elSize; p += elSize)
```

Accessing the iTH Object in a Block of Objects

Assuming that each object in the block is of size elSize, to access the i-th object, use:

```
p = block + i*elSize
```

Block of Pointers

For a block b of pointers, use b[i][j] to refer to the jTH object in a block pointed to by b[i].

Chapter 9

Memory Allocation for a string of n characters

```
if((s = calloc(n+1, sizeof(char)) == NULL) ...
```

iTH Character of a String

To refer to the iTH character in the string s, use s[i], where $0 <= i <$ length of s.

String Suffix

If s points to a string, then s+n points to the suffix of this string starting at the n-th position (here, n has to be less than the length of s).

Traversing a String

```
for(p = s; *p; p++)
    use *p
```

Read a Single Word (at most 9 characters)

```
if(scanf("%10s", s) != 1)
    error
```

Read a Line (at most n–1 characters) from a File

```
if(fgets(buffer, n, f) == NULL)
    error
```

Command Line

```
int main(int argc, char **argv) {
...
    switch(argc) {
    case ...

    default: fprintf(stderr, "usage: %s ... \n", argv[0]);
                return EXIT_FAILURE;
    ...
```

This idiom only checks the number of required arguments; it does not check their types or values.

Chapter 10

Compare Arrays of the same Size

```
for(i = 0; i < SIZE; i++)
    if(x[i] != y[i])
        different
```

Copy Arrays of the same Size

```
for(i = 0; i < SIZE; i++)
    x[i] = y[i];
```

Array Type

```
typedef ElemType ArrayType[size];
```

Prefix and Suffix of an Array

For a function f(T* arr, int n,...) operating on an array arr of size n, call f(arr+start, segSize) to operate on the segment of array arr of size segSize, starting from position start (here, segSize+start must be less than or equal to n)

Chapter 11

Member Access through Pointer

If p is a pointer to a structure that has a member w, then p->w gives access to w.

Memory Allocation for a Structure

For a structure s and a pointer p to this structure, use:

```
if((p = malloc(sizeof(struct s)) == NULL) ...
```

Traversal to the End of a List p

```
for(aux = p->first; aux != NULL; aux = aux->next)
```

Traversal to the Predecessor of the Last Object in a List

Assuming the list is not empty and has more than one element

```
for(aux = p->first; aux->next != NULL; aux = aux->next)
```

Opaque

In order to represent an opaque type `Abstract`, use the definition of the form

```
typedef struct Concrete *Abstract
```

in the header file. Define the structure `Concrete` in the implementation file.

Chapter 12

Conversion of Enumerated Type Values to Strings

Define an array `Arr` of strings; one string for each value, and a macro `TOINT` to convert these values into integers. Then a value `V` can be converted into a string using `Arr[TOINT(V)]`

THE COMPLETE LIST OF PROGRAMMING STYLE GUIDELINES

Chapter 3

1. My lexical conventions for comments are:

   short explanations are placed in comments at the right end of a line, for example

   ```
   if(isdigit)  /* error */
   ```

   Multi-line explanations are formatted like this:

   ```
   /*
    * Program to sort integer values
    */
   ```

2. The comments should never echo what is already in the code, for example

   ```
   k++; /* k is incremented by 1*/
   ```

3. Make every comment count.

4. Don't over-comment.

5. Make sure comments and code agree; there are few things that confuse code readers more than incorrect comments.

6. It is important to use a consistent style throughout your code. Variables should have meaningful names when appropriate (a control variable in a `for` statement may be called "i", but a variable representing a filename should not be called "r").

7. You are encouraged to mix cases to make your identifiers more readable, for example:

```
longIdentifier
```

8. Always avoid using two identifiers that differ from each other only by one character, or in case only, for example

```
setIns
```
 and `setInt`

Unfortunately, C does not follow this rule and uses both `ifdef` and `ifndef` as two of its preprocessor commands.

9. Since C does not have classes, you have to take extra precautions to avoid name conflicts. For example, it is best to avoid the general name

```
insert
```

because many functions may want to insert something. Instead, use specific names such as

```
insert_List
```

10. I recommend that
   1. A declaration of a different data type starts on a new line.
   2. The lists of identifiers are aligned so that they start in the same column.
   3. Each variable identifier (except the last one) is followed by one space.
   4. I discourage multiple initializations, such as:

   ```
   int i = 1, j = 2;
   ```

   or

   ```
   int i = 2, j;
   ```

   and instead recommend that each declaration that contains an initialization appear on a separate line, as in

   ```
   int i = 1;
   int j = 2;
   ```

   5. If comments are required, each declaration should be placed on a separate line, for example:

   ```
   int lower;    /* lower bound of the array */
   int upper;    /* upper bound of the array */
   ```

11. Names of constants will appear in uppercase throughout this book, and `const` always appears in front of the declaration.
12. I use exactly one blank before and one blank after the `"="` operator.
13. The lexical convention used for the main function is as follows:

```
int main() {      the left brace on the same line as the header
   body           body indented to the right
}                 the matching right brace aligned with int
```

14. I recommend that in order to specify long types, you use the uppercase `L` rather than the lowercase `l`, because the latter can be mistaken for 1, as in

```
100l
```

15. Don't use spaces around the following operators:

```
->          .        []     !      ~       ++        --      - (unary)
* (unary)       &
```

For example, write

```
a->b    a[i]    *c
```

but not

```
~ a     & c
```

In *general*, use one space around the following operators:

```
=       +=      ?:      +       <       &&      + (binary) etc.
```

For example, code should be written as

```
a = b;
a = a + 2;
```

not

```
a= b+ 1;
```

Although it is not necessary, you may skip spaces to show operator *precedence*. For example, you could write:

```
a = a*b + 1;
```

but you should avoid

```
a = a+b * 2;
```

16. Blank lines are used to separate logically related sections of code; for example the three sections of input, processing, and termination.
17. When specifying a new type using `typedef`, identifier names start with an uppercase letter.

Chapter 4

1. The body of the `if` statement is indented to the right, and all its instructions are aligned.

2. Some programmers always use curly braces within a conditional statement, even if only one statement is present:

```
if(condition) {
    single statement1
} else {
    single statement2
}
```

In my opinion, this clutters a program with too many braces.

3. Use indentation to improve readability of your code.

4. There are at least three alternatives to write the `while` statement, shown in the examples below:

```
while(expr) {
    stats;
}

while(expr)
{
    stats;
}

while(expr)
    {
    stats;
}
```

I will always use the first format in my code.

5. Some programmers prefer to use the `for` statement to represent a `while(1)` loop:

```
for(;;) {
    body
}
```

The two are identical.

6. Instead of writing

```
while(expr != 0)
    statement;
```

some programmers write

```
while(expr)
    statement;
```

but I find this style to be less readable and will not use it in this book. The same conventions apply to the expression in the if statement. For example, I will write

```
if(expr !=0)...
```

rather than

```
if(expr)
```

7. If the body of the loop is empty, then the corresponding semicolon is always placed on a separate line, indented to the right:

```
for(i = 1, sum = 0; i <= 10; i++, sum += i)
    ;
```

Chapter 6

1. Macro names will always appear in uppercase.

2. Any constant value, which might change during software development, should be defined as a macro or as a constant.

3. By using macros, you are adding new constructs and new functionality to the language—if you do this inappropriately, the readability of your code may suffer.

Chapter 7

1. Make sure comments and code agree; in particular, always carefully check that the function implementation meets its specification.

2. In general, a function definition should not exceed one page. Code should be broken up; in particular, lines that are too long should be avoided.

3. Either the function declaration or definition (or both) should be preceded by documentation, which describes the function. The required format of the documentation is as follows:

Function:	name
Purpose:	a general description of the function (typically, this is a description of what it is supposed to do)
Inputs:	a list of parameters and global variables read in the function
Returns:	value to be returned

Modifies: a list of parameters and global variables that are modified; describes any side-effects

Error checking: describes your assumptions about actual parameters; what happens if actual parameters are incorrect

Sample call:

In addition, there may also be a Bugs section, which documents cases that the implementation does not handle.

4. I do not write the code as follows:

```
if(n/10 == 0)
    return 1;
else return 1 + digits(n/10);
```

Instead, I write the code as follows:

```
if(n/10 == 0)
    return 1;
return 1 + digits(n/10);
```

In the above case, it is a matter of personal preference—some people, myself included, find the second code more readable, while others argue that by including the `else`, the code has a more logically understandable structure. In the case of a more nested `if` structure, extra `else`'s may make the code more difficult to understand.

5. Brackets in the `return` statement are unnecessary, and in my opinion clutter the code:

```
if(n/10 == 0)
    return (1);
return (1 + digits(n/10));
```

6. As always, the code is as clear as possible. For example, I could have written:

```
if(n /= 10)
    return 1;
return 1 + digits(n);
```

Although the outcome is the same, this is hard to understand, because of the side effect in the `if` condition.

7. Side effects in loop conditions should be typically avoided. As an example of a loop-side-effect, the code to print the digits of an integer n reversed could be written as follows:

```
do {
    printf("%d", n%10);
} while(n/=10);
```

A more readable solution avoids the side effect in the loop condition:

```
do {
    printf("%d",n%10);
    n /= 10;
} while(n != 0);
```

8. The code parameter of `exit()` should be one of the two values:

`EXIT_SUCCESS` or `EXIT_FAILURE`.

9. Global variables should be used with caution, and always carefully documented. In particular, changing the value of a global variable as a result of calling a function should be avoided; these side-effects make testing, debugging, and in general maintaining the code very difficult. If the function must change a global variable, it should document this clearly.

10. The placement of the definition of a global variable defines its scope, but also contributes to the readability of your program. I do not have strict recommendations, but *suggest* that for short files, all global variables are defined at the top, and for long files, they are defined in the logically related place (before definitions of functions that may need these variables).

11. A program typically consists of one or more files:
    a) each file should not exceed 500 lines and should begin on a new page.
    b) in each source file, the first page should contain the name of the author, date, version number, etc.
    c) avoid splitting a function header, a comment, or a type/structure definition across a page break.

12. Header files should only include function declarations, macros, and definitions of constants.

13. Avoid compiler dependent features; if you have to use any such features, use conditional compilation.

14. A header file should provide all the documentation necessary to understand the semantics of this file.

15. The documentation for the client is placed in the header file.

16. The documentation for the implementor is placed in the implementation file.

17. The documentation for the client and for the implementor may be different.

18. Global static variables have identifiers with a trailing underscore.

Chapter 8

1. The placement of the whitespace around the asterisk in a pointer declaration is just a lexical convention. All of the following are valid declarations of a pointer variable:

    `int* p;`   — implies that `p` is of type 'pointer to `int`'
    `int * p;` — no implication
    `int *p;`   — implies that `*p` (the value `p` points to) is of type `int`.

    Actual placement is not as important as consistency, and I will always use the last alternative.

2. `*(p+i)` is not readable and whenever possible should be replaced by `p[i]`.

3. Any memory allocation in a function must be documented clearly so that the client knows who is responsible for freeing this memory.

Chapter 10

1. To make code more readable, always use nested braces when initializing two-dimensional arrays.

Chapter 11

1. Names of structures defined with `typedef` start with an uppercase letter and end with the uppercase T.

2. Type names representing pointers to structures have names ending with TP.

3. For the sake of clarity, initializing arrays always use nested braces.

Chapter 12

1. Store all program messages in one place; it will be easier to maintain them.

2. When you consider various cases, do not forget to account for the "impossible" cases; they do happen.

THE COMPLETE LIST OF PORTABILITY GUIDELINES

Chapter 3

1. The documentation of programs, which are available to clients, should make it clear whether you are using identifiers whose length exceeds 6 characters. You should never use identifiers that have more than 31 characters.

2. To support portability, use only integers in the ranges specified in `limits.h` (see Appendix B). For example, you can always use plain integers in the range from −32,767 to 32,767, since this range is guaranteed by every implementation of C. Any other assumptions, such as that the size of an `int` is 4 bytes, must not be made.

3. In order to write portable code, you should explicitly specify `signed char` or `unsigned char`.

4. You should never make any assumptions about the code values of characters, such as that the value of `'A'` is 65. While this is true for the ASCII code of `'A'`, this assumption is not portable. Thus, use `'A'` rather than 65 in your code.

5. Use return codes: `EXIT_FAILURE` and `EXIT_SUCCESS` (other values will not be portable).

6. Do not assume that the evaluation of standard mathematical expressions, such as addition, is performed from left to right.

7. Use `typedef` to define synonyms for data types that are not portable.

Chapter 8

1. Programs that assume a particular architecture (for example, a big endian) are not portable.

2. Always pass `sizeof(type)` as a parameter to a `malloc()` call rather than the absolute value (for example, use `malloc(sizeof(int))`, instead of `malloc(2)`).

3. When you open binary files, you should always use 'b' in the second argument for `fopen()` (see Section 5.4); for example, use `"wb"` rather than `"w"`. While this will not make any difference under Unix, it will make your programs more portable.

Chapter 11

You can not assume that the size of a structure is the same as the sum of the sizes of all its members, because the compiler may use padding to satisfy memory alignment requirements. Any program that makes such an assumption is not portable.

Chapter 13

Perform shifts only on unsigned integer numbers. Do not use shifts with negative values, such as

```
x << -2
```

Appendix **H**

CROSS REFERENCE INDEX OF USEFUL CODE FRAGMENTS

Name and description	Where	Page
Hexadecimal dump	Chapter 2	9
Roots of quadratic equation	Section 4.3.2	75
Maximum of integer values	Example 4-5	79
Testing for various kinds of characters in the input stream	Example 4-9	86
Length of the longest line	Example 5-3	108
Reading from a file *or* stdin, writing to a file *or* stdout	Example 5-4	111
Copying a file	Example 5-4	137
Use of conditional compilation for debugging	Example 6-1	137
Converting characters into integer	Example 7-3	157
Stateless module Lines	Example 7-3	177
Extending stateless module Lines	Section 7.4.7	181

Name and description	Where	Page
Layer Module IO	Example 7-3	182
Module for caching data	Example 7-3	197
Module Ops for the counting of characters, words and lines	Section 7.4.7	197
Menu-driven program	Example 7-6	200
Function to find the size of a file	Example 8-3	248
Converting a binary file to a text file	Example 8-4	250
Converting a text file to a binary file	Example 8-4	250
Tabulate a function parameter	Example 8-8	264
Generic bubble sort	Section 8.18.3	286
Module representing a generic homogenous collection	Section 8.18.2	276
Enumeration (singleton)	Section 8.18.3	282
Shell sort for double values	Section 8.18.4	286
Module representing a concrete homogenous collection	Section 8.18.4	326
Sorting strings (insertion sort)	Example 9-11	328
Processing path expressions	Example 9-12	340
Module for string tokenization	Section 9.8	347
Displaying up to n lines from a file	Example 9-17	347
Reading a line of unlimited length	Example 10-3	372
Binary search for strings	Example 10-4	378
Largest value in a two-dimensional array	Example 10-5	381
Module representing concrete dynamic arrays (singleton)	Section 10.5	382

Name and description	Where	Page
Traversals of linked lists	Section 11.4.8	413
Modifications of linked lists	Section 11.4.8	413
Traversals of binary files	Section 11.4.9	416
Modifications of binary files	Section 11.4.9	416
Enumeration (general)	Section 11.5.2	423
Module representing generic dynamic arrays with shallow copy	Section 11.5.3	424
Module representing concrete lists with deep copy	Section 11.5.4	431
Clearing bits	Example 13-1	469
Setting bits	Example 13-1	469
Long jumps and applications for error handling	Section 14.2.2	475
Enumerations with shallow and deep copy	Section 14.3.1	481
Module representing generic lists with shallow and deep copy	Section 14.3.2	484

REFERENCES

[Aho83] Aho, Alfred V., John E. Hopcroft, and Jeffrey D. Ullman. *Data Structures and Algorithms*. Addison-Wesley, Reading, MA, 1983.

[Arn98] Arnold, Ken, and James Gosling. *The Java Programming Language*. Addison-Wesley, Reading, MA, 1998.

[Han97] Hanson, David R. *C Interfaces and Implementations, Techniques for Creating Reusable Software*. Addison-Wesley, Reading, MA, 1997.

[Har91] Harbison, Samuel P., and Guy L. Steele. *C: A Reference Manual*. Prentice-Hall, Englewood Cliffs, NJ, Third Edition, 1991.

[Joh78] Johnson, S. C. *Yacc: Yet Another Compiler-Compiler*. Bell Laboratories, Computing Science Technical Report #32 (July 1978).

[Ker78] Kernighan, Brian W., and Dennis M. Ritchie. *The C Programming Language*. Prentice-Hall, Englewood Cliffs, NJ, 1978.

[Koe88] Koenig, Andrew. *C Traps and Pitfalls*. Addison-Wesley, Reading, MA, 1988.

INDEX